MONTEREY PENINSULA COLLEGE LIBRARY

3 4262 00085 2695

S0-AKX-166

9797

DS
62.4
H82

Hudson, Michael C.
Arab politics

MONTEREY PENINSULA COLLEGE LIBRARY
980 Fremont Blvd.
Monterey, California 93940

BCL

ARAB POLITICS

The Search for Legitimacy

Michael C. Hudson

New Haven and London   Yale University Press

Published with assistance from
the Louis Stern Memorial Fund.

Copyright © 1977 by Yale University.
All rights reserved. This book may not be
reproduced, in whole or in part, in any form
(beyond that copying permitted by Sections 107
and 108 of the U.S. Copyright Law and except by
reviewers for the public press), without written
permission from the publishers.

Designed by John O. C. McCrillis
and set in Monophoto Baskerville type
by Asco Trade Typesetting Ltd., Hong Kong.
Printed in the United States of America by
The Vail-Ballou Press, Inc., Binghamton, New York.

Library of Congress Cataloging in Publication Data

Hudson, Michael Craig
    Arab politics.

    Includes index.
    1. Arab countries—Politics and government.
I. Title.
DS62.4.H82   320.9' 17' 4927   77–75379
ISBN   0-300-02043-0
          0-300-02411-8 pbk.

13   12   11   10   9   8   7   6   5   4

For Vera

Contents

Tables and Figures

Preface

My curiosity about Arab politics was aroused in the early 1960s when I was a graduate student working on a study of political modernization and political culture cleavages in Lebanon. While intrinsically interesting in itself, Lebanon was also the forum for a variety of movements and ideologies concerned with the Arab world as a whole as well as particular Arab countries. Two aspects of Arab politics, beyond their volatility, were fascinating and puzzling: the lack of congruence between "all-Arab" identifications and aspirations and the political realities of discrete political systems; and the multiple effects of rapid, uneven modernization on Arab political culture and subcultures. This study is addressed to these two concerns.

I soon discovered that attempting a systematic, unified comparative approach to modern Arab politics was not easy. Fortunately, I could draw upon some of the theoretical literature from the comparative politics of the 1950s and 1960s; and the work of scholars like Deutsch, Huntington, Easton, Geertz, and Rustow, among others, was of great help in devising an approach to my questions. Another source of assistance was to be found in some of the better work on Arab politics by writers such as Jacques Berque, Albert Hourani, and Malcolm Kerr, among others. But, in the Arab world, the problems of investigating legitimacy, authority, identity, politicization, and a number of other basic concepts still defy adequate solution. We still lack workable indicators for these phenomena and, as Manfred Halpern observed a decade and a half ago, we still lack adequate data. My interpretations, consequently, cannot be considered particularly scientific; they are instead judgments; I hope well-informed, arrived at by analyzing recent political events in terms of a variety of historical, ethnographic, sociological, demographic, and economic theory and data. In the absence of direct findings about attitudes, values, and motivations, inferences must be drawn from such material as is available. The only other alternative is to remain silent.

I have tried to identify the present malaise in Arab politics, as indicated by instability, cynicism, inefficiency, corruption, and repression, as the result (and, over time, through feedback, the cause) of insufficient legitimacy accorded by the people to ruling structures, ideologies, and leaders. The legitimacy problem in turn is the product of a complex set of historical, social, and cultural conditions, aggravated by imperialism and modernization, which have made it difficult for Arab political systems to achieve consensus on matters of identity, authority, social policy, and regional coordination. One basic element in the Arab legitimacy problem, like that in developing countries generally, is achieving structured political participation. A second main element, distinctive to the Arabs in its importance, is the impact of all-Arab "national" concerns for the legitimacy of particular state systems; in the Arab world the legitimacy problem extends beyond sovereign boundaries.

Of the many people who have influenced me in the preparation of this study, I must single out for special thanks my teacher Karl W. Deutsch who, because of his erudition and sense of history, never allowed his passion for precision to lead him into the sterility of excessive quantification. I must also acknowledge the benefit of a long and continuing dialogue with my friend and colleague Hisham Sharabi about the nature of social and political change in the Arab world. While our approaches (and many of our conclusions) differ, the exchange has been decidedly educational for me.

In addition, a great many other people—scholars, students, politicians, journalists, officials—both in the United States and in the Arab world have given generously of their time, expertise, and practical assistance. Many prefer to remain anonymous, but they know who they are and I hereby extend to them my deepest thanks. As to the others, I would like to mention particularly several former colleagues at Brooklyn College and the Johns Hopkins School of Advanced International Studies: Albert Gorvine, Benjamin Rivlin, Robert A. Lystad, Vernon McKay, Robert E. Osgood, John Badgely, and John Anthony; a number of former students and research assistants: John Bagnole, Solomon Brander, Richard Burns, Robert Butler, Montague Kern, Bassem Muallem, Albert Nader, Melhem Salman, Dan Smith, Dennis Williams, and, particularly, Joseph Gemayel and Mary Susan Ueber. Clement H. Moore made many valuable suggestions for improving the manuscript. Much of the first part of the book was drafted in Beirut during happier days, and I must record my deep appreciation for the hospitality accorded me by the American University of Beirut—its Political Studies and History departments, its Library, and not least its Mediterannean beach, where some of our most interesting seminars took place. Professors Munir Bashshur, Hanna Batatu, Yusuf Ibish, Adnan Iskandar, Walid Khalidi, Elie Salem, Kamal Salibi, and Mahmoud Zayid, among many others, made AUB an intellectual home away from home. I also spent many tranquil hours in the German Orient-Institut in Beirut, thanks to the kindness of its then director, Dr. Stephen Wild. During the latter stages of manuscript preparation, the new Center for Contemporary Arab Studies at Georgetown provided important support and a stimulating working environment; my thanks are due to Dean Peter Krogh and my other Center colleagues, Wallace Erwin, Ibrahim Oweiss, John Ruedy, and Irfan Shahid. Marian Ash of the Yale University Press was a wise and helpful editor. I am grateful to Eileen Donlin of SAIS and Mona Jallad of Georgetown for their patience and accuracy in typing various drafts of the manuscript.

Much of the material in this study, particularly in Part Two, is based upon interviews conducted over the past several years in all the Arab states except Sudan. In addition to the luxury of twelve summers in Beirut, there were four research trips. The first, in July through August 1968, was made possible by a grant from the American Philosophical Society and included Egypt, Libya, Tunisia, Algeria, and Morocco. The second was undertaken during a research leave supported by Johns Hopkins University in January through June of 1972 and included Iran, Kuwait, Iraq, Egypt, the two Yemens, Bahrain, Sa'udi Arabia, the United Arab Emirates, Oman, Jordan, Lebanon, and Israel. In February and March 1974, the opportunity arose to return to the UAE, Jordan, Syria, and Lebanon. Finally, a Guggenheim Fellowship in 1975–76 to study the politics of planning in several Arab states took me to Egypt, Kuwait, Qatar, Oman, the UAE, Sa'udi Arabia, Iraq, and the Yemen Arab Republic. It permitted me not only to improve my understanding of administrative processes but also to gain further perspective on the problems of legitimacy in general.

As to the transliteration of Arabic words, I have sacrificed accuracy for legibility. Most diacritical marks have been omitted except for an apostrophe indicating the medial *'ayn*. I have generally observed the common usage in spelling well-known proper names, which results in some inconsistencies, especially in Arab North African names where the French transliteration style is conventional.

I would like to absolve all those mentioned here, and all the others who have given me their help, of any responsibility for what follows. Many will disagree with my interpretation of the Arab legitimacy problem, but I hope that they find it at least stimulating.

Finally, I want to record my deepest gratitude to my wife, Vera Wahbe Hudson; our daughters, Leila and Aida; my father, Robert B. Hudson; my brother, Bob, and his wife, Kathleen; my father-in-law, George Wahbe; my sister-in-law, Tatiana Wahbe; and my brother-in-law, Boris Wahbe; for all their help.

Arab Politics

1

The Legitimacy Problem in Arab Politics

Without legitimacy, argued Max Weber, a ruler, regime, or governmental system is hard-pressed to attain the conflict-management
capability essential for long-run stability and good government. While
the stability of an order may be maintained for a time through fear or
expediency or custom, the optimal or most harmonious relationship
between the ruler and the ruled is that in which the ruled accept the
rightness of the ruler's superior power.[1] Contemporary scholars agree.
As David Easton puts it:

> The inculcation of a sense of legitimacy is probably the single
> most effective device for regulating the flow of diffuse support in
> favor both of the authorities and of the regime. A member may
> be willing to obey the authorities and conform to the requirements
> of the regime for many different reasons. But the most stable
> support will derive from the conviction on the part of the member
> that it is right and proper for him to accept and obey the authorities
> and to abide by the requirements of the regime. It reflects the fact
> that in some vague or explicit way he sees these objects as con-
> forming to his own moral principles, his own sense of what is
> right and proper in the political sphere. The strength of support
> implicit in this attitude derives from the fact that it is not con-
> tingent on specific inducements or rewards of any kind, except in
> the very long run.[2]

Ted Gurr, after identifying a number of common synonyms or near-
synonyms for legitimacy such as "political community," "political
myth," "support," "authoritativeness," and "system affect," proposes
that regimes are legitimate "to the extent that their citizens regard

---

1. Max Weber, *The Theory of Social and Economic Organization* (translated by A. M. Henderson
and Talcott Parsons; edited with an introduction by Talcott Parsons) (New York: Oxford
University Press, 1947), pp. 124–26; Reinhard Bendix, *Max Weber* (New York: Doubleday,
1960), pp. 294–95.
2. David Easton, *A Systems Analysis of Political Life* (New York: Wiley, 1965), p. 278.

them as proper and deserving of support."[3] It is the extent to which leadership and regimes are perceived by elites and masses as congruent and compatible with the society's fundamental myths—those "value-impregnated beliefs" (as Robert MacIver puts it) that hold society together.[4] The governmental system and leadership that is genuinely national, that partakes of the nation's history, that acts in accordance with the society's values, and that protects its broadest concerns is likely to be regarded as legitimate, even though particular decisions and leaders may be unpopular or unwise. A ruler, regime, or governmental process (procedures, arrangements for collective choice) that is not widely perceived as clothed in legitimacy is not able to function authoritatively.

The central problem of government in the Arab world today is political legitimacy. The shortage of this indispensable political resource largely accounts for the volatile nature of Arab politics and the autocratic, unstable character of all the present Arab governments. If one were called upon to describe the contemporary style of politics in the Arab world—a region that stretches from Morocco to Kuwait, organized into eighteen sovereign states (excluding Mauritania and Somalia, which recently joined the Arab League) embracing some 125 million people—the adjectives that immediately spring to mind include mercurial, hyperbolic, irrational, mysterious, uncertain,,even dangerous. Arab politics today are not just unstable, although instability remains a prominent feature, they are also unpredictable to participants and observers alike. Fed by rumor, misinformation, and lack of information, the Arab political process is cloaked in obscurity and Arab politicians are beset by insecurity and fear of the unknown. If their behavior appears at times quixotic or even paranoid, the irrationality lies less within themselves than in their situation. Whether in power or in the opposition, Arab politicians must operate in a political environment in which the legitimacy of rulers, regimes, and the institutions of the states themselves is sporadic and, at best, scarce. Under these conditions seemingly irrational behavior, such as assassinations, coups d'état, and official repression, may in fact derive from rational calculations. The consequences of such behavior, which itself stems from the low legitimacy accorded to political processes and institutions, contribute further to the prevailing popular cynicism about politics. These consequences, so dysfunctional for political development by almost any definition, are all the more damaging

3. Ted Robert Gurr, *Why Men Rebel* (Princeton: Princeton University Press, 1970), pp. 183–85.
4. Robert M. MacIver, *The Web of Government* (New York: Macmillan, 1947), pp. 4–5.

when juxtaposed against the revolutionary and nationalist values that are today so widely and intensely held by the Arab people. These values include liberation of the entire national homeland by regaining Palestine and throwing off indirect forms of external influence; fulfillment of Arab national identity through integration, if not fusion, of the numerous sovereignties; and the establishment of democratic political structures through which social justice and equality can be achieved. Such are the staples of virtually all political platforms in the Arab states, regardless of regime orientation; and such appeals have amply proved their political salience from one end of the Arab world to the other, as evidenced by the wave of independence and revolutionary movement throughout the region since World War I. So widespread are these appeals that every Arab politician of consequence has felt compelled to endorse and exploit them; and today, as we shall see, even the ideologically conservative monarchies have become fervent advocates of Arabism, democracy, and social justice. But such vast, if not utopian, ideals, held by so many with almost sacred fervor, contrast strikingly with the grim realities of political life. This incongruence cannot but complicate the task of building a legitimate order. Indeed, one observes from conversations with politicians and government officials across the Arab world a sense of frustration. They find themselves caught between ideology and political-administrative realities. They discover apathy, indifference, and corruption within their own bureaucracies and among the constituencies to be served. One also observes a widespread negative attitude, even fear, toward government among ordinary people. Even census taking in countries such as Sa'udi Arabia, Yemen, the United Arab Emirates, and, of course, Lebanon is regarded with suspicion. Such attitudes cannot be satisfactorily explained simply as the superstitions of "traditional" people but rather appear to be rationally derived from unhappy prior experience with "the authorities."

STRUCTURE OF THE ARAB LEGITIMACY PROBLEM

To analyze the Arab legitimacy problem most fruitfully, we must look beyond explanations rooted in the alleged uniqueness of the area itself. While it is easy to demonstrate the uniqueness of Arab culture, it is fallacious to assume that this uniqueness decisively shapes the political behavior of Arabs. Instead, we must seek our explanation in terms of universally applicable categories of analysis. Apart from the well-known objections to an area-oriented approach on general empirical grounds, an additional reason for looking to general theory is

the dubious character of existing reductionist concepts of the Arab or
Islamic mind, personality, and national character.

The legitimacy problem in the Arab world is basically the same as
that in most newly independent, rapidly modernizing states. In essence,
it results from the lack of what Dankwart Rustow has designated as
the three prerequisites for political modernity: authority, identity, and
equality.[5] The legitimate order requires a distinct sense of corporate
selfhood: the people within a territory must feel a sense of political
community which does not conflict with other subnational or supranational communal identifications. If distinct communal solidarity
may be understood as the necessary horizontal axis for the legitimate
political order, there must as well be a strong, authoritative vertical
linkage between the governors and the governed. Without authoritative political structures endowed with "rightness" and efficacity,
political life is certain to be violent and unpredictable.

Equality, the third prerequisite for political legitimacy, is specifically
a product of the modern age, which in the Arab world may be dated
from the Napoleonic invasion of Egypt in 1798. Certainly the nationalist stirrings in various parts of the Arab world, which began in the
late nineteenth century and came to fruition in the post–World War
I period, have been increasingly infused with liberal and radical
ideology. The ideas of freedom, democracy, and socialism are today
inextricable criteria for legitimate political order in the Arab world,
as in most of the Third World, and are, unfortunately, far from being
achieved. This singular failing, however, does not vitiate the importance of equality as a functional prerequisite for legitimacy in Arab
politics; indeed, I shall argue that it stands as the single greatest
impediment (though not the only one) to the development of political
legitimacy in the Arab world.

It is now virtually a truism that the process of modernization, or
social mobilization as Karl Deutsch has called it, has profound effects
on the politics of the new states, effects that are both functional and
dysfunctional for building political legitimacy.[6] The social mobilization
"package," which includes increasing urbanization, literacy, education, media exposure, and wealth, appears, on the one hand, to enhance
the possibilities of developing a civic, liberal political order inasmuch
as it broadens people's identifications and affiliations, integrates their

5. Dankwart A. Rustow, *A World of Nations: Problems of Political Modernization* (Washington,
D.C.: Brookings Institution, 1967), esp. chaps. 2 and 3.

6. Karl W. Deutsch, "Social Mobilization and Political Development," *American Political
Science Review*, 55:3 (September 1961), pp. 493–514, esp. pp. 498–502.

socioeconomic behavior, and standardizes to some extent their cultural norms. It also, in theory, enlarges the capabilities of government and administration. On the other hand, social mobilization is disruptive of traditional political relationships: the newly mobilized, politicized masses do not find old patterns of identity and authority relevant, and the process of developing new ones is rarely peaceful and sometimes revolutionary. Furthermore, rapid social mobilization certainly accentuates the importance of equality as a prerequisite norm for political legitimacy. The effects of social mobilization are discussed in chapter 6.

Specific Features of the Arab Legitimacy Problem

The politics of the Arab states can and should be analyzed in terms of the foregoing general framework, which is equally applicable to all modernizing polities. But there are several features of the Arab situation that require special attention for a full understanding of the Arab legitimacy problem. Indeed, to approach the legitimacy problem of any particular Arab state without reference to conditions and issues common and salient to all Arabs, or to what most Arabs refer to as the Arab nation, would result in a monochromatic, two-dimensional analysis. To put the matter in a slightly different way, Arab politicians and Arab political behavior are evaluated not solely according to internal, intrastate criteria. It is impossible to make an adequate diagnosis of the legitimacy of a particular Arab political system, regime, leader, or politician without reference to factors external to the Arab world. External sources of legitimacy, as we shall see in the comparative case studies below, are of two types: The first is the influence, defined largely in terms of the classical instruments of power, such as threat, coercion, promise, and reward, from contiguous or neighboring regimes and movements. For example, Syria or Egypt will "interfere" in the affairs of a neighboring Arab country by trying to enhance or reduce the legitimacy of a given politician or regime. The second type of external factor is more broadly identified as a set of evaluative standards that the noted Lebanese writer Clovis Maksoud has called all-Arab core concerns. The legitimacy of given leaders in a given state is determined to an important extent by their fidelity to these core concerns. At the present time, as I have indicated, Palestine is the foremost all-Arab core concern, although not the only one.

The fact that the Arab world in the late 1970s is divided into eighteen sovereign jurisdictions plus the Palestinian community enormously complicates the problem of developing two of the prerequisites of legitimacy—national identity and authority. National identity in the

Arab *umma* is at best multidimensional, at worst mired in irreconcilable contradictions. Legitimate authority is hard to develop within state structures whose boundaries are inherently incompatible with those of the nation. To make matters worse, the state interests of particular regimes are often incompatible with one another, so that conflict of varying degrees of severity often characterizes the relations between Arab states instead of the cooperation and harmony so obviously in the "national interest." One of the most perplexing features of contemporary Arab politics is the simultaneous growth of integrative cross-national behavior—as indexed by the proliferation of functional organizations and by flows of trade, finance, development projects, tourists, elites, and leaders—and the persistence of intrastate tensions, which have sometimes escalated into sabotage and armed violence, as in disputes between Syria and Jordan, Syria and Iraq, Egypt and Sa'udi Arabia, Sa'udi Arabia and the People's Democratic Republic of Yemen (PDRY, "south" Yemen), the PDRY and the Yemen Arab Republic (YAR, "north" Yemen), Libya and Morocco, and Algeria and Morocco—to take the most prominent examples from the mid-1960s through the mid-1970s. In recent years, particularly since the decline of Nasirism in the mid-1960s, some writers on Arab affairs have argued that the pan-Arab urge, never very successful, is now on the wane.[7] The failure of the highly touted unification or federation efforts by Egypt and Syria in the late 1950s and by Egypt, Syria, the Sudan, and Libya in the early 1970s would seem to support such a conclusion. But the fact that such efforts persist is surely as significant, if not more so, as the fact that they have thus far failed; and the fact that organizations with pan-Arab commitments such as the Ba'th party and the Palestinian national movement are now quite institutionalized without having forsaken their goal of all-Arab solidarity also suggests that pan-Arab perspectives have not lost their salience. Arab nationalism remains a formidable legitimizing resource for kings and presidents alike, and the considerable potential power of a revolutionary like George Habash derives in no small measure from his impeccable Arab nationalist credentials.

Given the fact that sovereign power in the Arab world today is distributed among several states, it is necessary to analyze the legitimacy problem of each within its own territorial context, but it would be a mistake not to recognize the importance of the pan-Arab environ-

---

7. For an interesting discussion of this theory, see Richard H. Pfaff, "The Function of Arab Nationalism," *Comparative Politics*, 2:2 (January 1970), pp. 147–68.

ment in both its power and moral dimensions for intrastate legitimacy. I attempt to give due consideration to this factor in the comparative case studies below. In doing so I also attempt to recognize that the salience of all-Arab concerns for political legitimacy varies within the Arab world.

LEGITIMACY AND CHANGE: THREE PERSPECTIVES

I have suggested that the problem of community and conflict in the Arab world today arises from a legitimacy shortage and that this shortage in turn is the result of the profound transformation occurring throughout Arab society and culture. As indicated above, scholars are less certain than they once were about the nature of modernization, particularly its political ramifications. One can discern three theoretical approaches that help reveal the implications of social change for building legitimacy. Broadly, each suggests a different range of possibilities for a legitimate political order. The "transformationist" model envisages the possibility, indeed to some the inevitability, of the complete displacement of traditional by rational sociopolitical systems through the cataclysm of revolution that in turn is induced by contradictions in the changing social structure. The Arab world political counterparts are several new republics with ideologies dedicated to a thoroughgoing social revolution surpassing in scope simple nationalist assimilation. The "mosaic" model emphasizes the persistence of primordial and parochial loyalties even during rapid modernization, and in some conditions even predicts their strengthening. The implication of this model for building legitimacy is that reconciliation, bargaining, and conflict management procedures are the only viable course short of brutal, forced assimilation for achieving community. Finally, the social mobilization model conceives of political outcomes, including ultimately legitimacy, as the product of a constellation of not necessarily harmonious social forces interacting with a given political culture. In its liberal version, the social mobilization model holds out the possibility of modernization giving rise to an educated, tolerant "civic" polity. In another version it is seen giving rise to efficient despotism or anarchy. I will discuss each of the three models briefly.

The transformationist model conceives of a fundamental system change from tradition to rationality through the medium of revolution. The revolution is a watershed that separates the new rational order from its traditional roots. Hisham Sharabi, discussing the Arab world, draws the distinction clearly: "Revolutionary leadership is 'rational,' choosing specific means to achieve specific ends, whereas patriarchal leadership is 'traditional,' accepting inherited values and goals and employing customary means to achieve them."[8] Sharabi, observing the coups d'état in the Arab world between 1949 and 1963, sees the transition process as relatively sudden and discontinuous through the traumatic event of revolution.[9] Power has to be seized; it is possible for men to transform a polity from the traditional to the rational by making a revolution; there is "a revolutionary wave" that is challenging both the remaining traditional states and the "intermediate" states.[10] It is noteworthy that in his recent writings Sharabi is consistent in maintaining his radical optimism, that is, his belief in the possibility of men creating a rational political order, despite the receding of the revolutionary wave in the Arab world after 1967 and the weakening of the Palestinian national movement in Jordan 1970–71 and Lebanon in 1976. Optimism is still possible because the Marxist liberationist position insists that Arab society, with its medieval disabilities, contains fundamental destabilizing contradictions which, when triggered, will generate the mass revolutionary consciousness that has been missing thus far.[11] Sharabi's analysis, which is partially correct, implies that once the revolution has been triggered a new and rational legitimacy formula will emerge, one that is deeply rooted and congruent with the new revolutionary worker and peasant class consciousness. The indisputably valid part of this analysis is the clarity with which it distinguishes traditional orientations from revolutionary ideologies and the significance it bestows on the revolutionary event in the transformation of political systems. Certainly once the revolution has occurred, there must be some change in the legitimacy formula. Less certain is whether revolutionary legitimacy formulas can sweep away traditional values and become deeply rooted themselves, that is, whether there can be a successful resolution of the revolution.

Similarly, Manfred Halpern invokes the metaphor of "the shattering of the glass" to depict the impact of secular modernism on traditional Islamic society.[12] Again, the image is one of the complete displacement of a system of balanced traditional beliefs and certainties by a disruptive force that, initially at least, offers no coherent system to replace it. One

---

8. Hisham B. Sharabi, *Nationalism and Revolution in the Arab World* (Princeton: Van Nostrand, 1966), p. 53.

9. Ibid., chap. 4.

10. Ibid., pp. 72–79.

11. Hisham B. Sharabi, "Liberation or Settlement: The Dialectics of Palestinian Struggle," *Journal of Palestine Studies*, 3:2 (Winter 1973), pp. 33–48.

12. Manfred Halpern, *The Politics of Social Change in the Middle East and North Africa* (Princeton: Princeton University Press, 1963), chap. 2.

does not need to accept Halpern's assertion that a new professional middle class is building a new, pragmatic science- and technology-based legitimacy formula to appreciate his insight into the profundity of the social changes that are taking place. Nor does one have to share Sharabi's radical optimism to benefit from his emphasis on the importance of the political sector in the process of change and of the very sharp contradictions in belief systems manifest in that sector.

The mosaic model, which has received renewed scholarly attention, questions the assumption underlying the transformationist and social mobilization models, namely that major sociopolitical development is likely or necessary. It questions even the possibility of revolution. The mosaic model asserts the persistence of traditional particularist identifications even under conditions of modernization or political revolution. It stresses the permanence of parochial and corporatist orientations. Among the most prominent social scientists to stress the deep-rootedness of "primordial" identifications, ethnic, religious, racial, and linguistic, is Clifford Geertz who, in a well-known article, indicated their possibly explosive salience for political developments in the new states.[13] Milton Esman asserts that "ethnic, racial, and religious solidarities are likely to touch deeper emotional levels" than other cleavages, implying that it cannot be easy for modernizing regimes to replace them with new loyalties.[14] Ronald Rogowski and Lois Wasserspring have challenged the logic of the Weberian secularization model (as expounded by Marion Levy).[15] That model, they suggest, asserts that with specialization, division of labor, and greater interaction of subsystems a society inevitably becomes more homogeneous, so that particularist, corporate subgroups lose their cohesion and distinctiveness. But they go on to argue that the assumption that the greater the social interaction, the greater the cognitive problem of distinguishing individuals and of placing them in society is erroneous, at least for societies that tend to be corporatist rather than individualist, that is, societies in which there are substantial identifiable majorities or stigmatized groups.

The implications for developing legitimacy that flow from the mosaic image are somber. Because ethnicity is so deep-rooted, the possibilities

13. Clifford Geertz, "The Integrative Revolution: Primordial Sentiments and Civil Politics in the New States," in Clifford Geertz (ed.), *Old Societies and New States* (New York: Free Press of Glencoe, 1963), pp. 105–57.

14. Milton Esman, "The Management of Communal Conflict," *Public Policy* 21:1 (Winter 1973), pp. 49–78, 54.

15. Ronald Rogowski and Lois Wasserspring, "Legitimacy and Stability in Corporatist Societies," paper delivered at the 1969 annual meeting of the American Political Science Association, pp. 1–7.

for the integration of new polities along modern lines, let alone revolutionary transformation, are remote; but insofar as assimilative, modernizing ideologies have an irreversible momentum of their own, the prospects for continuous conflict—a permanent legitimacy crisis—are far from negligible. The anthropologist M. G. Smith has developed a model of the plural society, characterized by deeply divided subcultures whose cohesion can only be maintained by a coercive elite.[16] Walker Connor, in a sharp attack on the assimilationist assumption in conventional models of nation-building, finds that only 10 percent of the world's states are ethnically homogeneous while in some 30 percent the largest ethnic group fails to account for half the total population. These are significant figures if it is also true, as he asserts, that "the prime cause of political disunity is the absence of a single psychological focus shared by all segments of the population."[17] Alvin Rabushka and Kenneth Shepsle propose a model of the essential instability of multiethnic polities, owing to a tendency toward "the politics of outbidding."[18] On the empirical level, in his cross-national study of civil strife in 119 polities, Ted Robert Gurr found that indicators of "group discrimination" and "political separatism" were "consistently and positively related to levels of civil violence."[19] Similarly, Douglas Hibbs, in his analysis of data from Charles Taylor's and my *World Handbook of Political and Social Indicators*, discovered a "powerful interactive impact manifested by the conjunction of social mobilization and ethnolinguistic fractionalization . . . (which provides striking evidence for theories arguing that a mobilized *and* differentiated population is a particularly explosive combination)."[20] Then of course there are the numerous contemporary intrastate conflicts that strikingly illustrate

16. M. G. Smith, "Social and Cultural Pluralism," in M. G. Smith, *The Plural Society in the British West Indies* (Berkeley: University of California Press, 1965), pp. 75–91. See also Leo Kuper, "Sociology: Some Aspects of Urban Plural Societies," in R. A. Lystad (ed.), *The African World: A Survey of Social Research* (London: Pall Mall Press, 1965), pp. 107–30; and Leo Kuper, "Plural Societies: Perspectives and Problems," in Leo Kuper and M. G. Smith (eds.), *Pluralism in Africa* (Berkeley: University of California Press, 1969), pp. 7–26.

17. Walker Connor, "Nation Building or Nation Destroying?" *World Politics*, 24:3 (April 1972), pp. 319–55, 320, 353.

18. Alvin Rabushka and Kenneth Shepsle, *Politics in Plural Societies* (Columbus, Ohio: Charles E. Merrill, 1972).

19. Ted Gurr, with Charles Ruttenberg, *The Conditions of Civil Violence: First Test of a Causal Model*, Princeton University Center of International Studies, 1967, p. 108. See also Gurr, *Why Men Rebel*, chap. 1 and Appendix.

20. Douglas A. Hibbs, Jr., *Mass Political Violence: A Cross-National Causal Analysis* (New York: Wiley, 1973), pp. 76–78. Data are drawn largely from Charles L. Taylor and Michael C. Hudson et al., *World Handbook of Political and Social Indicators*, Second Edition (New Haven: Yale University Press, 1972).

the salience of ethnic identifications and conflict: Northern Ireland, Pakistan, Nigeria, Sri Lanka, Philippines, Ruanda-Urundi, and Ethiopia, to name only a few of the most prominent.

What of the applicability of the mosaic model to the Arab world? This examination of Arab political culture will make clear that it is permeated with primordial sentiments and honeycombed with stigmatized groups—religious, ethnolinguistic, racial, tribal, and class; it thus tends toward the corporatist or segmented rather than the individualist type. At least half of the Arab countries exhibit politically salient (often conflict-ridden) divisions: Morocco, Sudan, Iraq, Syria, Lebanon, Jordan, the two Yemens, Oman, and Bahrain. In Arab society, then, "particularism can survive modernization."[21] The same is true of the non-Arab Middle Eastern states of Cyprus and Iran. The problems thus posed for developing political system legitimacy are serious indeed, especially in polities that have recently undergone modernizing coups or revolutions. Even under the comparatively optimistic transformationist and social mobilization models, it is not easy for elites to compose a strong legitimacy formula, but at least they can draw some solace from theories that predict the acceptance of universal symbols and norms sooner or later. The implantation of common revered loyalties and "rules of the game" can be expected. But if the political culture remains tenaciously parochial and segmented despite modernization (and the political ferment it generates)—if, indeed, modernization may in some cases actually exacerbate such separatist tendencies—then the problem of developing a political system legitimacy formula is not likely to solve itself as modernization continues; instead the nature of the problem itself is changed. In such cases, strategies of legitimacy based on transformationist or social mobilization models should be rejected, some scholars have argued, in favor of strategies of accommodation. For example, Iliya Harik asserts that "the new states of the Middle East are in need of accommodating particularistic tendencies and by constructive policy channeling them in the service of the civic order with patience and endurance."[22]

Perhaps the most satisfactory conception of the third model of change, the social mobilization model, is found in the work of Karl Deutsch.[23] His work, like that of other major development theorists such as Marion Levy, David Apter, and Gabriel Almond, falls within

21. Rogowski and Wasserspring, op. cit., p. 4.

22. Iliya Harik, "The Ethnic Revolution and Political Integration in the Middle East," *International Journal of Middle East Studies*, 3:3 (July 1972), pp. 303–23, 312.

23. Deutsch, op. cit. See also his classic *Nationalism and Social Communications* (New York: Wiley, 1953).

the Weberian tradition. This tradition (though not Weber himself) conceives of the transition from traditional to rational-legal societies through the process of secularization. In Deutsch's well-known formulation, social mobilization is posited as an interrelated set of growth processes including economic development, mass media exposure, interpersonal communications, urbanization, and the expansion of literacy and education. The implications of social mobilization for political system legitimacy are profound, especially in the Arab world where the growth rates are so high; but they do not all pull in the same direction. There are two areas of impact: the loads-capabilities equation, which relates the political system to the society, and the integration of the political culture itself. Social mobilization expands the politically relevant population by politicizing the masses and by both enlarging and fragmenting the elite. Thus it may create new and contradictory demands on government. The aspects of social mobilization bearing on infrastructure growth (urbanization, industrialization, etc.) may also generate heavier administrative demands on the decision-making apparatus and bureaucracy. On the other hand, the government and other structures of the political system may themselves grow, and their capabilities for institutionalizing participation, initiating development, and controlling subversion—in short, for coping with modernity—may be more than adequate to meet the new demands. Unfortunately, it is not easy to discern empirically whether the net effect is positive or negative in any particular case. Similarly, while the growth of communications networks associated with social mobilization may solidify the communal identity of groups having some primordial characteristics in common, such as language, race, ethnicity, or religion, it may actually divide societies in which there are several such semidistinct groupings: instead of all enhancing their identifications to the society bounded by the state, they may develop subnational or supranational affinities that weaken the state's legitimacy formula. The effects of social mobilization upon system legitimacy, therefore, are complex and even possibly contradictory, as Deutsch has always recognized. But his conceptualization of the process illuminates the possibilities more clearly perhaps than any other. It certainly illuminates the obstacles to legitimacy in fast mobilizing, culturally heterogeneous societies.

The psychological dimension of social mobilization also has important implications for the legitimacy problem. In his pioneering study of social change in the Middle East, Daniel Lerner suggests that empathy—the quality of an individual being able to imagine himself in somebody else's role—is one consequence of exposure to modernity (or social mobilization).[24] Empathy may ease the transition from tradition to modernity; it may promote the tolerance and ability to compromise, to associate together on instrumental and rational grounds instead of through primordial affinities. The implication is that new bases for community—a new legitimacy formula—are not only possible but predictable as a function of the rate of social mobilization.

But there is also a pessimistic side to this psychological coin. In modern society the social atomization of the individual produces apathy and alienation. These characteristics, Kornhauser argues, in turn facilitate the manipulation of the individual by the state or organized political movements.[25] His observations about mass society are based on the highly modernized societies of the West, and even the most modernized areas of the Arab world do not reach the same levels of industrialization or social differentiation. But they are relevant nonetheless. Even partial modernization generates severe pressures on the medieval mosaic of primordial affiliations that has always held Arab society together. And Arab society (perhaps because it is only partially modernized) lacks the web of secondary associations and cross-cutting group memberships of Western society so well celebrated by Tocqueville. Thus when old solidarities are broken down, Arab society probably lacks the "cushion" of secondary associations that in the West serve to some extent to counteract alienation. The implications for legitimacy are again ambivalent. On the one hand, mass alienation may be considered functional for establishing a new and rational legitimacy formula because it uproots people from old affiliations and renders them manipulatable, although this is not how Arab revolutionaries would describe the development of mass revolutionary consciousness. On the other hand, if alienation is a relatively permanent condition in a long period of social change, it may make the establishment of any permanent and active loyalties very difficult for the new regime as well as the old. An apathetic and perhaps unreliable population is an obstacle to the achievement of revolutionary objectives, and the nonachievement of objectives in turn is a new drain upon legitimacy.[26]

Granting that each of the three perspectives contains valuable insights, is it possible to ascertain which is the most valid for this

24. Daniel Lerner, *The Passing of Traditional Society* (Glencoe: Free Press, 1958), pp. 47–52.

25. William Kornhauser, *The Politics of Mass Society* (Chicago: Free Press, 1959), esp. chaps 4, 7, and 8.

26. Cf. Halim Barakat, "Al-Ightirab wal-thawra" (Alienation and Revolution), *Mawaqaf* (Beirut), 5 (1969).

inquiry? The radical ideological transformation in Arab politics is a fact of undeniable importance, notwithstanding the equally obvious fact that the Arab revolutions thus far have accomplished far less than they were intended to. Customary authority has sharply declined in importance at the national level in over half the countries of the area and is beginning to give way at the local level as well. In the Arab political vocabulary modern ideological symbols of liberation, democracy, and socialism are crowding out the parochial kinship and religious symbols of an earlier era as the basis for the legitimate political order. Ever so gradually centers of power are evolving that rest upon the egalitarian concerns not of a "new middle class" but of the great mass of urban and rural laboring people, as the established revolutionary movements seek to create a mass base to justify their rule. Imperfect as they may appear when judged against classical socialist standards, the revolutionary systems in Syria and Iraq, Algeria, Tunisia, the PDRY, and even post-Nasir Egypt, to mention the most notable cases, are indeed radical by comparison with the regimes that preceded them. Nevertheless, the radical optimism of the late 1950s and early 1960s that detected or anticipated a "shattering of the glass" and the creation of a coherent new basis for legitimacy on "modern" grounds was clearly mistaken. New legitimacy norms are not to be instantly and comprehensively implanted, and old values and attachments, whose incompatibility with modernity was exaggerated by the revolutionaries, are not going to be eradicated quickly.

But to admit that the validity of the transformationist model is only partial is not to concede superior validity to the mosaic model, for it too is defective. The chief merit of the mosaic perspective is its emphasis on the persistence of traditional solidarity patterns, with its obvious negative implications for radical sociopolitical engineering. But as the basis for a workable strategy for legitimacy, the mosaic model presents difficulties. On balance, there is little evidence to suggest that the Arab states are undergoing an "ethnic revolution." It is true that important ethnoreligious minorities, such as the Kurds, Sudanese blacks, and Lebanese Catholics, have been politicized perhaps to an even greater degree by social mobilization than the majority populations and have tried, with important Western help, to assert or defend their political independence. It is also true that other primordial groupings, such as the North African Berbers and the Alawite and Shi'ite Muslims of the eastern Arab world, exhibit the potential for political autonomy. But the spread of Arab identity and the imperatives to functional coordination arising out of technological and economic development suggest that Balkanization of the present Arab sovereignties and the larger Arab community, notwithstanding their own precarious and unconsolidated legitimacy, is not a deep-running trend. Even the Lebanese civil war has been a manifestation of sociopolitical rather than primordial-parochial cleavages. The image of an Arab Middle East dominated by particularist sectarian or ethnic elites is appealing to some for various reasons, but it is probably not an accurate forecast of the Arab future. The legitimacy of any new fragment-entities certainly would be severely challenged by the radical, secularist, assimilative, nation-building elements in Arab politics, which remain the strongest shapers of Arab goals and world views. Even though much Arab nationalist ideology of the 1950s and 1960s, with its calls for unity and social transformation, must be regarded as romantic and unrealistic, the trend is likely to remain toward assimilation rather than fragmentation, toward fewer and larger states, and toward greater functional coordination.

Is the social mobilization model, then, the most valid of the three? I feel that it is, in that it takes better account of the relevant factors. But I do not therefore conclude that the road to legitimacy in Arab politics is either smooth or short. It should be apparent from what I have said about the transformationist and mosaic perspectives that the social mobilization model, at least in its "melting pot" version, is seriously oversimplified. Thus this approach, like the other two, is unable to lead directly to a solution of the Arab legitimacy problem. Although this study ultimately concludes that the principal "cure" for the legitimacy problem is a significant degree of institutionalized participation through parliaments, parties, or equivalent bodies, it is not because social mobilization is producing bodies politic that are more individualized, liberal, educated, and tolerant, and thus "ready" for democracy. I cannot optimistically accept the old liberal arguments that a certain level of economic and social attainment (which the Arabs today are capable of reaching) are prerequisites for liberal democracy, as Lipset tried to demonstrate in general and Issawi tried to apply to Middle Eastern societies in particular.[27] Rather, it is because the political realities of an expanding, more differentiated, more organized, more sophisticated, politically mobilized population will require more representative institutions if a higher degree of political legitimacy is to be achieved. This is not to say, of course, that the requirement will be met, and it is entirely possible that higher degrees of legitimacy will

27. Seymour Martin Lipset, *Political Man* (New York: Doubleday, 1959), chap. 2.; Charles Issawi, "Economic and Social Foundations of Democracy in the Middle East," *International Affairs*, 32:1 (1956), pp. 27–42.

not be achieved. The two alternatives—chronic instability or more efficient despotism underpinned by fear and corruption—are equally foreseeable possibilities.

The particular merit of the social mobilization model lies not so much in its ability to predict a particular future as in its explication of the interplay of factors that will determine that future. Social mobilization is changing the structure of Arab politics. The possibility of assimilative nation-building remains real, though it will not occur within a short time; but, as I have indicated, the outcome is the result of the interaction between an expanding, more complex political arena, on the one hand, and the growth of government itself, on the other. These processes have profound implications for the development of government authority and political identity. Given the peculiarities of the Arab nation and the several Arab states and the sharply different levels of social mobilization in different parts of the Arab world and within particular states, it is no simple matter to sort out these implications. Consequently, it is easier to describe and analyze the struggle for legitimacy in different parts of the Arab world than it is to predict whether the Arabs are likely to develop more legitimate political systems in the future. I shall, however, hazard some opinions on this subject in the final chapter.

Strategies for Building Legitimacy

I have tried to expose the nature of the legitimacy problem in the Arab world in all its gravity and complexity. I turn now to another question: how is legitimacy developed under these difficult conditions? It might be argued that, for some regimes at least, no legitimacy whatever is developed. Indeed, John Waterbury, in an ingenious discussion of corruption in Morocco, goes even further and suggests that the system's stability depends on its pervasive illegitimacy.[28] But only the most cynical observers would contend that Arab political systems are totally devoid of legitimacy and thus completely dependent upon raw coercion for such stability as they may possess. Some systems enjoy greater legitimacy than others, and the legitimacy of particular ones fluctuates over time.

Leaders, regimes, and oppositions cope with the problem in various ways, using the instruments of legitimation at their disposal in varying combinations and trying to develop and maintain a reservoir of diffuse support as well as a specific coalition of supporters. What kind

---

28. John Waterbury, "Endemic and Planned Corruption in a Monarchical Regime," *World Politics*, 25:4 (July 1973), pp. 533–55.

of legitimacy resources can they rely on? Again, Weber's insights are germane. He states that the legitimacy of an order can be established by tradition, by positive affectual, emotional attitudes, by rational belief in its absolute value, or by recognition of its legality. In modern societies, he suggests, "the most usual basis of legitimacy is the belief in *legality*, the readiness to conform with rules which are formally correct and have been imposed by accepted procedure."[29] The difficulties confronting Arab politicians are obvious. First, Arab society is no longer traditional in the sense that any significant sectors can be swayed by appeals to custom, status, or superstition. Too much has happened in this century to disrupt customary authority relations and the status of old elites; too much social mobilization has occurred in the last generation for "primitive" superstition or fatalism to remain as reliable bases for rule. But if contemporary Arab society is no longer traditional, it is far from being fully modern; rather it is, in S. N. Eisenstadt's terminology, "post-traditional"—an obscure, ambivalent condition conducive neither to traditional legitimacy nor to rational-legal legitimacy.[30]

Second, the possibility of legitimacy based on rational belief in absolute values, expressed for example in the acceptance of natural law philosophy in the medieval West, is diminished in the modern Arab world because of the decline of Islamic jurisprudence as a significant factor in the formation of public policy. I am not suggesting that Islam is in decline as a popular religion; indeed, its importance as a solidarity bond and a component of Arabism remains undiminished. But the growing irrelevance of Islamic standards and criteria in the issues, conflicts, and policy processes of modern Arab politics and the diminishing influence of Islamic authorities in politics reduce the importance of an Islamic variant of Weber's "natural law" as a basis for legitimacy.

Third, as I have hinted, the struggle to develop legitimacy based on legality, which is the core of the Arab legitimacy problem, is only beginning. The norm that there should be "right rules of the game" is almost universally accepted by Arab elites, but the rules themselves in general have not been spelled out, have not remained permanent, and have been only sporadically effective. Given the newness of all the present Arab political systems (including the so-called traditional monarchies), it could hardly be otherwise. In short, Weber's "accepted

29. Weber, op. cit., pp. 130–32, 131.

30. S. N. Eisenstadt, "Post-Traditional Societies and the Continuity and Reconstruction of Tradition," *Daedalus*, 102:1 (Winter 1973), pp. 1–28.

procedures" are still largely absent. Little wonder, then, that what passes for regime support or popularity—transitory legitimacy—is so strongly infused with affect, emotion, and charisma. Little wonder too that it is so sporadic, mercurial, and insubstantial; it lacks solid institutional underpinnings.

I must now examine the instruments and strategies of legitimacy-building that politicians operating under the austere conditions of Arab politics can employ. What structural and cultural resources can they draw upon to generate citizen attitudes that the regime is "proper and deserving of support"?[31] David Easton has provided a useful threefold classification of legitimacy resources: personal, ideological, and structural. A strong personal leader may generate legitimacy for a regime or an entire system. The regime or opposition movement that succeeds in identifying itself with a highly salient ideological program may win positive support. Certainly in the Arab world those leaders who successfully associate themselves with the fullfillment of abstract but highly valued goals pertaining to sacred obligations, corporate identity, or deeply valued principles are likely to last longer and perform better than those who can induce compliance only on the basis of fear or expediency. Such leaders may even succeed in generating the scarcest but most enduring kind of legitimacy of all—structural or legal legitimacy, that is, a generalized respect for the rightness of the decision making and adjudicative roles and procedures of the political system itself. I will discuss briefly each of Easton's three types as they constitute the framework of analysis employed in the case studies in chapters 7, 8, and 9.

Personal

In systems "where the behavior and personalities of the occupants of authority role are of dominating importance," suggests Easton, the personal basis of legitimacy may be an important component of the overall legitimacy formula.[32] He goes on to suggest that the leader enjoying high personal legitimacy "may violate the norms and prescribed procedures of the regime and . . . ignore its regular structural arrangements." Moreover, "all political leadership, and not the charismatic type alone, if it is effective in winning support at all, carries with it this legitimizing potential; hence the concept of personal legitimacy covers a broader range of leadership phenomena than

31. Gurr. op. cit., p. 185.
32. Easton, op. cit., pp. 302–03.

charisma, in Weber's original sense, and includes the latter."[33] The political systems of the Arab world, as we shall see, have certainly assigned a strong role to personal leadership, historically and culturally. Furthermore, Arab leaders in the modern age, operating in systems that are poorly institutionalized and in the throes of ideological change, have had to carry more of the legitimacy burden than they can easily bear. Some, like Nasir and Bourguiba have exerted charisma (valid or spurious) over their followers and have single-handedly bestowed substantial coherence to their systems. Most of the region's numerous other strongmen have lacked comparable magnetism and failed to impart similar coherence, yet they have still accounted for much of whatever system legitimacy exists. One thinks of leaders like Ja'far al-Numayri of the Sudan, Mu'ammar al-Qadhafi of Libya, Hafiz al-Asad of Syria, Abd al-Karim Qassim of Iraq, and Houari Boumedienne of Algeria. That even those leaders incapable of casting magical spells over their followers can still perform a legitimizing function is due partly to the vacuum in legitimacy from other sources and partly to the historical-cultural importance assigned to personal leadership. Once again, strong leadership proves to be an unusually important common legitimizing factor in both the traditional and nontraditional regimes.

Personal leadership plays a major legitimizing role, of course, in the Arab monarchies; in fact, in all of them the king, amir, shaykh, or sultan does not merely reign but rules. It should be made clear that I am now speaking of personal, not structural, legitimacy. In traditional Arabian tribal polities we cannot say that "the office makes the man." On the contrary, the leader must demonstrate his personal competence if he is to earn the traditional oath of allegiance. What is perhaps more surprising is the persistence of monolithic personal authority structures in most of the revolutionary republican polities of the region. There is a curious continuity of personalist rule in the most traditional and the most rational systems—from Ibn Khaldun's concept of royal authority to the absolutistic presidential authority of a Nasir or Qadhafi. Since the Arab cases suggest that personal legitimacy is at least as salient in the nontraditional systems as it is in the traditional, it is difficult to accept Moore's opinion that "'personal legitimacy' is meaningless outside a traditional framework," even though he concedes that a charismatic leader can contribute

33. Ibid., pp. 303–4.

to rational legitimacy by articulating a rational formula.[34] Surely the leader's contributions to system legitimacy in Tunisia (and certainly in Egypt) are far more extensive and intensive in themselves than the rational ideologies that they propagate.

Notwithstanding the process through which new and dissonant values are taking root, the deferential orientations that support personalist rule seem to be little diminished. Yet theory would indicate that personalist legitimacy is increasingly vulnerable to erosion as societies modernize and become exposed to norms hostile to absolutism and dictatorship. If this proposition is sound, then—other things being equal—we would expect continued ferment in the monarchical and republican systems prevalent in the region. Such indeed is probably the long-term trend. But at present, personalist leadership is still a formidable legitimacy resource partly because of the absence of countervailing structures and partly because the leaders have been able to embody in themselves some of the diffuse legitimizing values arising out of political culture, most notably nationalism.

Ideological

Ideologies, Easton tells us, are "articulated sets of ideals, ends, and purposes, which help the members of the system to interpret the past, explain the present, and offer a vision for the future. . . . From a manipulative or instrumental point of view they may be interpreted as categories of thought to corral the energies of men; from an expressive point of view we may see them as ideals capable of rousing and inspiring men to action thought to be related to their achievement."[35] Ideology bulks large as a legitimacy resource in Arab politics. Indeed, political discourse in the Arab world over the past quarter century has been awash in ideology. If one were to measure frequency of symbols of nationalism, such as Islam, Palestine, democracy, liberation, and social justice, in the public speeches of Arab leaders, it would in all probability dwarf the discussion of policy alternatives, projects, and day-to-day politics; it would almost certainly exceed the attention given to comparably profound issues of identity, authority, and the ultimate good society in the political vocabulary of more settled political systems.[36]

The psychologically disruptive effects of social mobilization have

---

34. Clement H. Moore, *Politics in North Africa* (Boston: Little, Brown, 1970), p. 94, n.5.

35. Easton, op. cit., p. 290.

36. For a succinct essay on the language of Arab politics, see Hisham B. Sharabi, *Nationalism and Revolution in the Arab World* (Princeton: Van Nostrand, 1966), chap. 7.

generated not just an interest but a need for the masses newly interested in politics to identify with valued, meaningful collective goals and politicians who credibly associate themselves with these goals. The socially disruptive effects of social mobilization have created at the same time objective conditions of poverty and inequality among the rural and urban lower classes which render ideologies of socialism, redistribution, and social welfare more salient than they might have been fifty years ago. Furthermore, in the absence of structural legitimacy, ideological legitimacy assumes paramount importance almost by default. Ideology becomes a substitute for institutionalization. Perhaps, however, it serves to buy the necessary time for structural legitimacy to develop.

All the Arab regimes, whether "conservative" or "progressive," exploit ideology assiduously in their pursuit of legitimacy. But in the revolutionary republics it has been magnified into what David Apter calls political religion. To understand political religion it is necessary to extract from Apter's complex treatment of modernization his conceptualization of the consummatory and the instrumental aspects of legitimacy.[37] The consummatory aspects of legitimacy are solidarity and identity and the instrumental aspects are concerned with the effectiveness of policy making or political performance evaluated in terms of specified goals. Consummatory legitimizing values flow from Apter's "sacred-collectivity" model of the political system; instrumental ones pertain to his "secular-libertarian" model. Drawing his inspiration from Tolstoy, Apter suggests that through the mechanism of political religion, the political sector can communicate throughout society the symbols which may help satisfy the transcendental needs of individuals. These needs, which he identifies as the necessity of accepting death, establishing an individual personality, and identifying objectives, are doubtless acutely felt by people living through a period of rapid social change. The dilemma of successfully implanting new community values in societies undergoing political upheaval is obvious, and nowhere more so than in the Arab world where the religious character of society is so evident. One strategy for building a viable new mythology is to propagate a mythology that taps the need for the sacred without sacrificing the new requirements of modernity and rationality. Apter suggests that "the sacred may now be employed to develop a system of political legitimacy and to aid in mobilizing the community for secular ends."[38] The Arab, revolutionary

---

37. David E. Apter, *The Politics of Modernization* (Chicago: University of Chicago Press, 1965), p. 266, and chap. 8.

38. Ibid., pp. 39, 268, and 292.

regimes conform in theory to Apter's "mobilization system" type in which values of the sacred collectivity model are predominant to the exclusion of the secular-libertarian. Those that have come close include Iraq, Syria, Libya, the PDRY, and Algeria. Certainly "political religion" performs a central legitimizing function in these systems. It also performs a lesser role in those that have fallen short, which Apter might classify as the "neomercantilist" system—Egypt, Tunisia, the Sudan, and the Yemen Arab Republic. In all these cases the primary values invoked are secular nationalism and modernity, and their effectiveness has been enhanced by historical-cultural orientations and the powerful irritant of Western imperialism. In each system the ruling elite attempts to harmonize (in varying degrees, to be sure) religion and nationalism, kinship group and political movement, the legacy of the past and the promise of the future, the sacred and the secular, and the consummatory and the instrumental.

Political religion, however, is a problem as well as a solution from the point of view of those who favor the development of secular liberal democracies legitimized by law. As Apter puts it, "Can mobilization systems with political religions transform themselves into reconciliation systems, whose commitment is to a liberal framework of law? This is a question of great concern to the West." While such a complete transformation seems unlikely, the possibility exists for the emergence of a mixed neomercantilist system through the ritualization of political religion. Ritualization "would limit the functional consequences of religion without destroying its relation to authority." And, "If a mobilization system should begin to ritualize its leadership and traditionalize its consummatory values, by making them into a new and effective link between novelty and the past, this important alternative system becomes possible."[39] This process has been evident in the revolutionary regimes and may account in part for the superficial stability which several of them have displayed in recent years. But whether it can lay groundwork for structural legitimacy in the long run is a more doubtful proposition.

Structural

Political structures in themselves are also an important source of legitimacy. To the extent that they are seen to constitute the framework within which "accepted procedures" are carried out, they bestow legal legitimacy upon the system. In the traditional Arab polities, the offices of caliph, sultan, and shaykh generate respect

39. Ibid., pp. 305, 306–09.

based upon religion or custom, although such legitimacy is even more strongly affected by the personal reputation of the officeholder. The highly developed bureaucracies of some of the premodern dynastic Arab empires contributed to legitimacy by virtue of their pervasive presence and their control and extractive capabilities.

In trying to assess the impact of structural conditions on legitimacy in the contemporary Arab states, the concept of institutionalization as explicated by Samuel Huntington in his important study of political modernization serves as a guide. "Institutionalization," says Huntington, "is the process by which organizations and procedures acquire value and stability."[40] The more a governmental system or major structures within it are institutionalized, that is, exhibit adaptability, complexity, autonomy, and coherence, the more positively they will contribute to system legitimacy, that is, generate what Easton calls "independent belief in validity of the structure and norms."[41] Legitimacy is also enhanced by the scope of support accorded to structures; Clement Moore makes a strong case for the importance of this characteristic in his analysis of political development in North Africa.[42] The legitimizing constituency becomes larger and more widespread as society modernizes. The enlargement occurs on both the elite and mass levels. It is not easy for a political system to develop a legitimacy formula that will have wide appeal in both the enlarged mass and elite constituencies and also be capable of managing the new conflict cleavages within and between them that accompany the expansion of what Deutsch would call the population available for political participation. The extent to which the present-day Arab regimes can develop structural legitimacy is primarily a function of their ability to develop bureaucratic and party structural capabilities that extend government and politics from the settled area (the *bilad al-makhzan*) to the hinterland (the *bilad al-siba*) to perform service as well as extractive functions. Theory suggests that structurally based legitimacy may be the most durable, but of the three categories Easton proposes, this one has been the most difficult for contemporary Arab polities, whether patrimonial or republican, to develop.

Although the structural legitimacy of most of the modern Arab regimes is weak, it is also important to consider the possibility that it is getting stronger. It is easy for observers preoccupied by the feverish, conflict-ridden nature of Arab politics to forget that there has been a

40. Samuel P. Huntington, *Political Order in Changing Societies* (New Haven: Yale University Press, 1968), pp. 12–24.

41. Easton, op. cit., p. 287.

42. Moore, op. cit., pp. 91–93.

steady, unspectacular but very important development of a modern judiciary and public administration throughout the region. Unlike the early 1960s, there are today very few places in the Arab world where law and order and a governmental presence do not exist. Political scientists have not explored sufficiently the growth of modern civil and criminal codes alongside or in place of Islamic legal institutions. The considerable growth in the size of civil service and military bureaucracies in nearly all the Arab countries has added new weight to governmental authority. Furthermore, above and beyond the growing control capabilities of government there is also a growing service capability. If it is true that the growing, socially mobilized populations of the Arab world tend increasingly to judge politicians and evaluate the legitimacy of regimes by how well they perform, then it is important to consider policy formation and implementation in assessing overall legitimacy. Unfortunately, too little attention has been paid to policy outcomes, and so it is difficult to make comprehensive assessments of this complex subject.

For all the growth of bureaucratic structures, however, there has been little development of structures of political participation that are integrated within the formal political system. Parties and movements have appeared in most countries of the region, to be sure, but those that are not bureaucratized extensions of the leader or regime have usually played a dysfunctional, revolutionary, sometimes subversive role, challenging rather than consolidating such system legitimacy as may exist. Inasmuch as the liberal tradition in Arab politics was recent and of short duration, this situation is not surprising; the idea of "desert democracy" is too limited to a particular social situation to provide much historical precedent for participation in a modern setting. Nevertheless, this failing, while understandable, is of more than academic importance today because virtually all Arab politicians, conservative and progressive, whether in power or in the opposition, proclaim democracy as a central political goal. And the idea of popular participation has become widely circulated, and presumably widely accepted, by the socially mobilized masses during the last half-century. Today "government by the people, for the people, and of the people" is a criterion of political legitimacy in the Arab world, and the fact that none of the present Arab regimes meets this standard stands as a formidable obstacle to developing genuine structural legitimacy, as opposed merely to the extension of governmental control and patronage.

PATHWAYS TO LEGITIMACY

Burdened with many loads—identity problems, social change, radical ideologies, and incompletely integrated political cultures—the

Arab political systems function fitfully with their meager legitimacy resources. These systems cope with the pressures in two basic ways. One formula, in which traditional autocratic authority combined with diffuse nationalism and the ethos of development, is followed by the modernizing monarchies. The other, in which autocracy clothed in modern democratic norms and buttressed with more militant nationalism and a commitment to social equality as well as development, is practiced in the Arab republics. Most of these republics have been established recently through revolutions or struggles for independence.

The Modernizing Monarchies

With the exception of Morocco, the monarchies form a continuous group embracing most of the Arabian peninsula: Jordan, Sa'udi Arabia, Kuwait, the United Arab Emirates, Qatar, Bahrain, and Oman. Their authority is patrimonial both in theory and in fact, notwithstanding the accommodations that some of them have made toward democratic values and structures. The monarchies are legitimated primarily by the monarch's personal reputation and secondarily by the tradition of kingship (which in most cases is not firmly rooted) and an ideology emphasizing religious rectitude and kinship obligation. Ruling monarchs are nearly extinct outside the Arab world, but within this region their remarkable persistence suggests that the legitimacy formula that they embody exhibits greater congruence with sociocultural values than observers have thought. The monarchical legitimacy strategy may be designated as patriarchal in order to convey the character of the king's authority; in a fatherly way he governs each tribe and sect. King Hussein frequently speaks of Jordan as a "family." The metaphor has more than passing relevance for a culture in which the family is so central and revered and in which the father traditionally enjoys a high degree of deference from other members. Like many another father, however, Arab kings have frequently had to deal with rebellious children whose own growth and outside education incite them to challenge the established order. Historically, leadership in the tribal societies of the Arab world has fallen to chieftains whose authority has derived in part from their real or mythical kinship status, and in the Islamic polities of the past kinship has been an important legitimizing tradition.

The modern monarchies of the Arab world, not surprisingly, have exploited kinship and religion as legitimizing values: patriarchal authority is presented as normal, and the ruler's piety and dynastic proximity to the line of the Prophet Muhammad is often emphasized. But most of the present monarchs in the region have not been reticent about appropriating more modern values, presenting themselves as champions of economic development and pillars of secularized nationalism. In certain cases attempts have been made to align the monarchy with a form of parliamentary system although there has been little parliamentary independence.

Personal legitimacy, of course, bulks large among the sources of systemic legitimacy in the monarchies. Strong individual leadership as well as family or religious status are important determinants of the authority to be bestowed upon a king and, by extension, of the legitimacy of his regime. The office of monarch generates a certain structural legitimacy, but the performance of the incumbent is more important. Apart from the structural legitimacy of kingship itself, the contemporary monarchies have also succeeded in varying degree in institutionalizing their regimes more broadly. They have devoted considerable resources toward developing elaborate and capable administrative structures, particularly in the field of internal security. A different kind of structural embellishment was exemplified best until recently by Kuwait, which had developed a semiautonomous parliament and electoral system. I shall suggest that the surviving monarchies in general have been quite resourceful in exploiting the available systemic and symbolic building blocks of legitimacy.

In terms of their orientation to change, the patriarchal systems may best be described as conservative. They accept existing traditional group identities and accommodate them. They exploit traditional rivalries and play one group against another rather than trying to build a new order. The monarchs build their constituency on the traditional power holders: the upper-middle-class commercial and business elite, the large landowners, the clerical establishment, and the local notables of good families. As such they are pursuing a legitimacy strategy of accommodation rather than trying to assimilate traditional groupings into a new national identity; in this orientation they differ from the revolutionary leaders. Yet it would be misleading to suggest that the monarchs are insensitive to the legitimacy potential of certain nontraditional values. Several of the kings have sought to associate themselves with selected modern norms, particularly nationalism and development. But instead of building a new nationalism unfettered by tradition, the monarchs have simply superimposed nationalism onto existing political culture patterns without trying to eliminate them. Similarly, every monarchy in the region has set out energetically to show that it can deliver prosperity and growth just as effectively as progressive regimes. But they are wary of the more directly liberal, democratic, participatory values associated with modernity. Although they seek economic growth, they are reluctant to see the masses politicized and unwilling to permit significant mass participation or autonomous opposition groups. The Arab kings of the 1970s vary considerably in their benevolence, but they are fairly uniform in their refusal to open up their political processes in conformity with the ideals of democracy and egalitarianism, which are increasingly prevalent in their modernizing countries. Therein lies one of the principal weaknesses in the monarchical legitimacy formula.

The Revolutionary Republics

The Arab republics (with the qualified exception of Lebanon) share in varying degrees a revolutionary legitimacy. They share the traumatic experience of the revolutionary or independence event. This event serves as a watershed separating these new regimes from the web of traditional patterns of authority and influence one finds in the monarchies, and the patriarchal, deferential, sacred, and quasi-feudal values underlying them. The new regime confronts both an opportunity and a host of problems as it attempts to fill the legitimacy vacuum with modern, reformist symbols and myths. Several of the postrevolutionary regimes and leaders I shall analyze have derived considerable legitimacy simply through having participated in the independence struggle or revolutionary coup.

But beyond this exploitation of what might be called a fixed and diminishing legitimacy resource, the revolutionary republics have also sought to develop new and positive bases for government. In contrast to the conservative accommodation of existing identity and authority patterns, they have tried to break them down and integrate people into new ones. The authority problem is addressed with populist ideology and "popular organizations," bureaucratic parties and functional organizations subservient to the authorities. They have tried to build a new community committed to secular nationalism, strong central government, progress, and modernization. They seek their legitimacy through secular, rational, and universal norms. Yet, this nation-building is seriously impeded by the persistence of traditional primordial and parochial orientations. They emphasize Arabism and the importance of fulfilling hitherto frustrated national aspirations because they are well aware of the salience of these issues in Arab public opinion. But at the same time the quixotic, sporadic, uncoordinated, and usually unsuccessful efforts to achieve these ends also complicate the search for legitimacy. Indeed, the single most important delegitimizing factor for the regimes in what I shall call the pan-Arab core, has been their consistent failure to match words with effective deeds on the Palestine issue. Yet legitimacy requires at least that the words be uttered.

Under such circumstances it should be obvious why the building of structural legitimacy has been so slow, painful and as yet incomplete a process. In the absence of solid structural legitimacy, therefore, there has been an inordinate reliance on affective ideological symbols for legitimation, which accounts for the comparatively frenetic and hyperbolic style of revolutionary politics. This absence also helps explain the prominence of personalist leadership in the legitimacy formulas of the revolutionary republics.

It is useful to divide the revolutionary republics into two groups, those of the pan-Arab core and the republics of the periphery. The first group includes the older republics of the area in which Arab nationalism was born and the development of independent political structures and processes has been most complete. The politics of legitimacy in this area continues today to be shaped (and frustrated) by all-Arab concerns and by the Palestine question in particular. This group includes Egypt, Syria, Iraq, Lebanon, and the Palestinian community; in comparing their political behavior I attempt to evaluate the Nasirist, Ba'thist, Palestinian nationalist, and Lebanese pluralist approaches to the Arab legitimacy problem. The second group is more disparate, comprising Libya, Sudan, the two Yemens, Algeria, and Tunisia. Generally speaking, these political systems are newer than those of the pan-Arab core, having assumed their present forms from the late 1950s to the early 1970s. Geographically far removed from the pan-Arab core, their socioeconomic linkages with it until recently have been relatively tenuous. They share significantly in the Arab historical experience, but they also have their distinct local characteristics. Even though all-Arab concerns are becoming increasingly salient in all of the peripheral republics, and unmistakably so in Libya and Algeria, these values are not as overwhelmingly central as they are in the pan-Arab core.

As the Arab world advances toward the year 2000 is the legitimacy problem becoming more serious or less so? Scholars are divided on this question. Some are optimistic insofar as they predict the emergence of a new Arab man, or a new middle class, or new personalities embodying empathy and tolerance, or a new generation presumably more enlightened than its predecessors. Other scholars are pessimistic, seeing instead a vicious circle of praetorian instability, the monopoly of power by opportunistic military men, or even the persistence of inherent defects in the Arab mind that render modern civilized government difficult to achieve. But such visions, whether optimistic or pessimistic, must be treated with some skepticism since they suffer from a common analytical weakness: the reification of single-factor causes that lack convincing empirical support. In fact, to summarize and anticipate at the same time, the prospects for legitimacy depend on a more complicated set of conditions. On the one hand, the modernization process has sharply disrupted a political culture that even in its "traditional" state was parochial, fragmented, and dissonant. The social mobilization of the Arab masses, which is the most important fact for any political analysis of the region, has multiplied the often incompatible or contradictory policy demands made on the political system, and it has presented an array of new opportunities for opposition movements which regard existing regimes as illegitimate. Democracy, for example, is newly salient but conspicuously absent throughout the region. It has also placed additional administrative loads on governments insofar as social welfare and development responsibilities have become conventionally accepted, in conservative and progressive regimes alike. The new awareness of politics, moreover, has exacerbated the social and communal tensions latent in traditional Arab society, a development which, other things equal, suggests that ethnic and working class (urban and rural) upheavals will continue or be intensified in the coming years.

On the other hand, other things are not likely to remain equal, for the same modernization process will also generate conditions favorable for the development of legitimacy. The growth of a transportation, communications, and economic infrastructure has woven societies more closely together, thus enhancing the solidarity within specific countries and the Arab region as a whole. The new availability of the masses for politics has enhanced the integrative and legitimizing functions of Islam and even more so of Arabism. What was until only three decades ago primarily an intellectual movement, capable of mobilizing the masses only sporadically, has now developed into a significant wellspring of diffuse support for leaders and regimes skillful enough to identify themselves effectively with Arab-Islamic political goals. No less important is sheer growth in potential capabilities. The new power of governments facilitates legitimacy formation in two ways. One is through enhanced security. Although the legitimacy of a government is hardly proportional to the fright which it can inspire in its citizens, it is clear that a government with weak internal security is unlikely to generate either the support or the longevity necessary to convince people of its claims to legitimacy. Even more important is the dramatically expanded ability of Arab governments over the last two decades to make their administrative presence felt throughout their territories and to deliver new social services. Bigger governments and more secure regimes also may be able to satisfy some of the intangible value demands concerning national dignity, Palestine, and the Arab nation and in so doing yield perhaps the most important (though hardest to measure) legitimacy dividends.

I foresee neither a revolutionary leap forward into a new rational-legal consensus nor the resurrection of the Islamic polity with its ethnoreligious mosaics and stable class system. Despite the breathtaking socioeconomic development taking place in the Arab world, with all its implications for the growth of political system capabilities, the Arab political future seems cloudy. The fragmentation of the Arab nation into separate sovereignties appears largely irreversible, and only limited progress has been made toward inter-Arab coordination. So the chances for the advancement of all-Arab causes, notably Palestine, do not appear good, even as the salience of these causes in Arab public opinion intensifies. Thus, an important source of the Arab legitimacy problem, common to the monarchies as well as the republics, is not likely to diminish. Internally, the future of systems which rely mainly on traditional legitimacy is not bright, notwithstanding their unexpected durability; and the legitimacy potential of the revolutionary systems, while brighter than the analysts of praetorianism foresee, is still seriously marred by the intractability of the participation problem.

Part One

Political Culture and Social Change

2

The Elements of Arab Identity

The concept of political culture has been widely used by political scientists as a tool for interpreting political behavior. In its biological usage, a culture is a medium in which an organism lives; the nature of the medium will affect the viability and behavior of the organism. Culture, in its broadest social application according to the dictionary, is "the body of customary beliefs, social forces, and material traits constituting the distinct traditions of . . . a social group." Politics, David Easton has suggested, is "the authoritative allocation of values," and Harold Lasswell has defined it even more succinctly as the process that determines "who gets what, when, and how."[1] One can easily agree that the beliefs, forces, and traits that constitute a social culture must profoundly affect the society's political process. Even those aspects of culture which may not seem directly political—such as man's view of human nature and time, as well as his relation to nature and to his fellow man—influence political behavior.[2] An analysis of Arab political culture may help us understand more fully the legitimacy problem in Arab politics.

Sidney Verba has provided a useful explication of political culture. According to him, political culture refers to "all politically relevant orientations, whether of a cognitive, evaluative, or expressive sort . . ."; and such orientations can be held by all the members of a political system and can be directed to all aspects of politics. Verba suggests four dimensions of political culture: shared beliefs about national identity, about identification with fellow citizens, about governmental outputs, and about the decision-making process. Anticipating the problem that is obvious to any student of Arab political culture, he wisely

---

1. David Easton, *A Systems Analysis of Political Life* (New York: Wiley, 1965), p. 350; and Harold D. Lasswell, *Politics: Who Gets What When and How* (New York: Meridian Books, 1936, 1958), passim and Postscript, pp. 181–212.

2. Lucian W. Pye and Sidney Verba (eds.), *Political Culture and Political Development* (Princeton: Princeton University Press, 1965), pp. 521–22.

33

argues that the extent to which beliefs are shared is a crucial and open question to be investigated, not assumed.[3]

WHAT IS A NATION?

In his famous lecture in 1882, Ernest Renan posed the question, "What is a nation?" His answer was that nationhood resided in the collective will of the people to live together as a community. But that answer, because of its conceptual and methodological problems, was not definitive; and new generations of social scientists have felt compelled to ask it again, particularly in light of the emergence of "nations" in the Third World. Nowhere is the task of definition more difficult than in the Arab world where the multiplicity of primordial identifications includes kin group, sect, and universal religious community. In the industrialized West, these identifications are for the most part of only marginal significance to national politics and, in any event, are easily distinguished from nationalism. But in the Arab world all three are frequently closely related to a national identity. For example, the national identity of Jordanians or Kurds is colored with tribalism; the national identity of Lebanon and Yemen has been associated with a particular sect; and the national identity of Sa'udi Arabia and Libya or the Muslim Brotherhood is infused with Islamic symbols. And yet there remains a kind of group identification that cannot be subsumed under these categories. It is the prescriptive membership individuals hold in a people, their adherence to the idea of a nation, which, as Burke so eloquently put it, ". . . is an idea of continuity, which extends in time as well as in numbers and in space . . . made by the peculiar circumstances, occasions, tempers, dispositions, and moral, civil, and social habitudes of the people, which disclose themselves only in a long space of time . . ." We may think of the Arab nation as a group of individuals with a sense of their own collective distinctiveness vis à vis other individuals and collectivities who also recognize this group's distinctiveness. The principal dimensions of Arab nationhood appear to be a collective awareness of a common history, a distinctive language and culture (literature, art, folkways), a degree of similarity in appearance—which is not racial since the Arabs are an amalgam of races and do not practice racial exclusivity— and a historic, geographic homeland. "The Arab nationalism in which we believe," wrote Abd al-Rahman al-Bazzaz, "is based . . . not on racial appeal but on linguistic, historical, cultural, and spiritual ties,

3. Sidney Verba, "Conclusion: Comparative Political Culture," in Pye and Verba, op. cit., pp. 526–43.

and on fundamental vital interests."[4] Another characteristic which has particular salience in this age of modernization is a collective awareness of a common future and a collective motivation to build an ideal community through cooperative effort.

These dimensions should be understood as the most prominent outward, symbolic indicators of nationality. The political significance of a given nationalism may be a function of how many of these identity cues exist in a given situation and how salient they are to the individual compared with other identities and values. Deutsch speaks of nationalism as not just a function of differential quantities of social communication but also as a function of the complementarity of communication.[5] Persons of the same nationality communicate better with one another than with strangers: there are fewer misunder-standings, less "static." The reason is that language in general— concepts, references, style—carries a load of tacit meanings, nuances, and subtle keys to common values and experiences which differentiate assimilated from nonassimilated strangers. If this understanding of nationalism is correct, its implications for societies undergoing rapid modernization are important because it raises the possibility that the content, intensity, and scope of nationality are constantly being redefined. What differentiates national identifications from other types of community is the political content of the shared values: the shared values of nationalism are concerned with the governance of a community, issues of sovereignty, independence, power, and authority.

The Arabic nomenclature for different solidarity groups distinguishes the scope of various identity affiliations. The narrowest in scope are kinship groups—family, clan, and tribe—whose cohesiveness is cemented by a very strong sense of corporate solidarity known as *asabiyya*. *Qawm* and *watan* refer to two different shades of national identity, and both are used frequently in contemporary political discourse. The term *umma* refers to the broadest religious or national community, while the term *milla* up until recently designated a non-Islamic religious community living with the larger umma.

Asabiyya is translated in the *Encyclopedia of Islam* as "spirit of kinship." Franz Rosenthal, in his definitive translation of Ibn Khaldun's *Muqaddima*, calls it "group feeling."[6] Literally, the term

4. Quoted in Sylvia Haim (ed.), *Arab Nationalism: An Anthology* (Berkeley: University of California Press, 1964), p. 174.

5. Karl W. Deutsch, *Nationalism and Social Communication* (New York: John Wiley and the Technology Press, 1953), esp. chap. 4.

6. Ibn Khaldun, *The Muqaddimah: An Introduction to History*, translated by Franz Rosenthal, Second Edition, in three volumes, Bollingen Series 43 (Princeton: Princeton University Press, 1958, 1967), vol. 1, pp. cx, lxxvii–lxxx, 261–65.

refers to the male relations in the male line of the family or tribe, and designates the sense of solidarity which binds them to each other and promotes mutual cooperation against external forces. Anthropologists have charted the rigid hierarchy of obligations to which an individual is bound according to kinship proximity.

It was Ibn Khaldun who lifted this concept from its parochial tribal context to help explain the rise and fall of larger political dynasties. In so doing he employed the term in its broader context of "affiliation," without necessarily the blood connection of the strict interpretation. As such, asabiyya became in effect an indicator of the relative power of tribes and dynasties. Trying to explain the fragmentation of the Islamic polity up to his time (the late fourteenth century), Ibn Khaldun argued that dynastic change occurs because the outlying desert tribes maintain their asabiyya and can thus defeat the established dynasties. The latter, themselves once victors over a decadent, settled state, have now fallen victim because their asabiyya has faded and because other bases for solidarity are insufficient. And indeed, the victories of Muhammad's armies, of the Ummayads, the Abbasids and their allies, the various Persian, North African, and Turkoman dynasties, and of course the Ottomans lend plausibility to the thesis. It is note-worthy that Ibn Khaldun felt that the characteristics of the caliphate disappeared after the rule of Harun al-Rashid—the asabiyya of the Arabs had, so to speak, run dry.[7] But the interest of this analysis is not primarily with whether Ibn Khaldun's theory of desert vigor triumphing over urban decadence is acceptable, but rather in the importance that he placed on group feeling as an element of political culture apparently outranking in significance even such other bases as royal authority and religious merit. His emphasis on group feeling provides an important clue to one of the main roots of political legitimacy in the Arab world.

But what kind of clue? It would be tempting but dangerous to equate modern Arab nationalism with asabiyya. Certainly some of the modern ideologists of nation-building have cast about for alternatives to Islam as the primary legitimizing principle, and one of the principal ones (along with such ideas as liberal constitutionalism and socialism) has been the idea of a communal concept of peoplehood. The concept bears a superficial similarity with the Arab nationalist term qawm, which corresponds roughly to the German *volk*. Qawm, in turn, should be distinguished from watan, which is closer to the

7. T. W. Arnold, *The Caliphate* (Oxford: Clarendon Press, 1924), pp. 74–76.

territorial nationalism of the French *patrie*.[8] Asabiyya refers to the blood solidarity of a relatively small society, the tribe, in a unique historical-geographical context. *Qawmiyya*, on the other hand, is not a solidarity bond based on blood relationships but rather an ethno-linguistic concept of peoplehood. While tribes, clans, and extended families have become somewhat weaker than they used to be, parochial kinship solidarity groupings still exist. But they are hardly to be considered the sinews of modern Arab identity. On the contrary, asabiyya on balance is a powerful divisive force in the Arab world today, and it is dysfunctional for the development of a more integrated Arab political culture.

The word *umma* (from the root meaning "mother" or "source") has been used to designate the Islamic community—the organic family of Muslims; the word carries more of communal connotation than the more legalistic term *Dar al-Islam*, the domain of Islam. The word *umma* also has come to be used in twentieth century Arab nationalism to designate the "Arab nation," the *umma al-arabiyya*. This term is constantly used in the public pronouncements of all Arab heads of government, even though all attempts to achieve it have thus far failed. Do these failures indicate that the idea of the umma al-arabiyya is unimportant or declining? Perhaps not, for the warm, affective umma requires no more than this sense of brotherhood. Nor does it impose upon its members the same strict communal obligations that the narrower term asabiyya, tribal solidarity, does. Umma then is the broadest, most inclusive, least elaborated category of affective, primordial affiliation.

Umma should also be distinguished from the term *milla* (or millet) which is common in Arabic, Persian, and Turkish. A milla is a religious community in the *umma al-islamiyya*. To think of these sectarian groups merely as communities in the sense of neighborhood solidarity neglects the political content of the term. The Maronite Christian community of Mount Lebanon, for example, though technically a milla, regarded itself as a nation.[9] In the age before the idea of modern nationhood was current, the Maronites felt themselves to be a community, not exactly sovereign but autonomous and self-governing in their own territory. And while the fundamental linkages of sectarian solidarity were

8. Charles F. Gallagher, "Language, Culture, and Ideology: The Arab World," in Kalman Silvert (ed.), *Expectant Peoples: Nationalism and Development* (New York: Random House, 1963), pp. 199–231, esp. 217–19.

9. See Iliya Harik, *Politics and Change in a Traditional Society: Lebanon, 1711–1845* (Princeton: Princeton University Press, 1968), esp. chap. 6.

religious and communal, the long-term existence of the community in a particular area gradually led to an auxiliary notion of national territory (or watan). Thus, it was but a short step for some of these minorities to adopt the modern European idea of nationalism and ultimately to demand formal national independence from the Turkish Empire. Underlying the Lebanese civil war of the mid-1970s was the conflict between Maronite and various Arab nationalisms. The concepts of nation and ethnoreligious community then are closely related in their political character.

Albert Hourani has stated that the fundamental identity patterns of Middle Easterners in the eighteenth century were religious and ethnic.[10] Today, in the late twentieth century these patterns have by no means disappeared, but rather have been recast in modern nationalism and poured into the sometimes ill-fitting mold of sovereign, secular, territorial nation-state.

THE CORE OF ARABISM: ETHNICITY AND RELIGION

The hallmarks of modern Arab identity are, on the ethnic dimension, Arabic language and culture, and on the religious dimension, Islam. On both dimensions, the inhabitants of the Arab world are overwhelmingly homogeneous. Ethnographers look upon language as a key defining characteristics of ethnic communities, although physiognomy, skin color, and common historical experiences are also important. "The language of a people is closely tied to their ethnic background," says an authoritative Soviet atlas of ethnic communities. "Giving up one's native language—the basic means of communication among people belonging to the same nation, the basic means of preserving and developing their cultures—although not equivalent to complete ethnic assimilation, does testify to a very significant development of assimilating processes."[11] According to data from this atlas, the Arab states are among the most homogeneous in the world; only the Sudan (with its non-Arab southern provinces), Morocco and Algeria (with their Berber communities), and Iraq (with its Kurdish population) fall around or below the world median and mean. Of the rest, Egypt, Jordan, Sa'udi Arabia, the Yemens and postrevolutionary Libya are almost completely Arab in language and culture; and very

10. Albert Hourani, "Race, Religion, and Nation State in the Near East," *A Vision of History: Near Eastern and Other Essays* (Beirut: Khayat's, 1961), pp. 72–73.

11. *Atlas Narodov Mira* (Moscow: Department of Geodesy and Cartography of the State Geological Committee of the U.S.S.R. Academy of Sciences), p. 123; quoted in Charles L. Taylor and Michael C. Hudson, *World Handbook of Political and Social Indicators*, Second Edition (New Haven: Yale University Press, 1972), pp. 215–16; also pp. 271–74.

small ethnolinguistic minorities are found in Lebanon, Syria, Tunisia, Kuwait, and the Gulf states. In the post–World War II period, the only ethnolinguistic challenges to Arab political and cultural dominance have come from the south Sudan blacks and the Iraqi Kurds, and both of these uprisings, insofar as they were secessionist, failed, at least for the immediate future.

The Arab world today is also overwhelmingly Islamic. Save for the Sudan and Lebanon, each with nearly half its population non-Muslim, the Arab states are either almost wholly Muslim or contain small but important Christian minorities of around 10 percent, as in Syria, Jordan, Egypt, and the Palestinian community. A ranking of 136 countries in the world in terms of percentage of Muslim population finds the Arab states, except for Sudan and Lebanon, among the top 22.[12]

In emphasizing the ethnolinguistic and religious homogeneity of the Arab world (a point so obvious that its significance is sometimes overlooked), I do not mean to ignore the existence and political significance of the non-Arab, non-Muslim, and nonorthodox Muslim minorities in the Arab world; they are discussed in the next chapter. Now, however, having established the ubiquity of Arabness and Islam, it is necessary to examine each of these identity traits more closely and qualitatively.

The Roots of Arab Identity

According to Sati al-Husri, the most influential theorist of modern Arab nationalism,

> Every person who speaks Arabic is an Arab. Everyone who is affiliated with these people is an Arab. If he does not know this or if he does not cherish his Arabism, then we must study the reasons for his position. It may be a result of ignorance—then we must teach him the truth. It may be because he is unaware or deceived—then we must awaken him and reassure him. It may be a result of selfishness—then we must work to limit his selfishness.[13]

There is no doubt that contemporary Arab nationalists agree with this broad definition. Anyone whose native tongue is Arabic belongs to the umma al-arabiyya, the Arab nation, and partakes of *uruba*, Arabism.

---

12. Taylor and Hudson, op. cit., pp. 279–80.

13. Quoted in William L. Cleveland, *The Making of an Arab Nationalist* (Princeton: Princeton University Press, 1971), p. 127.

Divided today into twenty sovereign states, most Arabs, elites and masses alike, hope to achieve a greater degree of political integration in order that they may experience a renaissance that will equal or surpass the greatness of medieval Arab-Islamic civilization. The success of Iran and Turkey in achieving internal integration and coming to terms with the West still seems to elude the Arabs, at least in the view of many Arab intellectuals. Not that history of the Arabs is any less glorious than that of the Persians and Turks; indeed the problem seems to be that the past, glorified as it is in the current mythology, has given rise to expectations and dreams which the accomplishments of the present, impressive as they are, fall so far short of as to induce frustration rather than pride.

Just as the Jews consider themselves the people descended from Abraham and his son Isaac, the Arabs, another people arising from a group of tribes, claim prophetic ancestry. The mythical dualism between the north and south Arabian tribes finds the former party, or the descendants of Adnan, also related to Abraham through Ishmael, his first son by his wife's slave girl Hagar. The southern, or Qahtan, party, claims even more ancient lineage from the fifth generation after Shem, one of Noah's sons.[14] The terms Arab and Jew thus refer in myth at least to ancient kinship groups; and today it is not uncommon to hear Arabs and Jews refer to each other, not without irony, as "cousins". A distinguished and legendary genealogy is thus one dimension of Arabism. It is not heavily emphasized in contemporary Arab nationalist ideology, yet in Sa'udi Arabia today it is still common to identify people according to their northern or southern tribal origins.

Nor has the pre-Islamic history of the Arabs been strongly stressed. Although the modern Arab territories of the Nile and Tigris-Euphrates valleys are the cradle of civilization, there has been relatively little effort on the part of modern Arab nationalists to link these ancient civilizations to the heritage of the past. To be sure, local nationalists, particularly in Egypt, have made such efforts from time to time, but they have been marginal to the mainstream of Arab nationalism.[15] A visitor to Baghdad and its excellent museum which traces the impressive

14. Raphael Patai, *Golden River to Golden Road* (Philadelphia: University of Pennsylvania Press, 1969), chap. 7.

15. Note the relative paucity of pre-Islamic symbols and references in the Arab nationalist writings, particularly the more recent ones, assembled by Sylvia Haim in *Arab Nationalism: An Anthology* (Berkeley and Los Angeles: University of California Press, 1964). The principal exception is Edmond Rabbath's *Unite Syrienne et Devenir Arabe*. See Professor Haim's Introduction, esp. pp. 36–38, and selection No. 9 by Rabbath.

civilizations of Mesopotamia—Babylonian, Assyrian, Chaldean—
would observe that the Iraqis are increasingly interested in their
antiquity but would find little reference in modern nationalist ideology
to these pre-Islamic empires. By contrast, modern Iran strongly
emphasizes the uniqueness of Iran prior to and apart from Islam. The
difference lies in the special relationship between Arabism and Islam.
Islam arose among the tribes and towns of western Arabia and was
carried by Arab tribal armies who established their local rule in
Egypt and Iraq, as indeed they did all the way from Spain to Persia,
through exclusive Arab elites. From the beginning of Islam until the
fragmentation in the Abbasid caliphate we find a distinctively Arab
stamp on the empire. There is also a theological reason. Islam, embodying the final and most correct of God's revelations, was disseminated to bring to an end the era of ignorance—the *jahiliyya*—as
Islamic teachers described the pre-Islamic period. Inasmuch as all that
had gone before was now revealed as unworthy, it is not surprising that
Arabism should treat so summarily the preexisting cultures and
heritages. This tendency is an indication of just how strong the impact
of Islam on Arab identity has been. I consider the Islamic impact in
some detail below.

Some interpreters of Arab history, such as Philip Hitti, discuss it
in terms of political-military accomplishments, on the one hand, and
the contributions of its outstanding cultural and intellectual figures, on
the other.[16] The former include, as we have seen, the amazing conquests at the expense of the Byzantine and Sassanian empires. Every
Arab schoolchild knows not only of the remarkable accomplishments
of Muhammad as Prophet, leader, soldier, and diplomat, but also of
other heroes of that age: Umar ibn al-Khattab, the second caliph,
whose strong character and organizational talents made him, in von
Grunebaum's view, the master-builder of the "Arab-Muslim theocracy";[17] the great generals like Khalid ibn al-Walid, whose victory
at the battle of the Yarmuk (A.D. 636) drove the Byzantines out of
Syria, Amr ibn al-As, who captured Egypt in 639; Salah al-Din
al-Ayyubi (Saladin), who recovered Jerusalem from the Crusaders in
1187 and greatly reduced their territories, and the Mamluk general
Baybars who turned back the Mongol advance in 1260 at the historic
battle of Ayn Jalut in northern Palestine. The fact that certain of these

16. Philip K. Hitti, *Makers of Arab History* (London: Macmillan, 1968).

17. Gustave E. von Grunebaum, *Classical Islam: A History, 600–1258* (London: Allen and
Unwin, 1963, tr. 1970), p. 55.

heroes were not ethnically Arab (Saladin was of Kurdish origin, Baybars of Turkish stock) does not diminish their importance in contemporary Arab mythology.

The Arabs take as much pride in their cultural achievements as they do in their religious-military conquests. Materially, Baghdad of the Abbasids was a place of splendor. Through the *One Thousand and One Nights* the ordinary Westerner has obtained one of his few glimpses of medieval Middle Eastern society at its height; the exotic court of the Caliph Harun al-Rashid (786–809), for example, was a far cry indeed from the instability, corruption, and puritanism that was to come later. At this time Baghdad, according to von Grunebaum, may have had a population of 300,000 while Paris in 1380 had a mere 58,000 inhabitants.[18]

One important function of classical Arab civilization, particularly in the early Abbassid period, was to serve as a kind of cultural transmission belt, preserving Hellenic thought through translation into Arabic and ultimately passing it back to a Europe emerging from its post-Roman cultural decline. The Arab-Islamic civilization of those days, Constantine Zurayk has reminded us, was noted for a cosmopolitanism and tolerance—indeed, an open-mindedness and spirit of inquiry—that distinguishes a great and vital civilization.[19] To the Arabs' gifts of language, religion, and law were added, in addition to Greek philosophy, Indian contributions in mathematics and astronomy and Persian literary and administrative talents.

But the classical Islamic culture was more than a transmission belt; there were important original contributions as well. Philip Hitti, a distinguished historian of the Arabs, has catalogued some of them.[20] In the field of philosophy, where the central concern was the reconciliation of Greek rationalism with Islamic thought, scholars like al-Kindi (801–73) and al-Farabi (d. 950) made important contributions. These men, like most of the other intellectual giants of the time, were not just specialized in one field as in the modern age but were also accomplished in areas as diverse as music, optics, astrology, and alchemy. Men acclaimed primarily for their contributions in medicine such as al-Tabari (ca. 850) and Ibn Sina (Avicenna, 980–1037) are also known as historians and philosophers. Perhaps the last of the giants of the Arab-Islamic tradition was Ibn Khaldun, the

18. Ibid., p. 100.

19. Constantine Zurayk, "The Essence of Arab Civilization," *Middle East Journal*, 3 (April 1949), pp. 125–39.

20. Philip K. Hitti, *History of the Arabs*, Tenth Edition (New York: Macmillan, 1970), chaps. 24, 27.

fourteenth century Tunisian scholar, traveler, jurist, and diplomat, whose "Introduction" (*al-Muqaddima*) to the study of history, is acclaimed as a masterly sociological study of political power and authority. Others have compared him to his Italian contemporary Machiavelli: both were positivists concerned with the objective realities of human behavior; and both were able, remarkably, to free themselves from the prevailing theological perspectives. Thus their writings convey an uncanny sense of modernity to the twentieth century reader.

According to von Grunebaum, the Ummayad dynasty marks "the period of the self-destruction of the Arabs as a nation state,"[21] The exclusively Arab character of the Islamic polity was diluted during the Abbasid period, and Persian cultural influences became significant. The Abbasid revolution began around the turn of the eighth century in Iranian Khurasan. It ended with the defeat of Ummayad armies near Isfahan in 749 and the establishment of a new government in Baghdad by a member of the Abbasid family. No doubt Arab exclusivism contributed to the undermining of the regime in a political culture that was increasingly fragmented by Arab migrant settlers. According to one recent interpretation, the Abbasid revolution should not be understood as the "Persianizing" of the Islamic polity but as an indicator of Islam's success as a movement "above politics" to achieve "the assimilation of all Muslims, Arabs and non-Arabs, in the empire, into one Muslim community with equal rights for every member of the community."[22] Islam was now independent of any particular ethnically defined elite or dynasty. A number of separate, local dynasties appeared in North Africa and Persia in the ninth and tenth centuries, some claiming the caliphate for themselves, while the Abbasid caliphate lingered on, moribund, from the middle of the tenth century until the Mongol conquest of Baghdad in 1258. The Mamluks seized power in Egypt in 1260. They allowed the old Islamic culture in its Arabic form to survive until they were defeated by the Ottoman Turks in 1517. Then, for almost exactly 400 years, until the end of World War I, almost all of the Arabic-speaking lands were ruled by the sultan in Constantinople, and Arabism lay dormant.

But if the Arab nation-state had long since collapsed, the revival of the Arabs as a modern nation of states was now about to begin. In the nineteenth century, with the onset of modernization, the Muhammad Ali revolt in Egypt, the decay in the Ottoman Empire, and the

---

21. Von Grunebaum, op. cit., p. 64.

22. M. A. Shaban, *The Abbasid Revolution* (Cambridge: Cambridge University Press, 1970), p. xv.

local impact of Great Power rivalries, the first stirrings of a national political and cultural reawakening began to occur among the Arabs. Given the dynastic confusion and the long experience of alien rule, one can understand why the problem of building a new national identity on historical grounds has been a difficult one and why today's secular-modernist Arab movements like the Ba'th (Arab Socialist Renaissance party) have enshrined the medieval Arab-Islamic heritage in their ideology.

ARAB NORTH AFRICA

Although today a part of the Arab nation, the North African peoples historically have developed political identities somewhat different from the mainstream of Arabism. The political culture of North Africa is an amalgam of Berber and Arab traits, Islamic orthodoxy and heterodoxy, and dynastic parochialism. Consequently, as Gallagher and others have observed, its identity is not unambiguously Arab, African, or European;[23] nation and people are particularly elusive. Of the three, however, Arabism is uppermost. A review of the Maghrib's historical development may throw some light on this peculiar political subculture.

Glorious Carthage, strong and prosperous from the seventh through the fourth centuries B.C., finally fell to Rome in the Punic wars (264–146 B.C.). Rome imposed its own administration, economic system, and pagan religion; and when the empire was converted to Christianity, the indigenous Berbers were confronted with yet another alien belief system. North Africa and then Rome fell to the Vandals, but Eastern Christianity was restored in 534 in the reign of the Emperor Justinian and survived until the Muslim conquests a century later. The division of Rome and of Christianity into Western Latin and Eastern Greek factions was reflected in North Africa. The area's rugged terrain and fragmented Berber society made it propitious for heretics, mystics, and secret brotherhoods—a condition that was to frustrate the orthodox among the invaders, be they Christian or, later, Muslim.

The Muslims began their push across North Africa by capturing Cyrenaica in A.D. 642–43; in 670 the caliph's victorious general, Ukba ibn Nafi, began building the great mosque of Kayrawan in Tunisia; and by the beginning of the eighth century, the Muslims had reached Morocco. But Arab Islam was not to be impressed immediately upon

23. Charles F. Gallagher, *The United States and North Africa* (Cambridge: Harvard University Press, 1963), pp. 15–30.

the fragmented and turbulent North African society. The armies of the initial wave of conquest were small, their social impact was limited, and their mission of subjugation was difficult because of the incessant uprisings of dissident religious and tribal elements. Only with the second wave of Arab migration in the middle of the eleventh century was there sufficient settlement of migrant Arab tribes from the east to begin to make an impact. But the impact by that time was cultural rather than political, any semblance of centralized rule from the eastern caliphate having ceased by the end of the eighth century.

Faced with persistent local dissidence, the Abbasid caliph recognized the autonomy of the Aghlabids, an Arab dynasty centered in what is now Tunisia; this ninth century dynasty ruled over a largely Berber and Islamicized population. The Aghlabids were displaced by the Fatimids, an Arab-Muslim dynasty, to be sure, but Shi'ite. The Fatimids had been launched on their historic course by a Berber tribe of the modern-day Algerian Kabylia region. The Fatimids, reversing the direction of Islamic cultural diffusion, moved their caliphate to Egypt and founded the city of Cairo in 969. Their heterodoxy and power posed the most significant political challenge to Islamic orthodoxy until the expansion of Christian Europe. The Fatimids ruled from Cairo until 1171 when they in turn were dislodged by the orthodox Salah al-Din, the warrior who went on to subdue the Crusaders. The Fatimids belong more in the historical stream of the eastern Arab world than of North Africa; yet in linking the two briefly, they symbolize the limits of Islamic universalism.

In Tunisia the Fatimids were succeeded by a Berber dynasty, the Zirids. Meanwhile, in 788 the Shi'ite Idris ibn Abdalla, another heretic in eastern Muslim eyes, found refuge in Morocco and began to build a dynasty that would last a century. Idris was a *sharif*, a direct descendant of the Prophet's daughter and son-in-law, Fatima and Ali. This is the same lineage from which the present Alawite dynasty of Morocco, and its present King Hassan, claim descent and special legitimacy. Idris succeeded with the support of a Berber tribe, the Awreba, which he converted from its previous Christianity; his son and successor was the offspring of a Berber concubine.[24]

Up until the middle of the eleventh century, the Arabization of "Ifriqiya" was limited and superficial; and its Islamicization, though more widespread, was shot through with local variations and doctrinal deviances, especially Kharijite and Shi'ite. Then a new and far more

24. John K. Cooley, *Baal, Christ, and Mohammed: Religion and Revolution in North Africa* (New York: Holt, Rinehart, and Winston, 1965), p. 88.

substantial Arab migration occurred when the Fatimids (now in Egypt) expelled two large and troublesome tribes, the Beni Hilal and the Sulaim; others followed as well. The Arabization and Islamicization of North African culture, however imperfect, by now seemed permanent. Yet Maghribi politics remained essentially anarchic, consisting of perennial struggles between the great Berber tribal federations, the Sanhaja and the Zenata.[25] Then, at about the same time of the great Arab migrations, the first of the three dynasties that (in Gallagher's words) "gave classic dimensions to North African history" was established out of this tribal conflict.[26] It was composed of nomadic, puritanical Muslim Berbers from Mauritania (land of the "Moors"). This was the Berber-speaking Almoravid (al-Murabitun) dynasty, which ruled from 1056 to 1147 and was the first to unify Morocco. Its successor, the Almohad (al-Muwahhidun) dynasty, ruled until 1269 over not just Morocco but all the way to Tripolitania in what is today western Libya. It continued the mission of the Almoravids in trying to protect Muslim Spain against increasing Christian European pressure. It also reinvigorated the flagging Almoravid puritanism and managed to adapt the remarkably decentralized and egalitarian features of Berber tribal politics to the imperial level. In Tunisia, a branch of the Almohads, the Hafsids, established their own dynasty, which lasted from the early thirteenth century until the Ottoman Turkish take-over in the early sixteenth century.

A comparative decline in cultural vitality and political capability occurred throughout the area from the fourteenth century onward, particularly in Morocco under the Merinid dynasty. Maraboutism, the mystical Islamic revivalist movement, developed partly in response to the political decay. As the Spanish and Portuguese expelled Muslim rule from Spain and began even to occupy spots along the North African coast, the local rulers looked back to the east for help from the mighty Ottoman Turkish Empire. The Barbarossa brothers, between 1504 and 1529, led a revival of Muslim resistance and piracy against the Spanish depredations from Tunis and Algiers. They allied themselves with the Turks who had recently burst into Egypt and the eastern Mediterannean. By the end of the sixteenth century, Ottoman Turkey had divided its North African territories into the regencies of Tripolitania, Tunis, and Algiers—the Barbary coast.

Morocco, however, went its own way. Having virtually disinteg-

25. Neville Barbour, *A Survey of North West Africa*, Second Edition (London: Oxford University Press, 1962), p. 83.
26. Gallagher, op. cit., pp. 49–50.

rated by the end of the fifteenth century into a fragmented, disorganized collection of Muslim communities under the nominal leadership of the Berber Beni Wattas dynasty, Morocco was easy prey to the Portuguese and Spanish who occupied coastal enclaves. A new non-Berber dynasty arose in 1549 out of this confusion to resist the Europeans and hold Morocco together. This was the house of Sa'd, which claimed sharifian status and of course Arab lineage. The Sa'dis, influenced by the widespread mystical *sufi* maraboutism, viewed the Ottoman caliphate as an enemy of the true Islam. They also faced, internally, the enmity of the Berber tribes and, externally, the threats from the Spanish as well as the Turks. By 1660, during another internal crisis, the Sa'dis had been superseded by a new dynasty which also claimed Arab sharifian descent, the Alawites; this dynasty still rules Morocco, in spite of many vicissitudes, over 300 years later.[27]

On the eve of the modern age, the configuration of political and communal identities in Arab North Africa was highly fragmented. Soon a fundamental new complication was to be added: European imperialism. Out of this melange of commitments and experiences the Maghribi politicians, architects of independence in the 1950s, would have to build new structures of authority and myths of legitimacy.

THE ISLAMIC COMPONENT OF ARAB IDENTITY

The profound significance of Islam as a component of Arab identity lies in its pervasiveness in society, its integrating function beyond kinship, its adaptability, and its sociopolitical values. Islam is above all a confraternity of believers in the one true God, Allah, and his precepts as transmitted in most perfect form by Muhammad, his messenger. God's precepts are applicable to all spheres of life, and it is obligatory for Muslims to observe them in the Islamic community, the Dar al-Islam, and to extend its boundaries. In theory, there is no distinction between the worldly and the divine; the Muslim is not enjoined to render unto God what is His and unto Caesar what is his. In the domain of Islam, Caesar should be under God's divine guidance; alternatively, in certain branches of Shi'ism, a part of God's divinity is directly implanted in the leader, or *imam*. Worship, through prayer five times a day, is continuous, not episodic, and Paradise will only be attained through obeying God's precepts in daily life. This theological pervasiveness is matched by a symbolic pervasiveness. The symbols of Islam are ubiquitous: the mosques, the sound of the Qur'an being chanted from minarets, the arabesque character of decoration and

27. Barbour, op. cit., pp. 85–86.

architecture. Socially, Islam is manifest in charitable organizations, religious school systems, brotherhoods and orders, and the Friday address in the mosque. Studying or memorizing the Qur'an is the primary element in a young Muslim's education. Politically, the interpreters of the Law of Islam, the *Shari'a*, have always been close to the centers of dynastic power: the formal separation of church and state was until recent times inconceivable, and even today, although secular-minded rulers have to a large extent succeeded in reducing the power of religious leaders, the reaction of the Muslim judges and scholars, as well as masses of the faithful, to secular reforms is still significant. Individually, the Islamic ethic is a code of conduct whose observance commands respect and whose violation leads to censure and sometimes punishment by the community.

Islam's stress on the omnipotence of God and on the necessity for submission is indicated in the word *islam* itself, which means submission; a Muslim is one who submits. It has given rise to what many writers see as an attitude of fatalism among Muslims, not just toward God but more generally toward society and worldly circumstances. The pious Muslim accepts his fate knowing that a better world awaits him if he observes God's law. Contrasting with this fatalism, however, is what von Grunebaum called a "Calvinist paradox": the emphasis, particularly in early Islam on individual will and responsibility.[28] And even down to the moderate and radical reformers of the modern age, one senses an impatience with the seeming apathy or indifference of Muslims to rebuilding the Heavenly City on earth. There is thus a tension inherent in Islamic doctrine itself (not to mention Islamic history and current practice) between fatalism and dynamism, which makes it difficult to accept the usual generalization about Islam and political apathy. Indeed, much of the conventional wisdom about Islam and politics needs to be examined with skepticism.

Five obligatory pillars make Islam a constant and powerful factor in the normal life of the pious Muslim; he does not compartmentalize the religious sphere of his life from the other domains as do many Christians of the industrialized societies. At the same time, the pillars reinforce his sense of brotherly solidarity with his coreligionist. In the opinion of one writer, the profession of faith (there is no Divinity beyond the only Divinity, and Muhammad is the messenger of this Divinity) reveals Islam as "the religion of certitude and equilibrium, as Christianity is the religion of love and sacrifice."[29] Ritual prayers are per-

28. Von Grunebaum, op. cit., p. 33.
29. Frithjof Schuon, *Understanding Islam* (London: Allen and Unwin, 1963), p. 16.

formed at five specific periods during the day. Almsgiving is an individual obligation and is also carried out collectively by charities and landed charitable foundations (*waqfs*). The actual Islamic tax, the *zakat*, is still collected as such by some Arab governments such as the Yemen Arab Republic, and it underlies the philosophies of social justice that guide states such as Libya and Sa'udi Arabia where the influence of Islam is especially strong. The pilgrimmage is enjoined upon all who can afford to make it; in 1975 the number of pilgrims in the annual *hajj* season was 1.4 million. Special charter flights are scheduled from Arab and Muslim countries. Fasting occurs during the month of Ramadan and consists of total abstention from food or sexual activity between sunrise and sunset. The efforts of efficiency-minded governments, such as Tunisia in 1970 and 1971, to divert the piety of the fast into more socially useful and less economically draining forms have generally met with resistance.[30] Ramadan, however, did not prevent Egypt and Syria from launching the 1973 war against Israel.

Despite its elaborate structure and divine origins the Shari'a law has had only limited application in the Islamic lands; in fact, beginning with the fragmentation of the Abbasid period, it gave way increasingly to the worldly law and power of the dynastic rulers. According to Schacht, in modern times the Shari'a has "virtually ceased to demand actual observance."[31] Nevertheless, it remained theoretically paramount and did not disappear from the official codes in Turkey until 1928. Today Sa'udi Arabia is the only major country where there is extensive practical application of the Shari'a, although in many other countries the Shari'a and the Muslim judges (*qadis*) govern matters of personal status. But there can be no doubt of the long-term historical trend; and in most countries the central state with its European-inspired law codes inexorably extends its authority, circumscribing the Shari'a in its traditional urban and settled strongholds and replacing tribal customary law predominant in the wilder regions of desert and mountain.

Islam was a complete social system; membership—submission to God—admitted all on an equal basis before the demands, rewards, and punishments of God and thus created a certain brotherhood above

30. On President Bourguiba's effort, see *The New York Times*, November 7, 1971; and "The Ramadan Reform Controversy," selections by Habib Bourguiba and Kamil al-Shinnawi, in Benjamin Rivlin and Joseph Szyliowicz (eds.) *The Contemporary Middle East* (New York: Random House, 1965), pp. 168–78.

31. Joseph Schacht, "Shari'a," in the *Shorter Encyclopedia of Islam* (Leiden: E. J. Brill, 1953), pp. 524–29.

the immediate ties of kinship. It also conferred a stability, an equilibrium, on society as a whole, even to the point of supporting the passive acceptance of wrongs committed by the ruler who nonetheless deferred (theoretically) to the sanctity of the Shari'a. Unlike the history of Christianity in the West, there were no profound internal challenges to the Islamic way of life until the nineteenth century: instead of a conflict between church and state, the Islamic state absorbed the caliphate while reaffirming the unity of religion and politics. Instead of undergoing Christianity's fundamental doctrinal strife, Islamic orthodoxy retained its coherence, balance, and certainty. Perhaps it was the very certainty of the system that contributed to its tolerance of minorities. Although the esoteric nature of Islamic theological disputation draws the attention of Orientalists, for the ordinary Arab Islam is a creed that significantly defines his communal identity and obligations.

In trying to comprehend Arabism, therefore, it is essential to consider Islam, even though Islam had outgrown its Arab origin and political structures by early in the ninth century and spread far beyond the Arab peoples. That God chose to reveal His most perfect Word to Arabs, in Arabic, and that by God's will or historical circumstances it was the Arabs who spread Islam throughout the world is of deep significance to Arabs. In Turkey, Islam was almost broken as a political structure by the revolution of Kemal Ataturk; in Iran, which has been Shi'ite since Safavid times, the Pahlavi shahs have managed to circumvent it and emphasize monarchical symbols; but in almost all of the Arab states, including the relatively secularized ones such as Egypt, Algeria, and Tunisia, the force of Islam as a legitimizing principle is evident even at the highest levels.

To be sure, the caliphate has long since disappeared, the Shari'a law has been vastly supplemented almost everywhere by Western civil, legal, commercial, and international codes, and the former influence of the *ulama*, the scholars and interpreters of the Shari'a, has been decimated. Yet Islam remains a potent force for political mobilization, and Islamic notables are often politically influential. The shaykhs and ulama, for example, played a central role in the development of nationalist resistance in all the Arab North African states. In the Palestinian Arab strike and uprising of 1936–39, religious leaders helped organize armed struggle; and in the Palestinian resistance to Israeli occupation after 1967, the Muslim notables have once again played a prominent role. When an Israeli court in 1976 granted Jews access to the Mosque of Umar, which is built on the site of Solomon's temple, the decision set off waves of violent protest by Palestinian

Muslim Arabs. The Friday sermon in the mosques of Lebanon and Syria frequently touches on political matters and sometimes exhorts the faithful to certain kinds of political action. Throughout the Arab states, which as we shall see are generally lacking in the political infrastructure of parties, a free press, and associated interest groups, Islamic institutions continue to perform an important integrative and mobilizing function, sometimes serving to crystallize the opposition to a given regime.

There is scarcely a ruler in the Arab world who does not maintain at least the appearance of piety. Almost every Arab constitution makes Islam the state or official religion. In 1973 when the Ba'th regime in Syria wrote a new constitution that failed to declare Syria an Islamic state, there were serious disturbances. Colonel Qadhafi, leader of the Libyan revolution in 1969, has taken unprecedented steps to restore Islamic practices in a political system whose ideology is radical nationalist, modernist, and socialist. In Algeria, considered by many to be in the vanguard of Arab revolutionary states, a narrowly based technocratic-military elite seeks to broaden its legitimacy with a revival of Islamic culture. Even while he was destroying the Muslim Brotherhood, Gamal Abd al-Nasir emphasized his piety; and his successor Anwar al-Sadat (who is now referred to as Muhammad Anwar al-Sadat) has pursued the same stratagem even more vigorously. The emergence of Sa'udi Arabia, the heartland of the severest school of Islam, as a major power during the reign of the late King Faisal, according to local observers, has strengthened the conservative religious elements in almost all of the neighboring countries, notably in the Gulf, both Yemens, Egypt, Syria and even Iraq, the most ideologically rigid of the progressive regimes. The trend was strikingly illustrated when the Iraqi leader Saddam Hussein visited Sa'udi Arabia in 1976 and presented Prince Fahd with a copy of the Qur'an produced with the calligraphic excellence for which Iraq is famous. A Sa'udi newspaper commented approvingly on this "remarkable gesture," seeing in it a sign that Iraq was now going to emphasize Islamic solidarity in its foreign policy and by implication reduce its solidarity with atheistic powers.

The historical development of Islam illustrates that, by the force of its doctrine and by the wide scope of its concerns—psychological, social, economic, legal, and political—Islam has been an enormously significant integrating force for the Arabs. ". . . Islam had great success in integrating the political life of its adherents," writes W. Montgomery Watt, ". . . in the formation of the ummah or Islamic community. . . ." Islam harnessed tribal solidarity to the larger community and harmonized established tribal mores with the "beaten path" of the Sunna.[32]

Islam in the Arab world differs from religion in Western society: it permeates the daily life of the individual with its ritualistic obligations. It is an important part of socialization; it affects personal status; it plays a political role. Islam also serves to integrate Arab society by inculcating a sense of the Muslim's special relationship with God and in the brotherhood and mutual obligations of all believers. Because it has outgrown or circumscribed the historical-political structures of the area and because its core doctrine and demands are so clear, it has adapted itself to changing social conditions; despite a century of modernization and resolution, it still holds sway over the Arab masses. It is thus a powerful force for social and cultural stability. A contrapuntal strain is the commitment to struggle to perfect and defend the domain of Islam. Palestine is fundamentally a national issue for Arabs, but because of the sanctity of Jerusalem it is not without its religious significance as well.

ARAB IDENTITY AND ARAB POLITICS

In assessing the political implications of Arab ethnic consciousness and Islam, one should not go to extremes. It would be inaccurate to relegate Arabism to a marginal place, viewing it mainly as the artificial construction of a few intellectuals and politicians. Too much emphasis could be placed on parochial solidarity groups and the cleavages in Arab political culture. Too much stress could be placed on social background, notably the military, and calculations of personal interest and ambition as critical factors in explaining Arab political behavior. It is a mistake, however, to exaggerate the behavioral consequences of Arabism by reifying it into a set of character traits subsumed under appellations such as "the Arab mind."[33] Like most national character constructions, this one contains some kernels of truth but reveals more of the prejudices of the observers than the characteristics of the observed. Unfortunately, it lends itself to erroneous political inferences. Thus, the Arab is often portrayed as a religious fanatic, caring little about human life, capable of making only black and white distinctions, lacking in scientific curiosity, irrational, fatalistic, incapable of thinking clearly because of the allegedly imprecise nature of the Arabic

32. W. Montgomery Watt, *Islam and the Integration of Society* (Evanston: Northwestern University Press, 1961), pp. 174–75.

33. See, e.g., Raphael Patai, *The Arab Mind* (New York: Scribner's, 1973), and Joel Carmichael, *The Shaping of the Arabs* (New York: Macmillan, 1967).

language, burdened by an authoritarian personality, a "shame culture," and having a strong appetite for sex and power. Islam, too, according to some scholars, inhibits rational thought, accurate perception, and social innovation. Little wonder that a people sharing characteristics such as these should exhibit turbulent and irrational political behavior. Sharing the same monolithic Arab mind, the Arabs become a frighteningly cohesive entity whose capacity for satisfying their essentially negative urges is limited mainly by their collective weaknesses.[34]

The truth, of course, lies well between these two extremes. The salience of Arabism and Islam is far more than marginal. From Morocco to Oman, the sense of community at both the mass and elite levels is unmistakable. The reality of an Arab nation defined by strongly held common values and interests is far more than the idea of a few intellectuals. At the same time, anyone remotely familiar with the people of this Arab nation is likely to be skeptical of any common mind set among them. Rather, one is more likely to be impressed with the plasticity of Arab and Islamic identifications. To be an Arab does not exclude being many other things as well: Moroccan or Egyptian, Communist or royalist, black, brown, or white, Christian, Muslim, or even atheist. To be a Muslim requires a serious submission to God and the "right path," but the variety of Muslim practice in different parts of the Arab region and society is considerable. Whatever may have been the practice in previous centuries, it is impossible to detect today any discouragement of science and scholarship on the part of the Islamic establishment. Even in the most conservative society, Sa'udi Arabia, the ulama not only accept but encourage a program of educational development unprecedented, almost radical, in its scope. In Cairo or Amman, the urban middle-class Muslims rarely pray in public; in Riyadh and Sana they do; but they all share a spiritual and temporal sense of community. Women are veiled and restricted in Riyadh and Doha, while in Casablanca, Tunis, and even to a degree in Kuwait, they appear in the latest Paris fashions and are free to go about alone in public; yet they too share membership in the community of Islam. Within Arab Islam, most are of the orthodox (Sunni) persuasion, but some adhere to the various Shi'ite heterodoxies (which are considered in the next chapter), and a few belong to the mystical sufi orders. Among the Western-educated orthodox Muslims,

34. See Edward Said, "The Middle East Conflict: A Palestinian View," mimeographed, 1973; also his *Orientalism: A Polemic and a Counter-proposal* (New York: Pantheon Press, 1978).

many are "modernist" in the sense that they abjure Islamic ritual and follow Islam essentially as an ethical system, much the same way that Reform Jews or Unitarian and other modernist Christian congregations deviate from traditional religion.

There is, in short, such variety of expression of Arabism and Islam, and such tolerance of diversity and multiple identifications within each of the two ummas that few generalizations about the behavioral consequences of these identities are valid. Nor is it right to conclude that the existence of such pluralism negates the communal solidarity implicit in the ethnolinguistic and religious bonds which the Arabs share. The valid conclusion is simply that Arabs feel strongly that they belong to a specific ethnolinguistic and religious community; such feelings do not preclude a variety of other identifications, practices, and ideologies, nor are they precluded by them.

What are the implications of this rather complex configuration of identities for political legitimacy in day-to-day Arab politics? The widely shared values of Arabism and Islam have given rise to certain specific, widely shared interests. These include, first and foremost, the liberation of Palestine, the last part of the Arab homeland occupied by an alien power. They include the development of inter-Arab solidarity, though not necessarily political unity, so that the Arabs will be able to protect their petroleum riches and emerge collectively as a major world power. They include nonalignment with (and nonsubmission to) any of the Great Powers. They include, now that modernizing ideologies have become widely accepted by Arab elites, general commitments to economic and social development and a more equal distribution of wealth and power. They also include commitment to a renaissance of Arab-Islamic culture.

The Arab leader or politician desiring to win and hold power by maximizing his legitimacy will try to identify himself as an effective worker in behalf of all these interests, indeed, more effective than his competitors. Herein lies a clue to the turbulence of modern Arab politics. No politician can afford to be seriously outbid by others on the Palestine question. Similarly, all politicians must favor greater Arab solidarity, if not actual unity. They will be attacked both internally and regionally if they appear to be deviating from the path toward inter-Arab solidarity through isolationist policies. Politicians who seek to maximize development capabilities by accepting economic or military assistance from an outside power in return for that power's tutelage in matters of regional and foreign policy may find themselves under attack for submitting to outside interference. Regimes have been and will continue to be attacked by their internal and regional rivals for failing to implement effectively programs of economic and social development, or for enriching the ruling elite while failing to provide for the poor, or for showing insufficient interest in reviving and maintaining Arabic culture and Islamic practice.

Arabism thus imposes on the Arab politician both some general and some quite specific criteria for legitimacy. Were Arab political culture completely homogeneous and its institutions perfectly developed these would still be difficult criteria to meet. In reality of course, Arab society is in a ferment of rapid socioeconomic development. There are glaring inequalities of income and opportunity. There are the pluralistic features of culture and society that inevitably breed political tension. Furthermore, there is the fact that the Arab nation is now divided into twenty sovereign states. The incongruence between nation loyalty and all-Arab core concerns, on the one hand, and specific state loyalty and specific state interests, on the other, adds additional disharmony to the Arab political scene. Arabism is not intense or exclusive enough to eradicate—at least for the foreseeable future—the state political systems that have developed since World War I. Its diffuseness and its pluralism, which may be its greatest moral asset, is also a severe obstacle to the achievement of formal political unity. It is a measure of the lack of political integration in the Arab world that I must discuss Arab polities, as I do in the subsequent chapters, on a state-by-state basis. While there is growing machinery for inter-Arab decision making, it will be a long time before the preponderance of an Arab world "federal government" will render a discussion of the internal politics of Syria as unimportant as a discussion of Maryland politics is for an analysis of American national politics. At the same time, however, analysis of the politics of legitimacy in each Arab state shows how extraordinarily pervasive all-Arab concerns are in determining outcomes. All three types of legitimacy that I discuss—personal, ideological, and structural—reflect the salience of Arabism in general and all-Arab core concerns in particular. This is especially true for what I call the core states of the eastern Mediterranean, but it is also significant in the peripheral republics and the "traditional" Arabian kingdoms.

3

Cultural Pluralism in the Arab World

An underlying cause of the turbulence in modern Arab politics is the incomplete, unsettled nature of Arab political identity. To say that the Arabs are suffering from an identity crisis is probably going too far because, as I have tried to indicate, ethnic Arabism and Islam are very firmly rooted and ubiquitous. Together they comprise an unmistakable, distinctive identity, one to which its members have a deep commitment. Yet for all its basic simplicity and homogeneity, Arabism presents complex problems as a legitimacy resource and the Arabs remain a people hard to govern. For one thing, the Arabs are still in search of an adequate political expression for their nation in the modern world of nation-states. Boundaries and the legitimacy of existing sovereign entities are a recurring issue, especially in the Arab east. The Arabs have yet to consolidate themselves in a unified polity as the Turks and Iranians have done, and (as the country studies imply) it does not appear that they can erase many of these geographic sovereignty cleavages in the near future. A second kind of cleavage is social: as social mobilization and economic development continue, Arabs become more aware of their class identity and social inequalities. Ethnoreligious nationalism, if devoid of social policy content, loses its ability to generate overall legitimacy in a time of rapid modernization. I take up this important and relatively recent problem in chapter 6. The third problem, the integration of minority communities, is an old one and I examine it here.

I have pointed out that the Arab world is fundamentally homogeneous in terms of its widely shared national and religious values; moreover, the non-Muslim and non-Arab communities are very small. Nevertheless, the question of the political role of minorities in Arab polities is both important and unsettled. In a political culture noted for affectivity and the persisting salience of what Clifford Geertz calls "primordial" identifications, Arabism must coexist or compete with certain other parochial but intensely held corporate identifications.[1]

1. Clifford Geertz, "The Integrative Revolution," in Geertz (ed.), *Old Societies and New States* (New York: Free Press of Glencoe, 1963), pp. 105–57.

Comparative quantitative studies have shown that ethnolinguistic fragmentation, especially when mediated by subjective feelings of political separatism, helps explain political violence and instability.[2] Historians of the Arab world have long recognized the central importance of religious and ethnic identifications.[3] Although the recent conflicts in Lebanon, Iraq, and the Sudan have by no means been wholly sectarian or communal in origin, the fact that primordial affiliations become symbols of hostility suggests that the integration of minorities is as difficult to achieve in the Arab world as it is in other multicommunal polities. Where states or regimes are weak and subnational communities are strong, the minorities issue is sensitive, to say the least. In Lebanon social inequalities precipitated the struggle between a ruling Christian minority and a nonruling Muslim majority. The political leadership in Sudan and Iraq looked upon their black and Kurdish minorities, respectively, as subverters of civil order and tools of foreign powers, and not without reason. They also saw in the minorities a threat to national development. On the other hand, the minority leaders regarded the central government as intolerant and repressive, again not without reason. It might be added that scholars of the developing areas also find it difficult to avoid taking positions on the question: some would seem to expect and hope for assimilation while others appear to predict and defend minority self-determination.[4]

But it would be much too simple to assume that the relations among different communities must inevitably be hostile[5] just as it is too easy to assume that modernization is performing an assimilationist melting pot function in the area. Instead, it is necessary to proceed cautiously, looking at the traditional structure governing minorities and then at the condition of the principal non-Arab and non-Muslim communities today.

2. Douglas A. Hibbs, Jr., *Mass Political Violence: A Cross-National Causal Analysis* (New York: John Wiley-Interscience, 1973), chap. 5; Ted Robert Gurr, *Why Men Rebel* (Princeton: Princeton University Press, 1970), 188–92; and Gurr, *The Conditions of Civil Strife: First Tests of a Causal Model* (Princeton University, Center of International Studies, 1967), pp. 45–49, 56–59.

3. See, e.g., Albert Hourani, "Race, Religion, and Nation-State in the Near East," in *A Vision of History* (Beirut: Khayat's, 1961), pp. 71–105.

4. For an attack on those who allegedly fail to recognize the importance, and persistence, of ethnic identifications, see Walker Connor, "Nation-Building or Nation-Destroying?" *World Politics*, 24, 3 (April 1972) pp. 319–55. His point, on the whole, is well-taken; however, the accusation against Karl W. Deutsch of either "naive assimilationism" or inconsistency on this question is unpersuasive.

5. See the discussion and criticism of M. G. Smith's theory of the plural society in Leo Kuper and M. G. Smith (eds.), *Pluralism in Africa* (Berkeley: University of California Press, 1969), chaps. 1–3.

In the pre-Islamic period, the various minorities staked out a precarious existence in local dynastic kingdoms, often fighting with one another, and usually under a degree of vassalage to a multinational dynastic empire such as Rome, Byzantium, or Persia. With the coming of Islam, the Jewish and Christian communities fell under the special theological dispensation reserved for "people of the Book." They paid a head tax or tribute known as the *jizya*. Other minorities—clans, tribes, and larger proto-national entities—were won over but still retained their local identities and languages. The domain of Islam thus developed as a domain of tolerance for minorities, and the fanaticism for which Islam has rather unjustly been castigated in the West was reserved for the infidels on its geographic frontiers. With the rise of the Ottoman Empire, the last and most elaborate of the Islamic dynasties, this system of tolerance became regularized through the millet system. Sultan Mehmet the Conqueror, having captured Istanbul in 1453, appointed a patriarch to administer the civil as well as religious affairs of all Greek Orthodox, Armenians, and Jews. The word *millet*, originally Arabic and found in the Persian as well as Turkish languages, refers to a religious community. Under the system local communities of a particular sect were autonomous in the conduct of their spiritual affairs and civil affairs relating closely to religion and community, such as church administration, marriage, inheritance, property, and education. Communal disputes were settled by millet courts and enforced when necessary by the state. Local and central millet chiefs were chosen by the millets but were subject to the approval of the sultan. Furthermore, the top chiefs held high and influential posts in the state bureaucracy, the topmost among them enjoying the right of audience with the sultan.[6] Outside Istanbul local millet leaders were ex officio members of the provincial administrative councils. While the term originally applied specifically to religious communities (there was no Kurdish millet, for example), by the mid-nineteenth century it had become infused with broader ethnic connotations. In the Rescript of the Rose Chamber of 1839, it is used to refer to the whole Ottoman dynasty and nation in addition to the earlier usage to denote religious communities. This enlargement of the term was symptomatic of the influence of Western European nationalism, a force that was already undermining the bases of Ottoman Islamic imperial legitimacy.[7] With the rise of independent Turkish and Arab states, the

6. H. C. J. Luke, *The Making of Modern Turkey* (London: Macmillan, 1936), pp. 97–98.

7. Bernard Lewis, *The Emergence of Modern Turkey* (London: Oxford University Press, 1961), pp. 327–30.

millet of course disappeared, but the physical, cultural and legal distinctiveness of these communities remained largely intact. As long as minorities were not perceived as posing a collective threat to the existing political order, they were tolerated and their adherents sometimes achieved high positions.

Today the Arab nation and its sovereign states are honeycombed with minority groups whose communal identities, still distinct, lack either the Arab or the Islamic character, or both, which define the majority community. They may be divided into four categories: first, those which are Arab but whose Islam is not orthodox Sunni Muslim; these groups are generically Shi'ite and include the "Twelver" Shi'ites of Iraq and Lebanon, the Alawites and Druze of Syria and Lebanon, and the Zaydis of Yemen, among others. The second category includes groups which are Arab but not Muslim at all, and I include the various Christian sects of the Levant and Egypt and also the Jews from Arab countries (usually misleadingly referred to as Oriental Jews), most of whom now reside in Israel. The third group comprises communities which are Muslim but non-Arab, and the most prominent cases are the Kurds of Iraq and the Berbers of Algeria and Morocco. Finally, one finds indigenous corporate groups which are neither Arab nor Muslim. The animist and Christian Africans of the southern Sudan are the most prominent indigenous group of this sort. The Armenian Christians of Lebanon and Syria are also a prominent example.

I shall discuss each of these categories briefly. In doing so, however, it must be emphasized that the integration of these various groups with the majority community is a complex and subtle matter, one that defies linear quantification and easy generalization. There is a tendency sometimes to reify communal identities and to assume, falsely, that such identities are impermeable and exclusive. Cases of communal conflict notwithstanding, the reality is more complex. The modalities and possibilities of communal harmony are varied and usually successful; all of the seemingly communal conflicts of recent years have been triggered by sociopolitical issues and exacerbated by external interventions. Carleton Coon has neatly summarized the pluralist integrative process in the Arab world and elsewhere in the Middle East with his metaphor of the "mosaic" in which "people live together by living apart."[8] But useful as this metaphor is, it too is somewhat misleading in that it exaggerates the separateness of communal identities. The Arab world communities, even those in a state of conflict with others,

8. Carleton Coon, *Caravan* (New York: Henry Holt & Co., 1951), esp. chaps. 1 and 10.

are not watertight compartments, and their members do not have a singular and total identification with the primary community. Christian and Arab, for example, are not mutually exclusive categories: a person can feel affinities to both communities; the same may be said of Arab and Berber, Arab and Kurd, and even, though it might be disputed, Arab and Jew. To be sure, there have been times when Arabs thought that only an Arab could be a true Muslim and when a "Christian Turk" would have been a contradiction in terms; and there is certainly no doubt that conflict and exclusivism can indeed rupture a person's multiple identity, as the Arab-Israeli conflict demonstrates. But exclusivism is not the whole story. The anthropologist Lawrence Rosen, writing about Berber-Arab relations in Morocco, makes the point cogently:

> Ethnicity . . . distinguishes men as kinds of persons without at the same time separating them from rather full social intercourse. Indeed, in so far as there is a clear tendency to resist the establishment of any sharp lines of affiliation and identification in this part of Morocco, all studies that confront the question of Arab-Berber relations are forced to view them as the Moroccans themselves—as contingent and partial rather than complete and pervasive features of each man's social identity. To approach the question of social relations in Morocco mainly in terms of ethnic differences is to perpetuate the same error of misplaced concreteness of which the French themselves were so guilty: it is to give a reified and primary status to a distinction which, in actual operation, is of more ambiguous and subsidiary importance.[9]

While the plasticity of this particular case obviously is not exactly duplicated elsewhere in the Arab world, the observation still has broad general validity.

THE SHI'ITE MUSLIMS

Islam underwent a fundamental bifurcation following the transfer of the leadership of the community from Mecca to Damascus in the seventh century. On one side was grouped the supporters of the Ummayad line and on the other followers of Ali, the son-in-law of the Prophet, and his descendants—the unsuccessful claimants. The latter group has been given the generic name Shi'a, but it actually encom-

---

9. Lawrence Rosen, "The Social and Conceptual Framework of Arab-Berber Relations in Central Morocco," in Ernest Gellner and Charles Micaud, (eds.) *Arabs and Berbers* (Lexington, Mass: D. C. Heath Lexington Books, 1972), pp. 155–76, 173.

passes a diversity of parties and movements. Although differing significantly among themselves on matters of doctrine and political values, they all shared a fundamental dissatisfaction with the organization and leadership of the Dar al-Islam. All viewed the succession to the caliphate as illegitimate and the functions and divine basis of the office itself as irretrievably distorted and corrupted. One branch of Shi'ism, however, was far more radical and heterodox than the others; it encompassed a small number of sects known collectively as the *ghulat*, or exaggerators. Another group, the Kharijites, known as the first dissenters in Islam, was allied briefly with the Shi'a against the orthodox Ummayads, but then broke with the Shi'a over Ali's willingness to accept arbitration in his struggle with Muawiya, the Ummayad leader.

The Kharijites are today an extremely small part of the Muslim populations; they are found chiefly in the Ibadhi sect of Oman, with followers in Libya, Algeria, and East Africa. More important is the example of their dissent and their insistence that the imamate or caliphate is not necessary. Kharijite doctrine holds that the people can interpret and apply the Shari'a correctly. Moreover, the office of caliphate itself and the dubious succession process associated with it carries the danger that a given caliph might be bad or out of touch with his subjects. Certainly the succession to the Prophet's leadership that the first Kharijites witnessed, including the assassination of the Caliph Uthman, must have given them grounds for dissent. Nevertheless, as Elie Salem has noted, they realized that as a practical matter they did need a leader, an imam.[10]

Of the Shi'ites in the Arab world the most prominent and numerous are the "Twelvers" or the Imamis, whose conception of the imam is that of a mortal gifted with divine light. They comprise perhaps half the population of Iraq (and almost the total population of non-Arab Iran). A second branch, the Zaydis, found mainly in Yemen, have adhered to a more rationalist view of the imam, minimizing his miraculous qualities and the idea of the return of the Mahdi. The third primary grouping among the Shi'ites consists of movements that emphasize the divine and magical aspects of the imam and have developed doctrines which led them to be branded as ghulat by orthodox Muslims. These groups fall under the rubric of "Seveners" or Isma'iliyya, by virtue of their insistence that Isma'il, the son of the sixth revealed Imam Ja'far al-Sadiq (d. 765), was the last one and

10. Elie Adib Salem, *Political Theory and Institutions of the Khawarij* (Baltimore: Johns Hopkins University Press, 1956), pp. 51–53.

that he will return one day from his "concealment." By the end of the ninth century there were Isma'ili communities not only in Iranian Khurasan but also in Central Asia, India, and Syria. The Isma'iliyya persuasion engendered several distinctive movements, including the Qarmatians, and a similar radical sect in Iraq and Syria that led to the establishment of the Fatimid caliphate in the tenth century.[11] Under the Fatimids arose the Druze, the Nizaris (or Assassins), the Alawites (or Nusairis), and the Matawila of southern Lebanon.

The Nizaris

The best known of the Isma'ili groups are the Nizaris or Assassins, so called because of their fierce fanaticism under the influence of drugs. During the twelfth and thirteenth centuries a Nizari state was located on the southern shores of the Caspian Sea, and it survived for many years even though it lacked territorial contiguity and had to face the hostility of the surrounding dynasties. But these Isma'iliyya had developed a powerful communal solidarity that, as Marshall Hodgson has remarked, was more intense than the social integration and leadership legitimacy of the conventional dynasties.[12] Part of this solidarity was due to the esoteric, syncretistic, and neo-Platonic doctrine, which all initiates to the order partook of. The imam, in their conception, was entirely divine: the mortal in him was enveloped by the divine spirit, and he was thus incapable of error. The number seven had magical qualities. There were, for example, seven stages of emanation: (1) God, (2) the universal intelligence, (3) the universal soul, (4) primeval matter, (5) space, (6) time, and (7) the world of earth and man.[13] Part of their solidarity was due to their skill in organization: Isma'iliyya secret societies helped maintain the community long after the state of the Assassins had disappeared. Absolutely certain of the correctness of their belief, they welcomed death in its service.

The Zaydis

Among the other sects that have doctrinal, communal, and historical links with the Isma'iliyya are the Zaydis of Yemen and the Alawites and Druze, both of which are found in modern-day Syria and Lebanon. All play important political roles. The Zaydi sect was founded by the great-grandson of the Shi'ite martyr Ali. Like his father Hussein, Zayd

11. Dominique Sourdel, *Islam* (New York: Walker and Company, 1949, trans. 1962), pp. 90–92.

12. Marshall G. S. Hodgson, "The Isma'ili State," chap. 5 in *The Cambridge History of Iran*, Vol. 5 (Cambridge: Cambridge University Press, 1968), pp. 422–82.

13. R. Strothmann, "Shi'a," *Shorter Encyclopedia of Islam*, op. cit., pp. 534–41.

was killed by the Ummayads who had seized the standard of Islamic orthodoxy. Some of his persecuted followers made their way to East Africa and then to the Yemen mountains.[14] Theologically the Zaydis are distinguished from other branches of Shi'ism by their belief that Zayd (and not his brother Muhammad al-Baqir) was the fifth and last of the hereditary imams; henceforth they were to be elected. In contrast, as we have seen, the Isma'ilis believed in the divinity of Isma'il as the seventh and last revealed imam; their creed gave rise to the Fatimid caliphate, the Druze of Syria and Lebanon, and the Nizaris and Alawites of Syria. The cleavage between the Zaydis of the Yemen mountains and the orthodox Shafi'is of the coastal lowlands has been one of the main features of modern Yemeni politics, as I shall discuss in greater detail in the case study of Yemen below.

The Alawites

In Syria the Alawite community has won an important share of power. Yet Syria is the land where Arabism is at its most intense. Historically the seat of the Ummayad Empire, linguistically almost completely Arabic, Syria is perhaps 80–85 percent Muslim and perhaps 70–75 percent Sunni Muslim: in short it is quite homogeneous. But as Michael Van Dusen has observed, the small minority proportion is a deceptive guide to the importance of minorities in Syrian politics.[15] The most important minority in Syria's postindependence politics has been the Muslim Alawites. As Shi'ites, the Alawites belong in the tradition which stressed the divine authority and election of the imam and are closely related in doctrine to the Isma'ili persuasion. Unlike the "Twelver" Shi'ites of Iran, Iraq, and Lebanon, the Isma'ilis and the Alawites believe in only seven revealed imams, not twelve, and have developed a concealed, esoteric doctrine of successive divine emanations. The Alawites of Syria place Ali, the Prophet's son-in-law, on a higher plane than the earlier "Speakers" (Adam, Noah, Moses, Jesus, and Muhammad) and in this respect differ somewhat from other Isma'ilis.[16] They are among the poorest of the Syrians.

Surviving centuries of orthodox Muslim dominance, the Alawites briefly enjoyed a degree of autonomy under the French mandate,

14. Harold Ingrams, *The Yemen—Imams, Rulers, and Revolutions* (London: John Murray, 1963), chap. 2 and pp. 41–42.

15. Michael H. Van Dusen, "Political Integration and Regionalism in Syria," *Middle East Journal*, 26, 2 (Spring 1972), pp. 123–36; p. 136.

16. Dominique Sourdel, *Islam* (New York: Walker and Company, 1949, trans. 1962), pp. 90–93.

which, to facilitate control, divided Syria into ethnic states. But during and after independence, Alawite political identity dissolved considerably, so that it was not until the 1960s that it became factor.[17] During the sixties, however, a number of Alawites who had come up through the only channel of upward mobility accessible to them, the army, emerged as important political figures in the Ba'th party's Arab nationalist and social revolution. Sectarianism (or ta'ifyya in Arabic), a condition from which Syria had hitherto been comparatively free, began to manifest itself in a tangible degree of Alawite-Sunnite tension. While the Alawites do not exhibit marked linguistic or ethnic differences from other Syrians, they are regarded by the majority as different, secretive, and to some extent suspect. Indeed, the Isma'ilis (including Alawites) are known in Arabic as al-bataniyya, from a root meaning inward, hidden, or secret. A fascinating clue to the political culture of the Alawite region is found in the brief rise and fall of Suleiman Murchid in the late 1930s. Murchid apparently was given to epileptic seizures, and on one such occasion declared himself Mahdi, the promised redeemer who figures so strongly in Shi'ite doctrine. Before his rising was eventually put down by the French mandate authorities, he had mobilized substantial Alawite and Isma'ili followings in Syria.[18] In recent years an important part of the Syrian army and Ba'th party leadership has emerged from this region, one of the poorest in the country, and as a result there have been problems of acceptance by the Sunni orthodox majority.

The Druze

Concealment and esoteric ritual are also considered to be characteristics of the Druze, another sectarian offshoot of Shi'ite Islam found today in Syria, Lebanon, and Israel. In the early 1970s there were probably some 100,000 Druze each in Lebanon and Syria and some 36,000 in Israel. Like the Alawites, the Druze are an offshoot Fatimid Isma'ilism, having established themselves in Egypt in the eleventh century by deifying the Fatimid Caliph Hakim. In addition to practicing concealment of rites—the extent that only a small elected membership from the sect is permitted to study the sacred scriptures—the Druze have also incorporated in their doctrine the practice of taqiyya, or dissimulation: if threatened, the believer is allowed to

17. Van Dusen, op. cit., p. 134.

18. Jacques Weulersse, Paysans de Syrie et du Proche-Orient (Paris: Gallimard, 1946, Fourth Edition), pp. 275–78. See also Nabil T. Awad, "Al-Rabb," Middle East Forum (Beirut), October 1961, pp. 35–37.

conceal his Druze faith or to apostacize. In terms of doctrine, the Druze community may well merit Philip Hitti's characterization as "fossilized"; but this has not prevented them from assimilating and participating in the political and economic life of their areas. The Druze speak Arabic as their native language and are Arabized in their customs. During the social and political upheavals in Mount Lebanon in the middle nineteenth century, blood was spilled between Christian and Druze, as indeed there was between Christians and Sunni Muslims in Damascus; but in the modern postcolonial era, the Druze have not only assimilated to but have helped strengthen Arabism and socialism.

The Druze play a pivotal role in the institutionalized *ta'ifiyya* that pervades modern Lebanese politics; in Syria they were active in the nationalist resistance to French occupation; in Israel, where they were given special legal status and perquisites to differentiate them from the other Arab minorities, they were allowed to engage in police and military security duties. In the aftermath of the 1967 Arab-Israeli war, during which Israel occupied some Druze villages in the Golan Heights and seemed to be in a position militarily to sever the Druze-inhabited Hawran district from Syria, there were suggestions that a Druze political entity might be created to provide additional security for Israel. Such suggestions were reminiscent of the French effort to Balkanize Syria into a number of weak and manageable ethnic enclaves. The Druze again played a primary part in the Lebanese civil war in 1975–76: their principal leader, Kamal Jumblat, assumed the leadership of the "leftist-Muslim" forces against the "rightist-Maronite" side.

NON-MUSLIM ARABS

Islam accords to Jews and Christians a status of tolerance (*dhimmi*) and does not view them as aliens or enemies because of the considerable doctrinal similarities between these creeds and Islam; the Qur'an calls them "people of the Book" (*ahl al-kitab*). Throughout most of Islamic history, and particularly in recent times, there has been little religious conflict between Jews or Christians and Muslims. Early Arab nationalism had no difficulty in embracing both Christians and Jews indigenous to the Arab world. It must be admitted, however, that the coming of Western (Christian) imperialism and the Zionist settlement in Palestine at times clouded relations between Christian and Muslim Arabs and virtually displaced the indigenous Arab Jewish communities concentrated in Iraq, Yemen, Morocco, and several other Arab countries. Despite the negative political climate, however, there is nothing in the mainstream ideology of Arab nationalism nor in the dispositions of ordinary Muslim Arabs to hinder the cultural and religious freedom of either Jews or Christians.

THE ARAB JEWS

The Jews, as is well known, trace their tribal origins to Mesopotamia nearly 2,000 years before Christ. After their migration to Palestine, David established the first Jewish kingdom, which lasted for approximately seventy years. After the destruction of their Temple and the exile of the Babylonian captivity, they gradually migrated back and rebuilt the Temple; after another period of political autonomy, they were driven out of Palestine by the Romans and dispersed throughout the Middle East, North Africa, Europe, Russia, and eventually the United States. In Palestine only small communities remained, constituting a very small minority in the Byzantine and Arab-Islamic societies, which prevailed until 1920.

Although expelled from Palestine, the Jews did establish communities in several other parts of the Arab world. Many found their way back to Egypt and across North Africa, and Morocco became the seat of a particularly large community. Others found a livelihood along the trade routes to southern Arabia. Muhammad had dealings with the Jewish tribes around Medina and later expelled them. A thriving Jewish community developed in the Yemen. In Iraq, where many Jews had remained since the Babylonian captivity, the community also grew and prospered. Jews occupied high office and made important intellectual contributions to the great Arab-Islamic civilizations of the Middle Ages centered in Baghdad and Cordoba. For 2,000 years these communities lived in harmony with their predominantly Muslim-Arab neighbors. But after 1948, because of the outrage in the Arab world over the forcible establishment of Israel, these communities were both pushed and pulled to the new Jewish state. Thus today, the Jewish minorities outside of Israel are numerically very small indeed, constituting less than 1 percent of the various populations while comprising at least 85 percent of Israel (pre-1967 boundaries).

Even the Jewish community of Morocco, which since 1948 has enjoyed particularly conscientious protection from the authorities and close relationships both with the Berber and Arab population,[19] has steadily declined in size, mainly because of the continuing Arab-Israeli conflict: a study made for the U.S. army estimates that it

19. See Lawrence Rosen, "A Moroccan Jewish Community During the Middle Eastern Crisis," *The American Scholar*, 37, 3 (Summer 1968).

decreased from some 227,000 in 1948 to only 40,000 by 1970.[20] Certainly, the creation of Israel has drastically curtailed the influence that the wealthy mercantile Jewish elites once exerted in Egypt, Iraq, Morocco, and Lebanon. In Lebanon the Jews enjoyed full voting rights; in the Arab countries in active conflict with Israel, such as Egypt, Syria, and Iraq, they have had governmental protection against popular hostility, but they have also been subjected to surveillance for national security. Because there is a solid historical tradition of social harmony between Jewish and Muslim Arab communities, it is probable that they could once again live in harmony were a just solution to the Palestine-Israel issue to be implemented.

THE ARAB CHRISTIANS

The number of Christians of all rites in the Arab world today is probably between 5 and 10 million, the bulk of them located in the eastern part. The largest Christian community, the Coptic Church, is found in Egypt and it is said by various sources to include 2 to 4 million adherents, perhaps 10 percent of the population.[21] It still adheres to the Monophysite doctrine that was condemned at the Council of Chalcedon in 451. Christians of the Maronite Catholic and Eastern Orthodox rites are said to comprise at least 30 percent and 20 percent, respectively, of the population of Lebanon. In Syria approximately 8 percent of the population is Christian, primarily Eastern Orthodox; in Jordan the percentage is perhaps 6 and in Iraq, 4. According to 1970 official sources, some 12.5 percent of the population of Israel within the pre-1967 borders was non-Jewish (i.e., Arab) and of this group 82 percent was Muslim or Druze and 18 percent was Christian. Christians thus accounted for perhaps 3 percent of the total population, a majority being Catholic of various rites and the rest Greek Orthodox (32 percent) and Protestant (3 percent).[22] In North

20. Richard F. Nyrop, *et al.*, *Area Handbook for Morocco* (Washington: U.S. Government Printing Office, 1972), p. 78.

21. L. Humphrey Walz, "Christians in the Arab East," *The Link*, 6, 5 (November-December 1973). Dr Walz cites Clemmer and Rycroft, *A Factual Study of the Middle East* (Presbyterian, 1962), as giving a "conservative" figure of 1.18 million for 1960, but he also cites other estimates of from 2 million (according to the Egyptian census of 1960) to 6 million. In his thorough study, *Christians in the Arab East* (Athens: Lycabettos Press, 1975), p. 61, Robert Brenton Betts analyzes various figures and concludes that Copts number about 3.5 million, or 10 percent of the population.

22. Israel, Prime Minister's Office, Bureau of the Advisor on Arab Affairs, "Minority Groups in Israel," (Jerusalem: Publications Service, 1970). The figures are based on a book by Ori Stendel, *The Minorities*.

Africa, which was widely if superficially Christianized during the Roman occupation for some three centuries until the coming of Islam, a 1964 estimate placed the Christian population of Morocco at 250,000, Algeria 40,000, and Tunisia 40,000.[23]

The political identity and role of the Christian communities is more complex than that of the Jews. There can be little doubt in light of the events of the twentieth century that the Jews have become not just a religious and ethnic community but a political community with territorial claims, successfully implemented. The Christians, on the other hand, have largely become integrated in the predominantly Muslim populations without losing their religious identity or communal traditions. Nomenclature reveals the difference. Today one normally speaks of a Christian Arab but not a Jewish Arab. One rarely even hears the more accurate term Arab Jew but rather the euphemism Oriental Jew.

Christianity, as the official religion of the Byzantine Empire, was implanted in the Levant, Egypt, and much of coastal North Africa until the Muslim conquests of the early seventh century. As late as the eleventh century, a majority of the population of geographical Syria was Christian. It is noteworthy that the 2.5 to 3 million Eastern Orthodox Arabs of today take pride in their pre-Islamic identity and indigenous presence and claim that they therefore are coequal members with Muslims in the Arab nation. Byzantium, completely Hellenized since the seventh century, became more European, and Islam sank its social and cultural roots, as well as religious doctrine, throughout the Middle East and Northern Africa. The Christian communities of the east, both Orthodox and Latin, survived under Islam as "people of the Book" but not as autonomous "nations." The Maronites of Mount Lebanon were exceptionally cohesive, however, and accordingly they suffered periods of oppression (along with Shi'ites and Druze) during Mamluk period at the beginning of the fourteenth century. Although the political cohesion of the Arab-Islamic dynasties diminished, Christianity was never able to reestablish itself politically in the area. The Crusades of the twelfth and thirteenth centuries momentarily reestablished Christian kingdoms in Palestine and coastal Syria. From the middle of the eleventh to the end of the fifteenth century, Christian forces gradually reconquered Spain, and during the nineteenth and twentieth centuries the expansionist Christian powers succeeded in pushing back the Ottoman frontiers of Europe. But these were all externally mounted campaigns; internally, Christianity never suc-

23. John K. Cooley, *Baal, Christ, and Mohammed* (New York: Holt, Rinehart, and Winston, 1965), p. 8.

ceeded (outside of Lebanon) in recasting itself as a national political force because of its doctrinal fragmentation and the deep cultural division between the Hellenic and Roman worlds.

The various Christian sects adapted themselves to the millet status until historical forces were propitious for some of them at least to achieve greater communal, even national, autonomy. The convergence of two such forces beginning in the nineteenth century—the decline of Ottoman power and the spreading of European ideologies of ethnic nationalism—facilitated the establishment of national Christian communities in Mount Lebanon, Greece, and the Balkans. And as Christian European powers such as France moved into North Africa, and Austria and Russia entered the Balkans with their missionaries as well as soldiers, Christianity in a sense returned, but it was tainted with imperialism and won few converts.

NON-ARAB MUSLIMS

There are two substantial Muslim, non-Arab peoples in the Arab world today: the Berbers of the Maghrib and the Kurds of northern Iraq. Both, as we shall see, have a distinctive mythic history and folk culture, and both have occupied an identifiable, though not precisely defined, territory. But the Berbers are far more closely woven into the fabric of Maghrib society than the Kurds in the Arab east. Although they are for the most part Sunni Muslim, the Kurds' sense of tribal-national selfhood has driven them time and again to rise up against the Turkish, Iranian, and Arab states which Kurdistan lies athwart.

The Berbers

The Berbers are the original indigenous people of North Africa. They are thought to have migrated from Asia perhaps at the beginning of recorded history and to have developed a pastoral, agricultural, and tribal way of life that has changed little (in the isolated mountain areas at least) over the centuries.[24] The name Berber according to Gallagher, was originally applied to these people by the Greeks who considered them barbarians,[25] and it became established in Latin after the final Roman conquest of Carthage in 146 B.C. The Arabs who first conquered the area in the middle of the seventh century A.D. also used the word and it eventually fell into Western usage as well. Students of American diplomatic history recall the U.S. navy's skirmishes

24. Coon, op. cit., pp. 36–44.
25. Charles F. Gallagher, *The United States and North Africa* (Cambridge: Harvard University Press, 1963), p. 2.

against the Barbary pirates for fifteen years beginning in 1801 during Thomas Jefferson's presidency.[26]

Of the main ethnic populations of the Arab world, the Berbers are the most elusive to describe. Other peoples of the area can be identified and traced through their central political structures, their leaders, their law, and literature. But the Berbers have not one written language but a number of dialects confined to specific areas of the predominantly mountainous territories, as in the Rif, Middle Atlas, Kabylia, and Aurès mountains. In the middle 1960s, it was estimated that a third of Morocco's population is Berber-speaking while 85 percent speak Arabic (many people speak both, of course), and that Algeria is perhaps 22 percent Berber-speaking and 87 percent Arabic-speaking.[27] The number of Berber-speaking people in Tunisia is negligible. Arabic has clearly carried the day, yet the Berber culture remains firmly entrenched and extensive. Theirs is essentially a folk culture and their artifacts have remained "unchanged, reminding one observer of south-western American Indian crafts.[28] Berbers have professed Christianity, Judaism, Islam, and numerous heterodoxies of each without sacrificing their collective identity.

From a political standpoint, the most distinctive feature of Berber life is its carefully fragmented structure. Berber society is characterized by the absence of positive central authority. Instead, within a given tribal area some hundreds of families are grouped into settlements that are virtually autonomous cantons. These cantons are linked with other cantons of the same faction, or *liff*, while remaining in a state of precarious equilibrium with cantons of an opposing liff. An elaborate system of protections, immunities, and guarantees permits market activity to occur peacefully.[29] One of the underlying deterrents to conflict is the common mutual apprehension of the uncontrolled nature of a conflict should it occur because all the cantons in the alliance system would become involved. The Berber traditions of representation and decentralized, nonauthoritarian, independent political life and relationships have a strangely modern character. They may have provided the adaptability that has promoted Berber survival over the

26. See James A. Field, Jr., *America and the Mediterranean World, 1776–1882* (Princeton: Princeton University Press, 1969), pp. 49–58.

27. Charles F. Gallagher, "Language and Identity," chap. 4 in L. Carl Brown (ed.), *State and Society in Independent North Africa* (Washington: The Middle East Institute, 1966), p. 80.

28. Gallagher, *The United States and North Africa*, op. cit., p. 18.

29. Francisco Benet, "Explosive Markets: The Berber Highlands," chap. 10 in Louise Sweet (ed.), *Peoples and Cultures of the Middle East*, 2 volumes (New York: Natural History Press, 1970), vol. 1, pp. 173–203.

centuries, but they also may have inhibited Berber nation-building by retarding strong central authority patterns.

Along with their cultural resiliency, which has enabled them to withstand the numerous cultural waves that have washed over North Africa, the Berbers have a tradition of political activism which stretches back to the revolts of Masinissa and the two Jubas against Rome, and to subsequent risings against Byzantium, the Arabs, and the Turks. It continued into the modern period of the French and Spanish protectorates when the Berber tribal leader Abd al-Karim al-Khattabi rose up against the Europeans and created a state in the Rif mountains that lasted from 1922 through 1926. But in the face of growing nationalism among the Arabs, the French determined that separation of BERBERS AND ARABS WOULD BE ADVANTAGEOUS, THE RIF REVOLT NOTWITHSTANDING. THE BERBER *dahir* of 1930 was a French decree removing the Berbers from the jurisdiction of customary Islamic law and placing them under French law, but this blatant attempt at divide-and-rule became instead a rallying point for the nationalist movement. The dahir incident also showed that the linkages between Berbers and Arabs were more interwoven than the French wished to believe.

As the Arab North African states embarked on independence in the middle 1950s, they faced many problems, but Berber-Arab conflict was not among the most important. Algeria proved quite successful in integrating Berbers into the revolutionary elite, playing down ethnic identities, and applying its Arabization policies circumspectly.[30] In Morocco, where political integration is weak and instability a chronic problem, the kings (Muhammad V and his son Hassan) have sought to strengthen their authority by mediating Berber-Arab differences and relying upon the conservative mountain (Berber) elements as a counterweight against the modernizing nationalist sentiments on the coast and in the cities. Berber officer participation in the abortive military coups against King Hassan in the early 1970s complicated the task of maintaining royal authority.[31] Nevertheless, the editor of a recent collection of papers on Berber-Arab relations could still comment that "There is a remarkable consensus among the contributors . . . concerning the absence of a serious 'Berber problem,' at least in the present and foreseeable future."[32]

30. William B. Quandt, "The Berbers in the Algerian Political Elite," in Ernest Gellner and Charles Micaud (eds.), *Arabs and Berbers* (Lexington, Mass.: D. C. Heath Lexington Books, 1972), pp. 285–303.

31. A. Coram, "The Berbers and the Coup" in Gellner and Micaud, op. cit., pp. 425–30.

32. Charles Micaud, in Gellner and Micaud, op. cit., p. 433.

The Kurds

If relative tranquillity describes contemporary relations between Berbers and Arabs in North Africa, the condition of ethnic pluralism at the other end of the Arab world, in Iraqi Kurdistan, has been quite different. Like the Berbers, the Kurds are a people whose national history antedates Islam and whose identity has survived assaults over the years. Like the Berbers they are primarily a pastoral, herding, dry farming, and tribal society inhabiting an inaccessible mountainous region, geographical Kurdistan falls astride the Zagros range of southeastern Turkey, western Iran, and northern Iraq. But compared to the Berbers, the Kurds have a more cohesive national identity and more active national aspirations. The explanation for this difference is partly cultural and partly historical. The Kurds, first of all, are concentrated in one rather well-defined and remote area, while the Berbers are more widely dispersed into separate clusters, large and small. Linguistically, the Kurds are somewhat more homogeneous than the Berbers. While both peoples have a common language, both are divided into different groups of dialects that are not easily or mutually comprehensible; but the gap between the three main Berber languages seems to be wider than that separating the two main Kurdish linguistic groups. Kurdish, unlike Berber, has been a literary language, albeit a limited one, since the eighteenth century, and there have been Kurdish newspapers since the end of the nineteenth century.[33] In terms of social structure, the Berbers exhibit a more decentralized organization than do the Kurds even though both are tribal societies. Consequently, the Kurds have been able to undertake concerted action to a greater extent than the Berbers; the Kurds have a stronger tradition of leadership and rebellion than do the Berbers. Furthermore, the Berbers have been more prone to assimilation in domains such as religion and intermarriage with Arabs than have the Kurds.

The Kurds are of Indo-European racial origin and are thought to have entered the Zagros region in the second millenium B.C. They date their existence as a distinct people from the time of the Assyrian Empire and the Kingdom of the Medes in the seventh century B.C. They have been known by their present name since the Arab-Muslim conquest in the seventh century A.D. While accepting Islam they resisted the political and social influence of the Arabs, and as the Abbasid caliphate began to decay they established several quasi-autonomous petty dynasties of their own. During the Ottoman and

---

33. T. M. Johnstone, "The Languages of the Middle East," in Sweet, op. cit. I, pp. 121–22.

Safavid periods, a number of Kurdish principalities arose, some of which survived into the early nineteenth century. In the twentieth century the Kurds came within a hairbreadth of attaining statehood. In the Treaty of Sèvres in 1920, which was intended to divest the defeated Turkey of much territory, the Great Powers granted Kurdistan immediate local autonomy and forced the Turks to cede this territory to the Kurds within a year should the Kurds desire it. Unfortunately for the Kurds, the Turks under Mustafa Kemal (Ataturk) defeated the invading Greeks in 1921 and successfully demanded a revision of the agreement. The revised agreement, signed at Lausanne in 1923, promised tolerance for minorities but ignored any specific reference to the Kurds. In fact, the Kemalist government used force to suppress Kurdish political activity and insurrections in 1925, 1930, and 1937–38. At the end of the next world war, the situation was again fluid enough to provide an opportunity for Kurdish aspirations, and briefly during 1946 there existed an independent Kurdish republic with its capital at Mahabad in the Kurdish part of Iranian Azerbaijan. When the Soviet-Iranian crisis over Azerbaijan was resolved in favor of Iran, the Iranian army dissolved the republic's government and executed most of its leaders. In recent years, Kurdish political activity has been directed primarily against successive Arab governments in Iraq.

Mulla Mustafa al-Barzani, the Kurd's principal leader in recent times, was exiled to Moscow for more than a decade after the abortive republican experiment in Mahabad. Later he returned to Iraq to develop and lead the struggle against several governments in Baghdad in the 1960s and 1970s, until the collapse of the movement in 1975.

The Kurds numbered approximately 7 million in the mid-1960s, with 3.2 million in Turkey, 1.8 million in Iran, and 1.55 million in Iraq. Smaller concentrations could be found in Syria and Lebanon (320,000) and the U.S.S.R. (80,000).[34] Kurdish sources place the total number closer to 10 million, with 3 million in Iraq.[35] The social structure Kurdistan remains patriarchal and tribal with local leadership over a village or locale in the hands of an *agha*, or local clan leader, linked to a larger tribal community. As Coon notes, the tribal organization helps keep order among groups of adjacent and economically independent villages, and it also functions to mobilize warriors in the event of external threats, which, as Kurdish history indicates, are

34. C. J. Edmonds, "Kurds," in *The Encyclopedia Britannica* (Chicago, 1973).
35. John K. Cooley, *The Christian Science Monitor*, July 15, 1970.

chronic.[36] The fact that part of Kurdistan includes the major oil fields of the northern part of the Iraqi republic fueled Kurdish aspirations but also stiffened Iraqi resistance to any secessionist efforts. Nor were the outside powers disinterested in a game with such high stakes. The United States, Iran, and Israel provided Barzani with substantial covert assistance during his campaign against the Ba'thist regime in Baghdad in the early 1970s. But in a classical display of big power cynicism toward minority clients, Iran withdrew its support for the Kurds when it reached a rapprochement with Iraq early in 1975, and the revolt immediately collapsed. Operating at long last from a position of strength, the Iraqi government, having reestablished its control, proceeded to grant the Kurdish districts a limited degree of cultural autonomy and political representation, thus resolving for the foreseeable future this question within an Arab framework.

NON-ARAB, NON-MUSLIM GROUPS

The principal indigenous communities to the Arab world that share neither the ethnic nor the religious identity of the majority are the Armenians of Syria and Lebanon and the Africans of the Sudan's three southernmost provinces. Unlike the Arab Jews and Christians, whose physiognomy and use of Arabic has facilitated their integration, the Armenians are ethnically distinct and strongly attached to the Armenian language. Moreover, they are relatively recent arrivals. Yet they have on the whole found Arab Syria and Lebanon a comfortable refuge. The same cannot be said for the diverse tribes and sects of the south Sudan. Although they lacked communal cohesion, their economic condition was so poor and their political relations with Khartoum so unsatisfactory that they were driven to insurgency. Whether the compromise toward limited autonomy that ended the civil war can hold in the long run will be difficult if the basic and quite intractable problems are not also solved.

The Armenians

The Armenians are thought to have emerged as a self-conscious ethnic group in the sixth century B.C. in an area now part of north-eastern Turkey and the southern tip of Soviet Transcaucasia. Armenia became an independent kingdom in the first century B.C. and converted officially to Christianity in A.D. 301. The principal sect, the Armenian Apostolic (Gregorian) Church, adhered to the Monophysite doctrine.

---

36. Coon, op. cit., p. 303. See also Fredrik Barth, *Principles of Social Organization in Southern Kurdistan* (Oslo: Brodrene Jorgensen A/S Boktrykkeri, 1953), pp. 15–17, chap. 6, and passim.

The kingdom was ruled from Mount Ararat and extended its dominions and people well into Asia Minor to the Mediterranean and north to the Caucasus up until the Arab invasion of the seventh century. Armenia was thereafter administered by Arabs, Mongols, Turks, Persians, and Russians. Under the Turks, the Armenians had their own millet and, along with the Greeks, took on important financial and commercial functions avoided by Muslims. They even assumed important bureaucratic roles in the state. They were also a conduit for the intellectual and political ferment of Europe in the eighteenth century and after, by virtue of their Christianity, cosmopolitanism, and knowledge of Western languages.[37] In the nineteenth century, with the Turkish Empire in decay, Armenians were among those pressing for Western reforms and even Western intervention; and at the same time they were absorbing European ideas of nationalism and reviving the dream of an independent Armenia. As the empire continued to unravel at the hands of the Christian powers, the position of the Christian minorities with their Western connections and national aspirations became suspect indeed by the authorities. Armenian political organizations began to develop during the 1880s. Consequently, in 1894–95, Sultan Abd al-Hamid II sanctioned widespread and bloody pogroms in Turkish Armenia. In 1909, as the sultanate's authority crumbled, thousands of Armenians were massacred by Muslim militants. Then in 1915–16, the Young Turk government undertook the wholesale expulsion of Armenians; in the process over a million Armenians died and 450,000 fled to Syria. For a moment, from 1918 to 1920, in the aftermath of Turkey's defeat in World War I, there was an independent Armenian republic, but it disappeared with the rapprochement between Turkey and the new Bolshevik government in Russia. In 1938, when Turkey took control of Hatay Province from Syria by agreement with the French mandate authorities, additional thousands of Armenians—now refugees again— migrated further south toward Aleppo and Beirut.

Today there are an estimated 5 million Armenians in the world, of whom 2 million are in the Armenian Soviet Socialist Republic and 1 million in other parts of the Soviet Union. There are a half-million Armenians in the United States, notably around Boston and in California. Of the half-million in the Middle East there may be 200,000 in Lebanon and 165,000 in Iran. The Armenians remaining in the Arab world today are relative newcomers to their particular areas, even though, as we have seen, the Armenians are one of the oldest

37. Lewis, op. cit., pp. 61–62.

Middle Eastern peoples. Today in Syria, Armenians are secure and tolerated but completely removed from politics, and in Lebanon they have enjoyed both security and political power through their alliance with the Maronite Christian elite. Yet everywhere they remain a distinct and cohesive community. Although resisting linguistic or social assimilation, the younger generation of Armenians has increasingly learned colloquial Arabic and developed economic relationships with their Arab neighbors.

Unlike their Arab Greek Orthodox coreligionists in Syria, Lebanon, Jordan, and Palestine, the Armenians have kept apart from full participation in Arab politics; and unlike their Maronite coreligionists in Lebanon (many of whom deny their own Arabic language and culture), the Armenians have avoided challenging Arab nationalism. Their homeland, now under Soviet control, is somewhere else. And so they continue to enjoy cultural autonomy and legal equality as a kind of neo-millet in the Arab world today.

The Southern Sudanese

In February 1972, a cease-fire was declared between the government of the Sudan and the southern Sudanese rebel movement, ending a civil war that had begun in 1955 and cost between half a million and a million and a half lives.[38] At the height of the rebellion in 1968, there were 63,000 refugees from the southern Sudan in Uganda and another 40,000 in Zaire (Congo-Kinshasa), according to UN estimates.[39] This little-known struggle was the longest and probably the most costly struggle in human terms that the Middle East has known since the Armenian troubles in Turkey—vastly more so than all the Arab-Israeli wars put together, and possibly even more than the Algerian war which claimed nearly 1 million dead and missing.[40]

This struggle pitted the Sudanese government and ruling elite in Khartoum and the north, Arabic in language, culture, and political values, against an amorphous and faction-ridden coalition of southern elements speaking several tribal languages, black African in social structure and culture, and non-Islamic in religion.[41] Compared to the

38. Casualty estimates vary. According to Frederick Hunter in *The Christian Science Monitor*, January 14, 1971, a UN source put the dead at a half-million, but southern Sudanese sources estimated more than one million. Lawrence Fellowes in *The New York Times* of September 22, 1968, quotes a local official as thinking that a half-million was an inflated figure.

39. John K. Cooley, in *The Christian Science Monitor*, January 14, 1971.

40. Gallagher, The United States and North Africa, op. cit., p. 105.

41. A general survey by a Sudanese scholar is Mohamed Omer Beshir, *The Southern Sudan: Background to Conflict* (New York: Praeger, 1968).

religious and ethnic cleavages elsewhere in the Middle East, the north-south gap in the Sudan has been very wide. Linguistically, Arabic has penetrated little into the Sudan's southernmost provinces, while, as we have seen, Berbers, Middle Eastern Jews, Kurds, and even Armenians were Arabized to some degree even while maintaining their own first languages. Ethnically or racially, there is a far clearer differentiation between northern and southern Sudanese, compared to those between Arabs and the other minorities of the Arab world. It is true, as Ali Mazrui has observed, that the Arabs have been among the most tolerant and casual of peoples on the question of inter-marriage.[42] Certainly there is a substantial admixture of negroid features among the Arabs (or, if one prefers, the culturally, religiously, and linguistically Arabized peoples) of the Nile valley and southern Arabia; the Arabs of the northern Sudan are dark brown in complexion, distinctly darker than Arabs of the Fertile Crescent or the Maghrib. But the four million inhabitants of Sudan's southernmost provinces of Bahr al-Ghazi, Upper Nile, and Equatoria, are definitely black, not brown. They are also bigger and their head shape is more elongated. These physical differences reinforce the linguistic and religious differences. Approximately half a million of the southerners are Christians, mostly Catholics, but the great majority are pagan. The division is reinforced by an unequal distribution of wealth: in the middle 1960s the average per capita GNP for a southerner was estimated to be nearly ten times less than that of a northerner.[43] There were ten times as many students in northern schools as in southern schools. Even though tribalism is common to both north and south it is far more prominent in the south, which lacks an urban non-agricultural sector. The principal southern tribal groups, each with its own language, are the Dinka (with one million members), the Nuer, Shiluk, Anovok, Zandi, Latuko, and Bari.

When the British began their administration of the Sudan (in a nominal condominium with Egypt) in 1899, they instituted a separate "southern policy" to inhibit the social integration of the two parts of the country, and even today the infrastructure of roads and communications is meager. The British encouraged Christian missionaries to provide education in the South and discouraged cultural or commercial penetration by the Arabic-speaking northerners. With

42. Ali Mazrui, *Towards a Pax Africana* (Chicago: University of Chicago Press, 1967), pp. 112–13. Mazrui's discussion of Arab and African identities and interrelationships is unusually insightful.

43. Edouard Saab, in *Le Jour* (Beirut), August 6, 1965.

independence in 1956, friction was inevitable as the Khartoum government began to assert its authority and nation-building policies in the south. A bloody but brief rebellion in 1956 fanned separatist sentiments. In 1963, the Azania Liberation Front and its military arm, the Anya'nya, commenced a campaign of harassment that brought cruel reprisals by the government; caught between the two sides, many innocent people suffered. By early 1964, the government had expelled the 600 Christian missionaries operating in the south, accusing them of supporting the rebellion.[44] And in 1971, it was reported that Israeli military missions in Kenya, Uganda, Ethiopia, and the Congo were helping arm and train the rebels.[45] When Major-General Ja'far al-Numayri came to power in Khartoum in 1969, he took a more flexible approach to the southern problem than previous regimes, and by 1972 he helped bring about an end to the war. Khartoum de-emphasized Islam, agreed to a federal arrangement with greater regional autonomy, and allowed southerners to handle police and security functions. The southerners, by now weakened and divided among themselves, agreed to end the secession movement.[46] Several years later this settlement was still holding, but most of the economic and social problems remained, and it was clearly a severe test of Khartoum's limited administrative capabilities to try and solve them.

INTEGRATION OR CONFLICT?

What can be concluded from this survey of minorities in the Arab world about the prospects for integration and conflict? On the one hand, as argued in the previous chapter, Arabic culture and Islam are all-pervasive throughout the area, and if anything, the salience of these two wellsprings of political legitimacy is growing as modernization proceeds. Furthermore, there is nothing in modern Arab history or in Islamic principles conducive to exclusivist (or racist) political practices: on the contrary, tolerance of ethnic and religious minorities is not only the stated policy of all Arab governments, it is also supported by historical habit and to a large degree by modern practice. I have ranked the categories of minority groups (albeit somewhat artificially) in terms of their nominal distance from Arabism and orthodox Islam and have found significant examples of harmonious coexistence at each level. In the mid-1970s, there was general harmony between Shi'ite communities like the Zaydis, Alawites, and Druze and their orthodox

44. *The New York Times*, November 22, 1964.
45. John K. Cooley, in *The Christian Science Monitor*, January 14, 1971.
46. Colin Legum, in *The Observer* (London), February 27, 1972.

neighbors. Arab Christians and Jews were quite fully integrated. Orthodox Christians participate even at the political level, and the Jews, despite the problem of Israel, were reasonably secure—protected rather than persecuted by Arab governments, notably Morocco, Egypt, and Syria. In the non-Arab but Islamic category, the Berbers of North Africa appear to be highly integrated with the ethnic Arabs in numerous ways, including political participation. And the Armenians (in sharp contrast to their experience under the Turks) showed that even a non-Arab, non-Islamic community with a very strong sense of its own distinctiveness, could successfully "live together by living apart" with its Arab neighbors.

On the other hand, the recent past has been marked by four extremely violent conflicts between Arab-Sunni majorities and minority groups, and all of them appear to be primordial in nature. The Yemen civil war of the mid-1960s involved to some degree traditional rivalries between the ruling Zaydi imamate and the orthodox Shafi'is who provided most of the republican support. In the Lebanese civil war of 1975–76, Maronite Catholics were locked in brutal conflict with a coalition of mostly Muslim forces, contesting continued Maronite domination of the Lebanese state. A Kurdish independence movement finally was crushed by the Ba'thist government in Baghdad; and the south Sudan secessionist movement came to an end through a combination of armed combat and political compromise. If nothing else, these conflicts demonstrate that circumstances can arise in which communal solidarities can be triggered for political conflict. Since it is clear that no amount of modernization is likely to eliminate (through total assimilation) minority solidarity groups, the possibility for ethnosectarian conflict remains a constant danger should the conflict-precipitating circumstances arise. The Arab states most susceptible to this kind of problem are, of course, those with substantial minority groups: Morocco, Algeria, Sudan, Lebanon, Syria, Iraq, and Yemen.

What then are the special circumstances associated with communal conflict in the Arab world? Cultural distance per se, as we have seen, does not seem to be a common factor, for these major conflicts involve communities of varying similarity to one another. Geographical and demographic conditions are more important: in each case the contesting groups have a quite distinct territorial location, and one of the two usually has the topographical advantage of a mountainous base from which either defense or domination is facilitated, namely, the Zaydis, Maronites, and Kurds. The contending parties are not highly unequal in relative size, so that each poses a potential threat to the other. The origins of these conflicts are always political or economic,

rather than directly communal. Zaydis fight Shafi'is in Yemen not out
of doctrinal antipathies but because of a coup which breaks down the
existing authority structure. Lebanese Maronites and Muslims do not
fight a holy war but rather a battle about social and foreign policy
issues and the distribution of power in terms of class rather than sect.
Baghdad tries to crush Kurdish aspirations not because of any
particular antipathy toward Kurds as such but because it sees a threat
to its oil resources and national integrity. Communal hostilities are
perhaps more prominent in the Sudanese case, yet here too the main
issue is one of territorial integrity. There has also been an external
factor in each case that helped precipitate such quarrels into civil wars.
If one or both of the rival communities has a neighboring sanctuary
and supply line and if there are external powers with an interest in
promoting a conflict, then the possibility arises for protracted struggle
which eventually triggers communal stereotyping and generates
communal hatred. In Yemen, Sa'udi Arabia supported the Zaydi
royalist forces, while Egypt supported Shafi'i republicans. In Lebanon,
Israel and eventually Syria, along with the United States and certain
European countries, sustained and encouraged the Maronite forces,
while Libya, Iraq, and other Arab countries supported in varying
degrees the Muslim-progressive coalition. Iran, Israel, and the United
States supported the Kurdish insurgency as long as it suited their
interests. The southern Sudanese were helped by neighboring African
states and by Israel.

   None of this is to deny that communal tensions exist within the Arab
nation, but rather to argue that they do not in themselves generate
conflict. Thus the image of an Arab world seething with communal
hostilities and susceptible to Balkanization is closer to fantasy than
reality. To oversimplify the group identities of communities in the
Arab world can lead to misleading and mischievous interpretations.
One of the more pernicious effects has been to lend scholarly support
to neo-imperialist policies of divide-and-rule packaged in a liberal
philosophy of national self-determination. It assigns more coherence
and ethnic exclusivism for various minority groups than actually exists.
Thus, we have seen colonial or Great Power solicitude for the national
aspirations of Maronites, Jews, Armenians, Kurds, Druze, Alawites,
Assyrians, and African blacks at one time or another; but this solicitude
has so neatly meshed with imperialist designs as to raise skepticism
about its altruism. And the ease with which these powers abandon such
causes when they become politically unprofitable has frequently left the
client minority vulnerable to the understandable fury of the majority.

   However unfortunate the inflammatory activities of outside powers may be for generating communal conflict, they remain nonetheless a fact of life in the international system. And however inconvenient the corporate cohesiveness of minorities may be for Arab state policy makers, these minorities are most unlikely ever to be fully assimmilated. Nor is there any moral reason why they should be. Therefore, it would seem to be a proper concern of Arab policy makers and elites to continue to try and contrive structures through which the cultural integrity, prosperity, and happiness of the minority communities can be maximized, without detriment to the political values and the socioeconomic development of the entire polity. A policy of tolerance is not only ethically commendable but also may help to avoid future communal strife.

4

The Crisis of Authority

In the two previous chapters, I have attempted to analyze those dimensions of Arab political culture dealing with national identity and identifications among fellow citizens—the bases of corporate solidarity and intergroup relations. I now turn to those dimensions concerned with the attitudes of citizens toward government. Why do Arabs obey their rulers? The intention in this chapter is to reflect on the nature of authority in contemporary Arab politics.

The question of national identity and solidarity, we have seen, is complex, but the problem of authority is even more serious. It is no exaggeration, in fact, to state that the Arab nation and its constituent sovereign states are undergoing a crisis of authority. Few Arab regimes can count themselves as reasonably secure from attempted irregular changes of government through coups d'état, assassinations, rebellions, or armed uprisings. Since the beginnings of the independent Arab state system after World War II, there have been many challenges to established political authority. These challenges are analyzed in the country case studies which follow in subsequent chapters, and they are summarized for the period 1948–67 in the form of computer-drawn graphs in the Appendix. Since the late 1960s, Arab politics have been somewhat more stable than they were during this earlier period, but the crisis of authority is far from over, as study of the area during the first half of the 1970s makes amply clear. Among the monarchies, there were assassination attempts in Morocco, a civil war in Jordan, and a rural insurrection in Oman; and even in Sa'udi Arabia, the most stable of the kingdoms, the revered King Faisal died at the hands of an assassin. Among the republics of the pan-Arab core area, there were plots in Egypt, a coup d'état in Syria, at least one attempted coup in Iraq, and a calamitous civil war in Lebanon. The republics of the Arab world periphery fared no better; one could observe an attempted coup in Algeria, unrest in Libya, attempted coups in the Sudan, and a coup in northern Yemen.

The problem may be stated in Weberian terms. The traditional bases of authority have been weakened but have not disappeared, while rational-legal types of authority have arisen but are not strong. The coexistence of contradictory types of authority is a drain on overall system legitimacy. Arabs are still socialized into accepting traditional rationales for obedience based on kinship, religion, dynastic despotism, and feudalism. Yet at the same time, they are influenced by Western ideologies which justify authority on altogether different grounds like "the will of the people." But in the absence of effective structures of political participation, how is the will of the people to be ascertained? All sorts of politicians and groups can and do claim to be authentic representatives of the popular will. But there is usually no accepted, legitimized procedure for ascertaining which among them is the most authentic embodiment of this will. Accordingly, force is frequently the arbiter of the locus of authority.

Not only is there confusion over authority within the modern sector of the political system, there is also conflict between the modern and the traditional sectors. Politicians who base their authority claims on traditional grounds alienate the modern elements, and the modernists who try to justify their power on the basis of a popular mandate (which is often only hypothetical) do not easily win over the traditional elements. In the Arab world today it is easy to tear down old buildings and construct new ones, but it is quite another matter to destroy the traditional myths of authority and replace them with solid modern bases; thus, the life of politicians, traditional and modern, is permanently complicated by the need to appeal to very different constituencies, using for each symbols which are irrelevant, if not repugnant, to the other. In the absence of a coherent foundation for authoritative rule, there is a disproportionate reliance on personality and individual leadership to legitimize rule.

DIMENSIONS OF TRADITIONAL AUTHORITY

Traditional authority patterns in the Arab world are neither monolithic nor homogeneous. Not only are there tensions between traditional and modern criteria of authority, there are also contradictions among the traditional values themselves. Four dimensions of traditional authority can be discerned. The patriarchal dimension refers to the importance of kinship groups in Arab society and the habitual deference accorded to the father in the Arab family. The consultative dimension refers to the tradition in Arab tribal society whereby the leader's authority derives from communal acceptance and participation in decision making. The Islamic dimension consists of the moral precepts for right rule laid down in Islamic doctrine, with

its authoritarian and egalitarian tendencies, and the historical practice
of the Islamic dynasties. Finally, the feudal dimension refers to the
political economy of the later Islamic polities and the concentration of
authority in a class of notables. Despite modernization the patriarchal
family, tribal values, religious standards, and even neo-feudal relationships still exist in the Arab world and play a role in the determination
of legitimate authority. It is a role fraught with tensions and contradictions: on the one hand, it promotes absolutism and blind obedience—
a shepherd-flock relationship; but on the other hand, it engenders
demands for egalitarianism and participation.

Patriarchal Authority

At all levels of Arab politics, the family is an important political
as well as social structure. Political actors are frequently distinguished
by their family identity, and political authority even outside the
family is often paternalistic. From Morocco to Yemen, family or
family alliance parties are led by the senior members of the "best"
families in the area. The rural politics of south Lebanon, for example,
has long been dominated by the Asa'd family and its clientele of lesser
families, and the Sunni Muslim Mouseitbe quarter of Beirut is considered to be the "turf" of the powerful Salam family. At the national
level too, the family still bulks large among the various actors, even
though it has lost ground in the last quarter-century. Syria, before the
coups of the 1960s, had a forty family oligarchy. Analysts trying to
fathom the shadowy elite and patronage politics of Egypt or Iraq
before their revolutions in the 1950s had to keep track of family
positions and interrelationships. If the dynasty of Muhammad Ali
in Egypt in the first quarter of the nineteenth century could be described
as a family fief, the same description could also be applied in recent
times to regimes in Morocco, Libya, and Lebanon. In the Kingdom of
Sa'udi Arabia and the tiny Arab shaykhdoms of the Gulf, family and
polity reach the point of absolute congruence. Sa'udi Arabia of
course is named after the family that built it and administers it
exclusively. In the area of the modern United Arab Emirates, formerly
known as the Trucial Coast, the main ruling families and tribes were
the Qawasim (of Sharja and Ras al-Khayma), the Al bu Falah and
Al bu Falasa families of the Bani Yas tribe (of Abu Dhabi and Dubai,
respectively). In Oman, frequently racked by tribal factionalism and
sectarian conflict, the predominant family was (and still is) the Al bu
Sa'id. In what is now the People's Democratic Republic of Yemen,
the principal ruling families up until the revolution of 1967 were the
Qu'aitis, Kathiris, and the Wahidis in the former eastern protectorate,

and some twenty local sultans and shaykhs in the former western protectorate around Aden. Within all these ruling families there is a tradition of deference to the senior members (although power is not automatically bestowed on the basis of seniority). Patrimonial respect is the rule. The tradition of patrimonial deference extends beyond the family itself to the people who, in the ideal case, submit themselves as a flock unto a shepherd.

The implications of strong kinship affiliation for political authority in the modern Arab states are generally negative. Many Arab and Western intellectuals believe that it has impeded the development of modern political structures like parties and bureaucracies. One of the persistent and frustrating themes in the progressive movements of the twentieth century has been their inability to crush or to come to terms with ingrained habits of deference to paternal authority. At the nation-state level, parochial kinship loyalties are one of several subnational identifications that have inhibited national civic culture and public spirit. Islamic and desert traditions have merged to give the father's role preeminence in family affairs. The easy divorce provisions of Islam and the fractional shares (one-half of the son's share) allotted to daughters in Islamic inheritance laws are two of the most prominent symbols of the male's formal superiority over women. As for the children, studies of child-rearing practices find that the father's formal authority over sons and daughters is absolute. Furthermore, cross-cultural comparative studies indicate that the authoritarian personality traits are significantly stronger among Arabs than Americans.[1] Respect, deference, and strict obedience to the male head of household are sternly inculcated in children and wives. To be sure, the reality of power and authority relationships in Arab families, as elsewhere, does not conform exactly to these formal norms; for example, wives and mothers exercise rather more de facto influence than they have been given credit for. Nevertheless, the general pattern clearly is one of firm and virtually absolute fatherly rule.[2]

It would be simplistic to claim that there is a direct relationship between authoritarian, patriarchal family structures and the absolutist behavior of national governments—except perhaps in the few cases noted in which a ruling family and the national government are

1. L. H. Melikian, "Some Correlates of Authoritarianism in Two Cultures," *Journal of Psychology*, 42 (1956), pp. 237–48; and "Authoritarianism and its Correlates in the Egyptian Culture and in the United States," *Journal of Social Issues*, 15 (1959) pp. 58–68.

2. See Hisham Sharabi, with Mukhtar Ani, "Impact of Class and Culture on Social Behavior: the Feudal-Bourgeois Family in Arab Society," mimeographed, 1974, and Sharabi, *Introductions to the Study of Arab Society* (in Arabic) (Beirut: Dar al-Mutahida lil-Nashr, 1975).

virtually identical. Many other factors, including cultural values, class structure, nonkinship affinities, education, and the political arena itself, must also be considered. But it is permissible to conclude that the classical family situation at least does not seem to foster participant behavior or egalitarian norms. And while family solidarity is pervasive, there also appears to be a great deal of repressed rather than resolved conflict in Arab family life, thus explaining to a degree the paradox of family cohesion and simultaneous backbiting and feuding prominent in family life.

The implications of paternalistic authority are all the more important when it is realized that Arab kinship groups extend well beyond the size of nuclear families of the West. This difference is due not only to the fact that Arab nuclear families themselves are larger— with the average number of children between four and nine[3]—but, more importantly, because the bonds linking blood-related nuclear families are far stronger than in the West. Even the most Westernized, middle-class urban dwellers—that is, the least traditional population sector—exhibit these more extended affiliations, although they may not necessarily live in the same dwelling with their various cousins and their families. While these individuals would not seriously regard themselves as members of a clan, they would nevertheless retain close relationships with their near kin. Traditionally, cousin-marriage has been not only permitted but encouraged; and while this practice is declining somewhat in the more modernized locales, it is still widely practiced.

If kinship shapes the basis of authority even in the most modernized strata of Arab society, its role is even more important in the vast traditional sectors. In rural agricultural areas, for example, the clan is an important unit of social and political control. Here kinship is taken seriously indeed. While the terminology is sometimes imprecise, a clan may be defined as a group of families (households) in the same village or region, claiming common patrilineal descent. In his study of a Transjordanian village with three major clans, each comprising some thirty to seventy households, Richard Antoun records a number of cases of conflict in which the clan, led by its elders, enforced proper behavior upon its members: social ostracism of an individual from his clan could be as powerful a sanction as economic reprisals or even physical threats.[4] A daughter who dishonored herself dishonored the

3. The data are from a Jordanian survey, reported in the United Nations Economic and Social Office in Beirut (UNESOB) *Bulletin*, 5 (July 1973), p. 30.

4. Richard T. Antoun, *Arab Village: A Social Structural Study of a Transjordanian Peasant Community* (Bloomington: Indiana University Press, 1972), chap. 2.

clan and might pay for her indiscretion with her life; and while the government police might impose a sentence on the clan-notable who perpetrated a crime of honor, the ultimate resolution of conflict would require some compromise of the secular criminal code and local norms. Clan leaders would act as a delegation to arrange a *sulha*, or reconciliation, between one of its members and a member of a neighboring clan, providing a forum for mediation or arbitration and working out appropriate material restitution. The clans would select their own *mukhtar*, or mayor, who would in turn be designated by the national government as its local representative.

To be sure, family and clan are not the only shapers of authority in all domains of social behavior and certainly not in all geographic areas. Economic structure and religion also play crucial roles. Furthermore, paternalistic authority is increasingly diluted as physical and social mobility increases. Nevertheless, it requires little imagination to infer that a modernizing national government, such as that of Jordan, exploits both local authority structures and prevailing habits of paternalistic deference in building its legitimacy. By the same token, the progressive political movements desiring to mobilize the masses for revolutionary purposes can hardly ignore, much as they may deplore, the persistence of paternalism.

I have stressed the negative consequences (from a liberal point of view) of kinship on political authority. The congruence between patriarchal social values and patrimonial political values facilitates arbitrary rule and customary deference in modern Arab state politics, especially in those states where tradition is relatively unchallenged. In general, Arabs are not socialized either in their family upbringing or in the school to question the established centers of authority. Such socialization patterns are perhaps more inclined to produce followers than leaders. Worse still, they inhibit both effective leadership and "followership" in the predominantly nontraditional context of national politics: he who aspires to lead tends to be autocratic and inflexible, lacking in the skills to win a nontraditional following, while he who is supposed to follow tends to be apathetic and lacking in initiative.

There is, however, one characteristic associated with patriarchal authority which mitigates its authoritarian tendency. It is simply the multiplicity of kinship structures, which creates a kind of pluralism that limits the absolutism of a leader. This is the same condition that, from the point of view of an authoritarian nation-builder, is considered an obstacle to a civic culture integrated around a single national authority structure. The existence in all the Arab polities of numerous patriarchies, large and small—some with considerable functional or regional political autonomy—permits a limited degree of access.

Observers are impressed by the ability of ordinary Arabs to gain access
and favors from regimes and bureaucracies that are manifestly
unaccountable and officially remote; they do it by utilizing family,
clan, or tribal connections. In all the Arab states, especially the
monarchies, families or family alliances function like interest groups
or parties in industrialized societies. Even the most radical regimes
like Iraq and the PDRY have not eliminated this traditional pluralism
of authority structures.

Sometimes traditional pluralism degenerates into traditional anarchy. The Arabic proverb, "I and my cousin against the outsider;
I and my brother against my cousin," enshrines and summarizes what
is in fact a complex set of alliance rules graded by kinship proximity.[5]
Family honor is to be protected at all costs. Not unexpectedly, conflict
in areas without effective government takes the form of family feuds
and vendettas. Conflict resolution requires mediation by respected
neutral peacemakers between warring families, a procedure known in
Arabic as *wasita*. Even in areas in which government, with its secular
criminal codes, is slowly taking root, it is not uncommon for the criminal
convicted in the pursuit of family honor to get off with a light sentence.
If kinship thus serves to define security-communities in the traditional
Arab world, a corollary implication is that patterns of authority and
solidarity in broader political matters are also generated.

The Consultative Tradition

The second dimension of traditional authority also tends to inhibit
the basic patriarchal tendency toward absolutism and blind obedience.
Consultative mechanisms, a counterpoise to autocratic or ineffective
rule, are particularly a feature of tribal society in the Arab world; and
although the tribes are now but a small fraction of Arab society, the
consultative tradition is by no means forgotten. In fact, it is important
enough to dwell briefly on tribes and tribal politics in the Arab world
today.

The term tribe in Arabic has three common equivalents: *qabila*,
with a root meaning of kind, type, sort, specimen, or species; *ashira*,
meaning kinfolk, closest relatives, or bedouin tribes; and *ahl*, meaning
relatives, kinfolk, members, followers, or people. Precise figures on
Arab tribal populations are difficult to find, but one may obtain a
rough idea from some fragmentary estimates. Ibish reports that Syria

---

5. See Victor F. Ayoub, "Conflict Resolution and Social Reorganization in a Lebanese
Village," *Human Organization*, 24 (1965), pp. 11–17, and reprinted Louise E. Sweet (ed.), *Peoples
and Cultures of the Middle East* (New York: Natural History Press, 1970, 2 vols.), vol. 1, pp. 137–54.

in the early 1950s had a tribal population of some 450,000, or one-seventh of the total population, and that there were sixteen principal tribal federations, which would yield an average population of some 29,000 per federation. As some of these federations were subdivided into two to five main tribes, one might infer that a tribe in Syria could number between 5,000 and 15,000 members.[6] There are perhaps twenty-five major tribal confederations in the Arabian peninsula, among the most important being the Anaza, Harb, Atayba, Qahtan, Mutayr, and Rashid. The Shammar and Ruwalla federations historically have dominated the Tigris-Euphrates valley,[7] while in northern Arabia and the Levant the Huwaytat, the Druze, and the Ansariyya have played important roles up to the present day. Among the many tribes of the Sudan, the Beja federation and the Bisharin are the largest; and during British rule especially the tribes played a prominent part in national politics. In North Africa, the Berber tribes dominate the Atlas mountains, and the Moroccan Rif and Algerian Kabylia regions have historically resisted control by the central governments. The distinction in North Africa between the bilad al-makhzan (the settled, governed land) and the bilad al-siba (the land of dissidence or insolence) contrasts the land of tribal rule and conflict with that of order and government. The tribal way of life has been waning in the Arab world as modern transportation, communications, and the oil economy have taken root. Today perhaps less than 5 percent of the Arab world's population is actually nomadic,[8] with 2 to 2.5 million in North Africa, 1.5 million in Arabia, and 600,000 in Syria and Iraq. A far larger proportion, however, retains a degree of tribal identity; and the consultative aspects of tribal authority patterns are a part of the Arab cultural heritage in general.

The leader of a tribe is a *shaykh* or *sayyid*. A shaykh is "one who bears the marks of old age" and historically has referred to the patriarch of a family or tribe. In the modern period, shaykh (and in some localities, sayyid) have a more general application as a term of polite address and veneration. The shaykh of a tribe leads by virtue of his personal qualities as recognized by a council of the elders—the heads of the main families. Tribal leadership is not hereditary in principle, although the eldest or the strongest son of a chief often is the primary candidate, but even he must win the approval of the leading men of

6. Yusuf Kamal Husein Ibish, "The Problem of Minorities in Syria" (M.A. dissertation, American University of Beirut, 1951), p. 72 and chaps. 4 and 5.

7. Lady Ann Blunt, *Bedouin Tribes of the Euphrates* (New York: Harper, 1879).

8. According to W. B. Fisher in the annual reference book, *The Middle East and North Africa*, 1972–73 (London: Europa Publications), p. 11.

the tribe. When the men of the tribe swear allegiance to the leader through an oath called the *bay'a*, the leader is legitimized. Historically, the bay'a has functioned well in the legitimizing of dynastic sultans. In the present age, the acclamation of charismatic military leaders by unanimous plebiscites might be construed as a modern adaptation of bay'a for legitimizing purposes. Confidence can also be withdrawn through a similar procedure. The colorful leader of the Huwaytat tribe, Awda ibn Harb Abu Tayyih, who became known to the West through his collaboration with T. E. Lawrence in World War I, took over its leadership by virtue of his fighting skill and accomplishment: he was said to have killed seventy-five men, and Lawrence described him as the archetypical bedouin raider.[9] Effective tribal leadership depends upon superior personal strength demonstrated both in warfare and governance.

Yet the chief is not given license to rule arbitrarily; he must consult. Charles Doughty provides a glimpse of the tribal council or *majlis*:

> For the Beduins sitting in the coffee-tent of their menzil [dwelling-place], when the sun mounts, it is time to go over to the mejlis, 'sitting,' the congregation or parliament of the tribesmen. There also is the public coffee-drinking, held at Motlog's or some other one of the chief sheykhs' worsted 'houses'; where the great sheykh and the coffee companions may that morrow be assembled: for where their king bee is found, there will the tribesmen assembled together. . . . Let him speak here who will, the voice of the least is heard among them; he is a tribesman. . . . This is the Council of the elders and the public tribunal: hither the tribesmen bring their causes at all times, and it is pleaded by the maintainers of both sides with busy clamour; and everyone may say his word that will. The sheykh meanwhile takes counsel with the sheukh, elder men and more considerable persons; and judgement is given commonly without partiality and always without bribes. This sentence is final. . . . Their justice is such, that in the opinion of the next governed countries, the Arabs of the wilderness are the justest of mortals . . .[10]

In theory, tribal politics displayed significant democratic characteristics: election of the ruler, ruler accountability, and equal opportunity for participation in the majlis. A tribal shaykh, in the classical nomadic

9. George Rentz, "Huwaytat," *New Encyclopedia of Islam* (Leiden: E.J. Brill, 1971), pp. 642–44. The figure did not include Turks.

10. Charles M. Doughty, *Travels in Arabia Deserta* (New York: Boni and Liveright, n.d. [1888]), p. 248.

desert situation at least, could not rule for long without the consensus of the tribe. In practice too, these procedures had some reality as norms, especially in the purely nomadic tribal societies. But in the larger tribes, rule and influence was in fact restricted to the more important family heads, and as tribes became more settled the chiefs became more absolutist through their ownership of land, control of water supplies, and agricultural equipment. The principle of equal participation was also distorted by the inequalities of status and power within the families and larger kin groups that make up the larger community: thus patriarchal prerogatives, age, sex, and the pattern of interfamily connections and obligations made some men more equal than others. Nor was there any conception of a structured loyal opposition. Nevertheless, the practice of nomadic tribal consultation differs in its openness from the other traditional authority patterns such as feudalism, dynastic despotism, and imperial bureaucratic theocracy. Tribal democracy may be as remote from contemporary forms of government in the Arab world as the New England town meeting is to modern government in America, but in each case the earlier model expresses an ideal that retains some vitality.

The participant character of tribal government and the egalitarian social norms of Islam constitute two significant strands in Arab political culture, which has otherwise favored absolutism, that facilitate an open political system. I do not conclude therefore that tradition facilitates modern democracy. On the contrary, the contradictory values within the traditional sphere complicate the development of coherent bases for authority.

The Islamic Dimension

Islam, as argued in chapter 2, is a fundamental element in the national identity of the Arabs. It is scarcely less important as a factor affecting political authority where its effects are multiple. In terms of doctrine, it has been interpreted to justify virtually absolute rule, but at the same time it insists on equality. In terms of historical practice, the Islamic polity exhibited despotism punctuated by rebellion and chronic succession crises. In terms of its own heterodox offshoots, it embodied the idea of radical dissent.

As the political community of Muhammad and his Companions in Medina and Mecca gave way to the Ummayad dynasty in Damascus, a new political structure emerged—the imperial dynastic state. This institution, which attained its most elaborate form in the Ottoman Empire of the sixteenth century, was the ultimate arbiter of conflict and maintainer of order throughout most of the Middle East until the twentieth century. It was imperial in that it was driven to territorial expansion whenever possible (having no clearly fixed national territory as is the case today) because of Islamic ideology, dynastic ambitions, and internal sociopolitical pressures. It was dynastic in that succession occurred within the family, although rarely in an orderly manner, even though there was no clear sanction for such a procedure in Islam. It was also absolutist in that there were no checks, save those of God, upon the ruler, although there were consultative mechanisms in the form of the ministers and religious learned men. In the early history of Islam one might fairly characterize the imperial dynasties as theocratic, inasmuch as religion seemed to be central both in theory and in its affect on actual political behavior. But the transition from theocracy toward secular monarchy began to occur as early as the Ummayad dynasty according to Ibn Khaldun; certainly by the middle of the eleventh century, when the Abbasid caliphate had been shorn of its power by usurping Buwayhid sultans, there could be little doubt that the caliph's function was reduced to supplying theological legitimacy for the convenience of the ruler whose concerns were more practical than pious. Religion retained its formal centrality—indeed the office of caliphate was not abolished until 1924—but power rested with the sultan.

Even though the theory of the caliphate may have been a good guide to actual practice only momentarily, if at all, in Middle Eastern history, it is nonetheless instructive to examine it because it is the political expression of the Islamic culture that still permeates Arab society today. In simplest terms, the caliph was the successor to the messenger of God, the Prophet Muhammad. The caliphate was "to guarantee the maintenance of pure Islam in conformity with its law, to protect the faithful and defend them against heretics and unbelievers."[11] It was "to preserve the *Umma* intact, free from disunity, strife and heresy." According to al-Ghazzali (d. 1111), the most influential of the medieval Muslim philosophers, it was "an indispensable institution of Muslim life demanded by the *ijma* of the community after the death of Muhammad, when the maintenance of the religious and political order made the immediate investiture of the Imam imperative."[12]

But the Qur'an, the *hadith* (Qur'anic commentaries) and the ijma (the rule of consensus) were not explicit about the succession; the

11. E. I. J. Rosenthal, *Political Thought in Medieval Islam* (Cambridge: Cambridge University Press, 1962), pp. 22–24.

12. Quoted in E. I. J. Rosenthal, ibid., p. 38.

Arabic term for caliphate—*khalafa*—does not appear. There was thus no divine guidance as to whether it should be by heredity, election, or designation. The only point that does seem clear is that the successor was to be a guide to the divine law for ordinary men, as Ibn Khaldun later put it; that is, the executor of the Shari'a as interpreted through the consensus of the ulama. To what extent the caliph was to exercise royal authority (*mulk*) as against religious authority was uncertain from the beginning. According to Ibn Khaldun, interpreted by E. I. J. Rosenthal, "The decline of religion coincided with the transformation of the khilafa of that time into the *mulk* of Muawiya and the Ummayads, and it was also the time of the transition from a nomadic to a settled culture and the expansion of Islam into a vast empire . . ." The distinction between *siyasa diniyya*, based upon the divinely revealed prophetic law and represented by the khilafa, and *siyasa aqliyya*, founded by conquest, based on laws devised by reason and realized in mulk, the power state, is fundamental.[13]

In any event, the turbulent expansion of the empire created such pressures that a powerful and pragmatic leadership was required to hold it together; the religious sanctity of the caliphate alone would hardly be enough. The worldly character of the first Ummayad caliph, Muawiya, for example, has been illuminated by Julius Wellhausen, in the following terms:

> Piety was not his motive, neither did he follow the traditions of his murdered predecessor. . . . He had the faculty of winning over and retaining those whom it was expedient for him to have, and even of making those whom he distrusted work for him. . . . He was essentially a diplomat and politician, allowing matters to ripen of themselves, and only now and then assisting their progress, it might be by the use of a little poison. . . . He disliked to have recourse to compulsion, and he did not so much conquer Iraq as buy its submission. If he could reach his goal by means of money, he spent it lavishly, but he never spent it in vain, and it amused him to disappoint those who were counting upon his indiscriminate liberality, or thought they could cheat him. . . .[14]

It is significant that even with the presence of the Prophet so recent the political conditions required a strong, absolutist ruler concerned more

---

13. E. I. J. Rosenthal, *Islam in the Modern National State*, (Cambridge: Cambridge University Press, 1965), pp. 17–22.

14. Julius Wellhausen, *The Arab Kingdom and Its Fall* (Beirut: Khayat's 1963; reprint of 1927 edition), pp. 135–39.

with politics and war than with interpreting the Shari'a. If these rulers appear prototypical of contemporary Arab leaders, it may be because the conditions for governing are still difficult, perhaps even more so since Islam has declined as an integrative force.

The Ummayad caliphs also exploited the asabiyya of the Arabs, in addition to their holy office and their strong characters, to maintain the coherence of the empire. Arab officers and tribal chiefs constituted themselves as the ruling elite in the conquered territories; non-Arab local inhabitants, and to an important extent new Arab immigrants, were excluded. However much the resort to this exclusivity may have been dictated by political necessity, one result was the generating of hostility of the excluded national elements. The stressing of primordial Arab ties was necessary for coherence, but it conflicted with the universal values of Islam itself. The result was fragmentation and conflict. Such conflict was one of the reasons for the displacement of the Ummayad dynasty by the Abbasids in the eighth century.

The Abbasid revolution symbolizes the fundamental conflict between the orthodox Sunnis and the partisans of Ali, the Shi'a, over the nature of Islamic right rule. One element of the Shi'ites in particular, the Hashimiyya movement, had become disenchanted not just with the succession but with the nature of orthodox rule itself; the Hashimiyyas wanted to establish an imam, an ideal ruler, endowed with God's divine wisdom and able to execute it and to dispense with the all-too-worldly caliph-monarchs. They did not succeed, and the Abbasid caliphate remained orthodox. But Shi'ism did establish itself for a time two centuries later in the Fatimid caliphate of Tunisia and Egypt and finally in Persia in the sixteenth century with the Safavid dynasty. Elsewhere, various Shi'ite heterodoxies emerged from time to time, constituting in political terms a kind of radical alternative to the established bureaucratic orthodoxy.

Despite these deviations, the main lines of the Arab imperial dynasty were clearly drawn by the eleventh century. The shepherd (ra'iyy) was to look after the flock (ra'aiyya). As Lambton succinctly puts it: "All the sultan expected of his subjects was that they should pay their taxes, and pray for his welfare, while they expected from him security and justice."[15] Church and state were inseparable and so too were nonconformity and political opposition. Loyalties were accorded, on the one hand, to kinship groups, neighborhoods or guilds, and on the

15. Anne K. S. Lambton, "The Internal Structure of the Saljuq Empire," in *The Cambridge History of Islam*, vol. 5, *The Saljuq and Mongol Periods* (Cambridge: Cambridge University Press, 1968), pp. 203–82; p. 205.

other, to Islam and the Shari'a, but not to the state as such. As for the changing balance of power between caliph and sultan, the philosophers and theologians had by that time produced the necessary rationales. Al-Mawardi declared that the caliph's duties were the defense of religion and the administration of state but that he could hold office even if under arrest and could rightfully delegate some of his governing powers to others.[16] Al-Ghazzali proposed a cooperative relationship between caliph and sultan: the sultan would designate the caliph and the caliph would accept and legitimize the secular role of the sultan.[17] In terms of the rightful basis of government these distinctions were and still are important, but in terms of actual political behavior they were academic almost from the time they were proposed. Since the middle of the tenth century, when Baghdad fell under the Buwayhid kings, the caliphate had been reduced to the merest appendage of royal authority. Caliphs were jailed, humiliated, and exiled. Furthermore, by the thirteenth century local dynasts on both extremes of the Dar al-Islam were claiming the title for themselves.[18] As the Ottoman Turks burst into predominance, defeating the Egyptian Mamluks early in the sixteenth century, Sultan Selim I imprisoned the nominal Abbasid caliph and appropriated the functions of the caliphate into the office of sultan. There they remained until 1923–24 when the proclamation of the Turkish Republic led to the abolition of both offices.

Although the Ottoman state was always dominated by worldly as opposed to religious rule—a condition evident in the absolute superiority of the sultan's office compared to that of caliph—it is a fact nonetheless that under the Ottoman system, especially in the sixteenth and seventeenth centuries, the law of Islam reached its most elaborate and effective form. Under the administration of the Chief Mufti of Constantinople, the Shaykh al-Islam, the Shari'a was applied throughout the empire through a system of competent and independent judges—qadis; and it covered not only the domain of personal status but also commercial and civil law. However brutal, despotic, and unstable the politics of the sultanate may have been, the system remained to most of its subjects the domain of Islam. Even in its last days it is significant that the great majority of its Arab-Muslim subjects refused to take up the standard of the Arab revolt. Even the non-

16. Lambton, ibid.; and T. W. Arnold, *The Caliphate*, op. cit., pp. 70–73.
17. See Leonard Binder, "Al-Ghazzali's Theory of Islamic Government," *The Muslim World*, 45, 3, (1955), pp. 229–41.
18. Arnold, op. cit, pp. 107–20.

Muslim subjects enjoyed a substantial degree of security and autonomy by virtue of the millet system, Islam having accorded to the other "people of the Book" such protected status.

The Ottoman Empire maintained an unprecedented level of civil order and tolerance for minorities. Perhaps its most important achievement was the institutionalizing of government and administration legitimized by the principles of Islamic ethics and community. Notwithstanding the chronic defects in the succession process, the Ottomans developed a level of rational-bureaucratic performance, a set of structures for extending the imperial presence, and a measure of religious-legal legitimacy quite superior to preceding dynasties. It projected an overall coherence to an area fragmented into many small and fragmented ethnic and religious communities. Little wonder that some historians look nostalgically at the premodern days when all (or most) of the pieces of the Islamic cultural mosaic were "in place," before the time when assertive nationalisms introduced fear and conflict.[19] But for those leaders and peoples who did not want to be kept "in place," the empire, particularly in its last two centuries, was a stagnating influence and an increasingly oppressive master. In the post-Ottoman world of nation-states, the role of orthodox Islam in shaping political authority remains important but ambivalent. If historically it sanctioned despotism, spiritually it insisted upon the equality of all men under God and the obligation of the political leadership to work for a good society, one in which the poor would enjoy special benefits. If Islam historically failed to provide checks on despotism, it nonetheless clearly specified independent standards by which leaders should be judged.

Apart from the mainstream of Islamic authority patterns were the ultraorthodox reform movements and the radical dissenters within the Shi'ite confessions. Both are interesting inasmuch as they represented highly affective, indeed charismatic, alternatives to the existing bureaucratic-dynastic norms of the Islamic polity. As such they prefigure the revolutionary style of opposition to established government in the present age.

Within orthodox Islam the radical reformist strain has been most prominently symbolized by the Wahhabi movement. Wahhabism, which arose in the Najd region of Arabia in the middle of the eighteenth century, was intended to purify the established structures of the Islamic domain now ruled by the decaying Ottoman Empire. Its

19. See, e.g., Bernard Lewis, *The Middle East and the West* (London: Weidenfeld and Nicolson, 1963), pp. 44–46.

primary theological inspiration was the puritanical scholar Ibn
Taimiyya (1263–1328), who insisted upon the strict and literal
interpretation of the Qur'an and the hadith. Like Ibn Taimiyya, the
Wahhabi leaders rejected the possibility of modification or innovation
of the word of God to conform with modern circumstances. They
adhered to the strict Hanbali school of the Shari'a and preached the
virtues of the simple, austere life. They closely resembled the early
Kharijites even though there seems to have been no admitted historical
or theological connection between them.[20] Another significant example
of ultraorthodox leadership was Muhammad Ahmad of the Sudan.
He declared himself the Mahdi, committed to the establishment of the
universal Islamic umma. The Mahdi commanded the absolute
obedience of the masses; so great was his charisma and so loyal were his
followers that he was able to inflict heavy damage on the English,
including the death of General Charles Gordon at Khartoum in 1885,
and established a theocratic state that lasted until 1898. The most direct
expression of ultraorthodoxy in the modern Arab state system is the
Kingdom of Sa'udi Arabia, where the current ruling family continues
the Wahhabi tradition. Its leadership under King Faisal (but not his
successors) reflected a predisposition toward Wahhabi puritanism, and
its ideology still does. Of great significance too has been the development of puritanical orthodoxy outside of the Arabian peninsula,
notably in the Muslim Brotherhoods of Egypt, the Fertile Crescent,
and the regime of Colonel Mu'ammar al-Qadhafi in republican Libya.

The relevance of such dissenting movements for modern Arab
political culture lies in their conceptions of leadership and community,
which differ from establishment Islam. In place of the worldly rational
and absolutist sultan, held in check more in theory than in practice by
the word of God, there is an unswerving commitment among the
dissidents to the pure and the ideal in the notion of a religious leader.
This commitment is shared even by the relatively anarchistic Kharijites.
But the Shi'ite idea of a divinely inspired imam, whose divinity is
complete in the thinking of the Isma'ilis, stands even more sharply
against the orthodox gradualist acceptance of the worldly ruler. While
the idea of the Mahdi, the leader who will restore the faith, is found in
both Sunni and Shi'a Islam, the character of this leader, particularly
in Shi'ite doctrine, is magical and divine. He is infallible. If, as von
Grunebaum claims, the modern Muslim is frustrated by the weakness
and incoherence of the Islamic domain, he perhaps longs for the
deliverance of a charismatic savior. The Shi'ites in particular have

20. Elie Salem, op. cit., pp. 23–24.

been predisposed to welcome divinely inspired leaders, and their longing has had an impact on Islam as a whole. The charismatic leader who employs religious symbolism finds a receptive audience. The history of charismatic, chiliastic leadership in radical Islam suggests a predisposition in the political culture toward the utopian and the absolute, values which in the modernizing Arab world may support the movement of what Manfred Halpern has called "neo-Islamic totalitarianism."[21]

At the same time, however, the radical conceptions of community militate against arbitrary despotism. I have indicated a democratic tendency among the Kharijites in their selection of a leader. The Qarmatian sect also observed a high degree of egalitarianism, and the Isma'iliyya also exhibited a sense of communal equality. Heterodoxy survives today in mountainous areas, and in North Africa one finds the cultivation of saints, or *murabitun* (marabouts), in the Atlas and Rif. The marabouts play an important religious and even political role as mediators between God and man. Their persistence shows again that the totalistic and mystical qualities of heterodox Islam exert a considerable influence and that the idea of holy men or rulers possessing *baraka*, or magical protection, is deeply implanted. All these unorthodox elements share a deep commitment to an ideal society that is not adequately described by the term fanatical. Together, they have provided an alternative and radically different basis for authority and so have further complicated the development of consensus. Something of the impulse, form, and style of the Islamic radicals remains embedded in Arab political culture. It is a predisposition to welcome the divinely endowed Mahdi or his secular equivalent and to facilitate his mission of purifying the society, which in modern terms means making a revolution.

In an effort to compare the impact of the major religions on political development, Donald Smith finds that Islam has contributed strongly to the authoritarian culture of the Middle East, that it has submerged individual ego strength and self-determination through its insistence on submission, and that its egalitarian principles were in fact subordinate to the authoritarian tendencies.[22] From this discussion, one

21. Manfred Halpern, *The Politics of Social Change in the Middle East and North Africa* (Princeton: Princeton University Press, 1963), pp. 134–35. See also R. H. Dekmejian and M. J. Wyszomirski, "Charismatic Leadership in Islam: The Mahdi of the Sudan," *Comparative Studies in Society and History*, 14, 2 (March 1972), pp. 193–214.

22. Donald E. Smith, *Religion and Political Development* (Boston: Little, Brown, 1970), esp. pp. 184–89; cf. also pp. 21–23.

can see why many students of Islam and the Arab world basically accept these conclusions. But one should treat generalizations about religion with an extra measure of care. Clifford Geertz has noted the dilemma of the social scientist in studying religion, likening it to Freud's problem in analyzing dreams and to Plato's cave.[23] To be sure, the Islamic polity was characterized by the primacy of coercive force and instability in the succession process. Thus a case can be made for interpreting Islam as having contributed to an authoritarian political culture, but perhaps not to the degree that Smith and other writers assert. I am more inclined to agree with Watt that, while the ruling institution failed to preserve stability and unity, the failure is not obviously attributable to Islam but rather to the fragmented kinship society, poor communications, and quality of leadership of the time.[24] Furthermore, Islamic norms remained independent of rulers' whims, despite the impotence of the caliphate, and to a significant degree served to legitimize royal authority. Rulers and the ruled shared basic values; most rulers did not impose alien norms on their subjects, and so tyranny, in the sense of "wrong rule," was the exception. If authoritarian political culture implies acceptance of any authority, just so long as it is the strongest, then it is misleading to assert that Islam was a prime contributor to the authoritarian political cultures of the Arab world. Furthermore, as we have seen, the unorthodox dissenting movements in Islam militated against the dogmatic and scholasticist influence of the establishment ulama.

The Feudal Factor

The economic system, which distributes power as well as wealth, inevitably affects the nature of authority norms. In the Arab world the concentration of wealth, social control, and power in the hands of a small landed elite contributed over time to the legitimation of that elite's authority. With the development of trade and industry in modern times, the elite succeeded in extending its monopoly from agriculture into the newer urban economic domains. Thus today there remains, even to some degree in the revolutionary polities, a substantial substratum of deference on the part of ordinary people toward the notables of the good families—a kind of natural aristocracy, born to rule.

The political system of settled rural society in the Arab world until

---

23. Clifford Geertz, *Islam Observed* (New Haven: Yale University Press, 1968), pp. 108–09.
24. W. Montgomery Watt, *Islam and the Integration of Society* (Evanston: Northwestern University Press, 1961), p. 175.

quite recently could be described as quasi feudal. At once it must
be pointed out that Middle Eastern feudalism was not and, where it
still exists, is not identical with European feudalism of the Middle Ages.
Scholars have pointed out that the Middle Eastern system lacked one
of the main humanizing features of Europe's feudalism, namely, the
reciprocal, personal relationship between lord and peasant whereby
the lord, who was present on his land and worked it, knew his peasants
and felt responsible for them and the peasant felt a degree of loyalty to
his landlord. But in the *timar* feudalism of the Ottoman Empire, the
lord had no similar attachment either to his land or the sharecroppers
who worked on it because the land itself was a limited term concession
from the state in return for which the timar-holder (landlord) was
required only to make fixed periodic payments. The landowner, or
more properly, concessionaire, thus frequently was an absentee
landlord, and the peasant, who depended upon his impersonal master
for his seed, equipment, and livestock, was forced to pay enormous
rent in produce. Economically, the long-term results were bad,
because such a system discouraged agricultural development; politically, the system assured the predominance of a class of landed notables
and the exclusion of the masses of farm laborers.[25] The only prominent
exception to this arrangement in the Ottoman territories was in
Mount Lebanon, where the mountainous terrain, difficult to administer
from outside, encouraged the development of independence among the
cultivators; in 1858 an uprising among the Maronite peasantry against
their lords accelerated the collapse of feudalism. But generally in the
Ottoman state, even though feudalism had been steadily eroded by the
reforming sultans of the mid-nineteenth century, the political aspects
of the system survived. Even with the final demise of the Ottoman state
and the creation of independent states in the Middle East, rural
politics remained dominated by large landowning families; and these
notables have continued to play the key role in the hinterland down to
the most recent times.

Every village and region has its leading families, with their clienteles
who depend upon them for employment, loans, other business aid,
help in dealing with the government, and the favorable mediation of
quarrels. Not only is the support of a big family helpful to peasants and
laborers directly dependent upon the family for livelihood but also to
others of limited means in the notable's region, such as town laborers,
small businessmen, and other farmers. The rural notable's influence

25. Xavier de Planhol, op. cit., in the *Cambridge History of Islam*, vol. 2, 443–68, esp. pp. 460–
62; see also Iliya Harik in Richard Antoun and Iliya Harik (eds.), *Rural Politics and Social Change
in the Middle East* (Bloomington: Indiana University Press, 1972), esp. pp. 338–45.

has been essentially a product of his economic power—his land, capital, and control of transportation. But it also has resided in family reputation, military tradition, and in the capability to control his region physically, as in the case of "the lords" in Syria, Lebanon, and Iraq.[26] The notable's influence with the higher authorities of the empire would be exerted through his own access to local and provincial government officials. His influence with his clientele would be through the institution (mentioned earlier) known as wasita. Literally, wasita is a means, a linkage, between the patron and his client, a protective relationship not unlike that of the Sicilian mafia and its clientele. It is found at all levels (national and local) and sectors (urban and rural) of the political system. In return for favors only the notable can bestow, the client obligates himself to his powerful friend, perhaps promising him political support in some form or other.

If one facet of the feudal relationship is the relationship between notable and peasant, the other is that between notable and the central government. Again there are both similarities and differences in comparison to European feudalism. As we have seen, the Ottoman timar system (and its near-equivalent in Egypt) involved a limited land use grant from state-owned land to a soldier in service to the sultan. This system was economical in that it allowed the soldier to support himself directly from the land without draining the imperial budget, while at the same time, revenue was collected for it. It also permitted the maintenance of security and order in far-flung regions. But the Ottoman timars were subordinates and agents of the imperial administration, while the European barons were relatively autonomous vis-à-vis the kings, and the kings lacked the elaborate and far-flung bureaucracy and judicial system of the Ottoman rulers. As the empire weakened, however, the subordinate officials and notables became in fact rather more autonomous, and in the Arab world of the seventeenth and eighteenth centuries there was a resurgence of the authority of local rulers and notables. Despite a desperate and temporarily successful effort in the nineteenth century to reassert central authority, the social base of the notables' power remained. And when European control and independence came in the twentieth century, the notables reasserted themselves as the new political elite.

The politics, then, of a typical Ottoman province in the middle nineteenth century could be characterized by the subordination of

26. Albert Hourani, "Ottoman Reform and the Politics of Notables," in William R. Polk and Richard L. Chambers (eds.), *Beginnings of Modernization in the Middle East* (Chicago: University of Chicago Press, 1968), pp. 41–68, esp. pp. 48–49.

MONTEREY PENINSULA COLLEGE LIBRARY

peasantry to the landed notables in a *metayage* sharecropping system, and the theoretical subordination of the class of leading families to the imperial government. Within the province itself, politics involved the rivalries and alliances among leading families and clans; factions were linked horizontally by blood and interest and vertically by patron-client wasita ties. The similarity with the tribal polity, particularly in terms of the kinship bond, is clearly evident.

Only with the revolutions and upheavals of the 1950s and 1960s was the power of the rural landlords substantially curtailed in Egypt, Iraq, Syria, Algeria, Libya, and South Arabia in favor of that of the central government and ruling party. Although the landed class of notables has been emasculated in these countries in widely varying degrees, its authority has not so much been destroyed as appropriated by officials or by other families with acceptable political credentials; thus, the ordinary peasant today is not necessarily more autonomous politically than he was.

A parallel but more complex pattern of elite authority prevailed in Arab cities. An informal urban leadership structure has emerged that both fits the parochial, mosaic character of urban society and serves a mediating function between the neighborhood and the municipal authorities. Analyzing the leadership of nineteenth century cities in the Ottoman Empire, Hourani distinguishes three types of notable: the ulama or religious specialists, the military leaders of the local garrisons, and the secular notables (a'yan, aghas, or amirs) whose influence, like that of the rural notables, rested primarily on economic or reputational bases.

> Around the core of their own independent power they build up a coalition, combining other notable families, *'ulama*, leaders of armed forces, and also the organizations which embody the active force of the population at large: some of the guilds (in particular that of the butchers), the Janissaries in places where they have become a popular group, *shaykhs* of the more turbulent quarters, and those unofficial mobilizers of opinion and organizers of popular action who, under one name or another, go back into the distant past of the Islamic city.[27]

Today, the constellation of urban leadership still bears a marked resemblance to the nineteenth century. Religious leaders and organizations, for example, continue to play influential roles. Notwithstanding

27. Hourani, in Polk and Chambers, op. cit., p. 49.

its desert origins, Islam always flourished in the cities. The observance of ritual, attendance at the Friday speeches in the mosque, and the influence of the religious authorities is more evident in the cities than the countryside. In Arab countries, private Islamic charitable organizations support private schools, and the Islamic scholars influence curricula in the government schools. Mosques frequently become centers for demonstrations against (or for) the government, and religious figures continue to play important roles in organizing nationalist movements, mobilizing public opinion and legitimizing (or condemning) rulers and regimes.

The secular notable of the past has his contemporary urban (and rural) counterpart: the leader (*za'im*) of a good family who assumes responsibility for a certain quarter or neighborhood of the city. By virtue of his proven influence, his connections, his wealth, and family prestige, this "political broker" (to use Lucien Pye's term) provides wasitas for those who seek his help. In Arab cities the man who can obtain this kind of informal assistance may succeed, and succeed much faster, in obtaining this license or that permit, or expediting a piece of business, than the man who must go through official channels. An American observer of Arab urban politics would be reminded of the "boss" system that once prevailed in most American cities. Lincoln Steffens would have felt at home in the sitting room of Sa'ib Salam, one of the major Muslim leaders of Beirut, listening as this za'im dispensed wasitas, threats, judgments, and even the Lebanese equivalent of the Christmas turkey to the people who come to call upon him. Urban notables also have a certain coercive power at their disposal. In Beirut, for example, the *qabaday* is a kind of neighborhood strong man in the service of a notable. With a number of qabadays (and their gangs) at his disposal the notable or za'im has at hand an additional form of influence.

TENSIONS WITHIN THE TRADITIONAL AUTHORITY SPHERE

That the Arabs are a difficult people to govern is not due simply to the recent overlay of modern authority values on traditional patterns. The traditional patterns themselves are laden with tensions and contradictions. The patriarchal element is parochial, structured as it is by kinship groups, and is not conducive to integration within a larger political framework. Only in rare cases does a charismatic father figure succeed in turning his paternalism into a legitimacy resource; more often the culturally sanctioned paternal authoritarianism within every adult male promotes dissidence rather than compliance. Furthermore, to the extent that patriarchal authority relationships do prevail, they do not facilitate either the supple leadership or responsible "followership" that national politics requires.

The absolutist tendencies inherent in kinship authority are mitigated or contradicted to some extent by the parallel tradition of consultation which originated in Arabian tribal society. Leaders must prove themselves, and they must not act arbitrarily; yet, as we have seen, there is a cultural predisposition precisely toward arbitrary paternal authority.

Islam, which bulks so large in shaping Arab political culture, also bestows contradictory authority norms. Islamic doctrine insists upon the ruler following the right moral path and not indulging his own caprices. But Islamic political history (and the religious rationales for khalifal despotism) established a pattern of dynastic absolutism and diluted the idea of rebellion as a corrective recourse. At the same time, the emphasis on social equality and the ruler's obligation toward society introduces another theoretical check on arbitrary rule. Ultra-orthodox and heterodox elements provide almost a populist alternative to the main theme of the bureaucratic-theocratic polity.

Finally, the political economy of feudalism introduces a privileged, landed, and rich elite whose superior wealth and influence has generated deference to a quasi aristocracy. The bases of feudal authority are quite at variance with the other traditional authority patterns.

THE IMPACT OF MODERN AUTHORITY NORMS

The diversity of structures and values in the traditional sphere alone has hindered the development of authoritative government in the Arab world, but the factor precipating today's crisis of authority is, of course, the explosive intrusion of modern political ideologies into the area. The country studies below illustrate some of the grave problems arising from this development—problems which make the struggle for overall legitimacy difficult for traditional and modern political systems alike. Patriarchal, consultative, religious, and feudal norms basically are not compatible with the liberal, rational-legal, secular, democratic, and socialist ideologies now having such a significant impact on elites and masses alike. Because this ideological revolution is far from complete, the Arab world is living under dual systems of authority, and the problem of compatibility is chronic. It cannot be said that the traditional patterns have given way to the new ones. Moreover, just as there is diversity and incompatibility within traditional norms, so there is within the modern norms as well; and much of the conflict analyzed in the country studies concerns which of the modern values will prevail. Finally, to add yet another degree of complexity, modern ideological demands for participation have a certain echo from the traditional sphere, and traditional proclivities toward absolutism have their analogues in modern totalitarian ideologies, deepening the contemporary incoherence of authority norms.

Although no Arab state today fully exemplifies a pure type of traditional or rational-bureaucratic authority in the Weberian sense, for purposes of illustration one may compare Sa'udi Arabia and Iraq. In Sa'udi Arabia a royal family so numerous as to be almost a class enjoys authority on the basis of paternalistic kinship norms, tribal consultative practices, Islamic law, and neo-feudal royal patronage. The Sa'udi leadership is adamantly opposed to socialism or communism; it avoids democracy; it abjures what it considers to be immoral secularism. In Iraq, we see perhaps the nearest Arab approximation of the rational-bureaucratic ideal. An all-pervasive government manages most of the economy and social services. An all-pervasive party monitors regime security and mobilizes the masses through slogans, posters, and the controlled mass media. Objectives and means are precisely spelled out and widely publicized. Monarchy, feudalism, tribalism, and even religion (albeit delicately, as a political value) are castigated as reactionary. Instead, the party and the regime claim that their authority is derived from the objective will of the people. The will of the people is summarized by the slogan, "unity, freedom, and socialism." By striving effectively toward these goals, the regime legitimizes its rule.

Whatever one may conclude about the merits of either the Sa'udi or the Iraqi rationale, it is significant that each system has a serious authority problem. The problem is that participatory norms are widespread in both countries; yet the Sa'udi regime does not admit the merit of democracy even in theory, while the Iraqi regime does not allow it to exist in practice. Neither regime can allow open participation; both maintain elaborate internal security services. The Sa'udi elite, it might be inferred, correctly judges that the foundations on which its authority rests are being eroded. The regime's attempt at massive economic and social development, which give it a claim to modernity, probably only accelerates the erosion. The Iraqi leadership, one might guess, suspects that its rather abstract claims to legitimate authority—socialism, nonalignment, development, will of the people, etc.—do not arouse the fervent enthusiasm of all Iraqis. This is partly because many Iraqis still find traditional authority norms more salient and partly because the regime has no monopoly on these symbols. One of the advantages of traditional monarchical legitimacy is that the symbols are specific to a given family or individual, while in the case of regimes legitimated by modern ideologies, opposition groups can claim to be a more authentic embodiment of the sacred abstractions than the regime in power.

Both the traditional and the modern systems, therefore, face a crisis of authority that in more precise terms is a crisis of participation. Since neither the traditional nor the modern criteria are fully implanted at the present time and yet both are still very much in existence, the dilemma for all the politicians is serious. The basic solution is, of course, for both types of system to develop structures of participation which people will accept as credible embodiments of the democratic norm so widespread yet so unfulfilled. But for reasons that need not be detailed, this is a path fraught with dangers for those in power, especially in the short run. The alternative, which is practiced to one degree or another in all the Arab regimes today, is a strategy which emphasizes personal reputation, nationalist ideology, and structural capabilities. In the absence of solid norms and structures, traditional or modern, the personal leadership characteristics of the ruler take on great importance in building his authority. This is true both for kings and presidents. Furthermore, the most salient ideological symbols for Arabs today are nationalistic—particularly the questions of Palestine and Arab solidarity. These symbols, appear as far more powerful legitimizing resources than traditional norms such as monarchy and piety and modern ones such as socialism and development. Again, kings as well as presidents strive mightily to enhance their authority by identifying themselves as nationalists. The third element in this "muddling-through" strategy is the development of governmental structural capabilities, particularly in the fields of internal security and socioeconomic development. The development of structures for participation may lag, but the building of police forces, schools, mass media, and a healthy economy (with low unemployment) is just as helpful for regime authority in the Arab world as it is elsewhere. Thus, while the crisis of authority is a very serious one, there are ways to manage it, at least temporarily; and that is what much of modern Arab politics, as I show in the country studies, is all about.

5

The Legacy of Imperialism

When one observes the warmth of relationships at the elite level between Arabs and Westerners today, perhaps best symbolized by the embraces of Anwar al-Sadat and Henry Kissinger, one should not forget what most Arab schoolchildren know, that is, the history of the long, relentless, and sometimes brutal intrusion of Western powers into the Arab world. I say this not out of any commitment to historicism but because, as I shall demonstrate, Arabs today are more aware of their own history than ever before. Just as the golden era of the Arabs, which was touched upon in chapter 2, is a more salient legitimacy resource than before, so too is the grim history of Arab-Islamic and Western-Christian confrontation. Particularly when the latter period is juxtaposed against the glories of the former, it is easy to see both how anti-imperialism has become a salient legitimizing symbol and how the secondary—yet perhaps more profound—Western cultural challenge to Arab values has complicated the search for legitimacy.

The Assault of the West

The poignancy of the imperialist legacy for modern Arab politics is that the implanted values and instruments of social modernity were contaminated through the modalities of the implantation. The new modes of thought, politics, production, and commerce were of course disruptive in themselves, but because they were thrust upon a weaker, backward society in a manner that was inevitably brutal and manipulative, they became for generations of educated Arabs symbols of legitimacy yet, at the same time, deeply flawed symbols. Moreover, the conflict was not simply political or strategic but also cultural, and it dated not merely from the expansion of industrial Europe but from earlier times. Thus, one may surmise that the psychological disruption suffered by the Arabs from imperialist penetration was substantial. For in its fundamentals, it was a renewal of the ancient struggle between the partisans of Christianity and Islam which had ramifications in all domains of society—religion, economics, and politics.

The rise of Muhammad, as Henri Pirenne argued, forever divided the Mediterranean world: Islam developed its own exclusive cultural system, while European civilization and political development from the time of Charlemagne onward looked inward and northward.[1] For ten centuries the Islamic world and the West grappled, each threatening the territory and values of the other, until by the nineteenth century Europe's power prevailed and much of the Middle East fell under its control. The largely successful efforts by the Arab states in the mid-twentieth century to free themselves of Western domination thus are rooted in a very old cultural conflict.

Arab-Muslim victories against Byzantium and Christian Spain aroused deep hostility toward Islam among Europeans. The Crusades of the twelfth and thirteenth centuries, in which European settlements were established in the Holy Land and parts of North Africa, only deepened this image while of course arousing fear and hatred in the Muslim world. As Philip Hitti has observed, "Zoroastrianism, Buddhism and other less highly developed religions were never subjected to such a barrage of abuse and condemnation as Muhammadanism was. They posed no threat to the medieval West and offered no competition. It was, therefore, primarily fear, hostility and prejudice that colored the Western view of Islam and conditioned its attitude."[2] By the end of the fifteenth century the last Muslim enclave in Spain was eliminated, but the threat to southern central Europe from the rising Ottoman Empire was becoming acute: the Turks, it will be recalled, reached the outskirts of Vienna in 1529 and finally were decisively defeated there in 1683. Little wonder that the term "Turk" (which was synonomous with "Muslim" to Europeans) should have become a term of abuse in Europe,[3] just as the term "Arab" evokes extremely negative images in the United States today as a threat to that outpost of Western culture, Israel, and to Western security interests through control of oil.

But the tide was turning and Islam was coming under attack. The Arab and other Islamic lands became the object of Western state ambitions, interests, and rivalries. As I recapitulate the activities of Europe in the Islamic domain, I wish to emphasize their offensive character, in contrast with the passivity of a society losing control of its destiny. Out of this experience grew the mythology of anti-imperialism, which to this day is a central factor in the struggle for legitimacy.

1. Henri Pirenne, *Mohammed and Charlemagne* (London: Allen and Unwin, 1939).

2. Philip K. Hitti, *Islam and the West* (Princeton: Van Nostrand, 1962), p. 49.

3. Bernard Lewis, *The Emergence of Modern Turkey* (London: Oxford University Press, 1961), pp. 353–54.

The *reconquista* of the Iberian peninsula from Islam during the twelfth to fifteenth centuries was part of the expansionist religious fervor that had spawned the Crusades. The Portuguese and Spanish pushed beyond the peninsula, however, and established numerous colonial enclaves on the Atlantic and Mediterranean coasts of North Africa in the fifteenth and sixteenth centuries. The local Arab-Muslim dynasty in Morocco tried by itself to contain this persistent European penetration, while the rulers in neighboring Algiers, Tunis, and Tripoli turned to the growing power of Ottoman Turkey for support. In most cases the European raiders were animated by a violent anti-Muslim prejudice; atrocities and treachery were common.[4]

By the end of the fifteenth century, the political expansion of Europe was under way; in addition to the discovery of America, the last Muslim state in Spain, Granada, came to an end, and the sea route to India around Africa was opened. The Portuguese, by 1523, had established an exclusive and lucrative trade with India, the Persian Gulf, and Oman. But they had to fight the local Arabs and their Egyptian and Turkish supporters. The struggle for commercial advantage was all the more savage because of the anti-Muslim crusading spirit of the Portuguese. Vasco da Gama, having captured a ship carrying pilgrims to Mecca, is reported to have told the Captain, "Alive you shall be burned and I say that for nothing in this world would I desist from giving you a hundred deaths if I could give so many."[5] The Portuguese maintained a base at Muscat for nearly a century and a half until 1650 when the Arabs expelled them. The Dutch subsequently built up a position in the Persian Gulf shaykhdoms but by the latter part of the eighteenth century were gradually supplanted by the British, who were to become the principal power there until 1971.

The Seven Years' War (1756–63) between Great Britain and France, which secured Britain's position in North America, also set in motion the colonization of India. Britain's lucrative and strategic India connection led to its subsequent colonial involvement in the Middle East. Britain's two principal European rivals were France and Russia, and by the beginning of the nineteenth century, the competition had led to a scramble for territory and strategic advantage the would, by the end of the century, leave large parts of the Middle East under alien rule or domination. By the end of World War I even the former Ottoman Arab territories were under League of Nations mandates

---

4. John K. Cooley, *Baal, Christ and Mohammed* (New York: Holt, Rinehart and Winston, 1965), chap. 13.

5. Cited in Donald Hawley, *The Trucial States* (London: Allen and Unwin, 1970), p. 70.

instead of being independent. France had been thwarted politically
in America and India, but in 1798 Napoleon invaded Egypt. The
occupation was short-lived but important, for it signified the new
expansiveness of Europe and sowed the first seeds of modernization in
the Middle East. France probed into Egypt and the Levant under
Napoleon, and later into North and West Africa. British policy was
to blunt French encroachments either directly or through proxy local
powers on the approach to India. From the north, Russia posed a
threat from the Balkans through central Asia, which was evident from
Catherine the Great's efforts to expand toward the Mediterranean, the
Persian Gulf, and the Indian Ocean. The guiding principle of British
policy toward the Russian menace was to try and uphold the integrity
of the enfeebled dynasties of Turkey, Persia, and Afghanistan.

Britain's Impact

Governed by its far-flung interests and power, Britain's intrusion into
the Middle East became the most pervasive of the imperialist states.
To protect the southern and Western approaches to its lifeline to
India, the quasi-autonomous government of India secured for Britain
an exclusive and privileged position all along the coasts of Arabia. In
the Arab-Persian Gulf, British commerce was threatened by the piracy
and internecine raiding of the various shaykhdoms. The British were
also worried about the potential threat of the Wahhabi movement in
Arabia and by the expansionist activities of the powerful Egyptian
dynast Muhammad Ali, who posed a threat to his nominal suzerain,
the Ottoman sultan, and who seemed inclined toward France. In 1820
British naval power led to a general treaty between Britain and the
shaykhs (from Bahrain to Ras al-Khayma) prohibiting piracy against
British shipping. In 1853 the British effected the Perpetual Maritime
Truce establishing peace among the various shaykhdoms themselves,
from which document the name Trucial States was derived. And in
1892 another treaty guaranteed to Britain exclusively the right to
administer the states' foreign relations.[6] Kuwait entered into friendly
relations with the British in 1775 when it became a postal station on
the India route, and Britain consolidated its position there after 1903
by obtaining control of Kuwaiti foreign relations in return for protection.[7] In Muscat and Oman, the British also established a friendly
and exclusive position with the ruling Al bu Sa'id family toward the

6. Hawley, ibid., pp. 17–18, and *passim*.
7. H. R. P. Dickson, *Kuwait and Her Neighbors* (London: Allen and Unwin, 1956), chaps. 4
and 6.

end of the eighteenth century, although it was not formally established by treaty until 1891.[8] Britain was also concerned with southern Arabia. Even though the famous lifeline was the sea route around Africa (until 1869 when the Suez Canal was completed), the British were alarmed by Napoleon's incursion into Egypt in 1798 and later by the ambitions of Muhammad Ali; hence Aden became important to them, and a naval party from Bombay captured it in 1839. It was made a Crown Colony. They only left it in 1967, driven out by the nationalist rebellion. The twenty-odd sultanates up the coast from Aden also entered into special relationships with Great Britain later in the century and up to World War I.

The internal political consequences of Britain's presence on the Arabian periphery were to perpetuate and indeed strengthen the hegemony of particular families and tribes. At the same time the British studiously avoided any social or economic improvements beyond the port areas where they called. Significantly, it was at Aden where the first seeds of organized opposition took root and spread from the transient dock workers into the tribal hinterland. Characteristically, the efforts of liberal colonial officers to lay the groundwork for more participant government were too little and too late. In Oman and up the Gulf, British protection consolidated the patrimonial rule of certain families and a wealthy merchant class, while the small fishing, farming, and nomadic populations remained miserable. When declining fortunes finally forced Britain's withdrawal in 1971, the newly independent and rich shaykhdoms were left with little in the way of educated manpower or infrastructure and virtually no experience in participant politics beyond paternalistic tribal practices.

But it was Egypt that was to become the cornerstone of Britain's presence in the Arab world. British policy makers had long opposed the building of a canal at Suez, fearing the problems of keeping it secure from rival and local powers, but now that it was built (with French capital and expertise), the situation was different. Furthermore, Britain's influence over the Ottomans was waning. The ruler of Egypt, Khedive Ismail, had overspent in his effort to Europeanize his country and became indebted to European financiers. When his successor, Tawfiq, called together the Assembly of Notables to deal with the problem, this body objected to the debt-servicing requirements. The British and French refused to accept the assembly's position and, moreover, insisted on the sacking of a number of army officers as an economy measure. Anti-European disturbances broke out and

8. J. B. Kelly, *Eastern Arabian Frontiers* (New York: Praeger, 1964), p. 23.

the British navy bombarded Alexandria and proceeded to occupy the country "temporarily." The principal figure opposing the British, and the pliant Khedive as well, was the nationalist army officer Ahmad al-Urabi. He became another hero in the Arab antiimperialist pantheon and the first in a long line of officers in politics.[9]

On the coasts of Arabia, Britain's presence was limited. Egypt was a different story. Notwithstanding the antiimperialism of the Liberal Prime Minister William Gladstone, the British proceeded to take the leading role in the administration of the country. The British high commissioner, Lord Cromer, held the real power from 1883 to 1907, and he used it vigorously to fight bureaucratic corruption and inefficiency, to put Egypt's finances in order, and even to tame the Nile, among other things. Whatever progress may have been made, government was alien and autocratic; it nurtured a spirit of nationalism and anticolonialism. Indeed, precisely because progress had been made, the Egyptian people were mobilizable for political resistance. As we shall see in the discussion of modern Egypt, Britain's presence became the focus for the first modern nationalist movement in the Arab world. Without a Cromer, a Nasir, not to mention a Zaghloul, would have been impossible—or else long delayed in coming. It was not just an ideological imperialism which animated Egyptian policy makers as they tried to promote Egyptian-led Arab unity throughout the 1950s and 1960s. It was also an appreciation by these policy makers that there were rich lodes of diffuse support to be tapped among the Arab masses in all the areas under British tutelage. This support existed not just in Egypt but also in Palestine, southern Arabia, Libya, the Sudan, and the Gulf and would serve Egyptian state interests as well as Arab nationalist goals.

As London's involvement with Egypt grew, it was not long before the Sudan also fell under British control. From the time of Muhammad Ali at the beginning of the nineteenth century, Egyptian rulers had wanted to extend Egypt's dominions in Africa. Egypt had financial and political troubles of its own and was thus unable to established full control in this vast territory. The revolt of the Sudanese Mahdi and his followers in 1881 came at an awkward time for the Khedive. But two years later, with the Urabi rebellion crushed and Egypt under British occupation, the Khedive sent a British-officered expedition to

9. See Elizabeth Monroe, *Britain's Moment in the Middle East: 1914–1956* (Baltimore: Johns Hopkins Press, 1963), p. 17; Parker T. Moon, *Imperialism and World Politics* (New York: Macmillan, 1947), pp. 223–29; and P. J. Vatikiotis, *The Modern History of Egypt* (London: Weidenfeld and Nicolson, 1969), pp. 144–58.

restore order, but it was defeated. When the British sent Gordon the following year, he was killed and the Mahdiyya was established in Khartoum. In 1896, the British, alarmed by French and Italian activities in northeast Africa, sent Sir Herbert Kitchener at the head of a force that defeated the Mahdi and paved the way for establishment of the Anglo-Egyptian Sudan in 1899—a condominium in fact dominated by the English.

France and Italy

Although not as active as Russia and Britain in caring for the Sick Man of Europe, France had won, through the treaty of 1740, important legal and taxation exemptions for its subjects and their non-Muslim clients. In the Ottoman Empire, these were the humiliating Capitulations, and the other major powers obtained similar exemptions. France also retained what it considered to be a special relationship with the Catholic Christians in the empire, notably in Lebanon. After Napoleon's abortive occupation of Egypt, France played only a limited part in the early period of imperialism in the full flower of imperialism, it would assume a principal role. But initially French attention was directed to lands close at hand in North Africa. In 1830 a French expeditionary force landed at Algiers, ostensibly because the ruler, the bey, had struck the French consul with a fly whisk. In fact, the bey was on bad terms with France and other maritime powers, including the United States, because of raiding and piracy; and the regime of King Charles X was unstable and in need of a foreign diversion. (Furthermore, the fly whisk incident occurred in 1820, seven years before France actually declared war and ten years before it landed at Algiers.) The ruler surrendered, and the French established several coastal enclaves. As settlers moved in, the frontier was pushed back so that in forty years France had pacified all of what is modern Algeria. As usual, the colonial penetration was not without bloodshed and treachery. From 1832 to 1845, the Muslim tribal nationalist, Amir Abd al-Qadir, led a fruitless resistance against the colonization, but in the process he became one of the first nationalist heroes of the modern Arab world.

In March 1881, Tunisia was invaded by French troops from Algeria in retaliation for a tribal raid, and two months later the bey signed a treaty giving France a protectorate over the state. French businessmen, financiers, and farmers had already found Tunisia lucrative; colonizing it not only faciliated economic gain, it also kept the Italians from gaining the foothold there they desired. In addition, the appetite of the European powers for imperial prestige was aggravated by the

growing need to counterbalance the colonial achievements of one
party by compensating the rest; otherwise the risk of war in Europe
would be increased. Having gotten little from the Congress of Berlin,
France was encouraged to enlarge its North African domains.

Morocco did not fall under French protectorate until 1912, but once
again Great Power rivalries were as important as the intrinsic value
of the territory itself in shaping French policy. Germany's emergence
as an imperialist competitor with the other powers precipitated the
event. Britain and France in 1904 concluded an alliance to face the
growing German menace in Europe and to minimize their own
colonial rivalry by agreeing that England should remain in Egypt
and that France should look toward Morocco. Hoping to spoil their
plans, Kaiser Wilhelm visited Tangier in 1905 and proclaimed
German support for the sultan. The resulting crisis led to the state's
falling under the management of a consortium of European powers.
But then rebellions against the sultan and attacks on French and
Spanish residents provided the pretext for armed French intervention.
The Germans continued to foment local unrest and sent a gunboat to
Agadir in 1911, provoking the second Moroccan crisis. This crisis in
turn was resolved in the usual way by an agreement that allowed
Germany a free hand in equatorial Africa and gave France a free hand
in Morocco; and so France obtained its protectorate in 1912, and
Spain a small area in the north. It took the French two decades, how-
ever, before they had pacified the whole country.[10]

France's imprint on the political development of North Africa,
especially Algeria and Tunisia, was more profound than that of
Britain in its territories. One hundred thirty years of French settlement
in Algeria seriously disrupted the traditional society and economy, and
it created divisions within the elite that continue to bedevil Algerian
politics today. In Tunisia and Morocco the traditional ruling circles
eventually lost legitimacy by virtue of their collaboration with the
colonial authorities, giving way in Tunisia to a new bourgeois nationalist movement under Bourguiba and in Morocco to a nationalist sultan
who saved the monarchy by adapting an anti-imperialist position.
In all three countries, the occupation generated tensions and conflicts
within the educated elites over the value of Arab-Islamic culture in a
modern world, and it exacerbated ethnic and sectarian tensions.
Similar problems were raised when France assumed its mandate over
Syria and Lebanon after World War I: the chronic instability of Syria

10. Charles F. Gallagher, *The United States and North Africa* (Cambridge: Harvard University
Press, 1963), pp. 77–78.

under the mandate and after, and the ruinous civil war in Lebanon in 1975–76 are part of the French imperialist legacy.

Italy's imperial role may also be briefly noted. As the general scramble for colonies intensified in the 1880s, Italian governmental and commercial interests sought to carve out an empire in northeast Africa, from Eritrea across Ethiopia to the Somali coast of the Indian Ocean. Italy was encouraged in this to a degree by Great Britain, which sought an additional counterweight to the French. The Eritrean and Ethiopian venture collapsed when the Ethiopians destroyed an Italian force in 1896. The Somaliland concession lasted until 1941, when the British army began its push to liberate all of Somaliland and Ethiopia (which Mussolini had invaded in 1935). According to Touval, "Resentment against Italian rule was probably the most important factor behind the awakening of national consciousness."[11] Such indeed was the universal consequence of settler colonialism and direct rule throughout the Middle East. Libya was the other focus of Italian colonial ambition. Ever since the Congress of Berlin, when Italy received a promise of noninterference from the other powers, some of its politicians had longed to restore some of the grandeur of the Roman Empire. At the turn of the twentieth century, having made an alliance with Germany and having won Britain's tacit support for preempting a possible French take-over from Tunisia, Italy needed only a pretext to act. The pretext was the second Moroccan crisis of 1911. Italy handed Turkey, still the ruling power in Libya, an unacceptable ultimatum and then, after a sporadic and sometimes bloody war with Sanussi Arab tribesmen, occupied Tripolitania and Cyrenaica and named the conquest Libya after the ancient Roman province.[12]

ORIGINS OF THE PALESTINE QUESTION

Toward the end of the last century, the scramble for colonies developed in earnest. One important reason was Germany's dramatic rise as an industrial power challenging Britain, particularly in naval strength. The accession of Kaiser Wilhelm II in 1888 and the dropping of the prudent Otto von Bismarck signaled Germany's intention to compete vigorously with the other powers. The "eastern question" in European diplomacy, hinging on the disposition of Ottoman territories in the Balkans and beyond, had long exacerbated European rivalries. Now, with Germany wooing Constantinople, maneuvering for influence in Persia, and taking a growing interest in the Persian

11. Saadia Touval, *Somali Nationalism* (Cambridge: Harvard University Press, 1963), p. 71.
12. Moon, op. cit., pp. 218–21.

Gulf (where British geologists struck oil in 1908), the question was becoming far more serious. Twice, in 1889 and in 1898, the Kaiser visited Turkey and, on the second occasion, made a dramatic pilgrimmage to Jerusalem. German military advisers trained Turkish officers. Most spectacular was the Berlin-to-Baghdad railroad project. After years of maneuvering, the sultan and the Germans signed a concession agreement in 1903 to build the railroad from Constantinople, via Adana and Baghdad, to Kuwait. The line was never completed, mainly because of British and French government opposition, which dried up the needed financing.[13] The steady polarization of Europe's delicate balance of power from the 1890s onward was due in large part to Germany's vigorous new thrust eastward. By 1907 Britain, France, and Russia, despite their historic rivalries, were bound to one another over and against the German-Austrian alliance. Finally, a crisis in the Balkans ignited the First World War.

On the eve of World War I, Morocco, Algeria, and Tunisia were French; Libya was Italian; Egypt was now under a formal British protectorate; Iran was, in effect, partitioned by Russia and England; the shaykhdoms on the Arabian perimeter were in "special relationship" with Britain; and Turkey had thrown in its lot with the Germans. Great Britain and the other allies fought the Turks in Palestine-Syria and Mesopotamia, and also in the Yemen. Desperate for any victory against the formidable Central Powers, Britain made three fateful commitments in support of its Middle Eastern objectives. In 1915 it enlisted the aid of the sharif of Mecca to turn the Arabs against the Turks who had governed them for 400 years; in return it promised to support an independent Arab state, the western boundaries of which, however, were ambiguous. This commitment was made in the Hussein-McMahon correspondence. In 1916, to promote allied solidarity, Britain signed a secret agreement with France and other allies dividing the Ottoman-Arab territories into colonies and spheres of influence. Lebanon and Syria would go to France; Palestine, Transjordan and Iraq would go to England. This commitment was made through the Sykes-Picot Agreement. Finally, in 1917, the British foreign secretary, Lord Balfour, wrote a letter to Baron Rothschild stating that the British government "view with favor the establishment in Palestine of a national home for the Jewish people . . . it being clearly understood that nothing shall be done which may prejudice the civil and religious rights of existing non-Jewish communities in Palestine . . . "[14]

13. Ibid., 239–49.

14. Cited in Fred J. Khouri, *The Arab-Israeli Dilemma* (Syracuse: Syracuse University Press, 1968), Appendix, p. 360.

In addition to sentiment and domestic politics, considerations of wartime strategy lay behind the Balfour Declaration: British policy makers felt a Jewish Palestine would secure Britain's postwar position in the Arab world and thus protect the lifeline to India. It was also important to win the political and financial support of world Jewry, which the Germans themselves were actively courting. However logical the individual rationales for these three commitments may have been, the fact that they were incompatible with one another was to envenom the political development of the eastern Arab world and its relationships with the West. "The fundamental weakness of Britain's policy in the Middle East was that she never fully recognized the responsibility which her power and dominant influence imposed on her," writes Albert Hourani of Britain's "narrowly expedient" role in Palestine and throughout the Arab world.

> The tendency to support both parties in a dispute until the moment of inescapable choice, and then to incline towards the stronger, was fatal in an area where those disputes involved literally the life and death of communities and individuals, and where Britain, by virtue of her power, had the decisive voice . . . It ended in each side believing it had been betrayed by Britain, the victor because he saw or imagined the part which Britain had played in encouraging the resistance of his opponent, and the vanquished because, since Britain had final power, her intervention could have altered the balance of forces . . . [15]

Certainly, today there is honest disagreement among well-informed people as to the relative merits of the Arab and Israeli claims to Palestine. Some feel that the Zionist arguments are compelling; others judge that the claims of the two sides have equal validity. In the opinion of this writer, the moral superiority of the Arab claims, based as they are on continuous residence, overwhelming demographic, economic, and cultural preponderance, the principle of self-determination, national consciousness, and manifest resistance to Zionist colonization, is incontestable. I must agree with the assessment made by an eminent student of nationalism, Rupert Emerson:

> The conception of creating a Jewish national home in Palestine could not possibly be squared with the principle of self-determination, or, for that matter, of democracy, on the basis of any of the generally accepted criteria. Aside from the fact that many Jews wanted to establish themselves there, the only claim which had

---

15. Albert Hourani. "The Decline of the West in the Middle East." 2, *International Affairs*, vol. 29 1953 . pp. 157 58.

any conceivable status was that Palestine had been the ancient
Jewish homeland many centuries ago; but to accept the legitimacy
of claims to self-determination whose basis is possession broken off
two thousand years yearlier would be to stir up such a host of
conflicting and unrealizable demands as to totally discredit the
principle . . . . If self-determination were to be applied in the
customary fashion of seeking out what the people of the country
wanted, there could be no doubt where the overwhelming
majority lay nor of the rejection by that majority of both Balfour
Declaration and Mandate.[16]

It is difficult to emphasize sufficiently the importance of the Palestine
issue for the politics of legitimacy in the Arab world. Today Palestine
is as much, if not even more, of an issue ("our obsession" as the
Palestinian scholar Walid Khalidi has put it) than it was in 1917; for
not only is Palestine rich in national and religious symbolism for all
Arabs, it is also a crucial geographical linkage between the eastern and
western Arab world. In alien hands, Palestine has proved a barrier to
the integration of the Arab homeland. Even more important, it has
come to represent to all Arabs a national injustice of such proportions
that it cannot be laid to rest or—as some American diplomats once
liked to say—"put on the back burner." Four wars have intensified
the salience of the Palestine question, and as the growing capabilities
of the Arab world become more apparent to Arabs themselves, the
idea that Israel is "there to stay" is, one suspects, treated with more
skepticism than it once was. Whatever Israel's future may be, the
important point is that Palestine, which Arabs view as the last bitter
residue of the age of imperialism, imposes obligations on all Arab
leaders (especially those of the pan-Arab core) which can either
enhance or destroy their political legitimacy, depending upon how
successfully they are met.

By the end of World War I, the Western powers had extended their
influence over the former Ottoman territories of the Arab east. They
would have partitioned heartland Turkey itself if the Turks had not
resisted successfully. The newly formed League of Nations, although
dedicated to the principle of national self-determination, allotted
mandates to France over Lebanon and Syria and to England over
Palestine, Transjordan, and Iraq. The only area relatively free of
foreign influence was the heartland of Arabia and Yemen. World War I
marked the high point of European imperialism, but it also marked

16. Rupert Emerson, *From Empire to Nation* (Cambridge: Harvard University Press, 1962),
p. 313.

the beginning of an era of anti-Western nationalism in the Arab world. Henceforth anti-imperialism and national independence would be touchstones of legitimacy for Arab politicians.

ECONOMIC AND CULTURAL ASPECTS

I have dwelt mainly on the direct political implications of imperialism on Arab politics. The indirect effects were also important. European imperialism dislocated Arab society and culture. Foreign and indigenous merchants and financiers profited, creating a high bourgeoisie tied to the imperial economy. France introduced plantations and large-scale mechanized farming into North Africa. In Algeria, for example, *colons* or *pieds-noirs* steadily extended their holdings and forced the Muslim peasants off the land and toward the cities where they languished in poverty and unemployment.[17] Thus uprooted they were prepared in the most brutal way for politicization. The European bourgeoisie and favored local minorities, by virtue of their political connections, enjoyed business advantages unavailable to the indigenous middle class.[18] Such inequities laid the groundwork for future political upheavals.

Even the positive aspects of colonial administration were politically unsettling, such as increased agricultural and manufacturing output. The reforms of Lord Cromer in Egypt, for example, doubled the output of cotton, following construction of the first Aswan Dam in 1903, but the principal result was to enrich and enhance the political power of a small class of landowners. In 1913 nearly half the cultivated land of Egypt was held by 13,000 landlords while the remainder was shared by 1.5 million peasants.[19] Even in the societies not directly colonized, the reverberations of European power and the European economy had an important impact. During the Ottoman rule a combination of Islamic restrictions on commerce combined with the advantages conferred by the Capitulations on foreign businessmen and their local agents to retard the development of an indigenous economic infrastructure. Trade with Europe increased, but the benefits were siphoned off by the mercantile interests. Worse still, the reorientation of trading patterns virtually destroyed the nascent manufacturing sector of the Ottoman economy. In nineteenth century Syria, for example, steam navigation stimulated a revival of trade with Europe; but the cheap,

17. Jacques Berque, *French North Africa* (London: Faber and Faber, 1962, tr. 1967), p. 46 and passim; Pierre Bourdieu, *The Algerians* (Boston: Beacon Press, 1958), tr. 1962), chap. 6.
18. Berque, op. cit., p. 198.
19. Vatikiotis, op. cit., p. 241.

machine-made textiles of Europe blighted the local textile industry. Syria had little to export in return save precious metals in the form of gold and silver coins, which were soon exhausted. Local prices rose. The local silk industry in Lebanon and Syria collapsed and contributed to the sociopolitical violence of the middle nineteenth century.[20] Not only were these infant industries unprotected from European competition, their products were burdened with numerous shipping charges that eroded profits. In general, the economic impact of Europe's penetration (direct and indirect) of the Arab world, was profitable for a small upper-middle-class commercial and landed elite; and it was disruptive for masses of small peasants, the nascent industrial proletariat, and for the local manufacturing and handicraft industry. Against the real benefits of improved administrative efficiency, the infrastructure of roads, ports, communications, public buildings, and expansion of agricultural output had to be weighed these social dislocations.

Of all the facets of imperialism, the ones which may have had the most unsettling effect on indigenous Arab institutions were Western technology and thought. The superior quality of European machines and the superior power which flowed from European methods created a crisis of confidence among rulers and thinkers alike. One early response was to import technology in that most crucial of spheres, the military. For as the military balance turned against them, the leadership in Turkey, Egypt, and Persia began to realize that only Western technology could save them from Western encroachment. As early as the 1790s, the Ottoman Sultan Selim III encouraged the introduction of European military ideas and techniques. One reason for Sultan Mahmud's destruction of the Janissaries in 1826 was to clear the way for establishing a modern, European-style army. Throughout the nineteenth century, foreign military missions made regular appearances in Turkey. During the 1830s American naval architects rebuilt nearly the entire Turkish fleet, which had been decimated at the Battle of Naravino in 1827. In Egypt under Muhammad Ali officers were sent for training to England and France, and technical and military schools with European instructors were also established in Egypt. In 1870 Khedive Isma'il purchased American

20. Dominique Chevallier, "Western Development and Eastern Crisis in the Mid-Nineteenth Century: Syria Confronted with the European Economy," in W. R. Polk and R. L. Chambers (eds.), *The Beginnings of Modernization in the Middle East: The Nineteenth Century* (Chicago: University of Chicago Press, 1968), pp. 205–22; pp. 208–09, 218–19.

military supplies and engaged an American military mission to modernize his army; in fact, an American officer was named chief of the Egyptian General Staff.[21] In Persia, following a defeat at the hands of Russia in 1828, Fath Ali Shah's son Prince Abbas Mirza tried to organize a Persian army on European lines.[22]

The borrowing of military technology was not enough to prevent Europe's takeover of most of the Middle East, but it did contribute to the erosion of traditional elites and legitimacy values. It also shifted political power toward officers trained in European ways and exposed to liberal and nationalist political ideas. The diffusion of different standards of legitimacy that accompanied the first borrowings of military technology in the Ottoman Empire continues today at a greatly accelerated pace throughout the Arab world and particularly in the most politically traditional oil states of Arabia.

The social impact of imperialism was not confined to commercial or military matters. European advisers, administrators, diplomats, teachers, and missionaries brought with them ideas and policies designed to replace what they saw as the stagnant character of Muslim Oriental culture with modern standards and methods. The idea of uplifting the masses, which was also a comforting rationale for colonialist intervention, was formalized in concepts like the white man's burden and the *mission civilisatrice*. The attitude was symbolized by men such as Britain's Lord Cromer, the first viceroy of Egypt, or in Marshall Lyautey, the Frenchman who wanted to bring modernity to Morocco without obliterating its primitive traditional culture.[23] It was reflected more subtly in the educators and missionaries who sought to bring Western Christian enlightenment to backward societies. The political corollary of the Western impulse to civilize was, of course, the imposition of European institutions such as parliaments through the tutelage of colonial or mandate administrations.

The missionary movement was particularly important in the diffusion of Western culture. Missionaries went to work during the nineteenth century on a far greater scale than before. French Catholics and American Protestants were especially active. In French North

21. James A. Field, Jr., *America and the Mediterranean World, 1776–1882* (Princeton: Princeton University Press, 1969), pp. 390–91.

22. Peter Avery, *Modern Iran* (New York: Praeger, 1965), pp. 78–79.

23. The Earl of Cromer [Evelyn Baring], *Modern Egypt*, 2 vols. (New York: Macmillan, 1908). Cf. also Afaf Lutfi al-Sayyid, *Egypt and Cromer: A Study in Anglo-Egyptian Relations* (New York: Praeger, 1968). On Marshall Lyautey, see André Maurois, *Lyautey* (New York: Appleton, 1931), esp. 214–26.

Africa, Charles Cardinal Lavigerie organized a missionary order in
1868 that built hospitals and cared for orphans, among other things.[24]
In 1810 the American Board of Commissioners for Foreign Missions
was created to carry the gospel to "the heathen" wherever they might
be, including the "nominal Christians of Western Asia," and in 1819
Pliny Fisk and Levi Parsons set sail from Boston for the Near East.[25]
Subsequently, American mission churches and schools were established
in Lebanon and Syria, Turkey, Armenia, Persia, Egypt, Kuwait,
Oman, and North Africa. Able and well-intentioned as they were,
the missionaries (Catholic and Protestant alike) sometimes viewed
the "natives" and their culture with the condescension implicit in
the mission civilisatrice. For their part, the Muslims remained almost
completely immune to conversion. Among the Christians, there was
frequent conflict between their local clergy and the missionaries of
different rites.

The considerable significance of the missionary movement lay not
in its ability to convert the heathen but rather in the educational and
intellectual movements that it stimulated. The outstanding case is
Lebanon where, in 1834, Catholic and Protestant missionaries opened
schools and introduced a printing press. The missionary movement,
along with the modernist Egyptian administration ruling Syria at
this time, stimulated a literary revival that led to what George Antonius
called "The Arab Awakening."[26] In 1866 American missionaries
opened the Syrian Protestant College which later became the American
University of Beirut; up through the 1950s, it played an important
role in producing political leaders and stimulating Arab political and
intellectual activity. The Jesuits were equally active in establishing
schools in the area, notably Beirut's University of St. Joseph in 1875.
In Constantinople Robert College performed similar functions for
generations of the Turkish elite, as did the American University in
Cairo for Egyptians.

The influence of European ideas, most of them revolutionary in the
Middle Eastern context, also was diffused through the young people
whose well-to-do families sent them to Europe to study. By the 1820s,
there were small groups of Egyptian, Persian, and Turkish students
studying in Italy, France, and England. Out of this milieu came many
of the political reformers critical of the Ottoman sultanate, some of
whom formed the Young Ottoman movement and others, the Young

24. Cooley, op. cit., chap. 19.
25. Field, op. cit., pp. 92–93.
26. George Antonius, *The Arab Awakening* (London: Hamish Hamilton, 1938, 1961).

Turks.[27] Namik Kemal, a prominent Young Ottoman, had lived in exile in France; Midhat Pasha, another one, had traveled widely in Europe. Both were apostles of constitutionalism and popular sovereignty.

The response of indigenous elites to the Western cultural intrusion, in all its self-proclaimed benevolence, was understandably confused. Some intellectuals accepted and even welcomed Westernization in toto. But to others it was imperative to separate what they considered to be alien European values and alien political influence over their societies, on the one hand, from the fruits of modern industrial, technological, and social development, on the other. Thus the Islamic reform movement at the turn of the twentieth century, whose most influential exponent was the Egyptian Muhammad Abdu, argued that there was harmony, not conflict, between Islam and Western rationalism. He could support the form of government in Britain even while opposing the British protectorate.[28] The constitutionalist reformers of Iran and Turkey around the turn of this century even advocated the wholesale adaptation of parliamentarianism in preference to what they regarded as their own corrupt and stagnant despotisms; yet they still struggled against the Westernization of the Capitulations and other impediments to independence. Nearly a century later, we see the same distinction being drawn by most Arab elites. For example, in Algeria and Iraq today the ruling circles vociferously reject the neo-imperialist stratagems of the United States, but they simultaneously exploit American engineering know-how and marketing opportunities. Ironically, then, the alien ideological benefaction of imperialism triggered indigenous resistance to imperialism's raison d'être—political and economic exploitation.

A LEGACY OF CONFUSION

The heavy-handedness of the Western political assault on the Arabs, which was accompanied by a cultural assault more subtle and yet possibly more injurious to the formation of a self-confident Arab identity, greatly complicated the task of Arab politicians in building authoritative and legitimate political structures. By Western liberal standards the traditional Arab folkways and political forms were backward, and Western-influenced Arab reformers and revolutionaries proclaimed as much for almost a century. Yet Western parliamentary

27. Lewis, op. cit., pp. 39–40.
28. Malcolm H. Kerr, *Islamic Reform: The Political and Legal Theories of Muhammad Abduh and Rashid Rida* (Berkeley: University of California Press, 1966), chap. 4, esp. pp. 147–48.

forms proved unworkable because, some said, the Arabs were too
underdeveloped to make them work, or perhaps because these forms
could be manipulated by outside Western powers, directly or indirectly.
And, as the cases of Occidentophile politicians like Ferhat Abbas or
Nuri al-Sa'id showed, the adaptation of one's enemy's values and
practices, however progressive they might seem in the abstract, raised
fundamental crises of legitimacy. The legitimacy crisis raised by the
colonial confrontation was intractable: to cling to the past was
reactionary; yet to adopt advanced liberal practices was seemingly
impossible, given the assumed backwardness of Arab and Islamic
society. The imperialist experience forcibly imposed alien rule and
disrupted traditional society. It imposed new standards of legitimacy,
yet it hindered their achievement. It destroyed or manipulated old
elites and built up new ones compatible with imperial interests. It
carved out new political entities, forcing the independence movements
to conform to them. It exacerbated separatist tendencies among
religious and ethnic minorities. And in the two most egregious cases of
imperialist usurpation, France settled a whole French population in
Algeria, and Great Britain helped establish the Zionist settlement in
Palestine. Both became, and Palestine remains, vital all-Arab core
concerns. Paradoxically, then, along with the ambivalence, fragmentation, and contradictions which the colonial experience has
inflicted upon the search for legitimacy, it has made one important
though negative contribution: by constituting an objective alien
threat, it has stimulated a certain inchoate national consciousness and
generated a conflict from which more than one generation of Arab
politicians—as strugglers for independence—could derive legitimacy.
Modern Israel-in-Palestine, that remarkable residuum of classical
imperialism, that grain of sand in the Arab oyster, remains the single
most potent legitimizing force in Arab politics—and at the same time
the most potent delegitimizing force. For the politicians or regimes
which are marginally outbidden by their rivals on fidelity to the
Palestine cause often find themselves in the awkward position of one
whose grip on the tail of the tiger is slipping.

If Palestine remains the most consequential and paradoxical legacy
of the colonial past for modern Arab legitimacy, there are also other
dilemmas that have remained long after the colonial era has given way
to a subtler form of Western cultural domination. Arab elites from
Morocco to Iraq have been fragmented into a variety of ideological
extremes. Some seek legitimacy through statist technocracy—an end
of ideology; others see in this path the loss of the Arab religious and
moral heritage; and still others see in it the betrayal of socialism and

participatory democracy. Nearly all try to link a primordial national heritage with the goals of political modernity: a King Hussein demonstrates efficiency in a patriarchal context, in Sa'udi Arabia Islam is raised as a barrier to communist or socialist revolution; a Colonel Qadhafi insists on a return to Islamic fundamentals within the framework of Libya's populist, socialist revolution. Everywhere tensions persist and so do doubts as to the compatibility of such divergent values. In foreign relations the dilemmas are even more acute: Is encouraging Western investment compatible with national goals such as nonalignment? What are the costs and benefits for regime legitimacy, for example, in Egypt, for cooperating with Israel's patron, the United States? "Capital knows no religion," said a high Syrian Ba'thist to this writer in 1972, yet at the time the Syrian regime was risking its own nationalist legitimacy to adopt such a position; three years earlier it would have been treason. And on the level of long-term cultural values, as Sa'udi Arabian officials contemplated the invasion of foreign technicians and workers necessary to carry out the $142 billion 1976–80 five-year development plan, they wondered whether the kingdom's zealously guarded Islamic character—and indeed its Islamic political legitimacy—would survive.

6

Modernization and Its Consequences

Imperialism catalyzed new patterns of political identity among the Arabs, and it helped revolutionize authority structures. Modernization too is having a profound impact on identity and authority, but it is also generating important new criteria of political legitimacy. Modernization—by which I mean the interrelated growth trends in the economy, technology, education, urban lifestyles, and mass media exposure—has rendered salient for the Arab masses and elites alike questions about the output of the governmental process and, indeed, about the nature of the process itself. For the modernized Arab today, political legitimacy is not simply a function of what the government is but also what it does and how it does it. Development, equality, and democracy are the cardinal legitimacy values which the permanent revolution of modernization in the Arab world has created.

Confronted with these new criteria, the contemporary Arab governments, whether traditional or modern, are faced with serious problems. The objective realities of the modernization process include material and psychic dislocations. Peasants migrating to the great megalopolises of the Arab world must adjust to startling new conditions. Traditional certainties are challenged; new problems must be confronted. Even in the relatively favored societies, the byproducts of rapid economic growth are tangible and frustrating: inflation, housing, commodity shortages, congestion, pollution, sanitation. For the governors, the problems present themselves in the form of administrative overloads, bottlenecks, and political security dangers. In the ferment of social change, new and subversive ideas take root, and new kinds of organizations develop which can draw both upon the masses newly mobilized for political participation and the elites with the capability and possibly the motivation for dysfunctional political activity.

But if modernization carries dangers for the reigning leadership, it also creates conditions which, from the ruler's point of view, are more positive. In the Arab world, as elsewhere among developing countries, the government is perhaps the chief beneficiary of the technological and economic growth trends associated with modernization. The government gets the first computers, the latest military equipment, the best training for its officers and technicians, and the best advice from the experts of the industrialized societies on how to maintain regime security and develop governmental capabilities. In short, while modernization imposes new legitimacy demands on Arab governments, it also provides these governments with access to modern means for coping with them.

In trying to assess this race between demands and capabilities, I refer back to the concept of social mobilization advanced by Karl Deutsch and discussed in chapter 1.[1] Social mobilization is that process through which old values, habits, and commitments are broken down and replaced by new ones. The centrality of this process for an understanding of political integration and stability is obvious. Deutsch argued that this process could be indexed by a battery of aggregate-data measures like urbanization, education, literacy, transportation and communications networks, exposure to the mass media, and economic growth. He also asserted that while the process would promote assimilation and integration in societies that were already fairly homogeneous, it would exacerbate conflict and promote disintegration in societies that were deeply divided on communal, national, ethnic, or linguistic lines. Where this threshold of prior homogeneity might be has never been specified with existing data. But the proposition is clearly relevant to the Arab world where, as I have tried to indicate, there are powerful integrative cultural elements combined with pluralist and even separatist tendencies.

ARAB WORLD MODERNIZATION: EXPLOSIVE AND UNEVEN

The Arab world is growing in almost every way. Population growth itself is substantial: in the early 1970s only two out of fourteen Arab states for which data were available had annual rates under 2.5 percent, and one of these was Egypt where the population problem is the worst. None were less than 2.2 percent,-while eight were 3 percent or higher.[2] Urban growth rates in eight Arab states over the 1960–70 period averaged nearly 4.4 percent annually.[3] The number of motor vehicles

1. Karl W. Deutsch, "Social Mobilization and Political Development," *American Political Science Review*, 55, 3 (September 1961), pp. 493–514.
2. United Nations *Statistical Yearbook*, 1974, Table 18.
3. "Urbanization: Sector Working Paper," International Bank for Reconstruction and Development, June 1972; and J.I. Clarke and W. B. Fisher, *Populations of The Middle East and North Africa: A Geographic Approach* (New York: Africana Publishing Co., 1972).

in Egypt has doubled in the last two decades despite severe economic problems; in Lebanon the increase was eightfold, while in the oil-exporting states, it has been even higher. Airplane arrivals between the late 1950s and the early 1970s increased at Algiers by a factor of 5, Cairo by 8, and Kuwait by 8; and internal air travel is also growing fast: in 1976, for example, Sa'udi Arabian airlines planned to inaugurate a shuttle service every two hours between Riyadh and Jidda, using large wide-bodied planes. Media exposure via the transistor radio is now virtually total. Between 1950 and 1970, every Arab country at least doubled the proportion of school-age children actually attending school, and most in fact registered far more impressive increases, notably Sa'udi Arabia, Sudan, Kuwait, and Tunisia whose rates more than quadrupled. The average growth rate of GDP in the Arab countries between 1958 and 1965 was nearly 10 percent annually and per capita income, despite rapid population growth, has also risen substantially. When the price of oil increased fourfold during the early 1970s, it set in motion a process of explosive development, consumption, and related social dislocations, not just in the oil-exporting states but throughout the Arab world as well.

The imbalances associated with modernization, however, are also dramatic. Wealth is grossly maldistributed, both between and within countries. In 1974 the World Bank estimated the per capita income in the United Arab Emirates at $22,060, the highest in the world, while north Yemen's per capita income was about $100, one of the ten lowest in the world.[4] The vast gap between rich and poor within a given country was particularly striking in Egypt in the mid 1970s, as President Sadat began to relax the domestic austerity imposed by Gamal Abd al-Nasir: the return of luxury items like new Peugeot automobiles and expensive cameras for a tiny upper middle-class minority contrasted sharply with the prevailing mass poverty and delapidated infrastructure. There are other kinds of imbalances as well. Throughout the area, the rural agricultural sector remains relatively stagnant both economically and socially, resisting even the efforts of progressive land reform programs to improve the levels of education, literacy, and social services, not to mention production. In the traditional societies, mainly in Arabia, the social status and opportunities for women remains highly restricted compared to the comparatively liberated status of females in much of the Maghrib, Egypt, and the Fertile Crescent. Yet even in Arabia there are signs of change and contrast: Sa'udi Arabia exploits the technology of closed

---

4. The UAE figure is quoted in the *Baghdad Observer*, May 13, 1976; and the Yemen figure appears in several international organization reports, ca. 1975, dealing with Yemen.

circuit television to allow male instructors to lecture to female university students—women's higher education being a major social reform. In the computer center of north Yemen's Central Planning Organization, women, completely covered except for the eyes, operate advanced data processing machines alongside male colleagues. With the sharp impetus for development occasioned by the oil price increases of 1973–74, there has also emerged a number of vexatious imbalances and bottlenecks. Acute shortages of skilled and semiskilled manpower have occurred, and truck drivers are as much in demand as engineers. Congestion at ports creates delays and increases costs. Lack of housing for incoming workers drives up rents and land prices and creates other social pressures. Inflation is the inevitable result of sudden new consumer demand, and it imposes severe burdens on the salaried and lower classes. And all the while, the spread of radio and especially television, with its high proportion of American programming, continues to expose Arabs to very different values and behavior patterns. Finally, of course, there are the political imbalances: the Arab world is a kind of mixing bowl of ideologies. Monitoring the various Arab radio stations, one can hear the ideological conflicts played out in all their variety and intensity—a plethora of competing civics courses ranging from the conservatism of Islamic scholars on the Sa'udi radio to the secular socialism emanating from Baghdad. Not only are there Arab regimes of diametrically opposed types existing side by side, there are also frequently vicious propaganda wars between them. In short, along with the stresses induced by rapid change are the strains resulting from visible discontinuities and imbalances which accompany modernization in the Arab world.

On the psychological level people who are essentially traditional in their world views must increasingly cope with the demands of a modern society, while the relatively modernized individuals must constantly deal with traditional realities; and although I am prepared to argue that Arabs today have a remarkable facility for functioning in both milieus, there is no denying the psychic stress involved. On the social level, uneven modernization has accentuated the differences between classes: the gap between the illiterate and the literate, the rural and the urban, the commercial, landed upper middle classes and the new salaried technocrats, the old and the young, even women and men. On the political level, modernization has set in motion a bare-knuckled conflict of ideologies which contributes directly to the persisting instability of the region. In the long run, no doubt, the integrative aspects of modernization will prevail and Arab political culture will continue to grow more coherent, as has been the secular trend since the First World War; but in the short run, the disruptive characteristics of modernization appear to be the more salient, consequently the problem of legitimacy is rendered the more difficult.

I turn now to consider the principal dimensions of Arab modernization more thoroughly and to try and assess their political implications.

ECONOMIC GROWTH AND THE OIL FACTOR

The engine of social mobilization is economic development. The speed, scope, and intensity of social mobilization in its various dimensions depends heavily upon the growth of material resources. Even before the dramatic oil price increases of 1973–74, the Arab world displayed a relatively strong, albeit uneven, economic growth rate.

TABLE 6.1

Annual Compound Growth Rates of Total and Per Capita GDP, 1958–67
(percentage)

| Country | *Annual Growth Rates* | |
	Total GDP	*Per Capita GDP*
Libya	35.0	30.0
Kuwait	17.5	6.8
Sa'udi Arabia	11.4	9.5
Lebanon	10.6	7.9
Jordan	9.4[a]	6.8[a]
Egypt	8.7[a]	6.1[a]
Iraq	6.9	3.8
Sudan	5.1	2.2
Morocco	3.8	0.7
Tunisia	3.7	1.3
Syria	3.5[a]	0.6[a]

Source: Maurice Girgis, "Development and Trade Patterns in the Arab World," *Weltwirtschaftliches Archiv* (Review of World Economics), 109: 1 (1973), 121–67, 124; computed from *UN Yearbook of National Accounts Statistics,* 1969.
[a] 1958–65.

Maurice Girgis has pointed out, for example, that the annual compounded GDP growth rate for the Arab countries, 1958–65, was 9.6 percent, a figure higher than that for the developed countries (7.7 percent), the developing countries as a whole (7.1 percent), or Africa (6.6 percent).[5] His growth rate calculations for each country are presented in Table 6.1.

5. Maurice Girgis, "Development and Trade Patterns in the Arab World," *Weltwirtschaftliches Archiv,* 109: 1 (1973), pp. 121–69; pp. 122–23.

These rates are higher than those of the United Kingdom, Germany, the United States, and Japan during the industrial revolution.[6] The growth leaders have been the petroleum exporting economies of Libya, Kuwait, and Sa'udi Arabia. These are followed by Lebanon, Jordan, Egypt, and Iraq, a group in which manufacturing and services have accounted for rates from 7 to 11 percent. The slowest developers are the essentially agricultural economies of Sudan, Tunisia, Morocco, Syria and, one would add, the Yemens. The more recent period of the late 1960s and early 1970s has witnessed, on the negative side, the near paralysis of the Egyptian economy because of the 1967 war

TABLE 6.2

Estimated Total Population and Per Capita Income (ca. 1963 and 1973)

	Total pop. (millions) 1973	Per Capita Income (constant U.S.$)	
		ca. 1960–63	ca. 1970–73
UAE	0.2	—	7,224[a]
Kuwait	0.9	3,397	3,890
Qatar	0.1	—	3,159
Libya	2.1	399	1,850
Bahrain	0.2	—	902
Sa'udi Arabia	5.3[b]	204	833
Lebanon	3.1	412	631
Tunisia	5.5	202	433
Iraq	10.4	198	393
Syria	6.9	201	334
Jordan	2.5	168	334
Oman	0.7	—	297
Algeria	15.8	272	295
Morocco	16.3	158	279
Egypt	35.6	123	210
Sudan	16.9	91	125
PDRY	1.5	104	96
YAR	5.2[c]	52	77

Source: UN Statistical Yearbook, 1974, tables 18 and 188.
[a] K. G. Fenelon, The United Arab Emirates (London: Longman, 1973), p. 76.
[b] Non-UN estimate.
[c] Yemenis in Yemen, 1975 census.

and accumulated internal inefficiencies; but there has been a distinct improvement generally throughout the region stimulated in part by the revaluation of petroleum and a certain, probably temporary, measure of political stability. Thus, the formerly laggard economies

6. Ibid., p. 122.

of Syria, Morocco, Tunisia, and the Sudan have begun to register improvement.

Table 6.2 reports levels and changes in per capita income over, roughly speaking, the decade from the early 1960s to the early 1970s. In almost all cases—the least impressive being the PDRY and Algeria —per capita income has increased by at least half again as much, and in some—like Iraq and Tunisia—it has virtually doubled. Oil states like Sa'udi Arabia and Libya, of course, record quadrupled figures, even before the final round of price increases. The data on per capita energy consumption corroborates this generally high growth pattern. But the same table also reveals the imbalance of income distribution within the Arab world. The five states with per capita incomes of over $800 (ca. the early 1970s) comprise less than 9 million out of 129 million Arabs—about 7 percent. Ninety-two million Arabs—about 71 percent—live in countries where the per capita income is less than $300.

The economy of the Arab world has always been primarily agricultural, but there is now a shift toward other sectors. In the early 1960s, the agricultural share of GNP exceeded 50 percent in only two Arab countries for which data were available: Yemen and Sudan.[7] For the bulk of countries in the area, agriculture accounted for from 16 to 37 percent of GNP, while in Sa'udi Arabia and the small Arab oil states, the agricultural share was below 10 percent. The agricultural share of GNP in the Arab countries has fallen by from 5 to 10 percent from the early 1950s to the late 1960s.[8]

The labor force, however, is still predominantly agricultural. Approximately half or more of the labor force is employed in agriculture in at least two-thirds of the countries in the area.[9] Foodstuffs, mainly cereals, are the chief product, for the problem of food supply for a rapidly growing population precludes substantial diversification into other products. While the Arab world is more favored than south Asia or central Africa in terms of food, it has known serious famines in recent times, such as that in Lebanon and Syria during World War I and in North Africa in 1937. In recent years per capita agricultural production declined slightly in Algeria, Iraq, Morocco, Syria, and Tunisia. Today major countries such as Syria and Egypt, though well favored agriculturally, have had occasionally to import grains that

7. Charles L. Taylor and Michael C. Hudson, *World Handbook of Political and Social Indicators*, Second Edition (New Haven: Yale University Press, 1972), pp. 5–11, 338–40.

8. Girgis, op. cit., p. 137.

9. Taylor and Hudson, op. cit., tables 5–9, pp. 332–33.

they normally export. Estimates of daily calorie consumption per capita are two-thirds to three-quarters of the American average (3,140), and such figures doubtless understate the differences. For the ordinary peasants and laborers, meat is a rarity, and their one main meal a day consists mainly of bread, beans, onions, olives, and perhaps rice. The daily protein content for a great many Arabs is little more than half that of the average American.

Land tenure practices have been heavily responsible for the Arab world's lagging agricultural development. According to Doreen Warriner, the distribution of land in Syria, Egypt, and Iraq before the reforms was highly unequal, as Table 6.3 indicates.

TABLE 6.3

Land Distribution: Syria, Egypt and Iraq, ca. 1951–53

Syria ca. 1951		Egypt ca. 1952		Iraq ca. 1952–53	
Size of Holding[a]	Land Area (hectares)	Size of Holding[a]	Number of Owners[b]	Size of Holdings[a]	Land Area (hectares)
Small (under 10 hectares)	1,097,491	Small (under 2 hectares)	848,000	Small (under 5 hectares)	50,119
Medium (10–100 hectares)	2,892,414	Medium (2–8 hectares	465,600	Medium (5–150 hectares)	69,460
Large (over 100 hectares)	2,348,783	Large (8–20 hectares)	261,200	Large (150–5,000 hectares)	5,362
—	—	Very large (over 20 hectares)	817,200	Very large (5,000 hectares and over)	104

Source: Adapted from Doreen Warriner, *Land Reform and Development in the Middle East* (London: Royal Institute of International Affairs, 1957), pp. 30, 83, 140.
[a] Size of holdings not equivalent, owing to differences in statistical reporting procedures.
[b] Total land areas not available; number of owners affords a rough basis for reference.

Xavier de Planhol argues that the quasi-feudal land tenure system of the Ottoman Empire was disastrous for the development of rural society because it encouraged absentee landlordship and discouraged any incentive for improvement on the part of either owners or cultivators. W. B. Fisher compares the condition of Arab agriculture in the 1940s and 1950s with that of medieval Europe, noting that it exhibits little crop specialization. Instead of large-scale and efficient production of cash crops, one finds a mixed pattern of planting, typical of an economy where subsistence is the primary function.[10]

The political upheavals of the 1950s and 1960s brought major changes in the Arab agricultural economy, notably in Algeria, Egypt, Syria, and Iraq. In these countries, land reform has led to the disappearance or weakening of the powerful landed elite. Unfortunately, population growth and the inefficiencies that accompanied the land reforms did not markedly improve productivity, and there has been only limited introduction of the "miracle seeds" of the "green revolution." Still, the quality of life and social autonomy of millions of small farmers has been substantially improved through land redistribution and improved credit and technical facilities, such as access to fertilizers and tractors. Certainly the application of modern engineering to the land has contributed to the transformation. The High Aswan Dam, begun in 1956 and completed in 1971, increased Egypt's arable land by 35 percent and its hydroelectric power by 10 billion kilowatt hours; and the dam at Tabaqa on the Euphrates, the first stage of which was completed in 1973, is expected to double Syria's irrigated land and to quintuple its electrical energy production.[11]

As for the nonagricultural economy, the postcolonial period has seen a general flowering of commercial, financial, and service activities. Trade, particularly with the West, has grown sharply (far in excess of intraregion trade), notwithstanding various political problems. The number of business concerns has increased, as have credit and banking facilities. The gradual fusion of the old landed and newer commercial upper classes is nearly complete in those countries where they still function relatively unimpeded. Goods from all over the industrialized world—from cosmetics to computers—are easily available in Arab cities. Tourism and ancillary services have become major foreign exchange earners in several countries, notably Morocco, Tunisia, Egypt, and Lebanon. Manufacturing historically has been the smallest sector of the Arab economy and remains so today. Industrial production (excluding petroleum and construction) accounted for no more than 15 to 18 percent of gross national product in most countries of the area during the 1960s; Egypt leads the Arab world with around 18

10. Xavier de Planhol, "The Geographical Setting," in *The Cambridge History of Islam* (Cambridge: Cambridge University Press, 1970), vol. 2, pp. 443–68; and W. B. Fisher, *The Middle East and North Africa, 1969–70* (London: Europa Publications), p. 198.

11. *The New York Times*, January 16, 1971; *L'Orient-Le Jour* (Beirut), July 7, 1973; and Charles W. Yost writing in *The Christian Science Monitor*, February 7, 1974.

percent.[12] The percentage of the male labor force in mining and manufacturing for nine Arab countries averaged 9.9 percent.[13] For comparison, the U.S. percentage is 29.7, West Germany 43.7, and Denmark 30.9. Furthermore, the bulk of industrial production occurs in small shops with twenty or fewer workers, usually run by a single family. A glance at the size of the labor force in establishments of at least ten or twenty people (ca. 1969) shows how small the industrial proletariat is: Algeria, 104,500; Egypt, 545,400; Libya, 7,200; Iraq, 81,900; Jordan, 24,200. One may compare these figures with those of large companies in the industrialized world, such as General Motors (759,543 employees), U.S. Steel (176, 486), or the Exxon Corporation (141,000).[14] A visit to the manufacturing quarters of Cairo or Damascus reveals blocks of dark, one-room workshops, often with only three to ten workers—furniture makers, blacksmiths, tanners, metalworkers, cloth- and carpet-weavers. Only in Egypt so far has heavy industry begun to bulk large in the economy and society.

Oil, of course, is now the key economic factor in the Arab world, accounting for 60 percent of the Organization of Petroleum Exporting Countries' (OPEC) production, and its importance is hardly less for the area itself than it is for the industrialized nations like the United States, whose dependence on Arab oil rose from 16 percent in 1973 to 25 percent in 1975. In the early 1970s, Iraq was producing two million barrels a day, Kuwait three million, and Sa'udi Arabia—the emerging giant of the oil producers—eight million, with the capacity to rise to twenty million by 1980.[15] Other smaller Arabian-Persian Gulf producers include Qatar, Bahrain, Abu Dhabi, Dubai, and Oman. Egypt made a number of important oil discoveries during the 1960s and reached an annual output of twenty-one million tons in 1971, and in 1975 it recovered its Sinai wells, which had been under Israeli control since the 1967 war. Libya and Algeria are important North African producers because of their convenient location and the comparatively high quality of their oil and gas, respectively. Oil accounts for from about half of government revenues in the case of Algeria to two-thirds in Iraq to nearly all in Sa'udi Arabia, the Gulf shaykhdoms, and Libya.

Since massive extraction got under way during and after World War

12. Girgis, op. cit., pp. 126–27.

13. Taylor and Hudson, op. cit., pp. 329–31.

14. *Fortune*, "The 500 Largest Industrial Corporations," May 1973, p. 222.

15. Ronald Koven and David Ottaway, writing in *The Daily Star* (Beirut), July 11, 1973; and Jim Hoagland, writing in *The Daily Star*, July 31, 1973.

II, oil has been transforming the material life of the people of the Gulf
just as the Industrial Revolution did in Europe and the United States.
This transformation is plain to anyone who visited Kuwait or Riyadh
in, for example, 1946 and then again in 1973. Today one can see just
a few remnants of the mud walls that surrounded Kuwait city only a
few years ago, now a carefully preserved relic of the past, while the
city itself glitters with modernity. In Iraq the influence of oil is not
reflected so much in personal consumption and living standards as in
the development of infrastructure. The benefits of oil have extended
well beyond the boundaries of the main oil states: Lebanon's construction and financial boom, for example, was largely financed by
Arab oil dollars, as no doubt will be its post–civil war reconstruction;
and important intra-Arab development projects, such as schools, dis-
pensaries, and irrigation schemes, have been financed through the
Kuwait Fund for Arab Economic Development, whose lending power
in 1969 was $560 million. Aid from Kuwait, Sa'udi Arabia, and Libya
to the Arab states defeated by Israel in 1967 played an important role
in preventing their complete capitulation and economic relapse:
Libya's annual aid to Egypt was $150 million, and Sa'udi Arabia's
was reported to be from $100 to $300 million for 1973—excluding
additional aid in the October 1973 war.[16]

The already enormous influence of oil was dramatically accelerated
by the fourfold price increases of the early 1970s. Over the period from
1970 through 1974, the annual oil revenues of the seven Arab exporting
countries jumped from approximately $4.6 billion to $50.8 billion.[17]
In 1975 the total revenues of OPEC were $103.7 billion, of which
$62.6 billion (60 percent) accrued to the Arab producers alone: Sa'udi
Arabia $26.3 billion, Kuwait $9 billion, Iraq $7.7 billion, Libya $7.4
billion, the UAE $6.8 billion, Algeria $3.7 billion, and Qatar $1.7
billion.[18] This transfer of wealth from the West to the Arab world is
unprecedented, and its effects on economic growth, social patterns,
and the modernization process are only beginning to be felt.

How was the new capital to be used? The most decisive application
was in the military realm: the Arabian Gulf states provided some $2
billion to Egypt and Syria in support of the war effort against Israel

16. Jim Hoagland, writing in *The Washington Post*, September 2, 1973.

17. *The Middle East: U. S. Policy, Israel, Oil and the Arabs*, Second Edition (Washington:
Congressional Quarterly, October 1975), p. 30.

18. Farid Abolfathi and Gary Keynon, "The Absorptive Capacity of the Arab Members of
OPEC," Paper prepared for the Georgetown University Center for Contemporary Arab Studies
Symposium on Arab-American Economic Relations, Washington, D.C., April 3, 1976.

in 1973. Much of it went to finance (in 1975) over $25 billion worth of imports, including $5.5 billion from the United States. It went for increased investment in government securities, banks, industries, stock markets, and real estate. By early 1974, the Arab producers had established four financial consortia in cooperation with European and American banks, the Union des Banques Arabes et Françaises, the Banque Franco-Arabe d'Investissements Internationaux, the European Arab Bank, and the Compagnie Arabe et Internationale d'Investissement. Major American banks such as First National City, Chase Manhattan, and Morgan Guaranty were also becoming very active in Arab financial circles.[19] A not inconsiderable share was allocated for financial assistance to Arab, Islamic, and other countries of the Third World. According to Ibrahim Oweiss, the OPEC producers in 1973–74 pledged nearly $31 billion in foreign aid through international institutions (nearly 25 percent of all World Bank funds), multinational and national development agencies, and bilateral financial commitments.[20] Producers like Kuwait and Sa'udi Arabia were devoting up to 8 percent of their GNP for such assistance, far more than the developed countries. In the field of economic and social development, the Kuwait Development Fund invested some $344 million during the 1960s in projects throughout the Arab world. After 1971 three new development funds were established, the Abu Dhabi Fund for Arab Economic Development (capital, $125 million) and the Arab Fund for Economic and Social Development, with some $270 million subscribed by all the Arab states except Sa'udi Arabia. Iraq followed suit with its Fund for External Development in 1976. In 1973 the Council for Arab Economic Unity proposed channeling surplus private capital into the Arab world by guaranteeing against political risk. The Arab producing countries also showed interest in providing governmental and commercial loans and development funding for Africa and Islamic countries generally.[21]

The impact of the new affluence on the producing countries themselves, most of which have small populations, is already spectacular; and their modernization growth rates now outstrip the trends of recent years discussed above. In Sa'udi Arabia, for example, with its monetary

19. Ibrahim M. Oweiss, "Petromoney: Problems and Prospects," address before the Conference on the World's Chronic Monetary Crisis, Columbia University, March 1. 1974; *The Financial Times*, (London) April 18, 1974.

20. Ibrahim M. Oweiss, "Pricing of Oil in World Trade; With Special Reference to the Pricing of Middle Eastern Oil," (Washington, D.C.: National Association of Arab Americans, n.d. [1974] pp. 8–9.

21. Michael Field, "Investing Money Locally," *The Financial Times* (London), April 18, 1974.

reserves rising by $2.19 billion a month, a $142 billion five-year development plan for schools, roads, hospitals, airports, and communications was launched in 1976 to succeed the $10 billion plan just completed.[22] Television, automobiles, and expanded education are beginning to change the perspectives and lifestyles of Sa'udis; and Sa'udi women are on the threshold of a freer social role, the kind already experienced by women in Kuwait and the Arab countries to the west that had begun their modernization earlier. Among the other oil-exporting states the picture is much the same, and the boom has had reverberations in the neighboring nonexporting Arab states as well. The aggregate statistics do not yet reflect the dramatic socioeconomic improvements set in motion by the 1973–74 oil-pricing revolution.

But not all the consequences of this explosion are positive in terms of social and political stability. It has, in all probabilty, widened the real gap between the haves and the have-nots both between and within countries. A World Bank expert addressing Georgetown University's Center for Contemporary Arab Studies at a symposium in 1976 estimated that the 1974 Arab national product of $95 billion was apportioned in per capita terms as follows: $4,600 for the 40 million main beneficiaries of oil wealth and $360 for the 100 million other Arabs. Furthermore, within both the oil and non-oil countries, it is likely that the degree of income inequality has historically been highly skewed. Although income distribution data for most Arab countries are often incomplete and outdated, it can be inferred that considerable inequalities remain. Adelman and Morris, for example, estimated that in developing nations, on the average, the poorest 20 percent of the population holds only 5.6 percent of the national product. One Middle Eastern nation—Israel—falls well to the egalitarian side of that average, with 6.8 percent accruing to the lowest fifth of the population, but others are well below it: Tunisia 4.97 percent, Lebanon 3.0 percent, and Iraq (presumably prerevolutionary data) 2.0 percent.[23] The *World Handbook of Political and Social Indicators*, using UN data from the middle 1960s, estimated that Jordan and Egypt displayed above average income inequality, similar to many Latin American countries. Syria showed greater equality of distribution, close to that of Austria; while Israel was the third "most equal" country, ranking

22. *The Wall Street Journal*, April 12, 1974.

23. Irma Adelman and Cynthia Taft Morris, "An Anatomy of Income Distribution Patterns in Developing Nations—A Survey of Findings," Table 1, cited in A. J. Kanaan, "The Political Economy of Development Planning: the Case of Lebanon," Ph. D. Dissertation, University of California, 1973.

behind the United Kingdom and Sweden.[24] Of course aggregate figures do not tell the whole story. Many areas are favored with material resources that fail to be recorded in the GNP accounts: fertile soil which supports family fruit and vegetable gardens, salubrious climate and abundant sunshine for health, and the security for the sick and aged which traditional family norms provide. The new wealth is highly concentrated, but there is still some redistributive effect as it trickles down to the laborer, sharecropper, or small shopkeeper. Redistribution patterns cross class and even country lines through the channels of family and kinship, as typified by the man who has made good in the city and remits money to his village kinsfolk. In 1976, for example, Yemen officials estimated that Yemenis working in Sa'udi Arabia and the Gulf were sending home $1.6 million a day.

But even bearing in mind these compensating factors, one ought not to minimize the tensions and imbalances which accompany the new affluence. This picture indicates, first of all, that most Arabs are still poor; many live close to the subsistence level. Agriculture is the principal mode of livelihood, but farmers and peasants enjoy a disproportionately small share of national product. Although there have been land reforms recently, output is not keeping pace with population growth. The industrial sector is growing, but thus far not fast enough to absorb the constant migration into the cities. Furthermore, there are specific negative side effects to rapid growth. Inflation is one of the most vexatious, and in 1975 Sa'udi Arabia, Iraq, and the Gulf states were reporting cost-of-living increases well above 50 percent. Neighboring countries as well, such as Egypt, Syria, Jordan, and Yemen, while benefiting from the substantial inflow of oil capital, also experienced severe inflationary pressures. As national development planning and private investment leaped forward, serious shortages developed in the housing sector: one young Sa'udi complained that the new prosperity was preventing him from getting married. Iraq and other countries experienced occasional shortages in foodstuffs. Traffic congestion, municipal water supplies, and even environmental pollution were emerging as serious problems for Arab governments, which, in many cases, had hitherto allocated their limited capabilities primarily to maintain regime security and collect taxes. Public officials and religious authorities were becoming increasingly concerned over the moral consequences of the new affluence.

Oil is beginning to transform the Arab economy in fundamental ways. By the end of the century, Arab living standards will approach

24. Taylor and Hudson, op. cit., pp. 263–65.

the level in some of the industrialized countries. But the speed and direction of this transformation is problematical because the oil and oil wealth are so concentrated geographically and socially. A large proportion of oil revenue is being invested in the West, not the Arab world. In the future, oil is certain to be increasingly linked with politics—internal, regional, and international—as Arabs debate who shall control the oil and how the revenues should be used. Arab elites are aware of petroleum potentialities: oil can unquestionably do wonders in developing industry, modernizing agriculture, and expanding social welfare. But the critical question is to what extent Arab political systems will develop the will and capacity to utilize this unparalleled historical opportunity.

DEMOGRAPHIC CHANGE

Every state in the Arab world shows an annual population increase of over 2 percent and ten of them have rates of 2.9 percent or more. By comparison, the United States has had a rate of 1.1 percent, Italy 0.8, and Great Britain 0.4. The vast majority of this population is concentrated in the cultivable areas, which in the Arab world make up only 19 percent of the land.[25] Even in the desert countries like Libya were population density is very low, nearly all of the people are located in two or three coastal cities. Egypt's density of population to total area is only 33, but its density to cultivated area is 606; when one flies up the Nile, a deep green ribbon in the chalky desert, one sees the paradox of the empty, crowded Middle East at its most vivid.

Charles Issawi has observed that the Middle East—including the Arab world—is one of the most urbanized of the less-developed areas.[26] In this respect many of the Arab states are similar to developed countries like Italy, Denmark, and Bulgaria. Moreover, within the urbanized sector, there is a heavy concentration in one or two very large cities. Jordan, Lebanon, Iraq, Tunisia, Syria, Egypt, and the city-states of the Gulf exhibit among the highest concentrations in the world.[27] In several cases the concentration of urban population is specifically in the largest city, which (as Issawi notes) is a pattern characteristic of preindustrial Western Europe.[28]

---

25. Girgis, op. cit., p. 135.

26. Charles Issawi, "Economic Change and Urbanization in the Middle East," in Ira M. Lapidus (ed.), *Middle Eastern Cities* (Berkeley and Los Angeles: University of California Press, 1969), pp. 102–119; p. 113.

27. Taylor and Hudson, op. cit., pp. 222–24.

28. Issawi, op. cit., p. 116.

TABLE 6.4

Urban Population: Percentage and Growth Rates
(Population in urban settlements of 20,000 and more inhabitants)

Country	Urban population (1970, millions)	Annual urban growth rate (1960–1970)	Percentage urbanized (1960)	Percentage urbanized (1970)
Egypt	14,544	4.0	38	44
Iraq	3,954	4.0	39	44
Jordan	1,064	4.8	39	44
Lebanon	1,034	4.0	33	40
Libya	341	N.A.	18	25
Morocco	5,484	4.9	29	35
PDRY	325	4.2	28	33
Syria	2,351	3.4	37	39
YAR	301	5.9	3	6

Sources: "Urbanization: Sector Working Paper," International Bank for Reconstruction and Development, June 1972; and J. I. Clarke and W. B. Fisher, *Populations of the Middle East and North Africa: A Geographic Approach* (New York: Africana Publishing Co., 1972).
Note: Estimates of percentage of urban population for 1974, reported in the *UN Demographic Yearbook*, 1974, table 6, are as follows: Egypt, 44.3; Iraq, 62.6; Jordan (1973), 43.0; Lebanon (1970), 60.1; Libya, 29.8; Morocco, 37.9; PDRY, (1973), 33.3; Syria, 45.9; Sudan, 13.2; Tunisia (1966), 40.1; and Bahrain (1971), 78.1. It should be noted that the criteria for "urban population" appear to be those of the various national statistical organizations and thus may not be strictly comparable with one another. For the Yemen Arab Republic, according to its first census in 1975, the population of the 10 governorate centers was 6.7 percent of the total population within the country. Yemen Arab Republic, *Statistical Yearbook*, 1976, pp. 36–37.

The growth of cities, particularly primate cities, is proceeding even faster than the growth of population. As Table 6.4 shows, the average annual rate of urban growth in settlements of 20,000 or more inhabitants ranges from 3.4 to 5.9 percent. According to data compiled by Kingsley Davis, Cairo may be growing by some 224,000 people a year, which is more than the total population of the United Arab Emirates or of Haifa, Israel.[29] Riyadh, Sa'udi Arabia, is said to have grown from 69,000 in 1962 to 300,000 in 1968, or by some 10 percent a year, and Amman, Jordan, grew at the same rate during the 1960s.[30]

29. Kingsley Davis, *World Urbanization, 1950–1970*, volume 1; *Basic Data for Cities and Regions*, Population Monograph Series, No. 4 (Berkeley: Institute of International Studies, University of California, 1969). The estimated population of the UAE in 1968 was 210,000, according to *The Middle East and North Africa*, 1972–73, op. cit.

30. "Town Planning: A Centuries' Old Middle Eastern Problem," *The Daily Star* (Beirut), June 10, 1973.

Birth rates are as high in the cities as in the rural areas, but they cannot account for these enormous growth rates. Sociologists are generally agreed that migration from the rural areas is the principal cause.[31] Furthermore, they believe that migrants are pushed off the land more than they are pulled by the attractions of the cities. Peasants cannot afford to farm because of the very low income. It has been estimated that in recent years 51 percent of Egyptians earned their living in agriculture, but agriculture contributed only 25 percent to the gross national product; and in Lebanon where half the population was also in agriculture, only 10 percent of the GNP was accounted for by agriculture. In both countries the mechanization of agriculture, intended to promote production efficiency and levels, only exacerbated the flight of the peasant. Onerous land tenure practices in Iraq before its revolution contributed to the migration: shaykhs assumed control of tribal lands and reduced their tribes to poor tenant farmers. And in Jordan, Syria, and Lebanon, the migration of Palestinian refugees contributed to the swelling of the cities.

The political implications of this urban growth are serious. The number of unemployed and underemployed in the big primate cities appears to have increased faster than the size of the industrial labor force. Despite high unemployment in the megalopolis (as much as 17 percent in Tripoli, Libya, for example), people still stream in. Another negative characteristic is the concentration of migration to the single primate city and the lack of growth and economic development in medium-sized, intermediate cities: regional growth and autonomy are depressed by the maldistribution of infrastructure. The metropolis becomes burdened with problems: for example, the water shortage in Beirut or the transportation problem in Cairo, and the tin-shack migrant slums surrounding every major city, often adjacent to the most opulent quarters. Thus, the Arab world has experienced the growth of a poor *lumpenproletariat*, an economically marginal, semi-employed working class.

Given the low level of industrialization and the political weakness of most of the Arab countries, the political stresses generated cannot be dismissed as unimportant. To be sure, there has been some questioning of the prevailing belief that urban growth is a catalyst for social mobilization. Some recent research indicates, for example, that migrants from the countryside retain many of their rural value and behavior patterns. Instead of modernizing the country, urbanization

---

31. For a discussion of "push and pull" factors, see C. A. O. Van Nieuwenhuijze, *Social Stratification and The Middle East: An Interpretation* (Leiden: E. J. Brill, 1965), pp. 45–46.

to some extent is ruralizing the city.[32] Social mobilization has also spread to the rural areas through radio and television, improved transportation, and extended governmental services. Consequently, as L. Carl Brown has observed, "The Near Eastern urban-rural dichotomy can no longer be accepted as dogma."[33] Nevertheless, it is difficult to believe that the urban megalopolises of the Arab world do not multiply the opportunities for political involvement and significantly expand the political awareness of the migrants. The process may take longer than scholars once thought—perhaps a first generation of migrants has to come of age before politicization crystallizes—but even the persistence of parochial attachments does not necessarily stifle the exposure and eventual commitment to modern political norms, including participation. In the cities of even the most monolithic regimes (traditional and progressive), there are alternative sources of political information and opportunities for discussion, organization and, occasionally, action. In addition, as I have noted, urbanization creates serious administrative loads for the political system: housing, water, sewage, traffic, employment, and health. And so in times of political or economic crisis, Arab cities have exploded into violence: for example, Cairo in 1952, Baghdad in 1958, Casablanca in 1965. The catastrophic civil war in Lebanon in 1975–76, was to a very large extent the result of the unchanneled, unresolved social tensions arising from the chaotic social mobilization around Greater Beirut during the previous two decades.

To cope with such stresses requires authoritative, intelligent political leadership and a capable administration. In the urban areas of the politically institutionalized societies, one finds intermediate political organizations such as parties, neighborhood associations, and local councils, which in effect link the urban population with the political and governmental system; but in the Arab countries such organizations are not prominent and the linkages accordingly are weak. In Egypt the Arab Socialist Union is more effective in interest articulation and aggregation in the rural villages and provinces than in the great cities. In Lebanon's urban areas such functions have been inadequately performed by the traditional neighborhood bosses and by sectarian

---

32. See, e.g., Janet Abu-Lughod, "Varieties of Urban Experience: Contrast, Coexistence, and Coalescence in Cairo," in Ira Lapidus (ed.), *Middle Eastern Cities* (Berkeley and Los Angeles: University of California Press, 1969), pp. 159–87; "Urban-Rural Differences as a Function of the Demographic Transition," *American Journal of Sociology*, vol. 69 (March 1964); and *Cairo: 1001 Years of the City Victorious* (Princeton: Princeton University Press, 1971), esp. chap. 12, pp. 218–20.

33. L. Carl Brown (ed.), *From Madina to Metropolis* (Princeton: Darwin Press, 1973), p. 39.

organizations, and rationalized and comprehensive linkages were lacking. The result is that government and its planners are poorly informed and somewhat isolated; and there is little sense of efficacy, participation, or leadership accountability in the minds of the urban population. It is not surprising that urban areas exhibit a higher level of political apathy as measured by low participation in civic affairs or in voter turnout. But it is a mistake to equate this apathy with either contentment or indifference, rather it is an ominous sign of the irrelevance of established political structures.

THE REVOLUTION IN MOBILITY

The degree of change and contrast in physical mobility is particularly dramatic. Only in the last three decades has it been possible for Arabs in substantial numbers to move about outside their home villages or quarters—to visit, to work, to experience life in other places, and to get some sense of the dimensions of the Arab world. This is due not only to the rapid expansion of roads, motorized vehicles, and air transport but also to unique historical factors, of which the most important is the dispersion of the Palestinians to every corner of the Arab world. Over a half-million Palestinian peasants were forcibly uprooted and relocated into the sprawling refugee camps around Tyre, Saida, Beirut, Tripoli, Damascus, and Amman; and, even more significant politically, a substantial educated Palestinian elite was dispersed beyond these areas as well. In the early 1970s, the Institute for Palestine Studies estimated that there were sizeable Palestinian communities in Kuwait, Sa'udi Arabia, Egypt, Iraq, the Arab Gulf states, and even in Libya and the other Maghrib countries. Their presence and their problem have contributed to the broadening and deepening of Arab identity which has occurred since World War II. On the economic level, the petroleum bonanza has drawn not only Palestinians but also Egyptians, Syrians, Lebanese, Yemenis, and other Arabs to the oil-rich states; and there has been a massive seasonal inflow of Sa'udi and Gulf state tourists and summer residents to Egypt, Lebanon, Syria, and increasingly the Maghrib. While intra-Arab trade is miniscule compared to the value of the oil-commodities flows between the Arab world and the industrialized societies, there is nevertheless an identifiable eastern Arab trading community.[34] The mobility of people, however, is more impressive than the flow of goods. For example, the total number of motor vehicles in the Arab world in-

34. Michael C. Hudson, "The Middle East Regional System," in James A. Rosenau, Kenneth Thompson, and Gavin Boyd (eds.), *World Politics* (New York: Free Press, 1976), pp. 494-95.

creased by around 52 percent between 1963 and 1970–71, with states like Kuwait increasing threefold, Lebanon twofold, and even Egypt nearly doubling.[35] Thousands of hinterland villages are now accessible because of new roads. These developments represent a quantum jump in the physical mobility of Arabs and their exposure to the society and values outside the village.

Another important facet of the transportation revolution has been the dramatic spread of air travel. The fast-growing airline companies of the region have expanded intra-area communication to an unparalleled degree. In 1957 only two Arab airports, Beirut and Khartoum, recorded over 100 landings per week, but by 1973 there were 9 more in that category: Algiers, Bahrain, Cairo, Baghdad, Tripoli, Casablanca, Jidda, Damascus, and Tunis.[36] Compared with 1957 estimates, weekly flights arriving at Algiers have increased by nearly 5, Cairo by 8, and Kuwait by 8. Now even the more isolated capitals are easily reached: in 1973, for example, Muscat opened an international airport capable of receiving the largest planes, and in 1974 Sana opened its first modern airport where formerly there was just a landing strip. The pilgrimmages of Ibn Battuta across North Africa to the Arab east once took many months; now a Sa'udi Arabian Airlines Boeing 707 makes the trip weekly and scarcely a seat is empty. Until the Lebanese civil war, Beirut was the principal air transport center for the Arab world, and Middle East Airlines provided easy linkages to the major Arab cities and Europe; since then, Damascus, Amman, and Cairo have been expanding rapidly. The tiny United Arab Emirates has two busy international airports at Abu Dhabi and Dubai, and nearby Sharja is busy constructing a third. In Iraq, the government subsidizes twice- and thrice-daily flights from Baghdad to Mosul (on new American-made jets) for only $24 round trip.

The air travel boom has had an especially dramatic effect in Sa'udi Arabia. In 1957 the principal air link to Sa'udi Arabia was a daily Cairo-Jidda flight, and there was no scheduled internal service linking the kingdom's widely scattered settlements. But in 1973 there were twenty-eight flights weekly between Jidda and Riyadh, twenty-four between Jidda and Dhahran, and fourteen each between Jidda and Beirut and Jidda and Cairo. Perhaps even more significant was the fact that the national airline scheduled some forty-two local flights weekly between Jidda alone and nine smaller cities, not counting

35. Compiled from the *UN Statistical Yearbook*, 1972, table 150.

36. Figures for 1957 are from the *Oxford Regional Atlas of the Middle East*, pp. 56–57. The 1973 figures are from the October 1973 *ABC Official Airlines Guide*.

Riyadh and Dhahran.[37] In 1976 it was hard to obtain a seat even on the new 300-passenger jets flying between Riyadh and Jidda several times daily. The new Jidda international airport being built to replace the existing large but overcrowded facility would have—as one engineer described it—"runways so long that they will stretch all the way to Beirut." The kingdom that the great desert warrior Abd al-Aziz ibn Sa'ud had put together by force of arms and tribal diplomacy is now interconnected by the national airline. The authority of the central government and the ruling family undoubtedly has been enhanced by this aspect of modernization.

For the most part, air travel is for the elite, not the masses; but it is of more than passing interest that the physical circulation (and interaction) of elites is occurring at a far higher rate than ever before. On the mass level, too, the new physical mobility exposes people to society and its problems beyond the old parochial boundaries.

EDUCATION AND MASS MEDIA EXPOSURE

Among the most politically salient aspects of modernization is the exposure of individuals to nontraditional ways of life through education and the mass media. This movement of people into the pool of the socially mobilized may be indexed by the availability of radio and television, newspaper circulation, school enrollment and similar measures. The transistor radio has flooded the Arab world since the 1960s to such an extent that it is rare to find a locale without one. Even the once remote fastnesses of the Arabian desert and the North African mountains have been penetrated. The Voice of the Arabs radio station from Cairo is credited with playing a significant political mobilization role in the revolutions of both North and South Yemen in the middle 1960s. The bedouin commanded by Lawrence of Arabia could hardly have had but a parochial perspective on their rebellion against the Turks, but the nomad or peasant of the 1970s is possessed of a vastly broader, more complex and up-to-date world view of his area; and literacy is not a prerequisite for this new understanding. Television too is coming of age in the Middle East. As of 1973 all the major metropolitan areas were covered: there were an estimated 529,000 sets in Egypt, 331,000 in Morocco, 520,000 in Iraq, 320,000 in Lebanon, and 150,000 in Syria.[38] The Arabian Gulf oil states were moving heavily into television. Sa'udi Arabia, for example, with a population of between 5 and 7 million, had 300,000 sets, nearly three-fifths as many

37. *ABC Official Airlines Guide*, June 1973.
38. *UN Statistical Yearbook*, 1974, table 210.

as Egypt.[39] By 1973 Lebanon was broadcasting in color and Dubai was building a color television station. The young sultan of Oman brought color television to Muscat-Matrah and even Salala in 1976. A television watcher in Beirut with a good antenna could receive programs from Cyprus, Syria, Israel, and sometimes Egypt. Programming was diverse. In Lebanon, for example, it included a heavy proportion of American detective, western, and adventure serials, European sports events, and a growing amount of local cultural programming: drama, folk dancing, children's shows, and of course news. In Sa'udi Arabia 60 percent was locally produced, 20 percent European and American, and 20 percent was Egyptian and Lebanese.[40] An indication of the extent of cultural diffusion was the presentation of the American educational children's program, "Sesame Street," on Sa'udi Arabian television.

Exposure to the words and pictures of the mass media is one thing, but education through the study of the written word involves a more detailed and systematic learning experience. Literacy is still far from universal in most areas of the Arab world. Estimates of adult literacy in the late 1960s ranged between 20 and 25 percent for Algeria, Libya, Tunisia, Iraq, and the United Arab Emirates. Kuwait was approximately 57 percent literate. The estimate for Lebanon was around 80 percent.[41]

The press, a crucial element in the formation of public opinion, is limited by the extent of adult literacy, among other factors. Thus we find that most countries in the area lag far behind Europe and the United States in newspaper exposure. Circulation per 1,000 population in the United States in 1971 was 301 and in Italy was 146; but in the Arab world most countries were far lower. Kuwait was 66; Tunisia (1972) 28; Egypt 22; Sudan (1970) 8; and Sa'udi Arabia (1972) 7.[42] There has been little growth in newspaper exposure in recent years. Newsprint consumption per capita has more or less kept pace with the population increase. Only Lebanon shows an increase, while a few of the countries that experienced military coups (Algeria, Egypt, Syria) have actually declined—an interesting commentary on postrevolutionary priorities. As important as the quantitative penetration of the

39. According to *Television Factbook*, 1971–72 edition.
40. From data supplied by Dr. Abderrahman Al-Shobeily, Director-General of Television Programming, Ministry of Information, Riyadh, March 9, 1972.
41. Figures compiled from the *UN Demographic Yearbook*, 1971, Table 18; Taylor and Hudson, op. cit., table 4.5; and Michael C. Hudson, *The Precarious Republic: Political Modernization in Lebanon* (New York: Random House, 1968), p. 75.
42. *UN Statistical Yearbook*, 1972, table 210; and 1974, table 208.

TABLE 6.5

School Enrollment Ratios, 1950, 1960, 1970
(Proportion of school-age children enrolled, first and second levels)

Country	1950	1960	1970
Egypt	20	43	53
Sudan	4	11	18
Libya	9	37	73
Algeria	12	28	46
Tunisia	15	44	66
Morocco	9	26	32
Iraq	13	44	49
Jordan	21	52	52
Syria	28	44	66
Lebanon	—	49	73
Kuwait	17[a]	72	77
Sa'udi Arabia	2[b]	7	23
Bahrain	8	74[c]	91
Qatar	—	39	79
YAR	—	6	13
PDRY	7	15[d]	22[e]
United Kingdom	—	86	92
Nigeria	—	21	21
Brazil	—	47	68

Sources: UNESCO *Statistical Yearbooks,* 1961, 1969, 1971. Data for 1960 and 1970 kindly provided by Professor Munir Bashshur.
Note: Data for 1950 are unadjusted and calculated on a 5–9 year school-age range. The 1960 and 1970 figures are adjusted to the actual years covered by the primary and secondary levels, which are generally 6–17. The adjusted figures thus are slightly inflated compared to the earlier unadjusted figures.
[a] 1952.
[b] 1949.
[c] 1965.
[d] Unadjusted.
[e] 1967.

press into society is the quality and diversity of reporting and opinion. By the middle 1970s there was very little competitiveness or freedom from governmental pressures anywhere in the Arab world. In 1976 the two remaining cases of press freedom—Lebanon and Kuwait—both dried up. Most capitals were serviced by only one or two newspapers, and these for the most part operated under close governmental or military scrutiny. Compared with other modernization indicators like economic growth, urbanization, and electronic media exposure, the press in the Arab states is not advancing very rapidly. Quantitatively it is just keeping pace; qualitatively it has suffered a decline over the last two decades.

It is in the domain of education that Arab societies have made the most dramatic strides in recent decades. Social mobilization is occurring more intensely among the youth than the adult population. If, as social scientists believe, the school is almost as important as the home in the process of political socialization, then these dynamic trends in education growth are quite significant. Table 6.5 provides an overview of the rapidly increasing ratio of school-age children in school.

In 1950 no Arab country had primary and secondary school enrollment ratios of greater than 50, but by 1970 there were nine such countries. In fact, seven countries in 1970 had ratios of 66 or better: Libya, Tunisia, Syria, Bahrain, Qatar, Kuwait, and Lebanon. In 1950, eleven countries had ratios of 20 or less, while in 1970 there were only two such countries: Sudan and Yemen. All the Arab states at least doubled their school enrollment ratios between 1950 and 1970. Some countries starting nearly from scratch registered spectacular increases: for example, Sa'udi Arabia rose from 2 to 23; Sudan from 4 to 18; Kuwait 17 to 77; and Tunisia 15 to 66. Among the larger countries, Egypt made determined efforts ("a school a day") to expand the number of schools and to raise literacy levels, but because its population was so large, the rate of progress appeared less impressive than the actual accomplishment: at the primary level alone Egypt had some 3.6 million children enrolled in 1969–70. Unfortunately, however, according to Egyptian specialists, the Egyptian education effort began to falter after the 1967 war and the debilitating period of "no war–no peace." The problems of some of the very smallest states, while not involving huge expansion, were no less difficult because they involved building an educational system from virtually nothing. In the People's Democratic Republic of Yemen, for example, only one school had been built outside of Aden during the British rule, and that was just for children of the sultans. By 1972 there were primary schools in each of the six governorates and enrollment had increased by 400 percent, and there was a total school enrollment of over 153,000 pupils.[43] In Oman, at the time (1970) the reclusive Sultan Sa'id ibn Taymur was deposed by his son Qabus, there were only thirteen primary schools in the whole

43. Interview with Mr. Abdalla Ahmad Abdalla Baidani, Director of Planning and Statistics, Ministry of Education and Instruction, Madina al-Sha'b, PDRY, March 26, 1972; and PDRY Ministry of Education and Instruction, *Annual Education Statistics, 1970–71* (in Arabic).

country; but within the first two years of Qabus's reign, nineteen new ones were opened, including the first school for girls. By 1972 some 20,000 students were enrolled in all the schools in the sultanate.[44]

Girls are participating increasingly in the educational process despite traditional constraints on the proper role of women in society. Thus, in 1970 the school enrollment ratio of females was over 50 in Libya, Bahrain, Kuwait, Lebanon, and Qatar; and it was more than 30 in Algeria, Tunisia, Egypt, Syria, and Jordan.

What are these greater numbers of schoolchildren being taught? The curricula of former colonies or mandates bore a strong European influence, usually French; but they have been modified to take account of the importance of Islam and language in Arabic culture. Language and religion bulk largest in the curricula. In the Arab countries some 30 percent of elementary school time is devoted to Arabic. The time allotted to religion varies from around 10 percent in Egypt to 32 percent in Sa'udi Arabia. At the upper secondary level, about 15 percent of school time is devoted to Arabic for pupils emphasizing science and 20 percent for those in arts. In Egypt religion accounts for only 5 percent of the upper secondary curriculum, while in Sa'udi Arabia it ranges from 17 to 23 percent.[45]

The educational process, compared to the United States, is rigid and regimented; the all-important government exams, crucial to educational and social advancement, require rote learning. In Lebanon, for example, pupils must go through an extensive and highly structured program culminating in the government examinations for the *certificat* and the *baccalaureate*. Upper secondary students in Egypt take thirteen subjects concurrently, ranging from Middle Eastern history and philosophy to chemistry and physics to Arabic and at least one foreign language.[46] The former colonial areas have also seen the development of parallel private, usually missionary-sponsored, schools, which place particular emphasis on Bible studies and European history. In the Arab world, Egypt has served as both a model and a source for other countries: Egyptian schoolteachers and administrators are found in Sudan, Libya, and many of the developing countries of the Arabian peninsula.

44. Interview with Mr. Ali al-Qadi, Ministry of Education, Muscat, April 20, 1972; and unpublished statistical data prepared for the government.

45. From curriculum data kindly provided by Professor Munir Bashshur of the Department of Education at the American University of Beirut.

46. From curriculum data supplied by Prof. Bashshur.

It is interesting to examine the curriculum of a specific country, such as Kuwait. Kuwait's educational system has been influenced by the Egyptian model. The curriculum stresses Islam and Arabic. Islamic education is allotted four hours weekly in the six-year preschool and elementary cycle, two to three hours at the intermediate level, and two to three hours at the upper secondary level. Arabic language is allotted nine to thirteen hours at the preschool and elementary levels and eight hours at the intermediate secondary levels. Arithmetic and science are allotted eight to nine hours at the preschool and elementary levels and up to twelve hours at the intermediate level. Thereafter the student can choose between a sciences and an arts program, with the former requiring up to twenty-one hours and the latter two hours. Social sciences, beginning with history and geography, are not introduced until the fourth elementary year and one hour of civics is added at the intermediate level. In the arts program at the upper secondary level, there are thirteen hours of social studies a week, including history, geography, principles of society, principles of economics, and principles of philosophy, ethics, logic and psychology.[47] Notwithstanding the heavy emphasis on Islam and Arabic, the Kuwait curriculum introduces eight hours of English at an early stage, at the first year of the middle level, which is roughly equivalent to fifth grade in the American system. In the last two years of secondary school (in the arts program), five to six hours of a second foreign language are required.

The Kuwait system is roughly typical of curricula elsewhere in the area. The six-year elementary school cycle in Jordan, for example, teaches Arabic, religion (non-Muslims are instructed in their own religion), arithmetic, civics, history, geography, science, drawing (for boys), embroidery (for girls), music, and physical education.[48] In Oman the emphasis on religion is stronger, with eight to nine hours a week, and ten hours of Arabic.[49] In recent years governmental compulsory and free educational systems have come to supplement and to some extent supplant the traditional religious education offered by the shaykhs and imams of local village mosques, but the influence of the religious notables remains strong in the areas least penetrated by Western culture. In 1972 in the Yemen Arab Republic, for example, a

47. State of Kuwait, Ministry of Education, *Educational Programs and Plans*, 1971–72, pp. 7–12 (in Arabic).

48. Hashimite Kingdom of Jordan, Ministry of Culture and Information, *Education* (Amman, 1972), p. 14.

49. Interview with Mr. Ali al-Qadi.

governmental committee screened outside textbooks: it permitted the teachings of Darwin, but only preceded by a Muslim scholar's opinion.[50]

Political education is emphasized in most Arab educational systems, irrespective of ideology. In the new elementary school for girls in Lahij, outside Aden in the People's Democratic Republic of Yemen, the pupils learn patriotic songs that celebrate the flag and socialism and excoriate world imperialism, reactionaries, and Zionism. A civics text used in the fifth and sixth elementary grades in the Yemen Arab Republic begins with sections on the meaning, history, and principal components of Arab unity. It goes on to describe the development, aims, and organization of the League of Arab States, the Palestinian problem, Jewish aggression and expansionist aims in the Arab homeland, the problem of the Arab Gulf, and the obligations of Arab citizens in facing these problems. A final section deals with the United Nations, the Arab revolutions of recent times, and famous Arab-Islamic personalities.[51]

Higher education is both a symbol of and an avenue to elite status. In 1970 there were some 407,000 students enrolled in Arab institutions of higher education. The bulk of higher education manpower is concentrated in Egypt (218,300), Iraq (42,400), Syria (40,500), and Lebanon (38,100). If the whole area is taken as a single unit with a population of some 140 million, then the higher education enrollment is some 3,440 per million. It would then fall around the middle of a ranking of the world's countries, a long way from the top-ranking country, the United States, whose 1965 figure was 28,400. In terms of educational stock—the proportion of a total population that has had higher education—in the mid-1960s, the proportion for countries like Libya, Syria, and Jordan is only 1 percent or less, compared with 8 percent for the United States and 6 percent for Japan.[52]

The quantitative deficiencies in the higher education pool are steadily being reduced through the expansion of the educational plant. But there are also qualitative problems. One is the imbalance in skill specializations. According to an Arab scientist, a full 50–60 percent of higher education manpower in the Arab world is specializing in humanities, law, and social sciences. Only 10 percent are in engineer-

50. Interview with Mr. Muhammad Shahary, Director of Planning, Ministry of Education, Sana, March 28, 1972.

51. Yemen Arab Republic, Ministry of Education and Instruction, *Patriotic Education* (in Arabic), 1971).

52. Ibid., Table 4b, p. 207, using 1965 UNESCO data.

ing, 4–6 percent in medicine, and 6 percent in the natural sciences.[53] The same investigator discovered that the scientific research output of all the Arab countries, as measured in publications, was less than half that of Israel; that the government funds devoted to supporting research and development were less than 0.06 percent of GNP; and that Arab Ph.D. output in the sciences "is of such a low level as to be non existent in terms of practical effect."[54] Furthermore, the brain drain to the advanced countries was skimming off the best students, particularly in medicine and the sciences, and the flow increased in the years after 1967.[55] Until recently the governments have appeared indifferent to these problems or else incapable of solving them. The paradox of a simultaneous glut and shortage of trained manpower is explained in large part by the failure of the political systems to allocate the available resources to provide support and employment for existing manpower and to improve teaching and research capabilities. Libya and Iraq in recent years have made a significant effort to attract their overseas students home by placing them in well-paying jobs. There are signs that Sa'udi Arabia and the Gulf states are preparing to encourage a research and development capability in their countries and elsewhere in the Arab world. Nuclei for development research programs exist in Beirut, Amman, Cairo, Tunis and Baghdad around major universities and development-oriented government departments. While these promising indications have appeared since the late 1960s, they are only beginning to make an impact on the capabilities of the highly educated sector. There is, of course, a time lag between the expansion of the educated sector and the improvement of development capabilities. But one immediate effect is that it enlarges the political arena and expands the circle of relatively sophisticated individuals with the potential for influencing policy. There is no decisive evidence that the educators, journalists, bureaucrats, managers, and technicians that make up this group are socially coherent enough or possessed of enough common values to warrant being called a class. The educated elements in countries as ideologically different as Sa'udi Arabia and Iraq exhibit a remarkable diversity in political viewpoints. Such pluralism casts doubts on the hypothesis that an educated technocracy is introducing a new moderation and sobriety

53. A. B. Zahlan, "The Arab Brain Drain," *Middle East Studies Association Bulletin*, September 1972, pp. 1–16; 1.

54. A. B. Zahlan, "The Science and Technology Gap in the Arab-Israeli Conflict," *Journal of Palestine Studies*, 1, 3 (Spring 1972), p. 23.

55. Zahlan, "The Arab Brain Drain," op. cit., pp. 4–5.

into Arab politics. On the contrary, higher education does not prevent Arabs from becoming Muslim Brothers or Communists; and even high officials with Ph.D.'s in economics or advanced military training from the United States are capable of opposing their governments' pro-American policies. One thing, however, seems clear. As the educated stratum grows, it will generate increasing pressure on autocratic Arab regimes to allow wider political participation and to accommodate the new politically attentive publics with their diverse opinions. Regimes may try to resist this pressure by curbing political expression but they cannot stop it—in fact, through their social and educational development policies they actually feed it.

THE GROWTH OF GOVERNMENTAL CAPABILITIES

If some of the modernization theorists were too optimistic in assuming that social mobilization leads directly to assimilation and nation-building, they were certainly right in arguing that, at the minimum, it places great demands on the political system. Thus, in discussing Arab economic and social trends, I have emphasized their disruptive effects on existing political arrangements. But modernization also affects the structures of government. It may not enhance system legitimacy directly, but it may do so indirectly inasmuch as it strengthens governmental capabilities. Governments exploit modern technology to improve their ability to maintain political security and to expand their administrative presence and functions. Modernization undoubtedly accelerates the loads on the system, but it also enhances the ability of the authorities to cope with them. Today, the Arab governments, regardless of ideology, are striving assiduously to develop the administrative instruments to cope with the social mobilization ferment in their societies. Size and coercive potential obviously are not sufficient conditions for legitimacy, but they are necessary ones, and the growth of governmental structures has been a central feature of the overall development process in the Arab world.

In the post–World War II period, there has been a dramatic intervention by the state to direct the Arab economy and society. Part of the stimulus in this direction has been ideological. Following the pattern of the statist revolutions in Turkey and Iran in the early 1920s, several Arab states in the 1950s and 1960s moved to control and manage the major industrial enterprises and to implement agricultural reforms. Egypt took the lead in the Nasir revolution of 1952 and socialist reforms of 1961. In Tunisia and Algeria the state moved to replace or curb the economic imperialist legacy of France. In Iraq and

Syria liberal-bourgeois regimes were torn down by development-minded officer-politicians, and a whole mercantile class was displaced by state managers. Another part of the stimulus was economic. In the oil-rich states, the nature of the commodity itself and the patriarchal character of the social system stimulated the growth of autocratic, centralized administrations. In these traditional Arabian polities, which for the most part champion free enterprise and deplore socialism, the state has come to dominate in size and scope the nongovernmental sectors.

Government and public administration expenditures, presented in Table 6.6, account for 20–30 percent of gross domestic product in Jordan, Egypt, Sudan, Syria, Morocco, Iraq, and Libya, which puts these countries in the upper range in terms of governmental share of the economy.

TABLE 6.6

Government Final Consumption Expenditure as Percentage of
Gross Domestic Product, Selected Arab and Non-Arab Countries

Country	1960	1972
(Israel)	19	31
Jordan	27	29
Egypt	18	26
Sudan	8	25[a]
Syria	14	22
Morocco	9	20
Iraq	18	20[b]
Libya	13[c]	20[d]
(U.S.)	18	19
Kuwait	12[e]	16[b]
Tunisia	17	15
(Belgium)	13	15
Lebanon	10[f]	11[g]

Source: UN Statistical Yearbook, 1974, table 182.
[a] not strictly comparable to earlier figure.
[b] 1971.
[c] 1963.
[d] 1972.
[e] 1962.
[f] 1964.
[g] 1970.

These figures are higher than those for the United States, Canada, and the United Kingdom (19 percent), or Belgium and Italy (15 percent). The government share has expanded in recent years in most of the Arab states, especially Kuwait, Egypt, Sudan, and Libya. In absolute terms, central government expenditures have increased dramatically. Between 1967 and 1972, for example, Libya's expenditures increased by 404 percent and Syria's by 287 percent. Iraq's increase between 1968 and 1974—reflecting the oil price bonanza—was 199 percent. In the six years just prior to the oil boom, Sa'udi Arabian central government expenditures increased by 167 percent, and since then they have burgeoned even more. In just three years (1972–74) the newly created United Arab Emirates underwent a ninefold budget increase, and even the relatively impoverished Yemen Arab Republic increased by 63 percent. Over the same six- or seven-year period, the Moroccan budget increased by 61 percent, the Sudanese by 82 percent, and the Jordanian by 137 percent. Even the Lebanese budget increased by nearly two-thirds, and the PDRY, despite the closure of the Suez Canal, increased by nearly half. Only Egypt, crippled by the 1967 war and its consequences, lagged: between 1967 and 1973, its central government budget actually declined by 20 percent; but when the figure is calculated from 1968, an even worse year than 1967, there is a net increase of 20 percent.[56]

Many of the Arab governments allocate a disproportionately large share of public monies toward defense and security, a distribution motivated not only by the Arab-Israeli conflict but also by precarious internal security conditions. In 1965, for example, Jordan, Iraq, Sa'udi Arabia, Syria, and Egypt all devoted a higher percentage of their GNP (between 8 and 13 percent) to defense than did the United States (7.6 percent), and 8 Arab countries altogether ranked in the top 50 out of 121 countries on this indicator (along, incidentally, with Israel, Iran, and Turkey).[57] Six Arab states devoted between a quarter and a half of their annual central government budgets to defense in the early 1970s: Egypt, 45.2 percent; the PDRY, 43.3 percent; the YAR, 39.8 percent; Iraq, 30.0 percent; Jordan, 26.6 percent; and Sa'udi Arabia, 24.1 percent.[58] While in general the defense share of the budget has not increased much in recent years, the absolute increase in published defense allocations has been considerable. For example, in

---

56. Central government expenditure figures are calculated from data in the *UN Statistical Yearbook*, 1974, table 97.

57. Taylor and Hudson, op. cit., pp. 34–37.

58. According to the *UN Statistical Yearbook*, 1974, table 197.

the period roughly from 1967–68 through 1972–74, Iraqi defense expenditures increased by 194 percent, Sa'udi Arabian by 157 percent, Sudanese by 118 percent, Lebanese by 101 percent, Syrian by 98 percent, Egyptian by 58 percent, and Jordanian by 55 percent. Even discounting for moderate inflation (which has become much more serious only in the middle 1970s, it is clear that Arab governments have been considerably augmenting their coercive potential and no doubt improving the material position of the officer corps as well—a trend not unrelated to maintaining regime security. These figures for the most part do not reflect the enormous surge of arms purchases which the oil-rich Arab states began making for themselves and their neighbors in the middle 1970s, making the area perhaps the most heavily armed in the Third World. In terms of men under arms, Egypt in 1973 had an army of 260,000, Syria 120,000, Iraq 90,000, Jordan 68,000, Algeria 55,000, Morocco 50,000, and the Sudan 37,000.[59] National police forces also appeared to be very large. According to a ranking of 123 countries in terms of internal security forces per 1,000 of working-age population (ca. 1965), Libya, Egypt, Algeria, Jordan, and Iraq fell among the top 25 countries, and Tunisia, Syria, Yemen, and Morocco also fell on or above the mean value.[60] In short, the Arab states today have developed an extensive, if not always very efficient, coercive apparatus. Furthermore, nearly every Arab country has sought the best internal security advice available, either from the West or the Soviet bloc. From a technical point of view, therefore, it is probably harder today for elements outside and even inside the military-security structures to undertake to overthrow a regime. Mere numbers and equipment, however, cannot address the political issues that also figure in the stability equation. Indeed, the very existence of elaborate coercion structures raises new questions of control and makes even more imperative the need for a regime to generate legitimate authority over these organs of the state itself as well as the civilian population.

The modernization of government and administration, however, is not confined exclusively to strengthening the instruments of control. The Arab governments lately have embarked on far-reaching programs of socioeconomic development intended to improve the quality of life. Such programs, if successful, may also have positive political consequences, insofar as the popularity of the government and the prestige of its leaders is enhanced by improved conditions. While the share of

59. Figures reported in *The New York Times*, October 16, 1973.
60. Taylor and Hudson, op. cit., pp. 42–47.

central government expenditures earmarked for development (in industry, agriculture, health, education, and communications) has only increased in a few Arab states, the absolute increases in development expenditure are substantial indeed, reflecting the overall expansion of the government sector. Table 6.7 shows both the absolute increases and changes in the relative share of the development budget for several countries, as reported in recent UN statistics.

TABLE 6.7

Changes in Governmental Expenditures for Development

Country	Period	Absolute % increase in development Expenditures	Development expenditures as % of total central government expenditures	
			First year	Last year
Egypt	1966–73	25.2	28.6	36.5
Iraq	1966–74	250.9	24.2	25.6
Jordan	1965–73	620.7	25.5	55.0
Libya	1967–72	218.0	61.3	38.7
Morocco	1965–73	88.4	24.0	24.2
Sudan	1968–74	100.0	19.3	18.6
PDRY	1969–73	−87.4	0.1	0.01

Source: UN Statistical Yearbook, 1972, table 196; 1974, table 197.

One of the most remarkable countries in this respect is Jordan, which between 1965 and 1973 doubled the development share of the budget and experienced over a sixfold absolute increase in proposed development expenditures. Development expenditures in Iraq and Libya, recipients of oil largesse, more than tripled over recent years even though the development share of the budget remained nearly constant in one case and actually declined in the other. Relatively poor countries like the Sudan and Morocco nearly doubled their expenditures; and even Egypt, despite the burdens of a war economy, managed to enlarge its development budget by 25 percent and to enlarge substantially the development share of the total budget. Perhaps the sole exception was the even more underdeveloped PDRY, whose economy is strongly dependent on the Suez Canal, which suffered the virtual disappearance of its minuscule development allocations.

Regardless of ideology, every Arab state has taken significant steps toward central planning in recent years. The examples of Sa'udi Arabia, Iraq, and Egypt reveal three different roads to an increasingly state-dominated society. The case of Sa'udi Arabia is by far the most dramatic. The Sa'udi development plan for 1976–80 envisioned the expenditure of some $142 billion of which around 64 percent was to be devoted to the development of economic resources (especially industry), human resources, social services, and physical infrastructure.[61] It envisaged bringing in a half-million workers from outside and the construction of two brand new industrial areas and cities. Apart from its sheer magnitude, the most remarkable thing about the plan was that the Sa'udi authorities had agreed to undertake it at all, because the idea of planning to many of them was linked with Soviet-style communism. Indeed, in order to secure royal support for the first plan, the Sa'udi technicians were required to delete the term "five-year plan" because of its socialist connotation. Even before the first year of the new plan was over Sa'udi society was experiencing the growing pains of supercharged development—inflation, lack of housing and construction, and port bottlenecks. It seemed clear that the intended long-term improvements in the quality of life would be preceded by short-term frustrations which might be translated into resentment toward the planners, if not the government itself.

Like Sa'udi Arabia, Iraq is oil rich and its oil wealth is accelerating the ascendancy of the state over the economy and society. But Iraq differs in several important respects from its neighbor. It has a history of planning dating at least back to the Development Board of the early 1950s during the monarchy; and the post-1958 revolution governments, particularly the Ba'thist regime, have given the highest priority to central control and planning.[62] The state controls all the major business and financial enterprises, regulates the professions, and tries to increase its leverage over the private agricultural sector. It is committed to providing jobs, education, health care, and old-age security to every Iraqi—a far cry from the goals, let alone the capabilities, of the Baghdad government a generation earlier. Iraq possesses a relatively large skilled manpower pool both inside and outside the government and has the population and agricultural resources for diversified development. Whereas the Sa'udi planners must struggle to construct a rationale for their efforts compatible with Islam, monarchy, free enterprise, and the imperatives of the development

61. Kingdom of Sa'udi Arabia, Central Planning Organization, "Development Plan, 1395–1400," multilith, p. 600.
62. Jawad Hashem, *et al.*, *Evaluation of Economic Development in Iraq, 1950–1970* (Baghdad, Ministry of Planning, 1970; in Arabic, mimeographed), vol. 1, *The Experience of Planning*, pp. 29–94.

process, the Iraqis have an ideology which is relatively unambiguous and certainly all-pervasive: the centralized, hierarchical pursuit of specific goals laid down by the party, heavily influenced by Soviet socialist planning doctrine. The 1976–80 Iraqi five-year plan was budgeted at between $40 and $50 billion, depending on shifts in oil revenues—distinctly more modest than the Sa'udi plan but similar in its emphasis on industrialization, physical infrastructure, and human resource development. And like Sa'udi Arabia, Iraq experiences the frustrations and bottlenecks of accelerated growth but seemingly on a lesser scale.

If Sa'udi Arabia represents the neo-traditional approach to development and Iraq the centralized socialist approach, Egypt under Anwar al-Sadat is still groping for a strategy appropriate to a disenchanted, postrevolutionary society burdened with the most formidable economic problems of any Arab country. Sadat's Egypt has 800,000 new mouths to feed every year; so under the best of circumstances, development would have been difficult. But after the 1967 war there were also over a million refugees from Port Sa'id, Isma'ilia, and Suez to be resettled, and some $4 billion had to be spent on defense needs in the eight years following that war. Moreover, Egypt under Nasir had been committed to a broad program of social welfare which his successor could not cut back on without serious political repercussions. Lacking the religious and patriarchal legitimacy and the capital surplus to pursue the neo-traditionalist approach, and prevented from reembarking on a socialist-cum-austerity strategy by his "tilt" away from the Soviet Union toward the United States, President Sadat sought to improvise an approach based upon soliciting aid from the United States and wealthy Arab countries and encouraging foreign investment. Assuming adequate capital were forthcoming from these sources, it would be possible for Egypt to finance its proposed $17 billion 1976–80 five-year plan. But in the absence of a coherent, penetrative structural relationship between the regime and the society buttressed by a widely shared ideology—both of which exist, though in very different forms, in Sa'udi Arabia and Iraq—the Egyptian leadership and its planners faced real problems. Intraministerial rivalries, corruption, and a bureaucratically sluggish public sector (which embraces 80 percent of the economy) only compounded the basic political and economic weaknesses. Whether the loosely defined strategy of pragmatism, "The Opening" (*Infitah*) to foreign investment, and the encouraging of greater autonomy in public sector establishments would succeed in arresting Egypt's social and economic decline was considered a difficult task indeed, and President Sadat himself conceded in 1976 that no upturn was immediately in prospect. Thus, the Egyptian experience demonstrated both the positive and negative political implications of expanded governmental capabilities: a large, elaborate governmental apparatus committed to general social welfare can yield important dividends in popularity and even contribute to regime legitimacy, but a perceived lapse either in commitments or the ability to carry them out may have the opposite effect.

THE RACE BETWEEN LOADS AND CAPABILITIES

"At bottom," writes Deutsch, "the popular acceptance of a government in a period of social mobilization is most of all a matter of its capabilities and the manner in which they are used—that is, essentially a matter of its responsiveness to the felt needs of its populations."[63] Deliberate political and economic intervention in favor of more balanced growth and more even distribution of income may be necessary, he suggests, to prevent the instability that accompanies rapid social mobilization. Every Arab government, regardless of ideology or level of wealth, appears to realize the importance of this issue, if the efforts now being devoted toward planned development are a valid indication. The question remains, however, whether these efforts to enhance governmental capabilities are sufficient to cope with the ferment which social mobilization generates. There can be no doubt that virtually all the regimes now deploy a much more effective security and intelligence apparatus, and several have begun to administer social services that substantially improve the life of millions of people, especially in the urban, industrial-commercial, and governmental sectors. Oil money opens up a new range of possibilities both for the exporters and their neighbors, and it doubtless serves to some extent as a cushion for social tensions.

But, as we have seen, the currents of social mobilization are swift and deep. Uneven economic development with its attendant dislocations, the new physical and social mobility, and the information and education explosion all contribute to the ferment in Arab society. The tensions are especially acute within certain key role categories. In some of these categories, notably the students, urban workers, and skilled professionals, exposure to modernity is well advanced; in others, such as peasants and women, it is finally beginning to have an impact. Such exposure when combined with sociopsychological dislocation and exacerbated by the objective frustrations of growth—inflation, short-

63. Deutsch, op. cit., p. 502.

ages, and the like—turns the disinterested and quiescent into discontented, politically aware people. Far from breeding an end to ideology, this condition would seem to generate reformist and even revolutionary sentiments. The expansion of governmental capabilities is only a partial remedy for such discontents. Government by threat and coercion can temporarily hold people in check, but in the long run it probably exacerbates the basic grievances. Massive government intervention to improve the quality of life no doubt helps, assuming that it is perceived as successful; but even effective state intervention cannot address the moral and political issues which underlie so much of the cynicism and latent protest evident among the Arab citizenries. Political legitimacy basically cannot be bought. Unfortunately, as the country studies which follow show, Arab political systems, whatever their ideology, have been singularly unsuccessful in developing the kind of institutionalized mass participation that social mobilization requires. The prevailing norms which social mobilization generates are egalitarian and democratic, a far cry from the monolithic and often repressive conditions so widespread in Arab politics. Furthermore, social mobilization has broadened and deepened the salience of Arab national causes, especially the Palestine question; and the international and regional obstacles to progress along these lines adds an additional burden on the rather limited legitimacy possessed by most Arab regimes.

Part Two

The Politics of Legitimation: Case Studies

7

The Modernizing Monarchies

The political culture of the Arab world which I have tried to delineate in the foregoing chapters is a richly textured fabric of identities, myths, and folkways. But because of modernization and external political intrusions, it is being infused with new values and in the process has been subjected to severe strains. Arab political instability arises from the incongruity of primordial and particularist values with contemporary norms, notably those of modernity, and structures, foremost among them the state. Traditional identifications in some cases correspond with present-day sovereignties but in most they do not, being either subnational or supranational in scope. Class conflict has also developed: less deference is paid to the traditional landed, commercial and religious elements. The expansion of Arab elites, indicated by the spread of education, has added a new dimension to traditional intraelite conflict. Now younger "counter-elites" with modern skills and ideas challenge the old power holders. Consequently, there is not a state in the Arab world today that does not experience a problem of systemic legitimacy—not just routine political conflict "within the system" but conflict over the moral bases of the system itself.[1]

All Arab societies today, as I have suggested in Chapter 1, are post-traditional. The eight monarchies which I shall examine in this chapter are peculiarly vulnerable to the tensions of modernization. Their legitimizing values are essentially rooted in kinship, religion, and custom. But they are by no means wholly traditional; they do not conform precisely to the classical Middle Eastern patriarchy. In fact, we observe strong attributes of modernity in the legitimacy formulas of even the most traditional kingdoms, just as we shall discover persistent strands of traditional identifications in those systems that have crossed the revolutionary divide. Furthermore, there are significant differences among them. Some, like Sa'udi Arabia and the

1. Dankwart A. Rustow, in *A World of Nations* (Washington: Brookings Institution, 1967), Part One, discusses the essentials of the problem.

smaller Arabian shaykhdoms, are patriarchal in a distinctly familial way; others, like Morocco and Jordan are more bureaucratically developed. Fabulous petroleum wealth has transformed several of these kingdoms into advanced welfare states, yet they remain governed by medieval structures and values. The ruling monarchy is an anachronism in the modern world of nations, but those that have survived in the Arab world have proved more resourceful and adaptable than political theory would indicate. All of the kingdoms analyzed below have made a significant effort to modernize and develop their societies, although with varying degrees of success, and a few have even ventured to broaden political participation. So dramatic has been the example—indeed, the threat—of the revolutionary wave of the 1950s and 1960s that the monarchies of the 1970s appear to have learned from that experience. Consequently, they have become more competitive in the struggle to survive and˙ develop legitimacy than observers a decade ago would have predicted.

The King's Dilemma

In depicting "the king's dilemma," Samuel Huntington argued that the very centralization of power necessary for promoting social, cultural, and economic reform made it difficult or impossible for the traditional monarchy to broaden its power base and assimilate the new groups produced by modernization.[2] In the early stages of modernization, the monarchy's capacity to co-opt potentially subversive new elements might seem sufficient, but it would not continue to be a viable strategy. Earlier, Manfred Halpern had made a similarly pessimistic argument, referring specifically to Middle Eastern monarchies.[3] Assuming regime stability to command the highest priority, one way out of the dilemma, Huntington suggested, would be for the state to prevent or slow down the modernization process. Apart from this fundamental solution, Halpern saw two alternatives. One would be for the king to become the chief modernizer, turning this social force to his own purposes by controlling it himself. The other would be for the king to take the initiative in instituting a constitutional system with shared powers. Neither scholar, however, was particularly sanguine about the possibilities of avoiding or surmounting the dilemma. Underlying this pessimism are certain assumptions about royal authority in the modern Middle Eastern

2. Samuel P. Huntington, *Political Order in Changing Societies* (New Haven: Yale University Press, 1968), pp. 177–91.
3. Manfred Halpern, *The Politics of Social Change in the Middle East and North Africa* (Princeton: Princeton University Press, 1963), chap. 3, pp. 41 ff.

setting: (1) it is fragile, i.e., not deeply rooted; (2) it is structurally indivisible; and (3) it is incompatible with modernizing values. There is much to be said for these arguments and the assumptions underlying them. At the same time, those Arab monarchies that have survived have proven surprisingly resilient. To be sure, the erosion of the monarchies and shaykhdoms since World War II has been substantial: Egypt, 1952; Tunisia, 1956; Iraq, 1958; Yemen, 1962; south Arabia, 1967; and Libya, 1969. There has been no case of a monarchy displacing some other form of government. And yet the institution remains sufficiently viable in the middle-1970s to call for a reexamination of its prospects. To do this, I analyze the legitimacy problem in the several important monarchies that remain and their strategies for coping with contemporary challenges.

The ideal Arab monarchy, perfectly legitimized, entirely congruent with the values of the traditional political culture, would be an Islamic theocracy governed by the ablest leaders of a tribe tracing its lineage to the Prophet. The ruler would be guided by the substantive ethic of Islam and by the patriarchal-consultative procedures of tribal decision making. The ruler's authority would rest not only in his coercive power but in the respect of his people for a leader on the right path (the Sunna) who observes customary procedures of decision making. By his legitimate behavior alone, he would earn the deference of his people and thus acquire authority. The office of king itself would not confer upon him the requisite authority, nor would any particular mode of having acquired power, for there are no strongly legitimized succession procedures—neither inheritance nor election—in Arab culture. This is not to say, of course, that monarchs regarded as illegitimate could not rule effectively, for some did and some still do, but only that, ideally, the ruler's personal adherence to religious standards and kinship loyalties would be the principal criterion of his legitimate authority, not the office or institution of kingship itself.

The kingdoms of the Arabian peninsula are in reality not far removed from this ideal, and Sa'udi Arabia perhaps comes closest of all to it. The Middle East's biggest oil exporter and the world's second largest holder of international monetary reserves is a theocratic dynastic state in which family and religion are particularly symbiotic. The smaller principalities on the periphery of the peninsula—Kuwait, the United Arab Emirates, Bahrain, Qatar, and Oman—are structurally of the same species, but Islam is somewhat less salient as a political ideology and the political process is more open to external influences. Thus Kuwait, although still very much the state of the Sabah family, had until mid-1976 a parliament, elections, and a free press. Of the seven shaykhdoms that federated with some difficulty into the United

Arab Emirates, the five smallest ones are conservative but the two core states, Abu Dhabi and Dubai, have experimented with more liberal consultative mechanisms, recognizing that neither Islam nor traditional family authority is any longer a sufficient basis for legitimacy. Moreover, the federal structures themselves are slowly imposing a broader identity and more complex perspectives on obligation and participation. In traditionally cosmopolitan Bahrain, there has been pressure from labor and progressive political groups to reduce the formal monopoly of power held by the ruling Khalifa family. In tiny Qatar, the Al Thani dynasty leans closer to the classical Sa'udi model, but even here there is a realization by some ministers and officials that more adequate consultative and administrative mechanisms are needed. Oman has been the most isolated of the Arabian principalities, but even under the late Sultan Sa'id ibn Taymur, a veritable Canute, a variety of 'modern challenges to dynastic authority were gaining strength, notably the Marxist rebellion in Dhofar; so the new sultan, Qabus, who overthrew his father in 1970, searches for new ways to maintain the sultanate's legitimacy. In Jordan and Morocco, society is more complex and the vocabulary of politics more modern. The monarchs of these states are respected less as fathers than as strong, even ruthless, leaders. Governmental structures and capabilities, particularly in internal security, are highly developed. So too, relatively speaking, are parties and opposition movements, even though they are under almost continual suppression or intimidation by the government. If the Arabian family-states, blessed as they are with enormous wealth, are trying to circumvent the king's dilemma, the monarchs of the more complex societies are trying to meet the challenge head-on. As I examine each of these patriarchal systems, it will be seen that the legitimacy problem varies considerably from place to place, as do regime strategies of legitimacy.

SA'UDI ARABIA

When King Faisal ibn Abd al-Aziz was assassinated on March 25, 1975, by one of his young, American-educated nephews, there was apprehension in many world capitals, especially Washington, that Sa'udi Arabia might lapse into instability and confusion. Little wonder, since this austere desert kingdom of only 5.3 million people contains about one-quarter of the world's proven oil reserves and is the world's largest petroleum exporter. In 1974 it was estimated to have earned around $30 billion from its daily output of some 6.5 million barrels. Moreover, as the industrialized world slipped into deeper dependence on the Middle East exporters, they used their OPEC cartel to drive up prices; consequently, Sa'udi revenues jumped tenfold in just the two years 1972 to 1974, making this country a financial superpower and a formidable regional political force as well. The sudden death of King Faisal might have been the catalyst for revolution or disintegration into the traditional conflict that prevailed in Arabia before the revival of the House of Sa'ud at the turn of the century. But the transfer of power was accomplished smoothly. The Crown Prince, Khalid, half-brother of the deceased ruler, was installed on the throne and the offending relative was tried by a religious court, found guilty, and beheaded. The crisis had tested the stability of the monarchy, and the family had demonstrated its firm control of the situation.

The Making of a Tribal Theocracy

The durability of the Sa'udi political system is extraordinary compared with nearly all the surviving (not to mention the defunct) monarchies in the area, especially considering the fluid, conflict-ridden nature of traditional tribal political culture in the Arabian peninsula and the scale of social change which has been occurring there in the last half-century. In trying to account for it in terms of Easton's systemic sources of legitimacy, I must focus on the man who created the kingdom, one of the strongest leaders in Arabian history, whose accomplishments place him among the modern world's greatest nation-builders as well. Not only did Abd al-Aziz ibn Sa'ud (1881– 1953) embody unsurpassed personal legitimacy, he identified his rule with a strict adherence to Islam and utilized kinship affiliations to impose, for virtually the first time, political order throughout the Arabian heartland. All three types of legitimacy—personal, ideological, and structural—were cultivated within the traditional desert political culture. Rarely has a ruler exploited them so effectively, and none has matched Abd al-Aziz in generating a legend of heroic performance—a legacy which even the excesses of some of his offspring have not dulled.

Until World War I the Arabian heartland remained one of the last regions of the world largely unexplored by Western man. Only a handful of explorers such as Burkhardt, Burton, and Doughty had traversed its forbidding terrain, and no settled government had ever been implanted upon its nomadic and seminomadic population. Modern Sa'udi Arabia, which embraces four-fifths of the Arabian peninsula, contains approximately forty main tribes or tribal federations.[4] The Turkish Empire had included only the western and

---

4. See the tribal map of Arabia in Roy Lebkicher, George Rentz, Max Steineke, et al., *ARAMCO Handbook* (Netherlands: Arabian-American Oil Company, 1960), p. 62 and passim. The *Handbook* is one of the most authoritative and readable descriptions of the peninsula and its history.

northern peripheries of the peninsula, from Yemen around the Fertile Crescent to the head of the Arab-Persian Gulf; and the British Empire had exerted hegemony only over the ex-Turkish territories and the approaches to India—from Aden along the coast of Oman and the Gulf shaykhdoms. The interior remained an area of incessant raiding, shifting tribal sovereignties, and warrior norms. It was not, however, a place of anarchy, strictly speaking, for conflict was a functional part of the total system.[5] The last and most thorough of premodern Arabia's explorers, H. St. John Philby, has carefully described its society and customs—the very antithesis of a civic political culture.[6] By studying such writings one can appreciate the rigorous environment with all its uncertainty and dangers and its values of chivalry and (in the case of the Wahhabi Ikhwan Brotherhood) religious militance. One then begins to grasp the vast change that has taken place so recently and recognize just how successful the House of Sa'ud has been.

The Sa'ud family belongs to the Masalikh branch of the Ruwalla section of the great Anaza tribe of Najd, Iraq, and Syria. The Anaza enjoy sharif, or noble, status among the Arabian tribes by virtue of their claim to lineal descent from Ya'rab, the eponymous father of all the Arabs. In contrast, non-noble tribes such as the Awazim or Sulubba were only Arabized by intermarrying with noble lines.[7] The Masalikh and Ruwalla were located in Syria, near Damascus. According to Shaykh Hafiz Wahba, adviser to the late King Abd al-Aziz, the historical as opposed to the legendary origins of the Anaza date to the fifteenth century and the area around the Najd town of Dir'iya, near Riyadh.[8] By the eighteenth century the Sa'ud family had established itself as rulers of Dir'iya, and in 1745 Muhammad, son of Sa'ud ibn Muhammad ibn Muqrin, was proclaimed amir of Najd, thus formally initiating the dynasty's rule.[9]

The Sa'uds might have remained a minor local dynasty had it not been for the hospitality which Muhammad ibn Sa'ud accorded to a fundamentalist religious teacher named Shaykh Muhammad ibn Abd

    5. See Louise E. Sweet, "Camel Raiding of North Arabian Bedouins: A Mechanism of Ecological Adaptation," *American Anthropologist*, 67 (1965), pp. 1132–50. Reprinted in Sweet (ed.), *Peoples and Cultures of the Middle East* (New York: Natural History Press, 1970), vol. 1, pp. 265–89.

    6. See H. St. John Philby, *The Heart of Arabia*, 2 vols. (London: Constable, 1922), and his *Arabia of the Wahhabis* (London: Constable, 1928).

    7. H. R. P. Dickson, *Kuwait and Her Neighbors* (London: Allen and Unwin, 1956), chap. 3, pp. 82–87.

    8. Sheikh Hafiz Wahba, *Arabian Days* (London: Arthur Barker, 1964), pp. 101–02.

    9. A geneological tree of the Sa'ud family is found as an appendix in Dickson, op. cit.; see also the *ARAMCO Handbook*, pp. 54–56.

al-Wahhab. Abd al-Wahhab was a religious scholar from Najd who organized a movement militantly opposed to the alleged corruption, innovation, and laxity that had crept into the practice of Islam by the orthodox establishment since the time of the Prophet. The Wahhabis were, and are, Muslim fundamentalists. The destinies of the Wahhabis and the House of Sa'ud merged in 1744 when the head of the Sa'ud family joined forces with Abd al-Wahhab; and that year marks the founding of the Sa'udi political system, even though the state in its present form did not emerge until 1932.[10] Because of this historic union of a vigorous family with what was to become an awesomely influential religious movement, Islam even today has a special intensity in Sa'udi Arabia and—modern ideologies notwithstanding—lends a formidable legitimacy to the political system.

Galvanized by religious fervor, the Sa'ud-Wahhabi dominion soon spread far beyond the Dir'iya region. Riyadh was taken in 1773. By the 1790s all of Najd and Hasa was in their hands, and by 1812 they held the Hijaz (home of the rival Hashimite family) with its Holy Places as well as parts of Iraq, Yemen, Asir, and Oman. They were even preparing to move against Syria and Baghdad when Turkey decided to intervene. The Ottoman sultan, disturbed by the new Arabian power, delegated the ruler of Egypt Muhammad Ali and his son Ibrahim Pasha to curb it. By 1818 they had done so: the Sa'udi capital of Dir'iya was destroyed and the Sa'udi leader was executed in Constantinople. Sa'udi power was not completely eradicated, and the dynasty retained control around Riyadh and regained Hasa; but its fortunes remained in eclipse until the end of the century, owing in part to family rivalries. Indeed, in 1891, the Sa'udi amir Abd al-Rahman, father of Abd al-Aziz the Great (who was then a small boy), was forced out of Riyadh and into exile in Kuwait by the Rashid clan, clients of the Turks.

The epic revival of Sa'udi power and the emergence of Sa'udi Arabia as a modern state began in January 1902 with the daring capture of Riyadh by Abd al-Aziz. With subterfuge and daring, and against the advice of his father and his host the Shaykh of Kuwait, Abd al-Aziz and forty followers scaled the mud walls of the town by night, slew the governor, and began mobilizing the population for further conquests.[11] By 1912 he had recaptured all of Najd. In 1913 he began to drive the

10. George Rentz, "Saudi Arabia," in *Emergent Nations*, 2, 2 (Summer 1966), pp. 8–9.

11. The capture of Riyadh is described in Wahba, op. cit., pp. 160–64; Dickson, op. cit., pp. 138–39; and D. Van Der Meulen, *The Wells of Ibn Sa'ud* (New York: Praeger, 1957), pp. 49–53.

Turks out of Hasa, the eastern province, the location of yet-undis-
covered quantities of oil. In 1921 Hayil and Jabal Shammar were
captured from the remaining Rashids, and by 1926 Abd al-Aziz had
won the Hijaz, including all the Holy Places, from the Hashimites.
Ibn Sa'ud declared himself king of the Hijaz and Najd and its
Dependencies in 1927, and five years later the state, now roughly
within its present boundaries (although some of the eastern and
southern frontiers remained undemarcated), was renamed the Kingdom of Sa'udi Arabia. Having created the state through conquest and
blood, the Sa'ud family possessed the strongest possible customary
claim to ruling legitimacy. Uncontaminated by any substantial
colonial assistance and unhumiliated by colonial occupation—
afflictions that have sapped the legitimacy of the monarchy in Jordan,
Morocco, Iran, and the Gulf shaykhdoms—the Sa'udis enjoy a degree
of historical legitimacy unmatched by the other royal families.

The centerpiece and driving force of the expanded Sa'udi state was,
as I have indicated, that Arabian Charlemagne, King Abd al-Aziz.[12]
He is described by those who knew him as an imposing figure, muscular
and over six feet tall. Shaykh Hafiz Wahba speaks of his "magnetic
charm and endearing personality."[13] Embodying all the desert virtues
and skills—warrior, hunter, horseman—he was a generous man of
mild disposition who was ruthless only in battle. He was of course
pious, as befitted a Wahhabi prince. He would rise an hour before
dawn to read the Qur'an, then pray when the mu'adhin called out,
and finally return to his home to recite from the Qur'an and the hadith.
Only when these rituals were completed would he have breakfast and
attend to worldly matters of governance. Much of his daily work
consisted in making himself accessible to others—his advisers, relatives,
ulama, and ordinary subjects. The king also sired forty-one male
children, an accomplishment of no small political significance, for it
enabled the ruling family to develop into a formidable structure of
control and influence far beyond the confines of Riyadh. Rarely has a
leader generated such personal legitimacy, exploited religious values
as effectively, and used his traditional family structure so successfully
as instruments of conquest and consolidation.

Religious fundamentalism and royal politics were not always
compatible, however; and the revolt of the Ikhwan (1927–30)
illustrates both the problems and the skill of Abd al-Aziz in managing

---

12. A colorful biography is David Howarth, *The Desert King* (New York: McGraw-Hill,
1964).

13. Wahba, op. cit., p. 166.

his fanatical followers. The Ikhwan were a fraternity of several thousand tribal leaders who were militantly dedicated to the principles of Hanbali Wahhabist Islam. They established self-contained settlements known as *hijras*. They wore only the simple white turban; they enforced the strictest ritual observances and punished laxness on the spot. Although they had helped Abd al-Aziz in his most important conquests, their loyalties were to Islam above all else, and indeed they looked upon some of the king's activities, such as his dealings with English diplomats, with disapprobation. In the late 1920s the Ikhwan leaders, notably Faisal al-Duwish, Ibn Hithlain, and Ibn Humaid, unilaterally raided across the newly established Iraq-Sa'udi frontier. Although ostensibly religious in motivation, Ikhwan activities, like the Crusaders', were brutal and politically self-serving. These acts were in defiance of Abd al-Aziz's policy of accommodating (however reluctantly) the British and the Hashimites, and thus were a challenge to his legitimacy as ruler; but he was hard-pressed both on ideological and military grounds to oppose them.[14] Finally, however, when Ikhwan excesses had begun even to turn their own compatriots against them, the king raised an army and defeated them. Although destroyed as an organized force, it is well to remember that the Ikhwan represented a deep current of legitimacy in Sa'udi political culture, and that the family was vulnerable to attack from the religious right wing before as well as after the onset of oil wealth and social modernization. In 1975 King Faisal's assassin was identified with a family faction that had violently opposed the introduction of television to the kingdom several years earlier.

Sa'udi Arabia as a Petro-Power

In 1933 Sa'udi Arabia and the California Arabian Standard Oil Company (the predecessor of ARAMCO, the Arabian American Oil Company) signed a concession agreement. After several years of inconclusive prospecting around Dammam village on the Gulf a major find was made in March 1938. Initial production was modest, around 20,000 barrels daily, and growth was impeded by the onset of World War II. In fact, when the war also cut off the Mecca pilgrimmage—still the Sa'udi government's chief source of revenue—the United States mint advanced a supply of silver coins to meet basic expenses. But after the war, production increased dramatically, to

14. The Ikhwan are described in Wahba, op. cit., chap. 8. See also Sir John Bagot Glubb, *War in the Desert* (London: Hodder and Stoughton, 1960), esp. chaps. 13–19, for an account of the British-Hashimite campaign against the Ikhwan raids on Iraq.

over 500,000 barrels per day in 1949 and nearly 900,000 in 1951, the latter increase due in part to the Iranian oil nationalization crisis.[15]

The kingdom's and the family's wealth also skyrocketed. The unprecedented largesse overwhelmed the rudimentary bureaucratic and financial institutions of the system, which consisted essentially of the king himself and his close relatives. Money was squandered and unscrupulous outsiders reaped windfall profits. According to Elizabeth Monroe, on the eve of King Abd al-Aziz's death, the largest of the new palaces in Riyadh consumed three times the electricity of the entire city. She reports that although his health was failing, he realized that the new wealth was corrupting both his family and the whole order which he had brought to Arabia. On his deathbed he told Philby, "A man's possessions and his children are his enemies."[16] At the same time, events outside the kingdom were posing a challenge of their own: the Palestine war, the military coups in Syria, unrest in the Hashimite kingdoms of Jordan and Iraq, and above all the Nasir revolution in Egypt all indicated the rise of a new militant Arabism and growing public hostility to regimes closely linked to the Western powers. Then, on November 9, 1953, just at the moment when Sa'udi Arabia had been thrust into a position of great importance and even greater vulnerability by virtue of its new oil riches, the founder-king died.

Since that day the legitimacy problem facing the ruling family has remained much the same: how to maintain traditional historical and religious legitimacy under conditions of superaffluence, meager governmental capabilities, and the spread of modern political ideologies— secular nationalism, socialism, and democracy. The period of maximum vulnerability coincides roughly with the reign of Abd al-Aziz's son and successor, Sa'ud, from 1953 to 1964. A weak leader with extravagant habits, he was unable to arrest the social and moral dissolution of Sa'udi society; nor was he very skillful in meeting the revolutionary external challenges. By 1958, internal finances were in chaos and Sa'ud was under attack by Gamal Abd al-Nasir, then at the height of his popularity (Sa'ud was accused of paying $5 million to have Nasir assassinated). So the family leaders transferred the major executive functions to Sa'ud's brother, Crown Prince Faisal. Although Sa'ud recovered these powers in 1960, Faisal continued to demonstrate his greater strength and competence. Finally in March 1964 a sixty-nine-man royal family council, after due consultation with the Mufti

15. *ARAMCO Handbook*, pp. 139–50.
16. Elizabeth Monroe, *Philby of Arabia* (London: Faber and Faber, 1973), p. 274.

and the ulama, formally invested him with all ruling powers.[17] Several months later Sa'ud was deposed and Faisal designated as king.

Under Faisal the erosion of Sa'udi political legitimacy was checked, and the system he bequeathed to his half-brother Khalid in 1975 is far stronger than the one he inherited. While the long-term viability of the family monarchy is still questionable, the success of the Sa'udi chiefs suggests that this type of system is not completely helpless in coping with social modernization and political radicalism. Three mechanisms are particularly important in explaining the Sa'udi renaissance. First, King Faisal was able to reassert the personal legitimacy that is the sine qua non of patriarchal system legitimacy, and he was able to transcend the traditional tribal and family basis of support. Second, the Sa'udis were able to demonstrate a compatibility between traditional Islamic values and modern Arab nationalism. Third, the development of a technocracy parallel to the royal family control structure—interlocked with it and subordinate to it—has substantially enhanced system capabilities and performance.

Faisal's leadership, like his father's, was grounded in martial accomplishments and religious rectitude. As a youth he had led the successful campaigns in Asir and the Hijaz, and later on in the period of affluence he abjured the conspicuous consumption and dissolute behavior of many of the princes and lived a simple life in strict observance of Islamic precepts. Astute and cautious, he proved even more capable than his illustrious father in confronting the domestic and foreign challenges of the oil age. Under his guidance the kingdom drew up its first government budget in 1958. He brought in able advisers like Pakistani-born Anwar Ali, who directed the Sa'udi Arabian Monetary Agency. He encouraged the training of thousands of Sa'udis in the professions and sciences. He was instrumental in abolishing slavery and in modernizing the judicial system to supplement the Shari'a with modern commercial (and petroleum) law. In regional politics he accomplished the delicate task of neutralizing Egyptian penetration of Yemen and Sa'udi Arabia itself, despite Nasir's enormous charisma. Then after the Arab defeat in 1967 he seized the opportunity to project Sa'udi Arabia into the vanguard of the Arab nationalist struggle by providing financial assistance to the front-line countries. His decision to embargo oil shipments to the West in the 1973 war was a masterly stroke of legitimation. Along with Abd al-Aziz, Faisal ranks with the strongest leaders of the modern Arab world. His legitimacy lay less in popular adulation than in respect; less in rhetoric than in performance.

17. The text of the Royal Decree is in Wahba, op. cit., pp. 176–80.

With lesser leadership the system probably would have collapsed. The future of the Sa'udi system, accordingly, depends heavily on the quality of Faisal's successor, his half-brother Khalid and the other strong princes, particularly Fahd, the interior minister, who is regarded by some observers as the power behind the throne.

During the "Arab cold war" of the 1950s and 1960s (as Malcolm Kerr has aptly dubbed this ideological conflict), the Sa'udi dynasty was labeled as "reactionary" by the progressive regimes and movements. To secularist intellectuals, the primacy of Islam in Sa'udi society was inimical to enlightened development. To republicans the idea of a family-state was not only undemocratic but anachronistic. To nationalists the Sa'udi dynasty seemed only a step removed from being a client of the United States, a cat's paw in the American campaign against radical Arabism. Such attacks have originated mainly outside the kingdom. Inside Sa'udi Arabia of the middle 1970s, however, there is little sense of value dissonance on the principles of the Islamic polity and authoritative family rule; in this respect it differs conspicuously from most of the other surviving monarchies in the region, particularly Morocco and Jordan. The Qur'an and related texts stand unchallenged as the moral and legal foundation of the Sa'udi state. Although the judiciary is now headed by a minister of justice competent in both Islamic and European codes, the Shari'a remains the basic law. There is no constitution as such. Some Western-educated Sa'udis do not see a need for parliaments, elections, checks and balances, and other appurtenances of modern Western states. In a 1972 interview with this writer, a university official in Riyadh declared that there is no conflict between Islam and so-called progressive ideologies because Islam is the most progressive—even revolutionary—system in the world. It is certainly more satisfactory than the electoral systems of the West in which, he said, presumably educated voters are shown to vote on irrational grounds, parties express only narrow, selfish interests, and moneyed corruption is widespread. If such abuses and distortions affect Western democracies, the system would hardly be suitable for a less-developed society like Sa'udi Arabia.[18] Alluding to Rousseau, he asserted that the Islamic system of Sa'udi Arabia is a close real and practical expression of the General Will. The locus of legitimacy is not to be found in the people; instead, the Good Society (which the Sa'udis as good Muslims wish to create) emerges through a leadership imbued with Islamic values and a society governed by Islamic law and teachings. In short, the

18. Interview at the University of Riyadh, March 8, 1972.

totality and coherence of Islam is so ingrained in Sa'udi culture that it still serves as a potent integrating mechanism. The present leadership enjoys Islamic legitimacy; this is its most formidable political resource. Similarly, the idea of family rule is apparently still widely accepted, especially at the mass level. No matter to the average Sa'udi subject that Sa'udi Arabia is the only member-state of the UN whose very name denotes a family dominion. Moreover, the historical accomplishments of this particular family, as I have tried to indicate, give it a very strong claim to legitimate rule.

Arab nationalism presents something of a problem for Sa'udi Arabia's ideological legitimacy. It has to do partly with the focus of loyalty and political boundaries. The Arab nation today is divided into at least eighteen sovereign states each of which, while proclaiming its membership and loyalty to the Arab nation, also tries to develop its own identity and citizen patriotism—something the pan-Arabists condemn as "regionalism." Another part is ideological: today there are several different varieties of Arab nationalism. Some, like that of Libya's Col. Mu'ammar al-Qadhafi, are revolutionary yet Islamic in spirit; others, like that of the People's Democratic Republic of Yemen, are avowedly secular and hostile to religious influence in politics. The principal organized movement of Arab nationalism, the Ba'th party, has been unable squarely to reconcile Islam with its ideas of Arab identity and nation (just as earlier Islamic reformists failed to do so) and so the contradictions remain unresolved. Some types of Arabism are more compatible with the Sa'udi system than others. The type symbolized by Nasir in the 1950s and 1960s was one of the least compatible and most subversive of Sa'udi royal authority. Referring to the late 1950s, Richard Nolte observed that while a specific Sa'udi nationalism did not appear to evoke much enthusiasm, the symbols of Arabism in general and Nasir in particular were very popular.[19]

But the trend toward a polarization between Arab nationalism and Sa'udi kingship that seemed to be developing during those years was largely averted. Faisal was able to blunt Nasirist designs in the peninsula and yet win support from the more liberal elements in the kingdom for his comparatively enlightened policies. Moreover, Sa'udi Arabia's Islamic and tribal-ethnic character and its historical position made it the most authentically Arab of all the Arab societies. While the modernization of the Arab world has stimulated secularism among

19. Richard H. Nolte, "From Nomad Society to New Nation: Sa'udi Arabia," chap. 2 in K. H. Silvert (ed.), *Expectant Peoples* (New York: Random House, 1963). Nolte also speculated that nationalism might be developed into an additional support base for the regime.

some of the intelligentsia, it has also accentuated the primordial dimensions of Arabism among the masses. In short, far from being incompatible with the new Arabism, Islam and asabiyya were to many an expression of it; and so the traditional bases of Sa'udi legitimacy proved more adaptable to contemporary conditions than observers intent on the ideological revolution expected. But actions have probably been even more decisive than attitudes in building the positive linkage between pan-Arabism and Sa'udi legitimacy. King Faisal went far to dissipate the cloud of reaction when he showed his willingness to punish the United States with the limited oil embargo of 1973–74. In so doing, he demonstrated the regime's commitment to the core issue of contemporary Arabism, Palestine. At a single stroke he infused the Sa'udi system with more legitimacy at home and certainly throughout the Arab world than it had ever enjoyed.

The third factor explaining the Sa'udi success in coping with change falls in the category of structural legitimacy. In the last two decades Sa'udi Arabia has developed a large central government staffed increasingly with trained civilian and military professionals. According to one recent study, employment in the public sector rose from a few hundred under King Abd al-Aziz to more than 100,000 during the reign of King Sa'ud, and after Faisal assumed power in 1964 it increased by another 50,000.[20] A growing proportion of the top civil servants were holding university and postgraduate degrees from Western, Arab, and (increasingly) Sa'udi Arabian institutions. The ministries of Petroleum, Commerce, Information, Agriculture, Communications, and Finance were most strongly infused with secularized, well-trained cadres.[21] Along with the Monetary Agency, an important center of technocratic diffusion was the Ministry of Planning which in 1975 presented a gigantic $142 billion five-year development plan for the kingdom. The Institute of Public Administration was established in 1960 to assist in the training of civil servants, with special attention given to inculcating a spirit of bureaucratic responsibility and efficiency. In 1965 the Central Department of Statistics began publishing a comprehensive statistical yearbook.

It also appears that the military establishment was expanding quantitatively and qualitatively at a similar pace. Beginning in 1963, reflecting the impact of the Yemen civil war, defense expenditures began to rise. In 1962 they amounted to 7.8 percent of GNP, but by

20. William Rugh, "Emergence of a New Middle Class in Sa'udi Arabia," *The Middle East Journal*, 27, 1 (Winter 1973), pp. 7–20; p. 10.
21. Ibid, p. 13.

1965 the percentage was 11.6; and two years later, the year of the Six-Day War, they jumped to an estimated 17.4 percent.[22] During this time the GNP itself increased by about 25 percent. In the 1970s expenditures shot up astronomically because of continuing Arab-Israeli tension, the arms race in the Gulf, and the flood of new oil revenues: in the 1972–74 period, Sa'udi Arabia spent just over $1 billion in the United States alone, and projected expenditures for 1975 ranged from $1 to $2 billion.[23] Apart from the strictly military implications of these expenditures, it may be surmised that their social and technological impact on the officer corps and the regime itself would be profound, both in terms of increased control capabilities and changing political attitudes. Certainly, the 26,000-man National Guard (the former White Army of Ikhwan stock) and the 36,000-man army are far advanced in terms of capabilities from the Ikhwan raiders of the 1920s.

From a political standpoint, what is important about the sudden growth of technocratic government in Sa'udi Arabia is not just the magnitude of change but the fact that it seems to have taken place so far without jeopardizing the legitimacy of the ruling family. Indeed, it appears that the stability of the regime has been enhanced. It is perhaps premature, therefore, to speak of the development of a new middle class in Sa'udi Arabia whose interests and orientations are fundamentally at variance with those of the Sa'ud dynasty. This dynasty, it must be remembered, is not just a handful of princes resting on the laurels of King Abd al-Aziz: it is also in itself an effective and elaborate political organization. It now includes 2,000–3,000 males, and its various branches are represented by senior princes in a family council. Although little is known about its internal processes, it appears to be no less effective than the ruling single-parties of neighboring revolutionary regimes.

Kinship seems quite as cohesive an organizing bond as ideology. The family has taken great care to maintain its monopoly over the most important positions including the first and second deputy premierships, and the ministries of Defense, Interior, National Guard, Finance, and Foreign Affairs. It links the still-distinct regions of the country with a network of marriage and patronage connections. It serves as a penetrative information-gathering and influence-dispensing institution. Furthermore, under King Faisal and his successors, it has built

22. Data and estimates are from Nadav Safran, *From War to War* (New York: Pegasus, 1969), p. 189.
23. According to *The Washington Post*, January 30, 1975.

elaborate intelligence-gathering and internal security bureaucracies.

Certainly the pervasive surveillance apparatus, itself a product of the new modernity, discourages the formation of political opposition among the technocrats, civilian and military. But more significant are the positive factors. The new generation of secularly educated Sa'udis benefits handsomely from the system: it has an important stake in the security of the system in general and much to gain in personal terms—careers, status, wealth, and the rewards that come with building a modern society. In intellectual terms, too, many of the highly trained Sa'udis see little problem with the system's traditional values. A high official of the Central Planning Organization interviewed by this writer in 1972 asserted that it is "completely fallacious" to assume that rational development could not go hand in hand with traditional values.[24]

The Sa'udi solution to the legitimacy problems posed by modernity has on the whole proved more successful than expected. Islamic and customary values have been harmonized with modern nationalism and secular values of progress and development. The Sa'udi system has become structurally elaborate both in its traditional and technocratic sectors. But political development theory suggests modernization imposes various loads on the political system. In the previous chapter I commented on Sa'udi Arabia's "growing pains"—inflation, shortages, bottlenecks and frustrations. These are hardly neglible conditions, politically speaking, even in the presence of virtually unlimited capital. In addition, one may infer that the demand for participation is becoming increasingly salient. Even though King Faisal was relatively progressive in many spheres, there was virtually no development of structured participation during his reign apart from the traditional consultations, audiences, and petitions—all undertaken at the pleasure of the monarch. Unlike the monarchs in Kuwait, the United Arab Emirates, and Bahrain, King Faisal showed little inclination to liberalize the system. Certain symptoms of unrest, however, occurred during the 1960s which indicated that systemic opposition was not entirely absent. One involved the family itself: Prince Talal demanded a partial democratization of the regime, then went into exile in Cairo during the Yemen war and was subsequently reconciled with the royal establishment. Three other princes defected to Nasir in 1962 as did three Sa'udi air force pilots. In early 1967, during the last stages of the Yemen war, there were numerous acts of sabotage in various cities of the kingdom, reportedly inspired by Egypt. In 1969 the most serious

24. Interview in Riyadh, March 9, 1972.

incident occurred—an attempted coup and assassination, which led to the arrest of over 200 air force officers, among others.

Family unity continues to be a requisite for regime legitimacy and stability, and thus far the Sa'udi princes have proved to be a cohesive group, as the smooth succession from Faisal to Khalid in 1975 indicated. Neither old regional differences among the Hijaz-, Najd-, and Hasa-based branches surfaced, nor was there any evidence of the rumored rivalries between the Sudairi clan (offspring of Abd al-Aziz's principal wife) and the sons of Sa'ud and Faisal. Nevertheless, so little is known about internal family politics that future conflicts cannot be ruled out. If, for example, serious rivalry were to develop between Crown Prince Fahd and the next most powerful prince, Abdalla (second deputy premier and head of the National Guard), the coherence and legitimacy of the family's rule could be significantly impaired. Another requisite is the loyalty of the army and National Guard officers. This too appears solid, although the 1969 incident was serious. But the unprecedented development of the armed services could provide the setting and the opportunity for a coup attempt by nationalist officers, perhaps on the model of the 1969 Libyan coup. A neo-Islamic Sa'udi Arabian Qadhafi might legitimize himself without difficulty, once in power, but he would be faced with a far more difficult job of seizing power in the first place than his Libyan counterpart because of the comparatively greater size and competence of the Sa'ud family and its security forces. Perhaps it was King Khalid's and Prince Fahd's appreciation of the regime's vulnerability to possible populist tendencies in the techno-cratic elite that led to reported plans to establish a mostly appointive Consultative Council, an Organic Law, and administrative decen-tralization.

Sequence is important in the development of legitimacy, as Rustow and others have argued.[25] In Sa'udi Arabia royal authority was es-tablished and Islamic-kinship norms impressed upon the population prior to the onset of rapid modernization. Government had, as it were, a head start on society, so that the development of governmental capabilities (social, economic, coercive) may have occurred at a faster rate than the dissolution of traditional political culture. If so, this kingdom may be better situated than some of the other Arab kingdoms, like Jordan or Morocco, to cope with the strains imposed by the

25. Rustow, op. cit., pp. 120–32. Cf. also Leonard Binder, et al., *Crises and Sequences in Political Development* (Princeton: Princeton University Press, 1971), and Eric Nordlinger, "Political Development: Time Sequences and Rates of Change," in Nordlinger (ed.), *Politics and Society* (Englewood Cliffs, N. J.: Prentice-Hall, 1970), pp. 329–47.

introduction of new values and the politicization of new groups outside
the royal family.

KUWAIT

Kuwait in the middle of the 1970s is the richest and most politically
complex of the small oil shaykhdoms on the perimeter of the Arabian
peninsula. This flat little state (only 16,000 square kilometers in area)
of around a million inhabitants is the third largest oil producer in the
Middle East after Sa'udi Arabia and Iran, and its per capita income
in 1974 was estimated at around $11,000.[26] Its political characteristics
are even more remarkable. Power is monopolized by the easy-going
Sabah family, as it has been since 1710, and the tribes constitute the
politically preponderant sector of the elite. Society and individual
orientations remain colored by Islam, although of a less austere mode
than that which prevails in Sa'udi Arabia. Yet Kuwait is the only
monarchy in the peninsula (apart from Bahrain which held its first
elections in December 1973) to have held free elections and developed
a significant parliamentary system. It is the epitome of the modern
welfare state, with excellent health, educational, and social service
benefits available free to all its citizens. And ideologically, Kuwait
stands with the more militant of the Arab nationalist revolutionary
regimes. Neither in Sa'udi Arabia nor the other monarchies does one
find a more integrated and seemingly stable amalgam of political
tradition and modernity.

Traditional Bases of Legitimacy

Kuwait has been ruled by the Sabah family since early in the
eighteenth century. Originally part of the Anaza tribal federation,
which claims sharifian status, the Sabahs are supposed to have been
driven by drought from their homeland in the Najd region of Arabia.
According to legend, the Sabah amir, Shaykh Abdalla, demonstrated
his aristocratic qualities by refusing to allow his beautiful daughter
Mariam to marry a suitor from a lesser tribe, even though it meant
going to war against a stronger adversary whom the Sabahs defeated.[27]
Skepticism has been expressed as to the validity of the family's aristo-

26. According to calculations made by the Union Bank of Switzerland, published in *The
Financial Times* (London), May 7, 1975.

27. Dickson, op. cit., pp. 26–28 and passim. The author, a long-time British political agent
in Kuwait and his wife, Violet Dickson, are considered leading authorities in the field. See also
the recent study by their daughter, Zahra Freeth, H. V. F. Winstone, *Kuwait: Prospect and Reality*
(New York: Crane, Russak and Company, 1972).

cratic lineage and the veracity of such heroic legends,[28] but the fact remains that the family was able to maintain continuous settlement and rule and thus establish customary authority. In any event, no other clan has been able to establish an earlier or superior claim.

That the family could maintain itself so successfully was due less to its aristocratic claims than its ability to deal with neighboring rivals and the great powers. By the end of the nineteenth century, Kuwait was one of the focal points of European imperialist competition. The Berlin-to-Baghdad railway actually would have terminated in Kuwait. The British, accordingly, were concerned that this neglected corner of the Ottoman Empire, which was beginning to tilt toward Germany, not fall under hostile influences. At the same time a particularly strong Sabah prince, Mubarak, seized power by the ruthless but effective method of murdering his two half-brothers who were too much influenced by their pro-Turkish Iraqi-born chief minister. Although Kuwait had maintained a connection with the British since the late eighteenth century, Shaykh Mubarak placed it formally under Britain's protection on January 23, 1899. The shaykhdom's special relationship with Britain helped it to survive the upheavals in the peninsula which the collapse of Turkey and the revival of Sa'udi Wahhabism stirred up. The new Kuwaiti amir, Shaykh Salim, even contemplated enlarging his domain to include part of the Sa'udi-controlled Hasa coast. But he was quickly disabused of that notion by the Sa'udi Ikhwan who nearly destroyed his dominion. So in the final settlement of 1922 his successor Ahmad needed British diplomatic support simply to hold fast. Nor was it the last time Kuwait would need British help, for in 1961, just after independence, Shaykh Abdalla called in British troops to deter Colonel Abd al-Karim Qassim of Iraq from enforcing his claims to the shaykhdom.

Ever since Mubarak's accession in 1896, the politics of the Sabah family, synonomous until recently with Kuwait politics in toto, have been relatively tranquil. Mubarak ruled for nearly two decades and Ahmad (1921–50) for nearly three. Shaykh Abdalla, the "father" of modern Kuwait, ruled peacefully from 1950 to 1965, a period of momentous change in which Kuwait was transformed from family-state to petro-state; and his brother, the present amir, Shaykh Sabah Salim al-Sabah, has ruled peacefully for over a decade. The principal line of factional cleavage in the family sets the Jabir line against the Salims, but in the main an amicable division of power has been arranged.

28. See Ralph Hewins, *A Golden Dream: The Miracle of Kuwait* (London: W. H. Allen, 1963), pp. 11–51 and passim, for an iconoclastic but informative analysis.

Since 1950 the amirs have come from the Salim branch, but in recent years one of the most dynamic leaders has been a son of Amir Ahmad, Crown Prince Jabir, who has been finance minister and prime minister.

While the legitimacy of the Kuwaiti system is strongly grounded in the personal leadership exercised by the amirs and the deference accorded by custom to the ruling family, it also derives from religious values. The Islam practiced in Kuwait is less rigorous than that of Sa'udi Arabia, even though the Sabahs trace their origins to the Sa'udi heartland. The families are distantly related, and the Kuwaitis once gave Abd al-Aziz ibn Sa'ud refuge from the Turks. But the puritanical Sa'udis have always regarded the Sabahs as insufficiently pious. And the Sabahs, who learned to fear and had to fight the Sa'udi Ikhwan, were never much enamored of the idea of Islamic theocracy. Moreover, the geographical and economic character of the emirate—open to the sea and dependent on maritime trading—has contributed to its relatively cosmopolitan religious and political character. To make this distinction, however, is not to deprecate the substantial imprint of Islam in Kuwait's political culture. The constitution stipulates that Islam is the official religion and that Islamic law is the principal source of legislation. The traditional prohibitions of alcohol and other forms of excess remain in force publicly, although observance is sometimes lax. Even the political and social reforms of recent years, such as in popular representation and women's rights, have taken place within the Islamic context. Nobody has called for a secular order.

Therefore, the Kuwaiti polity appears to be solidly grounded in the traditional legitimacy value resources of kinship and religion. In terms of Easton's systemic sources of legitimacy, Kuwait, like the other Arabian principalities, is distinguished by the strong personal legitimacy of the leaders of the ruling family. Tribe and family are the principal legitimizing structures. And Islam, although not elaborated as a formal and comprehensive ideological code in the sense that it is in Sa'udi Arabia, provides at least a substratum of common identity and moral values. Kuwait, however, has become more than a traditional tribal polity, and its legitimacy formula today is more complex than I have indicated thus far.

Confronting Modernity: A Liberal Nationalist Approach

The tribal city-state would seem to be an anachronism, its future uncertain, in a region like the Arab world which has been swept by social modernization and revolutionary ideology. In the case of Kuwait there is, additionally, a long-standing territorial claim by Iraq, as successor to Ottoman Turkey, to the entire shaykhdom—a claim which

Iraq has revived twice in recent times, in 1961 and 1973–74. Kuwait has chosen a more adaptive course than some of its monarchical neighbors like Sa'udi Arabia and Oman in coping with these loads on the system: it has opened the door to modernization by creating a welfare state and a climate of liberalism. Instead of using Islam as a barrier to social change and modern political values, the Kuwaiti elite has tried to merge it with modern Arabism and make it functional for the regime's domestic legitimacy. It has abjured the repressive, police-state approach of its neighbor Iran, the regional superpower. Kuwait, in short, epitomizes what might be called the liberal-nationalist model among the patriarchal strategies for legitimacy. The liberal-nationalist approach as practiced by the Sabah family consists of a well-calculated strategy of benevolent personal rule, representative structures, and nationalist ideology—all of which are widely perceived as congruent with traditional as well as modern values.

Compared with some of their royal counterparts, the Sabah amirs in recent decades at least have been mild, unflamboyant, and astute. While not averse to the worldly pleasures, they have exhibited a sense of civic responsibility as well. The present amir, Shaykh Sabah Salim al-Sabah, is the ultimate authority, and he consults with some fifteen of the most influential members of his large clan. Unlike the Shah of Iran, he rules indirectly and delegates most policy issues and routine matters of government to the premier and cabinet. A retiring man, Shaykh Sabah received a secondary education in Kuwait and some training in England for police work. Subsequently he became head of the Kuwait police force. Apart from summer vacations in Lebanon, the amir has traveled outside Kuwait only infrequently. His personal legitimacy derives neither from piety, like King Faisal's, nor charismatic nationalism, like Nasir's. It rests instead upon competence and custom. Although since independence there have been occasional stirrings of resentment at the family's monopoly of power, there has been no serious challenge. The principal cleavage, as indicated, remains within the family; and the Jabir branch represents the main "alternative" to the Salim branch.

Perhaps the most innovative facet of Kuwait's legitimacy formula, compared to the other monarchies, was its fourteen-year experiment with limited parliamentary democracy, which lasted until August 1976. In 1962 a constitution was enacted which called for a cabinet-parliamentary form of government, although ultimate powers remained with the amir. The Kuwait National Assembly, like many parliaments in the world today, had little autonomy and rarely initiated policy. But it did function as a constant and vociferous forum for criticizing the government, as a visitor to one of its sessions would quickly ascertain. Moreover, it had given an institutionalized means of expression and access to the main sociopolitical elements in contemporary Kuwait—the nomadic and sedentary tribes, the urban merchants and businessmen, and the politicized, nationalist intellectuals and professionals. The tribes had become increasingly important in electoral politics as a conservative counterweight to the businessmen and nationalist intellectuals. According to a member of the royal family, who in 1972 described Kuwaiti politics as "democracy in a tribal setting," at least one of the big tribes would hold what was in effect a primary election in its district to select, within a traditional framework, its candidates; the official election then became a somewhat pro forma event. The businessmen, although sometimes impatient with the family's rule, had such an advantageous economic situation that they did not agitate for major reforms. The nationalist intellectuals, led by Dr. Ahmad al-Khatib, were sympathetic to pan-Arab and reformist movements elsewhere in the region. As long as this group refrained from attacking the ruler or infringing upon what the family considered to be the security of the state, there was a substantial measure of free political expression. The progressive image which these nationalists provided probably contributed significantly to the legitimacy of the whole system.

Kuwait is also distinctive in comparison with the other Arabian monarchies in terms of the extent to which its leaders have tried to embody modern nationalist ideology. It is not just the small nationalist minority in the assembly that supports Arab and progressive causes; it is also the ruling family itself. The Kuwait constitution declares the state to be Arab and its people part of the Arab nation. Arabism is a powerful yet somewhat ambiguous legitimizing force. The dimensions and concerns of the Arab nation are far broader than those of particular Arab sovereignties, and it is incumbent on the Kuwait leadership to demonstrate its fidelity to that nation by supporting pan-Arab causes. After the 1973 Arab-Israeli war, Kuwait disbursed $1 billion to the Arab confrontation states for rehabilitation and new arms. Its Arab legitimacy at home is reflected in the degree of its acceptance elsewhere in the Arab world. Moreover, the latent conflict within Arab nationalism between ethnic Arabism and secular-socialist Arabism, casts an additional ambiguity on this dimension of Kuwait system legitimacy. In the early 1960s, for example, "radical" (i.e., democratizing) pressures were brought to bear on the newly independent state from Nasirist and Ba'thist elements. But the ruler responded effectively with generous regional aid programs. He established the National Assembly and created the freest political climate in the Arab world outside Lebanon. Thus, in Kuwait up until late 1976 one could see the most significant attempt by a patriarchal regime to acquire modern sources of legitimacy. Even more than in Sa'udi Arabia and the United Arab Emirates, Arabism serves as a link between traditional and modern principles of legitimacy; but in Kuwait the secular and democratic content of Arabism is more pronounced than in the other kingdoms. And as for the other modernizing legitimacy principles, Kuwait's head start in building a welfare state has made the realization of many development goals an accomplished fact.

Capabilities and Loads

Oil wealth, of course, has provided the wherewithal to pursue this relaxed liberal-nationalist course. The oil began flowing in quantity in 1949. By 1952 output had more than doubled, reaching 37 million tons, partly as a result of the Iran crisis. A year later Kuwait had become the world's second largest exporter and fourth largest producer.[29] By the time of independence and constitutional government less than a decade later, the oil bonanza had made the state (and its ruling family) the primary economic and political institution in the country, reversing the former predominance of the merchant class. By the early 1960s the public payroll (excluding the armed forces) was swollen to some 53,000 employees.[30] Wise management on the part of Amir Abdalla during the 1950s laid the groundwork for a social welfare system so comprehensive that few native Kuwaitis or immigrant Arab workers entertained political grievances, ambitions, or revolutionary ideas. In 1952 Abdalla established a Development and Welfare Board to implement the program. He also undertook a farsighted program of overseas investment in 1952 when he created the Kuwait Investment Board in London. When and if Kuwait's oil deposits run dry early in the next century, Kuwaitis will be able to live comfortably off the interest from these long-established overseas investments. Furthermore, with an eye to its external vulnerability, Abdalla and Finance Minister Jabir Ahmad established the Kuwait Fund for Arab Economic Development (KFAED) in 1962, an organization designed to provide development assistance and funding to the poorer and more underdeveloped countries in the region. The shaykhdom's generous assistance, subsequently expanded through

29. Hewins, op. cit., p. 236.
30. Fakhri Shehab, "Kuwait: A Super-Affluent Society," *Foreign Affairs*, 42, 3 (April 1964), pp. 461–74; pp. 462–63, 471.

other institutions as well, placed it in a more favorable light among the nationalist-revolutionary movements and regimes, notably Nasir's. An outright donation to Iraq helped dampen that neighbor's acquisitive designs. In 1974 Kuwait quintupled the capital of the KFAED to $3.4 billion, increased its contribution to the Arab Fund for Economic and Social Development, and was supporting major projects in Egypt, Sudan, Syria, and other countries.[31]

And yet, capable though it has been, the Kuwait experiment in "tribal democracy" is not without its weaknesses. They were evidently serious enough for the crown prince and the ruler to disband the parliament and curb the free press in 1976 for a four-year period of "reexamination." On the internal level, the system of tribal democracy was too tribal for some and too democratic for others. Liberal critics objected to the attempts of the ruling family to preserve its power base through enfranchising conservative, uneducated nomads, many of whom were not Kuwaiti at all. At the same time, these critics observed that hundreds of thousands of long-time Kuwait residents were being excluded from political participation. A 1972 census revealed that 54 percent (some 400,000) of the resident population was non-Kuwaiti— mostly expatriate Arabs, and of these at least a quarter were skilled Palestinians occupying important technical and administrative positions. These non-Kuwaitis suffered economic and social discrimination, and they were politically disenfranchised. Only male Kuwait citizens over twenty-one could vote; and after various ineligible categories (such as the armed forces) are subtracted, the number of eligible voters was only between 30,000 and 45,000. In the 1971 elections only around 15,000 votes reportedly had been cast. Furthermore, political parties were prohibited. According to liberal critics, therefore, the threat to system legitimacy in Kuwait was from not enough democracy. The prevailing view, however, held that Kuwait's liberal institutions were a net liability for continued system legitimacy. This view objected to criticism from the parliamentary opposition and the press concerning waste in domestic politics and the government's insufficient support for the Palestinian and other Arab nationalist causes. It was critical of the dilatory character of the parliament itself and the behavior of some of the deputies.

Kuwait's external problems also contributed to the tightening of patriarchal absolutism. The leaders of Sa'udi Arabia, whose growing weight in Gulf affairs could hardly be ignored by the Kuwaitis, were reportedly disturbed at the radical Kuwait press criticism of the new

31. *The Financial Times* (London), "Middle East Banking Survey," March 24, 1975, pp. 23–24.

conservative trend in Arab regional affairs, particularly the tough stance being taken toward the militant Palestinians by Sa'udi Arabia, Syria, Jordan, and Egypt. A small state surrounded by large and potentially predatory regimes could ill afford too much domestic embarrassment or indiscipline. While Iraq has relaxed its claims to the whole of Kuwait, it still claims two Kuwaiti islands (Warba and Bubiyan) which impede Iraqi port development on the Gulf. Iran's emergence since the middle 1960s as the preponderant military power in the Gulf raises the possibility of a quick take-over, although the political circumstances favoring such a move seem remote. Nonetheless, Kuwait remains vulnerable militarily, notwithstanding its efforts in the 1970s to build up its armed forces. It is also vulnerable to externally supported subversion. When Iraq settled its differences with Iran in 1975 and began improving its relations with Sa'udi Arabia, Kuwait's vulnerability may have increased another notch.

On balance, it must be concluded that Kuwait's rulers were singularly successful during the first decade and a half of independence in fostering system legitimacy through a strategy of liberal-nationalist accommodation. But the reversion to patriarchal absolutism in 1976 suggests that even here, in this wealthy welfare state, structural legitimacy is more illusion than reality, while traditional patriarchal legitimacy is by no means permanently established either.

THE LOWER GULF STATES

Until recently political life in and around the shaykhdoms on the northeastern perimeter of the Arabian peninsula was Hobbesian in its anarchy. This is the area once known as the Pirate Coast, where piracy and slavery were common practice until the British imposed a series of truces on its warring families in the nineteenth century. Constant feuding within and between the clans which ruled the undemarcated little territories along this coast made life precarious and orderly government impossible.[32] But a political scientist observing the same area today might be reminded instead of Plato. Bahrain, Qatar, and the United Arab Emirates resemble the classical Greek or Italian city-states in a modern setting. A wise and benevolent ruler presides over a small society in which everybody knows his place: the bureaucrats administer, the merchants trade, and the workers work. Patriarchal

---

32. For examples, see J. B. Kelly's carefully detailed study of the Buraimi Oasis dispute between Sa'udi Arabia and the Trucial states, *Eastern Arabian Frontiers* (New York: Praeger, 1964). On the history of the ruling families of the area, with special attention to the British connection, see Donald Hawley, *The Trucial States* (London: Allen and Unwin, 1970).

rule is accepted as the norm, and the amir enjoys high personal legitimacy. The prevalent ideology, if any, is pragmatism; and a small but
growing technocracy assists the ruler in the development of his domain.
There is little evidence of unrest or revolutionary ideologies because
the material rewards for most individuals are so attractive that few care
to take the time or incur the risks involved in political participation.
There is much validity in such an image, but the reality is somewhat
more complex.

Compared to the other shaykhdoms—Bahrain, Qatar, the states
of the United Arab Emirates, and Oman—both Sa'udi Arabia and
Kuwait are well-established political systems. They have been functioning longer as independent entities (Sa'udi Arabia since 1932, Kuwait
1961), whereas the lower Gulf states attained formal independence
only in 1971. They are more structurally elaborate, having begun to
develop bureaucracies, budgets, and interest groups or parties outside
the ruling family. Because Sa'udi Arabia and Kuwait have been major
oil exporters since the late 1940s, they have been experiencing intense
social and economic modernization for over a generation, while the
others (except for Bahrain) are around a decade behind them. To the
young elites of the formal Trucial Coast, Sa'udi Arabia and Kuwait
stand as alternative developmental models.

The lower Gulf shaykhdoms have much in common with one
another. They are all very small, with populations ranging from
170,000 in Qatar, 216,000 in Bahrain, 230,000 in the United Arab
Emirates, to some 435,000 in Oman. Like Sa'udi Arabia and Kuwait
they all have very large expatriate communities. They are also wealthy
oil-exporting economies. Until recently (Bahrain again excepted) they
lacked the most rudimentary social infrastructure: there were almost
no educational, health, or social facilities, and little in the way of
transport and communications. Politically, they are family states:
Bahrain is ruled by the Khalifas, Qatar by the Al Thani, the two
principal emirates of the UAE by the Al bu Falah of Abu Dhabi and
the Al bu Falasa of Dubai, and Oman by the Al bu Sa'ids. They all
share in varying degree the problem of maintaining legitimacy under
conditions of superfast modernization and regional tension. Historically, each ruling family has been plagued with intrafamily
rivalries which often were resolved by assassination. The separate
emirates were frequently at war with one another. Now, with rapidly
expanding populations (Abu Dhabi grows by 25 percent annually)
including large numbers of expatriate Arab professional people and a
new generation of educated citizens, there is a problem of justifying not

only the ruler's authority, but the legitimacy of the ruling family itself.

Although they are basically similar, the shaykhdoms vary considerably in terms of the seriousness of their legitimacy problems and the approach their leaders take toward coping with them. Roughly speaking, legitimacy is a function of size and wealth: the very small, very rich states like Qatar and the UAE have managed very well, while the larger and less affluent ones like Bahrain and Oman have experienced difficulties. Bahrain in particular stands out in terms of the exposure to modernity of its people. Its first school was established in 1919 and by 1970 its primary and secondary school enrollment ratio was the highest in the Arab world.[33] Not surprisingly, therefore, it has experienced a degree of modern student and labor unrest unknown elsewhere in the Gulf. Oman's problem is quite different. Long the most isolated country in Arabia, Oman until recently faced a rural Marxist insurgency in Dhofar province and a vulnerability to urban subversion because of low regime capabilities and narrowly based support for the family. Another variable contributing to system stability and legitimacy is the size and homogeneity of the ruling family; Qatar is a positive case in point. The shaykhs also differ in their approach to the social change taking place around them. At one extreme, there was the late sultan of Oman, Sa'id ibn Taymur, who, until he was deposed by his son Qabus in 1970, actively opposed all modernization. He did all in his power to keep foreigners out of his country and his countrymen insulated from foreign ideas. At the other is Shaykh Rashid of Dubai, the second most powerful ruler in the UAE, a veritable merchant prince, whose liberal and cosmopolitan outlook has helped make Dubai the Beirut of the Gulf. Qatar and Oman would seem to emulate the conservative Sa'udi model, while Abu Dhabi, Dubai, and Bahrain somewhat reluctantly follow Kuwait. Some of the rulers have been rather more cautious than others about opening up their domains to participation by people outside the family, but today every one of them embraces development planning as a way to dilute potential ideological opposition to family rule.

Bahrain

Like Kuwait, Bahrain is a tribal polity founded by a clan that emigrated from Arabia: the Khalifa family of the Utab tribe drove out the Iranian rulers in 1783 and has remained in control virtually

33. According to data compiled from UNESCO sources and kindly provided by Professor Munir Bashshur of the American University of Beirut.

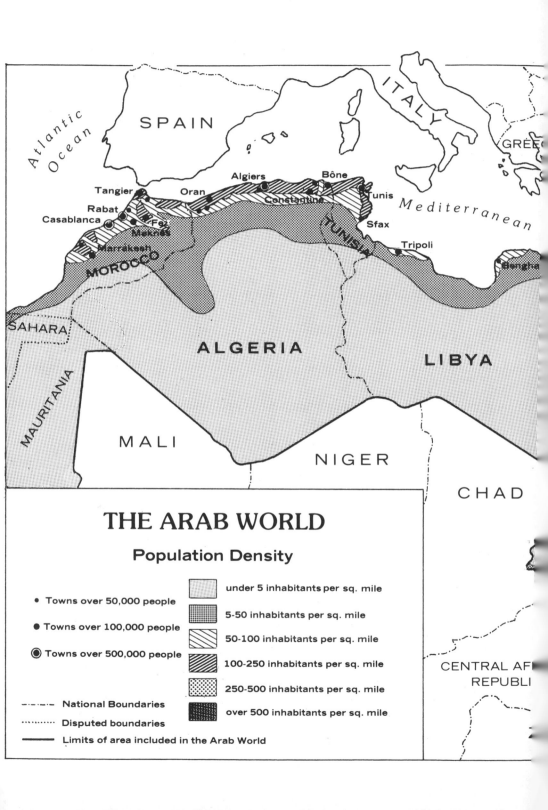

THE ARAB WORLD

Population Density

- • Towns over 50,000 people
- ● Towns over 100,000 people
- ◎ Towns over 500,000 people

—·—·— National Boundaries

··········· Disputed boundaries

———— Limits of area included in the Arab World

under 5 inhabitants per sq. mile	
5-50 inhabitants per sq. mile	
50-100 inhabitants per sq. mile	
100-250 inhabitants per sq. mile	
250-500 inhabitants per sq. mile	
over 500 inhabitants per sq. mile	

Black Sea

Caspian Sea

TURKEY

Aleppo Mosul
Latakia SYRIA Kirkuk
LEBANON Homs
Beirut Damascus
ISRAEL IRAQ Baghdad
Karbala
Alexandria Amman Basra
Jerusalem
Port Sa'id JORDAN Kuwait
Suez KUWAIT
Cairo Dhahran BAHRAIN
Hofuf QATAR
Riyadh Muscat
EGYPT UAE

SA'UDI

Red Sea Jidda Mecca ARABIA OMAN

Omdurman YEMEN PDRY
Khartoum Sana
SUDAN Wadi Medani

Eritrea Aden
DJIBOUTI

ETHIOPIA Djibouti

SOMALIA

Indian Ocean

E UGANDA KENYA Mogadishu

CYPRUS SYRIA
LEBANON Damascus
Beirut
ISRAEL
Tel Aviv Amman
Jerusalem
EGYPT JORDAN

SA'UDI
ARABIA

without interruption to the present.[34] Unlike the other shaykhdoms, however, Bahrain is relatively mixed religiously. The ruling family and others that accompanied it were, of course, orthodox (Sunni) Muslims while the indigenous islanders were predominantly Shi'a, reflecting 180 years of Persian rule. Furthermore, approximately one-fifth of the present population is foreign; and the foreign population includes an influential, well-to-do Iranian community of over 7,000, which inevitably provides some additional leverage for Iran in local politics. There are also some 10,000 or more Indians and Pakistanis, many of whom occupy good positions in the labor force. And as Bahrain was long an important British outpost, until the end of 1971, the British business, military, and diplomatic community carried considerable weight in local affairs. These strategically placed non-Arab and largely non-Sunni communities gave Bahrain a certain cosmopolitan, indeed Western, character quite different from neighboring shaykhdoms. The British presence, which dates back to 1820, became more influential in the 1920s, particularly after Sir Charles Belgrave became adviser to the ruler, Shaykh Hamid al-Khalifa. The collapse of the pearling industry and the discovery of oil in 1933 made Bahrain the first welfare shaykhdom of the Gulf, and with the assistance of British advisers, the ruler expanded the educational facilities. In the 1970s Bahrain's oil reserves, never major, were beginning to dry up, but its stock of educated and sophisticated young people remained very high. Thus in addition to the vertical primordial cleavages in the system, there were also horizontal stress lines. High social mobilization and exposure to modern political values, combined with limited economic opportunities, have eroded the traditional legitimacy of this patriarchy.

The society and culture of Bahrain are not just extensions of the ruling family as in some other patriarchies where one can almost say that system and family are coterminous. Not only is Bahrain probably the site of the mysterious civilization of Dilmun of the third millenium B.C., it has been a center of trade and commerce ever since then; and in the sixteenth century, before the Iranians, Arabs, and English, it was ruled by the Portuguese. The Khalifas consolidated their rule, to be sure, but there has always been an underlying population somewhat culturally alien from the ruling clan. Thus, kinship does not have the

---

34. For a general survey of the history and culture of Bahrain, see James D. Belgrave, *Welcome to Bahrain* (Manama: Augustan Press, 1970). I am also grateful to Dr. Ali Taky for discussing with me in Manama in March 1972 his dissertation presented to the Sorbonne on the political development of Bahrain.

fortifying value in Bahrain that is does elsewhere in the Gulf. As for religion, its legitimizing power in Bahrain is diluted by the division between Sunni and Shi'a. Furthermore, Bahrain's relatively long and thorough modernization and its need for a modern legal order has reduced Islam as a legitimizing element. Early in this century the British introduced their own extraterritorial legal system for non-Bahrainis, and it was gradually extended into many fields requiring legislation. Only matters of personal status, for Bahrainis, were left exclusively in the hands of the Muslim religious authorities and the shari'a.[35] Shaykh Issa ibn Salman al-Khalifa's proclamation of independence in 1971 did not speak of Islam as the source of rule but instead declared fidelity to more modern and immediate causes: Arabism and Palestine.[36]

Bahrain's advanced level of modernization has been a source of pride to Bahrainis. But education and political awareness have also accentuated the Khalifa family's legitimacy problem. As early as the middle 1950s, when Nasir was challenging the British at Suez, Bahrainis took to the streets in demonstrations of support, which the British suppressed. In 1965 there was violent labor unrest with political overtones at the BAPCO petroleum refinery. In the spring of 1972 another labor dispute involving Gulf Aviation's hiring of Indians and Pakistanis rather than Bahrainis provoked disturbances which although minor indicated once again the demand for broader political participation. In 1975 there was prolonged worker unrest in the country's major factory, the ALBA aluminum plant. As in southern Arabia a decade and more previously, the labor movement was the structural core of this discontent.

The response of the Khalifa family until recently has been to ignore or play down such demands. To some, the family's alleged religious laxity, the unseemly social deportment of some of its members, and its close past relationship with the British have tarnished its authority. Above all its unwillingness to share authority and its repression of some opposition elements (Ba'thists and Arab nationalists) has created discontent. But the present amir, Shaykh Issa, born in 1934 and ruler since 1961, has gradually taken a more liberal position. In January

35. W. M. Ballentine, "French-Egyptian Pattern for Future Legislation," and Dr. Husain M. al-Baharna, "Judical System is Put on a Sounder Footing," *The Times* (London), special section on Bahrain, December 16, 1971. Dr. al-Baharna is Minister of State for Legal Affairs and author of *The Legal Status of the Arabian Gulf States* (Manchester: Manchester University Press, 1968).

36. See the text of the proclamation in *L'Orient-Le Jour* (Beirut), August 14, 1971.

1970 he created a twelve-man advisory Council of State which was subsequently transformed into a Council of Ministers. One of its tasks was to draw up a constitution that would allow for at least limited popular participation in government. In 1972 a forty-four-man constituent assembly (half appointed, half elected) drew up a constitution which was approved by Shaykh Issa. And in December 1973 Bahrain held its first parliamentary elections, and among the winners were a number of relative progressives. It appeared that Bahrain's rulers were belatedly following Kuwait's liberal example. But this parliamentary experiment faltered after only a year and a half. In the wake of the National Assembly's refusal to pass a security law, the government cracked down on left-wing politicians and dissolved the council. Bahrain lacks the superaffluence of Kuwait, and its population is more divided and more attuned to modern political ideologies than that of Kuwait; so the future struggle for legitimacy is not likely to be easy.

Qatar

Until 1949 when oil began flowing in quantity, Qatar was one of the least developed spots on the Trucial Coast.[37] Long enmeshed in the ceaseless feuds of rival clans, it was subservient to the Khalifas of Bahrain from around 1776 until the 1860s when the present dynasty, the Al Thani, was installed with British help.[38] The religious and cultural orientation of the Al Thani is more akin to that of the Sa'udis than the rather more cosmopolitan Khalifas of Bahrain or Sabahs of Kuwait. The Qatar peninsula is small both in size, 4,000 square miles, and in population, around 170,000. But the ruling family is the largest among the lower Gulf emirates, which helps account for the stability and institutional simplicity of its political system today.[39] The Qatari economy is built almost exclusively on petroleum. Oil exports account for 90 percent of the emirate's income. Oil revenues rose from $59 million in 1963 to $397 million in 1973. Production in 1973 was around 600,000 barrels per day.[40] Although its production is far smaller than that of Kuwait or Abu Dhabi, it is well ahead of Oman, Dubai, and Bahrain; certainly it is wealthy enough to provide very well indeed

37. Hawley, op. cit., p. 260.

38. Belgrave, op. cit., pp. 106–10.

39. According to *The Economist* (London), "Survey of the Arabian Peninsula," June 6, 1970, p. xxii, which also reported that "the Doha telephone book has page after page of Shaikhs with the name Al Thani."

40. Data reported in "Qatar," a pamphlet published by the League of Arab States, Arab Information Center, New York, September 1974, p. 4.

for its small population and to project considerable influence in Gulf affairs.

Although Qatar began building up an administrative structure during the 1950s as oil revenues began to accumulate, it was not until 1970 that the emirate began to take on the structural appurtenances of a modern state. A provisional constitution was promulgated and a cabinet created. An Advisory Council "of 20 prominent Qataris representative of the commercial, industrial and professional sectors" (as a government press release described it) was permitted "to debate legislation, make recommendations, and request ministerial statements. . . . "[41] These innovations, although less liberal than those of Kuwait or Bahrain, were quite substantial for such a traditional dynasty and, in fact, well in advance of Sa'udi Arabia.

The principal pillar of ideological legitimacy in Qatar is Islam, the state religion, and the Al Thani, like most of the emirate's population, adheres to the rigorous Hanbali code of the Wahhabis. Since independence and the withdrawal of the British protectorate in 1971, the Al Thani family has emphasized its linkages with the rest of the Arab world. The provisional constitution asserts that Qatar is a part of the Arab nation. As in the other shaykhdoms, the ruling dynasty seeks to enhance the customary and religious bases of legitimacy by identifying itself with the concerns of modern Arab nationalism. A few Qatari officers have been sent to the Israel front. More important, the emirate has been generous in its aid to the frontline Arab combatants, particularly Syria.

Qatar's future is as uncertain as that of any of the other rich ministates in the Gulf, but the source of the uncertainty is regional rather than internal. Internally, the dynasty would seem to have little to fear from popular discontent of the kind that exists in Bahrain, Oman, or potentially even in Kuwait. Its population is small and homogeneous and its territory is compact, unlike Oman, which faces rural insurgency. The family has the financial capabilities to curb the nascent radical liberation movement in the Gulf and the security capability to thwart a take-over by elements outside the family. Even with its liberalized structures, the family still holds around two-thirds of the cabinet positions. Politics, accordingly, remains very much a family affair; and instability, should it occur, is more likely to be a product of intrafamily rivalries, as it always has been, than of a popular insurrection. In point of fact, the present ruler, Shaykh Khalifa ibn Hamad Al Thani, came to power in February 1972 in a family coup which

41. Government of Qatar press release, *The New York Times*, January 27, 1974.

overthrew his cousin, Shaykh Ahmad ibn Ali Al Thani. Because there are distinct factions within the family Amir Khalifa has refrained from designating his favored and able son Abd al-Aziz as his successor, reportedly for fear of antagonizing important personalities. In the meantime, the huge inflow of capital stimulates development, and the burdens on the amir and his rudimentary administration accordingly increase. The need to plan, to execute projects, to curb corruption and develop trained manpower becomes more acute daily. These factors are causing an expansion of government, which means that educated young men outside the royal family are beginning to gain influence and may in time bring pressure for political change.

The United Arab Emirates

At the beginning of 1968 Great Britain announced that it would withdraw from its special protective relationship with the nine oil-rich Gulf shaykhdoms in 1971. The announcement set in motion efforts to establish a federation in order to reduce their vulnerability to subversion and increase their capabilities for modern government. The project was not easy because the little emirates had a long history of conflict and rivalry with one another. Originally, it was planned that the larger shaykhdoms of Bahrain, Qatar, Abu Dhabi, and Dubai would join with the five tiny (and much poorer) emirates. As it happened, however, the federation that came into being in December 1971 included only six states: Abu Dhabi, Dubai, Sharja, Ajman, Umm al-Qaywayn, and Fujayra. A seventh, Ras al-Khayma, subsequently joined. Bahrain and Qatar at the last minute refused to join, each demanding a more central role than the others were willing to grant. Bahrain, with much the larger population, had demanded the largest share of seats in the proposed federal legislature. The cosmopolitan Bahrainis, mindful of their higher levels of modernization, exhibited a certain condescension toward the other relatively underdeveloped emirates, particularly Qatar with which they also had a territorial dispute. In addition, Bahrain's candidacy was clouded at first by an Iranian claim to the island. The Iranian claim had special force in light of her military power and her close relationships with the ruling families in Qatar, Dubai, and Ras al-Khayma. Even after Iran renounced her claim in May 1970, abiding by the results of a UN-sponsored plebiscite, the pro-Iran emirates continued to be suspicious of Bahrain as a potential source of subversion, radicalism, and decadence. As for wealthy Qatar, it wished a voice in the Federation's affairs commensurate with its expected financial contribution and was unwilling to join unless other sensitive issues like the location of the capital and the voting procedures were settled definitively prior to establishment of the union.[42] The withdrawal of Qatar was a disappointment to Dubai because the two ruling families were linked by marriage and commercial ties. They had even shared the same currency, the Qatar-Dubai rial. Dubai was thus left without a major counterweight to Abu Dhabi, which was now by far the strongest unit in the federation; and Abu Dhabi and Dubai had been at war with one another as late as 1948. The withdrawal of Bahrain was a disappointment to Abu Dhabi, reportedly because Shaykh Zayid hoped its membership would have given added weight and capabilities to the federation as a whole and greater leverage for Abu Dhabi in its dispute with Sa'udi Arabia over the Buraimi oasis.[43] But considering the disparities in size and wealth among the emirates (the smallest, Umm al-Qaywayn has a population of only 4,000) and the history of incessant conflicts among them, it was no small accomplishment that a federation of seven states finally did come into being.

Abu Dhabi is the most important emirate in the federation, contributing about 90 percent of the federal budget in addition to financing separate development projects in the poorer member-states.[44] The amir of Abu Dhabi, Shaykh Zayid ibn Sultan al-Nihyan, is president of the UAE. The vice-president is Shaykh Rashid ibn Sa'id al-Maktum, amir of Dubai (75,000 inhabitants in 1972), the most commercially developed of the emirates. The remaining five emirates are considerably smaller, poorer, and less powerful. Sharja is ruled by Shaykh Sultan ibn Muhammad al-Qasimi and has a population of some 45,000. Ras al-Khayma (population 28,000) is ruled by another branch of the Qasimi family headed since 1948 by Shaykh Saqr ibn Muhammad. Fujayra (population 10,000) is ruled peacefully by Shaykh Muhammad ibn Hamad al-Sharqi who came to power in 1952. Ajman (population 4,500) has also enjoyed relative tranquillity and has been ruled since 1928 by Shaykh Rashid ibn Humaid. And Umm al-Qaywayn has been governed since 1929 by Shaykh Ahmad ibn Rashid.[45]

Until quite recently the main basis of legitimacy, such as it was, in these states was the personal reputation of the ruling shaykh. The

---

42. *Al-Nahar* (Beirut), April 7 and 10, 1971, published a statement by the ruler of Qatar on his state's position concerning the proposed federation. It was one of a series in which the official positions of the other major emirates were presented.

43. Phebe Marr, in *The Christian Science Monitor*, December 8, 1970.

44. United Arab Emirates, Ministry of Information, "United Arab Emirates: Second Anniversary," 1973, p. 42.

45. Hawley, op. cit., Appendix C, pp. 333–50; see also John Duke Anthony, "The Union of Arab Amirates," *Middle East Journal*, 26, 3 (Summer 1972), pp. 271–88.

structural basis was the family, and the ideological or value basis was Islam and tribal norms of conduct. On balance, as we have seen, this formula more often than not was unable to sustain stable or settled government. Five of the seven amirs in the new federation had come to power through an irregular seizure of power. Shaykh Zayid of Abu Dhabi had overthrown his brother Shakhbut in 1966; Rashid of Dubai had deposed his uncles in 1932; Ahmad of Umm al-Qaywayn had shot an uncle who had just murdered his father; Saqr of Ras al-Khayma had expelled his uncle in 1948; and, in the most recent coup, 1972, Shaykh Sultan of Sharja assumed power after his brother Khalid had been shot by his cousin and the former ruler, Saqr ibn Sultan.[47] In Abu Dhabi, the core state of the federation, eight of the fifteen amirs in the Al bu Falah dynasty of the Bani Yas tribe, which has ruled uninterrupted since the 1760s, have been assassinated; the bloodless deposition of Shakhbut thus was considered a relatively positive development.[48] Compared to the Sa'udis and Kuwaitis of the twentieth century, the petty dynasties of the Trucial Coast, while firmly established vis à vis other families, were unable to develop legitimate, effective intrafamily political procedures; or, to put it another way, force and assassination were legitimate "rules of the game."

This grim condition appears to have changed dramatically in the last decade. One reason is that the vast oil revenues pouring into the area have changed it from a zone of political and economic scarcity to one of affluence and security. Another is that the departure of the British at the end of 1971 was an event which awakened the individual emirs to the dangers of continued division and feuding. By the 1970s the stakes of politics in the Gulf had risen markedly and larger neighbors like Iraq, Iran, and Sa'udi Arabia were taking a new and not entirely benevolent interest in the little shaykhdoms. And so, notwithstanding their rivalries, the seven amirs banded together to build a more durable order. Shaykh Zayid of Abu Dhabi was the principal force behind the federation; and Shaykh Rashid of Dubai, although harboring some misgivings for reasons mentioned above, acquiesced to play the secondary role. Together they comprised the heart of a system that is already developing beyond the patriarchal structures on which it is based.

46. G. Dardaud, "Fujairah, un pays arabe presque inconnu," *As-Safa* (Beirut), July 21, 1972. The Abu Dhabi per capita income projection is reported by Ray Vicker in *The Wall Street Journal*, April 30, 1974.

47. "UAE Crosses its First Hurdle," *Middle East International* (London), March 1972, pp. 24–25.

48. Hawley, op. cit., pp. 335–37.

Personal reputation—royal authority—and kinship still play the central legitimizing role in the Federation but the setting is new. Instead of the tribal chieftain operating in a quasi-warlike environment according to the desert warrior ethic, the petro-princes of the 1970s are respected as upholders of a settled, civic order. Their authority is enhanced by their technocratic expertise more than their martial characteristics. They are still defenders of the faith, but more important politically, they are now apostles of development and dispensers of immense patronage. In Weberian terms their leadership is no longer just traditional or charismatic, it is also becoming increasingly legal-rational. Shaykhs Zayid and Rashid are cases in point. Shaykh Zayid of Abu Dhabi, the UAE president, is basically a bedouin desert chieftain, reputedly more at home around the Buraimi oasis, where he was born in 1917 and grew up. He enjoys the manly pastimes of hunting and riding. The shaykh is respected for his bedouin virtues: simple tastes, strength of character, and impulsive generosity. He remains a tribal leader with a mainly tribal constituency, and he has taken care to observe the consiliar custom of shaykh rule, consulting with tribal notables and making himself accessible to ordinary people. But nobody is more aware than Shaykh Zayid that the tribal character of Abu Dhabi is changing. Native Abu Dhabians are outnumbered by foreigners—mainly expatriate Arab professionals—by two to one, and even the indigenous residents of Abu Dhabi and the neighboring emirates are getting educated and settling down as the petro-money pours in. Accordingly, this ruler has taken up the challenge by modernizing his government and seeking to expand his legitimacy base beyond the classical tribal norms. Lacking a formal education himself, he has brought in a group of highly trained advisers and administrators to handle the emirate's burgeoning governmental revenues and activities.

Shaykh Rashid of Dubai is no less respected and if anything even more adaptable to change than Shaykh Zayid, but the style is different. He belongs to the Al bu Falasa, another section of the Bani Yas tribe, which seceded from Abu Dhabi in 1833.[49] Whereas Shaykh Zayid is a tribal leader, Shaykh Rashid is more the Levantine entrepreneur, more cosmopolitan than heroic. According to one of his high-ranking subordinates, there is a saying in Dubai that Shaykh Rashid knows what every citizen has in his stomach. Indeed, the ruler observes with a microscopic eye the affairs of his little principality. For example, during a two-hour interview with a visitor the ruler's financial adviser received three telephone calls from Shaykh Rashid: the first was an

49. Ibid., p. 339.

inquiry over a temporary electrical power failure. If it had been planned, the ruler wanted to know, why hadn't he been notified in advance? A second call was to warn that there would be a very severe rainstorm shortly, and there was. The third was to alert the proper department that His Highness had observed a power pylon in danger of falling. Attention to detail, however, does not distract Shaykh Rashid from weightier matters. Long before commercial oil production started in 1969 he had developed Dubai into a prosperous commercial center whose principal receipts were derived from the import and export of gold. Although he too lacks formal schooling, he is widely regarded in Dubai, by local people and foreigners alike, as most astute in international finance and trade and a capable administrator as well. The ruler's typical daily schedule, as recounted by one of his aides, reveals another important facet of his personalist leadership style—his accessibility. He rises every morning at 6 A.M., before anybody else is up, and after prayers takes an inspection drive around the town. Then, after coffee, he is off to the office for a morning of routine royal duties: receiving distinguished visitors and petitioners, checking the status of various projects, and signing checks (for he handles the shaykhdom's financial affairs personally). After lunch and two hours of rest or reading, Shaykh Rashid turns his attention to new projects and planning, and in the evening there are usually a couple of dinner parties.

While the personal leadership of the shaykhs is central to the evolving legitimacy in the emirates, scarcely less important is the development of more elaborate structures for administration and, to a limited extent, participation. Both the royal and the technocratic sectors of the elite seem convinced that future legitimacy will depend upon the building of a modern governmental apparatus. In Abu Dhabi, Shaykh Zayid decreed a major reorganization of the emirate's government in July 1971. One decree established a Council of Ministers with a prime minister. It also streamlined the administration from a conglomerate of twenty-eight offices, each directly responsible to the ruler, to fifteen ministries responsible first to the Council of Ministers and ultimately, of course, to the ruler himself.[50] In Dubai, Shaykh Rashid's administrative structure has been simpler and perhaps more efficient. It consists of three offices: the ruler's office, the Department of Ruler's and

50. The text is found in Abu Dhabi, Ministry of Information and Tourism, "Decrees and Laws Reorganizing the Government Structure in Abu Dhabi," 1971. For an analysis, see Christian Dallaporta, "Les Transferts institutionnels et politiques dans l'Emirat D'Abou Dhabi (1)," *Politique Etrangère*, 6 (1974), pp. 689–717; esp. pp. 691–97.

Petroleum Affairs which is responsible for income, and the Central Accounts section which keeps track of expenditures. In 1972, Mahdi Tajir, a Bahraini, was in charge of Ruler's and Petroleum Affairs, and W. R. Duff, an Englishman, was in charge of Central Accounts. Other high-ranking officials are Palestinian and Indian. All are responsible solely to Shaykh Rashid. But growth has necessitated an expansion of this compact administration. To the basic offices of customs, courts, passports, post office, and police were added, in the 1960s, the municipality, central accounts, water supply, and the state engineer; in 1970–71 public health, sewage, and civil aviation were added. The shaykh's major public works projects, the hospital, the port enlargement, and the international airport, added more infrastructure. In the smaller emirates the administrative structures are far more rudimentary than in Abu Dhabi or Dubai.

With the establishment of the Federation, a new structural layer has been grafted onto the traditional emirate governments. The highest executive body is the Supreme Council, consisting of the rulers of each emirate (with one vote apiece) and presided over by Shaykh Zayid, with Shaykh Rashid as vice-president. Below this is the Council of Ministers which is gradually taking over most of the functions of the local emirate administrations, not without some confusion. A particularly important step was the creation of a union defense force in addition to the local armed forces. In December 1973 a single federal cabinet was formed and the local (Abu Dhabi) cabinet abolished. The premier was Maktum, son of Shaykh Rashid, and the deputy premier was Khalifa, the son of Shaykh Zayid. Its large size—twenty-seven portfolios—reflected the need for broad representation; at least sixteen ministers were from the various ruling families, but certain key ministries were manned by able technocrats such as Ahmad al-Suwaydi (foreign affairs) and Mana Sa'id al-Utayba (oil and minerals).[51]

Structural development in the realm of participation has lagged behind bureaucratization, and the UAE has been more cautious in this respect than Kuwait or Bahrain. Nevertheless, beginning in 1971, certain steps were taken to strengthen system legitimacy in terms of popular representation. In Abu Dhabi, at the same time he reorganized his administration, Shaykh Zayid also decreed the creation of a National Consultative Council consisting of fifty "notables of the country, who are reputed for their sound judgement and standing, and those who have rendered distinguished services to their country."[52]

51. For the list, see "Chronology," *Middle East Journal*, 28, 2 (Spring 1974), p. 167.
52. Abu Dhabi, Ministry of Information and Tourism, "Decrees and Laws" op. cit., Article 1.

Its functions were to discuss topics of public interest and advise the Council of Ministers, but it has no autonomous power. In Dubai, the representative process was more informal, consisting of a kind of "kitchen cabinet" of notables to whom Shaykh Rashid would turn for advice. At the federal level, the provisional constitution (itself a major innovation) established a Federal National Council, consisting of forty delegates nominated by the rulers of each emirate. Abu Dhabi and Dubai were allotted eight seats each, Sharja and Ras al-Khayma six each, and the remaining emirates four each. Its powers too were limited to recommendations concerning legislation prepared by the Council of Ministers.

Turning to the ideological basis of legitimacy in the emirates, we do not find a formal ideological code designed to generate acceptance of the existing authorities. But certain widely held values are appealed to by the shaykhs. Most basic and obvious is the customary deference accorded to the traditional leading families. Islam is also stressed, although the social impact is less evident in Abu Dhabi and especially Dubai than in Sa'udi Arabia. Not only is the piety of the ruling family taken for granted, Islam is the official religion, according to chapter I, article 7, of the UAE provisional constitution of 1972, and the Islamic Shari'a is the "principal source" of law.[53] Arabism is emphasized even more strongly, for article 6 proclaims the UAE to be a part of the great Arab homeland (watan) and its people to be a part of the Arab nation (umma). Arabic, of course, is the official language of the state. Furthermore, a visitor to Abu Dhabi and the other shaykhdoms is struck by the enthusiasm and intensity of the commitment to Arabism, not in its secular or socialistic forms but as a primordial ethnic identification; indeed, it seems stronger and less complicated than in the urban heartland of Arabism—the Fertile Crescent and Egypt. The shaykhdoms have contributed hundreds of millions of dollars ($600 million to Egypt alone, 1973–75) for the Arab struggle against Israel. To be sure, it is prudent for the rulers of tiny, rich shaykhdoms to demonstrate their legitimacy to powerful and potentially hostile constituencies in the Arab world beyond their borders, but their generosity is more than the paying of protection money. Two additional factors must be considered: expatriate Arab influence and the conception of legitimacy held by the ruling families themselves. It is true that domestic public opinion, of any structured type, is very weak in most of the shaykhdoms, the principal exceptions being Kuwait and Bahrain. And in all of them

53. "The Provisional Constitution of the United Arab Emirates," (in Arabic), Abu Dhabi, mimeographed, July 18, 1971.

(and to a lesser extent in Sa'udi Arabia), there is a substantial expatriate population, including a large proportion of non-Arabs such as Baluchis, Iranians, and Pakistanis, which is relatively apolitical and certainly not committed to Arabism. Even the Arab expatriates generally refrain from politics, especially the poor Yemeni laborers. But the thousands of middle-class Egyptian, Lebanese, and Palestinian professionals and businessmen exert an indirect politicizing effect. Many are school-teachers and others are skilled government employees; all of them, particularly the Palestinians, carry values, perspectives, experiences, and even simple information, that are influencing the traditional political world views in Arabia.

The second factor is the traditional conception of honor held by the ruling families themselves. They perceive themselves as Arabs, with all the obligations that this entails in terms of brotherhood, mutual assistance, and honor. Public (nonelite) opinion may indeed be ill-formed, but the rulers must also observe the values held by the family elite, and these constitute another distinct source of Arabism's salience as a legitimizing principle in the Arabian patriarchies.

The shaykhdoms of the UAE in the middle 1970s appeared to enjoy strong legitimacy based on personal leadership, kinship, custom, and religion. Arabism is serving as a legitimizing bridge, because of its salience both to the traditional and modern sectors. That ethno-religious Arabism will have to give way to secular-socialist Arabism as the mobilized sectors expand is a distinct possibility, but whether secular-socialist Arabism will be as supportive of patriarchal rule is more problematical. As for the modern values—social justice, develop-ment and democracy—so far they have not been very salient. Like the other petro-kingdoms, the shaykhdoms of the UAE certainly are developing the capability for rapid economic and social welfare development. The principal inequality lies between citizens and non-citizens. But two questions remain unanswered. One is the unity of the federation itself. Following the renewal of the provisional constitution in December 1976, the prospects were for a further integration of administrative and political structures. An important step in that direction was Shaykh Rashid's agreement in the spring of 1976 to integrate the Dubai Defense Force into the federal army. Nevertheless, traditional and generational cleavages among the amirs still exist, and the interests of particular emirates are not always congruent with those of the Federation. The other question involves political participation. So far there has been little demand for democracy, either on the elite or mass level. In the UAE it is still not clear how representative structures will develop. As of the middle 1970s the radical movement for the liberation of the Gulf had caused only sporadic and minor disturbances. But if Bahrain and Kuwait are any example, it is likely that demands will arise for parties, elections, and a more participant political life. One may see the emergence of coalitions of nonroyal notables cutting across the old emirate boundaries. Already the influence and the constituency of figures like Ahmad al-Suwaydi, whom many consider one of the most powerful men in the federation, or the multimillionaire Mahdi Tajir exists on a federationwide basis and might serve as the precursor of more formalized structures of interest, articulation, and aggregation. Eventually, it would seem, some further elaboration of institutionalized participation will be necessary.

Oman

The sultanate of Oman shares the tip of the Masandam peninsula with the UAE. It also shares a turbulent history and a traditional patriarchal form of government. But in terms of developing a viable legitimacy formula for the late twentieth century, Oman's situation is considerably more difficult than that of the emirates. The personal legitimacy of the sultan is relatively precarious; his regime has been out of step with ideological currents in the Arab world; and the structure of his government has been too rudimentary and intermittent to generate much system legitimacy across such a vast (up to 100,000 square miles) and rugged territory.

Until the family coup of July 23, 1970, when Qabus ibn Sa'id succeeded his xenophobic father as sultan, Oman was the most isolated polity in the Arab world. Virtually devoid of infrastructure, communications routes, social services, and education, the sultanate's political life continued to be governed by clan and tribal factionalism overlaid with religious sectarianism. The rugged mountainous interior of the Jabal Akhdar range and the monsoon-fed jungle country of Dhofar facilitated the persistence of these traditional divisions and frustrated political integration and centralization. Nevertheless, Oman could not remain unaffected by the quest for oil, which was discovered in commercial quantities in 1967. Furthermore, traditional conflicts with outside powers like the Sa'udis and the Qasimis of the Trucial States were intensified during and after the 1950s by the ideological convulsions in the Arab world and the increasingly important quest for oil. The discovery of oil in commercial quantities in the hinterland of Oman added an entirely new dimension to Oman's internal cleavages and its regional strategic position. The implications for political system legitimacy were considerable: a country whose society and political values in the 1970s were probably much like Morocco or Transjordan at the turn of the century was now catapulted into the age of Marxist liberation movements and electronic warfare.

Even without the shock of modernization, the nature of the political identity and legitimacy in Oman has been contested and continually redefined over the centuries. The latest redefinition occurred with the accession of Sultan Qabus: he changed the name of the state from the Sultanate of Muscat and Oman to the Sultanate of Oman. The change symbolized his stress on integrating the entire territory under his rule and minimizing the historic cleavage between the hinterland of Oman and the coastal areas directly ruled by the sultan in Muscat. It is true that the ruling Al bu Sa'id family is one of the oldest continuous dynasties in the world, its reign dating from 1749; but its rule has been persistently challenged, particularly from the tribal chieftains of the interior around Nizwa, who have long struggled to maintain a politically autonomous imamate—an Ibadhi theocracy.

On the structural level this regional cleavage has involved traditional tribal coalitions. Roughly speaking, one faction was a federation led by the Bani Hina and composed by Yemeni tribes originally from southern Arabia and linked epogynously to Qahtan; the other was led by the Bani Ghafir and consisted of the Nizari tribes from northern Arabia who are descended by legend from Adnan. The former was largely Ibadhi, the latter largely Sunni. In modern times this classical distinction has become blurred because certain tribes have shifted their allegiance, but the process of coalition formation along tribal lines remains, even though legendary ancestry and sectarian affiliation have become overlaid with some startlingly modern ideological identifications.

The Al bu Sa'ids, while Ibadhis themselves, have traditionally been more secular and outward-looking in their values and interested in developing power through sea trade. The greatest of the Al bu Sa'id kings, Sayyid Sa'id ibn Sultan (1806–56) actually moved his capital to Zanzibar and ruled a territory that included parts of the coast of East Africa and southern Persia as well as Dhofar and coastal Oman. The Ibadhi sect dates to the earliest days of Islam and the first Ibadhi imams established themselves in the Jabal Akhdar early in the ninth century. Ibadhism, an offshoot of the Kharijite movement, has been described by one active observer of contemporary Oman as "Presbyterian" in comparison to the fundamentalism of Wahhabi Islam: there are few points of doctoral difference, and both are rather more austere than the mainstream of orthodox Islam. In the complex series of invasions and fluctuations of tribal coalition rule that Oman has known over the centuries, the fortunes of the Ibadhi imamate have waxed and waned, but one of its high points was in the seventeenth century under the Ya'ariba imams. After a civil war that had precipitated a Persian invasion, the Al bu Sa'ids took over the imamate and drove out the Persians, but, as we have seen, this family in turn became estranged from the Ibadhi leaders of the interior. Another period of unrest occurred at the end of the nineteenth century, and a new imam from the interior challenged the dominion of the Al bu Sa'id sultans Faisal and Taymur. Britain, now actively concerned to keep the approaches to India in friendly hands, supported the sultan in checking the challenge of the imam and the tribal leaders behind him; and by the Treaty of Sib (1920) the sultan's nominal suzerainty over the interior was acknowledged in return for guarantees of the free movement of goods (at low duty) and people between the interior and the coast. Though rather vague in its delineation of authority, this arrangement led to a period of relative internal peace until the 1950s.[54] When in 1949 Sa'udi Arabia renewed its claims to the Buraimi oasis (to which the shaykhdom of Abu Dhabi also held a claim), the old struggle broke out again. Moreover, geologists now suspected there were oil deposits in the adjacent area. The new imam, Ghalib ibn Ali and his brother Talib allied themselves with the Sa'udis against Sultan Sa'id ibn Taymur, hoping to divert the expected oil revenues from the interior. In 1952 the Sa'udis, with the encouragement of American oil interests, occupied part of the Buraimi oasis area, and in 1954 Imam Ghalib proclaimed an independent Ibadhi state and pressed for membership in the Arab League. British-led forces acting in the name of Abu Dhabi and Muscat and Oman expelled the Sa'udis in 1955, and at the end of that year the sultan of Muscat and Oman made an historic journey through the interior to Buraimi to reassert his somewhat cloudy authority.[55] Temporarily defeated, the rebel leaders fell back upon Sa'udi Arabia, Egypt, and the Arab League to press their case through diplomacy, and in 1957 Ghalib's Oman Liberation Army opened up a major rebellion. Again the British-supported forces of the sultan prevailed and the rebellion was crushed within two years. But in 1963 rebellion broke out yet again, this time in Dhofar, the southern-

54. On the history of Oman, see Robert Geran Landen, *Oman Since 1856: Disruptive Modernization in a Traditional Arab Society* (Princeton: Princeton University Press, 1967); also Joseph J. Malone, *The Arab Lands of Western Asia* (Englewood Cliffs, N. J.: Prentice-Hall, 1973), pp. 211–24.

55. The expedition is vividly chronicled in James Morris, *Sultan in Oman* (London: Faber, 1957).

most province, which was gradually taken over, not by religious
leaders but by Marxist-nationalists. Once more, British mercenaries
and military assistance were pressed into the service of the Al bu Sa'ids,
but the rebellion has continued inconclusively into the middle 1970s,
placing a substantial drain on the sultanate's budget.

The concept of political system with its Western connotations can be
misleading when applied to Oman inasmuch as it suggests a distinct
territorial sovereignty, political coherence, and common membership
in the polity. Until recently, Oman has shown few of these qualities.
Thus it is hard to speak of political legitimacy in the normal sense,
supportive of a nation-state entity. Notwithstanding the long, continuous rule of the Al bu Sa'id dynasty, the high fragmentation of the
country, socially and culturally, and the virtual absence of socializing
institutions like schools have required a very high coercive content in
the maintenance of the sultan's authority. Certainly, however, the
trend in the twentieth century has been toward the improvement of
the coercive capabilities of the sultan, the extension of his authority
in the country and with it a degree of legitimacy. But the legitimacy
base of the system is very small and almost exclusively rooted in the
family's longevity in rule. It can claim little religious legitimacy
inasmuch as the hinterland rebels have historically been able to
preempt that value. And its successes in expanding its control have
depended very heavily upon outside British support. The reign of
Sultan Sa'id ibn Taymur during the eventful period from 1932 to 1970
was marked by a degree of absolutism and isolationism probably without parallel. It was one of the most successful and resolute efforts by
any ruler to prevent modernization and so provides one of the purest
real-world tests of the proposition that a monarch can buy stability by
retarding modernization. For four decades the stratagem (if that is
what it was) worked well: it bought precious time to build the authority
of the sultanate and to enhance the possibility that its legitimacy might
also increase. But it had its costs. One was that by the 1960s the old
sultan himself, formidable ruler that he was, was so isolated that he
failed to perceive the dimensions of political change in the area.

The Dhofar rebellion crystallized the dilemma. When the British
realized that the sultan was an increasingly vulnerable "reactionary"
target, they arranged for his son to succeed him in hopes that the son
would be able to cope with these new political challenges more
effectively. But the son is now left, so to speak, holding the tail of a tiger.
To reverse strategies and try to master rather than dam up the currents
of modernization is risky because the old strategy placed the family in
conflict with nearly every modern legitimacy resource. At odds with

important forces in the Arab world, conservative as well as revolutionary, the sultanate cannot easily exploit Arabism as a bridge to
modern legitimacy as most of the other patriarchies have sought to do.
The inordinate dependence upon British military and civil advisers,
even after Britain's formal withdrawal from its position of influence
east of Suez in 1971, placed the regime in a vulnerable position. The
solicitation of Iranian counterinsurgency forces to maintain the road
to Salala in Dhofar may have been tactically successful but costly in
terms of legitimacy. With respect to the legitimizing values arising out
of modernization—development, social justice, and democracy—
the legacy of the old sultan is particularly negative. Little wonder that
in the early 1970s the highest priority was being placed on internal
modernization. British and American development experts were
working energetically to improve the regime's capabilities for housing,
health, education, light industry, and of course defense. For a civil
service of only 4,300 it was a formidable task, considering that up to an
estimated 90 percent of the national income was distributed among the
10 percent of the population in the Muscat-Matrah area, and that
nearly half the government budget (some 3 million out of 6.4 million
Omani rials in 1971) was spent on defense. Fortunately for the government, the price of oil increased fourfold between 1972 and 1974. At the
same time Chinese support for the Dhofar rebels sharply diminished
as Peking sought to improve its relations with Iran. It seemed possible,
therefore, that the sultanate might be able to afford both guns for
Dhofar and butter for development.

But many uncertainties remained. There was some concern among
some of the sultan's advisers whether the young monarch, whom they
hoped would develop into a strong leader like King Hussein of Jordan,
possessed the strength of character necessary to carry the regime
through its difficult circumstances. Although Qabus appeared to be a
benevolent and popular ruler, he was also known to be at times
moody and introverted and at others impulsively extravagant. In 1975
the Western press reported that the sultanate was overspending on
development projects at a time when world oil consumption was falling
off. Oil revenues account for 95 percent of the government budget.[56]
While the rebellion in Dhofar was officially declared crushed in
December 1975, it was still not dead, and the sultan's use of Iranian
troops to combat it was bitterly opposed in Arab nationalist circles.
Similarly, the continuing British presence on the Masira island base

56. According to an economic survey prepared for the sultanate in 1972 by the Whitehead
Consulting Group, a British firm.

and in the officer corps of the sultan's armed forces cast a certain shadow over regime legitimacy, as did the sultanate's growing relationship with the American military and intelligence community. Occasional acts of sabotage in the Muscat-Matrah area and reports of government arrests and executions indicated a degree of subversive ferment. The sultan needed to neutralize or come to terms with populist and nationalist ideological currents without undermining the traditional bases of his own personal legitimacy. And over the long run he faced the difficult task of trying to build structural capabilities for development and participation, difficult because of the socio-economic stresses and demands which will be an inevitable part of Oman's very rapid modernization.

THE HASHIMITE KINGDOM OF JORDAN

The considerable success in building legitimacy which we have observed in the Arabian desert kingdoms is due not only to strong leadership happily united with technocracy. It also depends on two important environmental factors. One is the relatively unpoliticized character of their rather sparse, tribal-oriented populations. Education and exposure to modernity—and to political ideologies subversive of patriarchal rule—have begun to spread only recently. The other is wealth. Oil revenues have sharply accelerated the growth of central government with all its security and surveillance apparatus, its educational and propaganda facilities, and its substantial services and patronage. While modernization is fraught with future dangers for the monarchs, it has certainly facilitated their coming to terms with the present.

I turn now, however, to two Arab monarchies in which these two conditions do not carry the same positive weight. In Jordan and Morocco, there is less wealth and there are larger and more politicized populations. These societies are also less homogeneous than the desert kingdoms in terms of primordial affiliations and national identifications. Over half of Jordan is Palestinian, and Morocco has long experienced dissidence between the mountain people of Berber background and the Arab culture of the coast. Consequently, for Kings Hussein and Hassan the monarch's dilemma is particularly acute. Yet in spite of difficult circumstances these two regimes have survived and, to a limited degree, gained ground over the forces that deny their legitimacy and seek to destroy them. In trying to understand how they have, so to speak, beaten the odds against them, at least for the present, the factor of personal legitimacy—strong, authoritative leadership— is even more crucial than in the oil kingdoms. One also senses a greater reliance on the instruments of repression and coercion because of the existence of politicized elements actively opposed to the system—notably student and labor groups. Each regime has sought as well to inculcate ideological legitimacy to counteract antiroyalist doctrines. The Hashimites have emphasized, in addition to their sharifian status, their role in the Arab nationalist movement. King Hassan tries to project his religious sanctity to the pious masses of Morocco as well as the legacy of his illustrious father's role in the struggle for independence from France. Each appeals selectively both to the traditional elements and the new, educated elites by invoking, on the one hand, sacred and primordial symbols and, on the other, by taking the lead in the material development of their societies.

Nowhere are the paradoxes of Arab legitimacy more apparent than in Jordan. Every positive legitimizing asset casts a shadow of negativism. How can a political system created only recently (1922), and almost fortuitously by British diplomats as a byproduct of more important strategic decisions find legitimacy as an indigenous, traditional polity? The task has not been easy, and the kingdom has suffered chronic tension and subversion; but it has survived the assaults of internal antiroyalist groups, external Arab states, Israel, and—most recently in 1970–71—organized, armed, militant Palestinian nationalists. It has also confounded numerous economic experts who have solemnly decreed that the state was "not viable." And yet, after having suffered the amputation of the West Bank in 1967 at the hand of Israel and the pyrrhic victory over the Palestinian fida'iyin in "Black September" 1970, the Jordanian government discovered a new Jordanian nationalism based on east Jordanian tribal and Islamic values, loyalty to the royal family and to the king's army, and more pertinently, cleansed of Palestinian, pan-Arab, and progressive ideologies. This rather bitter redefinition of political community—particularist, isolationst, anachronistic—was replete with ironies, coming as it did from the family that launched the Arab revolt against Turkey in 1916 and that for decades sought to monopolize the Arab national movement and create a great Arab state in the Fertile Crescent. But the question of legitimacy and identity in Jordan must be treated in the context of the rise and decline of the whole Hashimite family in modern Arab politics. And the fortunes of the family—once the amirs of Hijaz and the Islamic Holy Places, and the monarchs of Iraq, West Bank Palestine, and Transjordan—are in turn linked to the fortunes and misfortunes of the British in the Arab east. This Western connection, in which the Americans succeeded the British, has proved to be the curse as well as the lifeline of the royal family.

A Traditional Desert Emirate

There is no doubt that the Hashimites can stake out impressive claims to the three pillars of traditional legitimacy that I have identified: kinship, religion, and historical performance. Indeed, had not their kingdoms become so embroiled with the turmoil of Western penetration and social mobilization, it is possible that they would have attained the political dominions, stability, power, and wealth which their bitter rivals in Arabia, the Sa'ud dynasty of Najd, did in fact achieve in the building of Sa'udi Arabia. The Bani Hashim, a clan of the Quraysh tribe of Mecca, to which Muhammad had belonged, had ruled Mecca and the Hijaz district since the tenth century; of course they bore the aristocratic status of sharifs, and their reputation was further enhanced by their rule over the Holy Places of Islam. There were of course, as we have seen, many sharifs and amirs in Arabia, and indeed throughout the world of Islam; and in the turbulent tribal politics of the peninsula, a family that aspired to rule had continually to prove itself in combat no matter how distinguished its lineage. But the Hashimites were as brave and strong as the rest, and their special status singled them out as rulers with ambitions and potential power well beyond the barren and backward Hijaz. It was not surprising, therefore, that the Hashimites should have introduced themselves to the British in Cairo at the beginning of World War I, and that the British should have taken note of a possible ally against the Turks. For in addition to their military value as a tribal guerrilla force, the Hashimites carried the stamp of Islamic legitimacy and might serve as an ideological counterweight to the sultan-caliph in Constantinople, who had declared a jihad against Britain and its allies.

Secure and even preeminent in the ascribed legitimacy of family and Islam, the Hashimites came to play a regional and international political role far beyond the limited horizons of the Hijaz. The outbreak of war in 1914, involving Britain against Turkey in the Middle East, thrust upon Hussein ibn Ali (great-grandfather of the present Jordanian ruler) an historic opportunity. The sharif and his three sons became the standard-bearers of the hitherto latent Arab nationalism by rising up against the Turkish garrisons of northern Arabia and Syria; in return for this assistance against a mutual enemy Great Britain agreed to support the Hashimites as rulers of an independent Arab kingdom—such was the agreement in the famous but sloppily worded Hussein-McMahon letters of 1915. I have already described how Britain's conflicting wartime commitments aborted the birth of this Arab kingdom. Nevertheless, in an effort to reward at least partially its Hijazi ally (or client), Great Britain did manage to create a kingdom in Mesopotamia (Iraq) for one son, Faisal, after he had been driven out of Damascus by French troops. It was Faisal who was entrusted with ruling the ill-fated Kingdom of Greater Syria, which from late 1918 until July 1920 actually functioned from its capital in Damascus and claimed sovereignty over Palestine and Lebanon. A second son, Abdalla, who had been helpful in linking his father's movement with the secret urban Arab nationalist groups and also in dealing with the British, was rewarded after some delay with the emirate of Transjordan. Until the Cairo Conference of 1921 nobody had ever thought of Transjordan as a political entity, tribal or otherwise. But as Abdalla had settled himself and a tribal force in Ma'an and thus become a potential problem both against British mandate Palestine and French mandate Syria, it was expedient that he also be rewarded and that some formal structures be created east of the Jordan river that would allow a Jewish home in Palestine to develop without the harassment of Arab desert warriors.[57] Thus two Hashimite kingdoms were created, neither on the ancestral territory of the family, and both under the tainted aegis of British imperialism. As for Sharif Hussein himself, he continued to rule the Hijaz from Mecca for six years after the war, but he was unequal to the challenge of Abd al-Aziz ibn Sa'ud and his militant Wahhabi fighters, the Ikhwan. In 1924 the Sa'udis attacked the Hijaz; Hussein abdicated in favor of his son Ali who in turn was driven out by the Sa'udis in December 1925. The Hijaz became part of Sa'udi Arabia, adding new fuel to the traditional conflict between the two royal families, a conflict that would be suspended some three decades later as all monarchies came under fire from the new wave of radical republicanism in the Arab world.[58]

Under King Abdalla the emirate of Transjordan, with a population of less than a half million and largely bedouin enjoyed order and tranquillity until the Palestine upheavals in the 1940s. A British subsidy and the British-officered Arab Legion (whose second commander was the famous Sir John Bagot Glubb "Pasha") contributed to this happy state. The amir was granted a greater degree of autonomy by Great Britain in 1928, although the British after their usual fashion kept the last word on foreign affairs and decisive influence over the

57. On this period, see Sir Alec Kirkbride, *A Crackle of Thorns* (London: John Murray, 1956); and George Antonius, *The Arab Awakening* (London: Hamish Hamilton, 1938, 1961).

58. James Morris, *The Hashemite Kings* (New York: Pantheon, 1959), provides an insightful portrait of all three generations of the monarchs, both in Jordan and Iraq, and their problems.

treasury. The king also proclaimed a constitution which formalized his absolute authority in internal matters. Full independence was granted in 1946 and a new constitution was written.

Modernization and Challenges to Legitimacy

The political system of Jordan was dramatically transformed after the 1948 Arab-Israeli war. The Arab Legion had managed to hold the West Bank and the eastern part of Jerusalem (including the old city with its Holy Places), and in December a conference of West Bank notables met in Jericho to proclaim Abdalla the king of Palestine; by 1950 Abdalla had formally annexed the territory and the emirate had a new name—Jordan. But the period of tranquillity was over. The new state now had a mixed population of largely sedentary and better educated Palestinians, on the one hand, and a traditional desert tribal society, on the other, which greatly complicated the ruling family's legitimacy problem. Middle-class, educated Palestinians of Jerusalem and the other West Bank towns who had thought of Transjordan as a desert backwater (if they thought of it at all) and who had never seen any reason to visit Amman, now found themselves subjects of the Hashimite king. Transjordanian tribal leaders and village notables, imbued with the values of the desert kinship society and Islam, looked with equal disdain on the devious Palestinians and with some apprehension at their penetration of Jordanian administration and society. In fairness, it must be added that these unflattering stereotypes remained mainly latent and that there were many linguistic, cultural, commercial, religious, and familial bonds linking the people on either side of the Jordan, so the two groups were far from alien to one another. Nevertheless, the sense of regionalism with its undertones of the classical Middle Eastern distinction between the desert and the settled societies, did pose a political problem.

This problem was compounded by the legitimacy problems on the external level.[59] Isolated for two decades from the quiet but deep-running currents of Arab nationalism, Transjordan had been able to exist relatively untroubled as a desert shaykhdom, very much the way in which several of Britain's Arabian Gulf shaykhdoms existed into the 1960's. But as the Palestinian conflict between Jews and Arabs moved toward its climax, the emirate found itself sucked back into the maelstrom of Arab national ferment from which it had emerged in World War I. Only now the situation was more difficult. We have

---

59. The importance of external factors is stressed by Naseer H. Aruri in *Jordan: A Study in Political Development (1921–1965)* (The Hague: Martinus Nijhoff, 1972), part 3.

noted how certain Arab Gulf shaykhdoms have managed with some success to exploit Arabism as a bridge between traditional and modern legitimacy, Kuwait being the outstanding case. But for the Hashimites in Jordan the matter was more complex because Jordan was no mere bystander to the Palestinian trauma; it was directly involved. Against the creditable showing of the Arab Legion in the 1948 fighting had to be weighed the debit of the close Hashimite association with Great Britain, universally regarded as the midwife of the State of Israel.[60] Furthermore, the rivalries among the newly independent Arab states, now envenomed by their disastrous performance against the Jews, meant that the regime's Arab nationalist credentials were certain to be loudly challenged by competitors. From Egypt, Syria, and even Sa'udi Arabia, malicious observations were made about how the same family that won two kingdoms out of the defeat of Arab nationalism in World War I had now joined the new Jewish state in the partition of Palestine. Suspicions deepened as word got out about King Abdalla's secret postwar meetings with Golda Meir. This is not the place to assess the validity of competing claims to the mantle of true Arab nationalism, except perhaps to remark that there was little honor to be shared at all. To this day loyal followers of the Hashimites insist that it is they who kindled the flame and carried the torch, seeking realistic goals through pragmatism rather than empty and inflammatory ideological ranting. In any case, it is clear that for Jordan the issue of fidelity to Arab nationalism—and Palestine was the core issue at stake—was highly salient and that the family's record was, inevitably, a mixed one.

The achievement of modernity, I have suggested, can itself be a legitimizing factor, and on this criterion the political system of Jordan also has come to show mixed results. In terms of material development the performance was good. After 1948, the integration of eastern Jerusalem and the West Bank and thousands of skilled Palestinians into the kingdom led to a development boom. The boom was substantially facilitated by British and American and a small amount of outside Arab aid and investment. Jordan ranked number one among all countries in terms of U.S. aid per capita, $226 between 1958 and 1965, and the total of combined military and economic aid came to $447 million.[61] Confounding the economic pessimists, Jordan experienced a

60. See Sir John Bagot Glubb, *A Soldier with the Arabs* (London: Hodder and Stoughton, 1957).

61. Charles L. Taylor and Michael C. Hudson, *World Handbook of Political and Social Indicators*, Second Edition (New Haven: Yale University Press, 1972), p. 207.

rate of economic growth of 9.3 percent annually between 1960 and 1965. The city of Amman nearly doubled between 1952 and 1961, increasing from 218,000 to 433,000.[62] Tourism on the West Bank, agriculture and light manufacturing on the East Bank, and the development of good roads and communication brought an unprecedented level of prosperity to the kingdom. Travelers between Lebanon and Jordan by way of Damascus during the 1960s often observed that Jordan was more visibly developed than Syria even though the latter country in theory had greater development potential. The loss of the West Bank to Israel in 1967 of course was a severe blow to development capabilities. Yet, as we saw in the previous chapter, Jordan's development in the middle 1970s has been dramatic. Jordan's competent administration and planning and its development accomplishments no doubt lent a certain legitimacy to the system.

But in terms of the nonmaterial values associated with modernization, the system's performance was less impressive: there was little progress made toward greater social justice or redistribution of wealth —no major land reform, no progressive taxation, and few curbs on private enterprise aside from the informal patronage and influence dispensed by the family itself and its closest retainers. The privileges of Jordan's wealthy commercial and landed class have been preserved, not tempered. Indeed, free enterprise ("the freedom to acquire property, the right of ownership, and the right to work") is one of the three main rights written into the Jordan constitution.[63] While the prerogative of the government to direct and regulate the economy is also stated, the thrust of this right of free enterprise is clearly the dominant theme, and as such is opposed to ideologies calling for state action to redistribute wealth. It must be added, however, that despite considerable material inequalities in income and land distribution[64] there has been little manifest public dissatisfaction with social conditions (unrest has focused on political frustrations), particularly in comparison with several neighboring countries. The regime's unprogressiveness in this domain, therefore, has probably not seriously eroded system legitimacy. Two sectors from which a serious threat

62. J. I. Clarke and W. B. Fisher (eds.), *Populations of the Middle East and North Africa* (New York: Africana Publishing Corporation, 1972), p. 207.

63. Hashimite Kingdom of Jordan, Ministry of Culture and Infromation, *The Government of Jordan* (Amman, 1973), pp. 1–5.

64. Taylor and Hudson, op. cit., p. 263; Raphael Patai, *The Kingdom of Jordan* (Princeton: Princeton University Press, 1958), pp. 121–23.

could emerge—the tribes and the army—receive generous patronage, salaries and other benefits; and the regime makes a special effort to emphasize their political status by giving their representatives privilaged access to the palace.

The legitimacy crisis in Jordan is political, not social. The monarchy has resisted the determined efforts of various politicized elements— Arab nationalists, Ba'thists, and Palestinian nationalists—for meaningful participation and power sharing. Formally, Jordan is a constitutional monarchy, but in fact the king holds absolute power. There is a parliament but its autonomy has been minimal, and except for a brief period in the middle 1950s, political parties have been banned. Because political crises, arising usually out of the Arab-Israel question or inter-Arab politics, have been so frequent, martial law has been more the rule in Jordan than the exception: specifically, the years 1957–63, 1966–67, and 1970–73 were periods of martial law (the king of course is commander-in-chief of the army). In 1976 pro-Palestinian critics of Syria were summarily (though temporarily) jailed. It may be objected that interpreting Jordanian absolutism as a drain on system legitimacy involves a double or even triple standard of evaluation, considering that every other patriarchal system in the Arab world is also absolutist—and yet some, at least, seem to be regarded as more legitimate than the Hashimite family is in Jordan. Furthermore, as one high Jordanian official, who was formerly a Ba'thist sympathizer, pointed out in an interview, Jordan's government is surely no more absolutist than those of neighboring Arab republics ruled by military officers. The necessity for periods of strict control, he noted, was due to crisis situations originating outside the country. But Jordan is more thoroughly socially mobilized than the other monarchies: its stock of educated people, its exposure to modern political values, and its political experiences in the maelstrom of conflict and revolution have intensified the salience of democracy as a legitimizing principle. Apart from the chronic precariousness of the monarchy, as indicated by nearly constant crisis and numerous assassination attempts, the fact that the King and the ruling circles have themselves gone so far in giving the kingdom a constitutional and parliamentary *form* of government is indicative of the importance attached to participatory values. As for the dictatorial character of neighboring systems that are republican in form, that point must readily be granted; indeed, I shall argue below that the value dissonance between form and reality in the modern systems is very much a drain on their legitimacy too, particularly in those in which social mobilization has penetrated the sectors of potential counter-elite development.

Coping with the Challenges

Jordan's legitimacy problem can be observed from the local and national levels. In his valuable study of politics in Karak in southern Jordan, Peter Gubser finds an inconsistency in the monarchy's approach to legitimizing itself with the local people.[65] On the one hand, the king inculcates loyalty to himself through the traditional mechanism of dispensing patronage to the shaykhs and tribal notables. On the other hand, he projects himself as a modern leader whose authority rests theoretically on representative institutions and whose central government provides tangible services. But few people believe the parliament to be representative because of the evident corruption in the electoral process. There are, according to Gubser, two contradictions in the Hashimite approach: first, parliament is the symbol of democracy but is perceived as nonrepresentative; hence its contribution to system legitimacy is minimal. Second, "the combination of traditional and modern systems of political authority, i.e. tribal and state, creates confusion as to where authority is supposed to lie."[66] Looking at Jordan's political processes from the national, whole-system perspective, Naseer Aruri observes that

> whereas the task of state-building was achieved in a few days, that of nation-building remains unfulfilled until the present day. Jordan stands out as a state by virtue of its monopoly of the instruments of violence, its power to settle disputes, and allocate goods, services, and values. But it is not a nation since this power has never been a consensual one. Jordan has not been able to develop a consensus as to the legitimate means and ends of political action.[67]

While this is tantamount to asserting that the system is fundamentally illegitimate, an opinion that is perhaps exaggerated, there can be no disputing the cleavages that divide the Jordanian family within itself and from its putative father. The suppression of the Arab nationalist government of Sulayman Nabulsi in 1957 and the curtailing of political freedoms indicated serious disaffection within the two-thirds of the population that is Palestinian, sedentary, and educated. Another round of rioting occurred in 1963 and 1964 as Jordan refused to support the Arab unity campaign in Egypt, Syria, and Iraq. In late 1966 and early

---

65. Peter Gubser, *Politics and Change in Al-Karak, Jordan* (London: Oxford University Press, 1973), chap. 5, esp. pp. 149–52.

66. Ibid., p. 150.

67. Aruri, op. cit., p. 187.

1967, following Israeli border raids, civil unrest among Palestinians in the West Bank cities of Jerusalem, Nablus, and Hebron resulted in harsh suppression by the royal army. After the catastrophic Six-Day War, the rise of an organized Palestinian national movement came to pose the severest challenge of all to Hashimite authority. As the Palestinian organizations went about building up a structural base from which to attack Israel, they created "a state within a state" in Jordan. Finally, in Black September 1970, the royalist officers and tribal army, led by Sharif Nasir and Habis al-Majali, assaulted the Palestinian urban strongholds, resulting in some 4,000 deaths, and eventually drove the guerrillas out of Jordan. Since then Jordan has returned to normal, but domestic political activities and press freedom have remained curtailed. Borrowing a leaf from the authoritarian revolutionary regimes, a government-sponsored single party, the National Union, was established in 1972, but its effectiveness, like that of the other representative structures, seems marginal. But few Jordanians (and even fewer Palestinians in Jordan) doubt the effectiveness of the *mukhabarat*, the royal intelligence apparatus.

In light of all this past instability and bitterness, the only possible conclusion would seem to be that the last remaining kingdom of the Hashimites can only survive by coercion. But the reality is more complex, and there are two factors which mitigate an otherwise praetorian situation. Despite all that has happened the king retains significant personal legitimacy. Some of his popularity, ironically, appears to arise from the fact that he has survived so many challenges. By surmounting crisis after crisis, King Hussein has acquired a measure of respect which helps support the system itself. There is a strong interrelationship between legitimacy and strength of leadership in the traditional Arab systems. Nowhere is this interrelationship clearer than in the case of the Jordan monarchy. It is thus no accident that the surviving monarchies of the Arab world are ruled by exceptionally strong men. Hussein, moreover, is impressive in his demeanor: although short in stature he is eloquent in Arabic, has a reputation for personal incorruptibility, and is known for his courage and daring. He is an expert marksman, hunter, pilot and athlete. The patriarchal system today owes much of its apparent vitality less to traditional patriarchal values than to the sheer force and intelligence of royal personalities.

The second factor that might ease the Jordan regime's legitimacy crisis is more a potentiality than an existing condition. It falls under the rubric of ideological legitimacy. As we have observed, external events, particularly in inter-Arab politics, have profoundly affected Jordanian legitimacy, usually in a negative way. But on those rare

occasions when the king deemed it politic to align himself with progressive nationalist forces against the British or the Americans, his
popularity mushroomed. After the 1967 Arab-Israeli war, the death
of Nasir in 1970, and especially after the 1973 Arab-Israeli war and
oil boycott, a new climate of optimism appeared briefly in the Arab
world, and a new opportunity arose for Jordan to escape from its past
difficulties. At the summit conference in 1974 at Rabat, the Arab
governments unanimously endorsed the Palestine Liberation Organization's claim to represent the Palestinians in the former Jordanian
West Bank. By acquiescing in this decision, King Hussein went far
toward healing the wounds of Black September. The most dramatic
example of Hussein's flexibility was his movement in 1975 toward
integration with Ba'thist Syria in a number of domains—commerce,
transport, education, tourism, and military policy. According to one
interpretation, the move was a belated effort by Jordan to shoulder
its all-Arab responsibilities by helping shore up the Arab "eastern
front" against Israel. As such it may have been intended to dissipate
the antiroyalist feelings emanating from Arab nationalist and Palestinian elements inside and outside the kingdom. Another interpretation,
however, held that the Jordanian-Syrian rapprochement indicated
less a pan-Arab tilt by King Hussein than a retreat toward "regionalist
isolationism" by the Syrian president, Hafiz al-Asad. Certainly Jordan
stood firmly behind Asad's 1976 intervention in the Lebanese civil war
which seemed designed to muzzle the Palestinian resistance movement.

Whatever the correct interpretation, the events of the middle 1970s
indicated the continuing linkage between the Hashimite regime's
internal legitimacy and the unresolved all-Arab concerns agitating
the immediate region. They also indicated its tactical skill in coping
with these concerns, even though it remained fundamentally hostile
toward militant pan-Arabism and any truly autonomous Palestinian
movement. Barring the always present possibility of a military coup,
either from progressive or conservative officers, or a serious dispute
within the family itself, such as between the king and his powerful
brother Crown Prince Hassan, the prospects for the Hashimites restor-
ing some of their historical legitimacy could not be ruled out.

MOROCCO

On July 10, 1971, the king of Morocco, Hassan II, was giving a party
to celebrate his forty-second birthday at his summer palace at Skhirat
when a force of several hundred military cadets stormed the palace.
Before the abortive coup attempt was contained, 100 of the king's
guests, 350 soldiers, and 10 of the army's 15 generals lay dead. The

king miraculously escaped, by virtue of what some Moroccans termed divine grace (baraka) and others called his remarkable sang-froid.[68] A year later the king incredibly emerged unscathed when his Boeing 727 airliner was attacked in midair by would-be assassins; and in the resulting purge the regime's feared *éminence grise*, Col. Muhammad Oufkir, died by what the government spokesman called self-inflicted gunshot wounds. And less than a year later, on March 3, 1973, the twelfth anniversary of his accession to the throne, yet another abortive plot to overthrow the monarchy—a military revolt in the Middle Atlas mountains and the Sahara Desert—was put down. Perhaps 2,000 arrests were made. As ominous as these events in themselves was the singularly apathetic reaction of the Moroccan people to them. Not that the Moroccan people are naturally undemonstrative. The fervent popular acclaim for Hassan's father, Muhammad V, upon his return from forced exile in France in 1955 stands in dramatic contrast, and the contrast raises questions about the legitimacy of the present monarch and his regime.

Traditional Bases of Legitimacy

Any such inquiry should begin with an appreciation of the unusually fragmented character of Moroccan political culture, a fragmentation perpetuated by the rugged and inaccessible terrain which historically has constituted a barrier for the penetration of centralized government. Morocco in this respect is very much like Iran and Oman. In considering the problem of government and ruler legitimacy in Morocco, therefore, it is helpful to recall the polarities, the passions, and the discontinuities in its society and culture: the historical cleavages between the settled, coastal culture and the mountainous, tribal culture of dissidence; the differences between Berbers and Arabs and among Berbers themselves; and the varieties of Islam, from orthodox and cosmopolitan to mystical and particularist. As Clifford Geertz puts it, describing traditional Morocco,

> the basic style of life . . . was about everywhere the same: strenuous, fluid, violent, visionary, devout, and unsentimental, but above all, self-assertive. It was a society in which a very great deal turned on force of character and most of the rest on spiritual reputation. In town and out, its leitmotivs were strong-man politics and holy-man piety, and its fulfillments, small and large, tribal and dynastic, occurred when, in the person of a particular individual, they momentarily fused.[69]

68. *The Washington Post*, December 12, 1971.
69. Clifford Geertz, *Islam Observed* (New Haven: Yale University Press, 1968), p. 8.

It is not suggested that Morocco is lacking in overall national identity, for the development of nationalism since the 1930s has achieved at least this basic level of integration,[70] but rather that the discontinuities in orientations within this political culture are still very great. Accordingly, the problems for both government and the opposition are unusually difficult.

The resources of traditional monarchical legitimacy, I have suggested, include deference and respect for family rule and for the ruling family, religious rectitude, and the national historical experiences. Theoretically, the king of Morocco should be well endowed in all these respects, more so indeed than several of his more secure royal counterparts further east. In fact, however, the widespread mass apathy and elite hostility toward both the man and the office seems to suggest not only the usual problem of monarchies coming to terms with the legitimacy of modernity, but also an erosion in the traditional resources as well. The Alawite dynasty, as I observed in an earlier chapter, emerged as the ruling family in 1664, and from the core of its territories around Meknes and Fez, it gradually extended and consolidated its rule under the leadership of Sultan Mulay Isma'il (1672–1727)—remarkable military and political feats, considering the anarchy prevailing in this rugged land. In the 300 years of Alawite ascendency there have been many periods of instability and almost constant challenges (for instability too is a tradition in Morocco); and in 1912 the sultan, although he did not lose his office, was forced to submit to the French protectorate. Nevertheless, it can be said that this is a dynasty with roots in Moroccan history; compared to the Hashimite monarchies in Jordan and Iraq which date from the early 1920s, the Alawites of Morocco may be designated truly traditional.

The Islamic basis of the Moroccan political system is also well established in theory. The imprint of the first Islamic invasions, the loyalty to the early caliphates in Damascus and Cordoba, and the religious fervor of the indigenous local dynasties of the medieval period, such as the Almoravids, stamped the Moroccan polity with a profound and distinct Islamic character. The Alawite family, moreover, claimed sharifian status, although it was not unique in this respect among Morocco's great families. The office of the sultan,

70. Elbaki Hermassi, *Leadership and National Development in North Africa* (Berkeley: University of California Press, 1972), pp. 144–49 and 208, asserts that the problems of Morocco (and Algeria and Tunisia) are not national identity or social integration, for these states are "integrated, centralized and patterned along the lines of contemporary Europe" (pp. 144–45). Rural rebellions should not be analyzed as manifestations of primordial politics but rather as pressure exerted through traditional means upon the state to provide adequate modern services. The real problems concern the efficacy and legitimacy of regimes, he writes.

therefore, combined temporal authority and spiritual legitimacy. In Morocco the religious legitimacy was especially pronounced, inasmuch as the country remained beyond the jurisdiction of the Ottoman Empire, in whose sultan the historical universal caliphate nominally resided from the sixteenth century to the twentieth. As the imam and commander of the faithful, therefore, the Alawite sultans laid the strongest possible claims to Islamic legitimacy.[71]

As we have observed, however, Islam in Morocco is not the monolithic and coherent value system that it is in most other parts of the Arab world. One of the principal cleavages distinguished the orthodox, urban, classical tradition—and it is this tradition in which the Alawite family (notwithstanding its Shi'ite origins) finds its legitimacy—from the Islam of the mountains, the marabouts (local saints), and the mystics of the Sufi orders. This particularistic Islam has frequently taken on political significance and structures, and until recently the brotherhoods and orders (*zawiyas*) have lent a dimension of religious legitimacy to the hinterland opponents of royal authority. In the early twentieth century the Salafiyya movement of Islamic reform, led by the Egyptian scholar Muhammad Abdu, began to penetrate the Moroccan elite and later, in the 1930s, influenced the Moroccan Arab nationalists, notably Alal al-Fassi, founder of the Istiqlal party.[72] Because the French colonial penetration was widely interpreted as a new Christian assault on Islam and because several of the Sufi orders (committed to other-worldly, nonpolitical pursuits) had cooperated with the French, the theological differences between these two tendencies in Islam was exacerbated by modern nationalist, colonial, and religious issues. The Alawites may have been the preeminent family in Moroccan Islam, but the legitimacy conferred by that status was neither complete nor unchallengeable.

As for the legitimacy conferred by historical memories, the record is ambiguous, for the interior, the bilad al-siba described in an earlier chapter, has persistently challenged and only unwillingly acquiesced in the extractive rule of the coastal bilad al-makhzan. In this context, of course, dynastic longevity alone is something of an accomplishment; but the discontinuity of authority and the general turbulence of the reign render it on balance something less than a major legitimacy

71. Neville Barbour, *A Survey of Northwest Africa*, Second Edition (London: Oxford University Press, 1962), p. 100.

72. Jamil Abun-Nasr, "The Salafiyya Movement in Morocco: The Religious Bases of the Moroccan Nationalist Movement," in Albert Hourani (ed.), *Middle Eastern Affairs, Number Three*, St. Antony's Papers, Number 16 (London: Chatto and Windus, 1963), pp. 90–105.

resource, despite the hallowed legends of the great Mulay Hassan and other notable sultans. The French occupation did not help either, for the supine acquiescence of the sultan in the imposition of the protectorate and the concomitant rise of nationalist and anti-French sentiment reduced the legitimacy of the sultanate in the eyes of many to zero.[73] But the accession of Muhammad V in 1927, although initially inauspicious, led to a renaissance of royal legitimacy as the nationalist forces and the new sultan began increasingly to support each other. The crowning event in this renaissance was France's ill-advised decision to deport Sultan Muhammad in 1953. His exile only exacerbated the civil unrest which had prompted it in the first place, and the French were forced to allow him to return two years later. Suddenly the sultan had become the symbol of resistance and rectitude, of independence and a new nationalism. A hero partly by his own virtues and partly by the misjudgments of others, Muhammad V, through his actions, not his office or status, generated intense legitimacy for a new and independent political system, replete with parties and a constitutional ideology.

The kingdom which was admitted to the United Nations in November 1956, a year after Sultan Muhammad's triumphal return, was a political system fraught with contradictions. It was the product of four elements: the French, the traditional rural-Islamic notables, the nationalist movement, and, most important, the sultan. In the struggle for (and against) independence, they had maneuvered themselves into two unlikely alliances. The French, apostles of modernity (and colonialism) had long sought to enlist the most particularistic and conservative elements in behalf of the colonial enterprise. The Berber dahir (decree) of 1930 had been the most decisive effort to induce rural, Berber separatism as a counterweight to urban Muslim-Arab anti-colonialism. In 1953, still true to form, the French had actively encouraged the traditional qa'ids (local chiefs) and pashas, led by Hajj Tihami al-Glawi, pasha of Marrakesh, to force Sultan Muhammad into exile.[74] The nationalist movement, led by Fassi, was strongly Islamic: it had seized upon the Berber dahir and its threat to Islam to arouse concerted resistance among elements normally antagonistic to one another. The new sultan himself turned out to be their most important ally, even though the postindependence monarchy envisioned by many nationalists would have been stripped of its traditional

73. For an example, see André Maurois, *Lyautey* (New York: Appleton, 1931), pp. 187–213.

74. Stéphane Bernard, *The Franco-Moroccan Conflict* (New Haven: Yale University Press, 1960), pp. 122–85; esp. pp. 163–78.

absolutism and tempered with constitutional limitations. The fusion of the nationalists with the monarchy and, especially, the subsequent take-over of the nationalist movement by the monarchy is extremely important for evaluating the legitimacy problems faced by King Hassan in the 1970s for it indicates the strength and personal legitimacy of Muhammad V and the growing centrality of the royal institution. "The importance of the charismatic relationship between the King and the people," wrote Douglas Ashford, "is undoubtedly the most striking characteristic of Moroccan politics."[75] And as Geertz insightfully observes, by the time of his exile and return, Muhammad V had become "something no Alawite sultan, however powerful, had ever been before, an authentic popular hero ... a maraboutic king."[76] He effectively fused into his own personality and office the powerful legitimizing values of Islam, nationalism, and even secularism. Unlike the independence struggles in most Arab countries, this one resulted in a restoration rather than a nationalist revolution; and the forces of liberalism—the nationalist parties—were relegated to a secondary place in the postindependence political system. By making the monarchy the hub of all political forces in the country, Muhammad V bestowed upon that institution a degree of concentrated authority and superior leverage which the scattered and divided opposition could not compete with.[77] While he could not bequeath to his son and designated successor his own enormous charisma, he did leave him an office and a strategic position on the commanding heights of Moroccan politics that helps account for Hassan's surprising survival into the middle 1970s.

King Hassan's Quest for Legitimacy

Since King Hassan ascended the throne after his father's unexpected demise in January 1961, there has been a steady erosion of system legitimacy. In what writers such as Clement Moore and John Waterbury describe as an historic throwback to the premodern, preprotectorate sultanate, the Moroccan kings rejected the promising stratagem of an alliance with the constitutional nationalists to bridge the transi-

75. Douglas E. Ashford, *Political Change in Morocco* (Princeton: Princeton University Press, 1961), p. 412.

76. Geertz, op. cit., pp. 80–81.

77. Hermassi, op. cit., chap. 5, emphasizes the marginality of the Moroccan elites, their narrow urban bourgeois base and "their structural incapability to undertake rural mobilization." (p. 111.) The monarch held the advantage.

tion from traditional to modern legitimacy.[78] Instead, the monarch sought to capitalize, indeed monopolize, upon his preeminence as the national symbol and to exclude even conservative nationalist parties such as the Istiqlal of Fassi from effective participation. Hassan II dallied briefly with parliamentary politics but then went on to accelerate their decay. The constitution promulgated in 1962 gave the king broad powers, but it also called for an elected parliament. In the 1963 election, Morocco's first, a government-sponsored party, the Front for the Defense of Constitutional Institutions (FDIC), won the most seats, but the two main opposition parties, the Istiqlal and the National Union of Popular Forces (UNFP), a more progressive group with strong trade union support which had split from the Istiqlal in 1959, also did well. But the Istiqlal was denied seats in the cabinet and governmental patronage and so lost influence. From the king's point of view, the UNFP was much the more threatening opposition movement. It was supported by the large Moroccan Labor Union (UMT) led by Mahjoub Ben Seddiq and was strong in the cities. But it was incapacitated just after the election when the government accused some of its leaders of fomenting a plot to assassinate the king and overthrow the regime; several of its leaders were jailed. Urban unrest and political instability continued, and over 100 were killed during the Casablanca riots of March 1965. Finally, in June 1965, King Hassan disbanded the parliament altogether on the grounds that it was paralyzing the work of government.[79] In October 1965, Mahdi Ben Barka, principal leader of the UNFP, under sentence of death in Morocco and living in exile in Europe, was abducted on a Paris street and never seen again. Ben Barka had been involved with various Third World progressive movements in Africa and Latin America as well as the Arab world, raising the suspicion that his kidnapping and presumed assassination transcended the Moroccan political scene; but the King's trusted interior minister, Colonel Oufkir, was found guilty of complicity in the crime by a French court.

During the state of emergency which he had declared, King Hassan assiduously strengthened his preponderance vis à vis the opposition. In a 1968 interview with this writer in Rabat, a well-placed Moroccan

78. Clement H. Moore, *Politics in North Africa* (Boston: Little, Brown, 1970), pp. 107–18; John Waterbury, *The Commander of the Faithful* (New York: Columbia University Press, 1970), chap. 7, and part 3.

79. Stuart Schaar, "King Hassan's Alternatives," in I. William Zartman (ed.), *Man State and Society in the Contemporary Maghreb* (New York: Praeger, 1973), pp. 229–44.

journalist stated categorically that politics was a "one-man show." Slowly, the king began to restore the forms of liberal government: a new constitution was approved (by 98 percent) and new elections were held in 1970. A third constitution was promulgated in 1972, more liberal than the previous one in that two-thirds instead of one-third of the seats were filled through direct election. But the parties— indeed, all groups with a potential for organized opposition—were kept divided and off balance, tempted by patronage, compromised by corrupting relationships, harassed by the various arms of the regime. As John Waterbury has observed, the king was making himself the arbiter of all political issues and groups, acting to retard the mobilization of any nationwide elements (even friendly ones) for fear that they could turn against the monarchy. Instead, the king exploited the large rambling Alawite family with its multitudinous connections and wasitas.[80] Beyond the family was a large constituency of the pious, led by the ulama, with their special veneration for the office and the family. Rural notables with noble status, businessmen locked into the web of patronage and obligations manipulated by the palace, and above all the army officer corps, completed the structure of royal authority. The principal representatives of the peasantry, the urban industrial workers, the students, and the professional classes—the Istiqlal and the UNFP (now itself factionalized)—were left outmaneuvered and frustrated. Then, against a background of student demonstrations, unemployment, and labor unrest, came the first of the coups.

Of all the remaining monarchies in the Arab world, King Hassan's regime in the early 1970s appeared to be facing the most serious difficulties. Lacking the abundant financial resources of the petro-kingdoms, yet plagued with a dissatisfied, politicized urban proletariat and educated stratum, the king, after the 1971, 1972, and 1973 crises, could no longer even count with confidence upon the loyalty of the army officers. Trends outside the political sphere were hardly more promising. Morocco had displayed one of the lowest economic levels and growth rates in the Arab world during the 1960s.[81] There had been a decline in per capita food consumption. An estimated quarter of the urban work force was unemployed, and there was a surplus of educated and semieducated manpower.[82] At the same time, colossal private

80. Waterbury, op. cit., chap. 7 and pp. 148, 152.

81. Maurice Girgis, "Development and Trade Patterns in the Arab World," *Weltwirtschaftliches Archiv*, vol. 109, 1 (1973), pp. 121–69; p. 124. The growth rate was 3.8 percent and the per capita income $225.

fortunes had been amassed. According to a French observer, the rich indulged in the most conspicuous consumption—from luxury villas in Casablanca to caviar flown in by special plane for parties.[83] The king and his entourage reportedly pursued a lifestyle far removed from the puritanical austerity of a King Faisal. One scholarly observer spoke of the "permanent crisis" and the "corruption and hopelessness" of the Moroccan situation.[84] Another portrayed the regime as cynically pursuing a course of planned corruption in order to paralyze all possible elite opposition.[85] Unfortunately, he argued, the corruption was not functional (as some theorists have suggested it can be) in building governmental rationality and capabilities or in encouraging economic development or democracy. Its only function was to promote the survival of the regime. King Hassan's dilemma, concluded Waterbury, was "whether, in the short term, his survival can be made compatible with rational administration and economic development, or whether, in the long term, it can be made compatible with planned corruption."[86]

Yet the king was not to be counted out so quickly. Although his basic dilemma—choosing between the perils of modernization and the perils of stagnation—remained unsolved and perhaps unsolvable, he demonstrated a surprising ability to recover from adversity during the two years following the 1973 revolt. Indeed, as we have noted in the case of King Hussein, adversity seemed actually to strengthen the mystical regard in which the office and its occupant were held by thousands of uneducated Moroccans. In 1975 a reporter for Le Monde wrote that he had often heard people in rural areas say that "if our king miraculously escaped death twice, it is because he has baraka. God's with him."[87] Furthermore, he added to his personal popularity by identifying himself once again with the Arab struggle to recover Palestine. Just before the 1973 war he sent a Moroccan contingent to Syria, and it subsequently distinguished itself in the fighting on the Golan Heights. In the postwar period he benefited from an enhanced status in Arab affairs and was host to the important Arab summit conference at Rabat in 1974. His old nationalist opponents could hardly outbid him on Arabism. Even

83. Guy Sitbon, "Les Marocains en procès," Le Nouvel Observateur (Paris), August 13, 1973, pp. 28–29.

84. Hermassi, op. cit., pp. 211–12.

85. John Waterbury, "Endemic and Planned Corruption in a Monarchical Regime," World Politics, 25, 4 (July 1973), pp. 533–55.

86. Ibid., p. 555.

87. Paul Balta, "Hassan's Morocco: New Prestige, Old Problems," The Manchester Guardian Weekly, March 22, 1975, p. 12; reprinted from Le Monde, March 4 and 5, 1975.

closer to home was the dispute with Spain over Spanish Sahara and
the Mediterannean coastal enclaves of Ceuta and Melilla. Once again,
the king took the initiative, depriving the opposition of exploiting a
highly salient issue. Melilla and Ceuta had been Spanish since 1497
and 1581 respectively, and the phosphate-rich Sahara had been held
by Spain since 1884. Spain's cession of the poor Atlantic enclave of Ifni
in 1969 had not muted Moroccan demands for the other more valuable
territories as well. After the World Court in October 1975 rejected the
Moroccan claim to Spanish Sahara, King Hassan acted unilaterally
to take over the phosphate-rich territory. He organized a mass march
of Moroccans into the territory and sent in Moroccan troops to secure
the prize. In the process he astutely aroused Moroccan nationalist
fervor and successfully identified himself with the cause. He also
restored to some extent his rather frayed relations with the officer
corps. As a legitimacy building device, the king's Sahara initiative
was a brilliant stroke, well worth the risk of war with neighboring
Algeria. The only problem was whether the guerrilla activities of the
Algerian-backed Polisario Liberation Front, the movement striving
for the territory's independence, might not prove to be a long-term
burden on the Moroccan army and treasury—and thus an eventual
drain on royal authority.

On the internal level, King Hassan generated ideological legitimacy
of a progressive coloration by nationalizing foreign landholdings in
March 1973. He then relaxed the restrictions on political expression
and promised late in 1974 to call new elections at a future unspecified
date. The Communist party, now known as the Party of Progress and
Socialism, was permitted to function. The main opposition parties, the
Istiqlal (led since Fassi's death by Muhammad Boucetta), the old
UNFP of Abd al-Rahim Bouabed (now known as the Socialist Union
of National Forces), and the new UNFP (led by Abdulla Ibrahim)
resumed their activities and their strong criticism of the corruption in
the Moroccan system with the permission of the king. And so, despite
the three nearly successful attempts of the early 1970s to overthrow
the monarch, there was by 1975, in the view of many, a greater degree
of freedom of speech in Morocco than in any other country of the
Maghrib or Arab Asia except for Lebanon and Kuwait. Freedom of
political action, however, was another matter, and opposition leaders
were aware that the king's secret police were monitoring their activities
carefully.

Finally, King Hassan's position was significantly strengthened by
an exogenous factor of the greatest importance: at the beginning of
1974 the price of phosphate tripled and six months later it increased

again by 50 percent. Morocco is the world's third largest producer of phosphates and the largest exporter.[88] What this meant in the short run was a considerable increase in the patronage "pie" to be distributed throughout the system, and in the long run it created at least the potential for an expansion of political and economic capabilities that could ease some of the social discontent so prevalent throughout the country.

Faced with a more severe legitimacy crisis than any of the other monarchies, King Hassan could still rely upon the deep regard which Moroccans feel toward the throne, so richly legitimized with religious and nationalist values. At the same time, he showed himself to be extremely skillful in using popular issues to his own advantage, thus fortifying the ideological legitimacy of the regime. If analysts like Waterbury are correct, it is inappropriate to assign much structural legitimacy to the regime; indeed it seems to thrive on the tacit sense, shared by all participants, of its illegitimacy, but there is no denying its efficacy as an instrument of manipulation and control. There are no competing structures with the same scope of support. With the loyalty of the military and security chiefs uncertain and the perpetuation of the inequalities and discontents in the urban working class, the new stability may be illusory, but the mere fact of King Hassan's survival into the late 1970s is in itself an indication that monarchies may not be as immediately vulnerable to modernization as some theory suggests. The monarch who is astute and strong can pursue and even create options which will at least delay the day of reckoning. The Moroccan case also suggests, however, that royal survival requires a considerable amount of luck.

88. Jonathan C. Randal, in *The Washington Post*, October 1, 1974.

8

The Republics of the Pan-Arab Core

The principal problem which the Arab monarchies face in trying to preserve or enhance their legitimacy is establishing a linkage with modernity. But for the revolutionary republics, the legitimacy problem is one of maintaining connections with the past. Jacques Berque, discussing the Arabs, has observed that despite all innovations of the recent past, "modern view-points still have to take the past into account, all the more as the masses are under its influence in many respects, and the people still look to it as a form of safeguard."[1] One of the themes that we shall encounter as we compare legitimacy in the revolutionary states is the ambivalence of the modernizing politician: on the one hand, his raison d'être as a modernizer requires the elimination of what are sometimes called the shackles of tradition; on the other, his instincts as a politician sensitize him to the importance of his being congruent with a traditional culture. The point is illustrated in the almost identical comments made in interviews by officials in the revolutionary regimes of Iraq and the People's Democratic Republic of Yemen (PDRY). Each said that their governments were frustrated in pursuing their policies of development and social justice because they were compelled to accommodate a religious mentality and organized religious influence at the grass-roots level. Not that their regimes were opposed to religion per se, as the Soviet authorities have been; for religion has its place in the Arabic heritage. It was just that the badly needed reforms take so much longer and are so much more difficult to implement because of these deep-rooted perspectives.[2]

The ambivalence of commitments to tradition and modernity of course, is hardly unique either to this area or to the present time. The Western observer of the political debate in the Arab world might be reminded of the debate between the radicals of the French Enlightenment and the conservative reaction. The ambivalence among

1. Jacques Berque, *The Arabs* (London: Faber and Faber, 1960, tr, 1964), pp. 268–69.
2. Interviews conducted by the writer in Baghdad on February 27, 1972, and in Aden on March 22, 1972.

Middle Eastern intellectuals is far from being a phenomenon only of the mid-twentieth century, of course; the debate dates from the late eighteenth century. As Niyazi Berkes and Albert Hourani have shown in their definitive studies of Turkey and the Arab east, respectively, the challenge of Western secularism, nationalism, liberalism, and socialism has roiled the intellectual currents so profoundly that the harmony of traditional political orientations at the elite level has been destroyed.[3]

But the struggle has been inconclusive. Even at the elite level these exogenous influences have not eradicated traditional perspectives, as I shall show in each of the postrevolutionary republics that I examine. Old certainties doubtless have been eroded but they have not disappeared. Among intellectuals there has emerged no coherent and integrated orientation to modernity analogous to the timeless, parochial, authoritarian, and sacred traditionalist world view.[4] And even if there had, there would be no grounds for supposing that a modern integrated political community was therefore imminent, because the intellectuals hardly constitute the sole determinant of the values that underpin legitimacy. One must emphasize the non-intellectual aspects of political culture, in the republics as well as the monarchies. In the former, however, the impact of formal and rational theory and ideology is comparatively greater. Modern ideology has not welded a completely modern political community in the polities which have crossed the "revolutionary divide" that I am about to consider. Religion, kinship, and history itself still shape political identities in the most transformationist among them. Many progressive Arab politicans and intellectuals have assumed too easily that traditional identifications and values could be definitively shattered. This faulty assumption, as I remarked in chapter 1, has led on the scholarly level to an exaggeration of the potency and speed of modernization as a solvent of tradition, while on the operational level it has led to a consistent underestimation of the political strength of the traditional sectors. The ease and frequency with which coups have been carried out has in this respect been somewhat misleading; coups are not difficult to organize and carry out—coups themselves are something

3. Niyazi Berkes, *The Development of Secularism in Turkey* (Montreal: McGill University Press, 1964); Albert Hourani, *Arabic Thought in the Liberal Age: 1798–1939* (London: Oxford University Press, 1962).

4. Dankwart Rustow, in his excellent study, *A World of Nations* (Washington: The Brookings Institution, 1967), pp. 11–13, sees tradition (because of its diversity) as a residual category. Without denying the diversity of traditional polities, I would simply suggest that the diversity of structure and complexity of legitimizing formulas in modernizing polities is considerably greater.

of a tradition in the Arab world—but to build a viable order on modern legitimacy bases after the coup has proved to be an extra-ordinarily intractable task. The postcoup dismay attributed to Gamal Abd al-Nasir, when he discovered that the old patterns persisted, has been felt no doubt by revolutionary leaders and elites from one end of the Arab world to the other.[5]

Another distinction must be drawn. Not only are traditional and modern values intermixed in both the monarchies and the republics, but also the relation between the two orientations is one of tension rather than complete opposition. Thus I spoke of the ambivalent rather than contradictory commitments which a revolutionary politician or civil servant may hold in trying to achieve progressive values in a society and culture still deeply infused with primordial identifications and orientations. Social theory often conceives of social change in dichotomous terms: *gemeinschaft* versus *gesellschaft*, tradition versus modernity. But it is difficult to find among all of today's develop-ing nations any that have been completely transformed from one to the other; and so it has been necessary to interpret them as being in transition. Committed by the either/or imperatives of the prevalent typologies and an assumption of the universality of progress, it is difficult to conceive of mixed polities that are not necessarily going anywhere at all. This observation, however, should not lead to the assertion that the Arab systems have entered into equilibrium and achieved community. The mixed legitimacy formulas observed in both the monarchies and the republics may not be able to end the legitimacy shortage that I have spoken of.

In trying to blur the tradition-modernity distinction, it must be remembered that there is a profound difference between states which have experienced a revolutionary, modernizing event or trauma and those which have not. To be sure the Arab world has known so much instability in the twentieth century that one could reasonable doubt whether any fundamental change was occurring at all. By one count, there were thirty-two successful coups d'état in the Arab world between 1949 and 1966,[6] and even the most enthusiastic radical would hesitate to describe them all as revolutions. If the term revolution is understood in its most profound sense, as an upheaval that not only overturns a political regime but also changes sociocultural values and

5. Gamal Abdel Nasser, *The Philosophy of the Revolution* (Buffalo: Economica Books, 1959), pp. 31–35.

6. Michael C. Hudson, "Some Socioeconomic and Political Conditions of Irregular Power Transfers, 1949–1966," mimeographed, September 1973; table 1.

the distribution of wealth, then one could argue whether the Arabs have experienced any revolutions at all.

But somewhere between the political hiccough and the social earthquake there is the revolutionary event that replaces one set of authoritative institutions with another, such as monarchies with republics; or that replaces one ruling elite with another, as when a landed-commercial-religious oligarchy gives way to a professional-industrial-military elite. Such events may transform the social order only partially, but they do constitute major transformations in the structures and legitimizing values of the political system. All the Arab republics of the middle 1970s except Lebanon have experienced such revolutions. Although the event of achieving independence from colonial rule is not necessarily a system-transforming act (Morocco, Jordan, and the Arab shaykhdoms being cases in point), the struggle against Western imperialism, direct or indirect, has been a feature in each one—hence, the familiar dilemma of the modernizing revolutionary who is driven by Western political values and goals (often against the indigenous values of his people) and yet who is repelled by Western politics and culture.

In every case the revolution has required the development of a new legitimacy formula. The need has arisen out of the novelty of the situation of independence and the legitimacy vacuum left by the destroyed ruling structures. The development of a new formula is complicated, however, by two factors: the ideological fragmentation within the growing elite (particularly the growth of counter-elites within the intelligentsia, military, and labor sectors) and the differential social mobilization occurring among the masses. The effect of the latter factor in some cases stimulates an accentuation of traditional values (as in the phenomenon of the Muslim Brotherhood in Egypt), but in general it is not pervasive enough to provide fertile soil for the widespread legitimizing of a revolutionary regime. My task in assessing the legitimacy formulas in the revolutionary Arab republics is to see how the building blocks of legitimacy, such as kinship, religion, history, nationalism, and modernity, are exploited to accommodate the new stresses brought on by the revolution, in addition to the traditional cleavages and tensions.

I must also reemphasize another dimension of the legitimacy problem which is distinctive for the Arab states as a whole, and especially the revolutionary republics. This is Arab nationalism in its most inclusive sense—that set of widely held values and preferences concerned with achieving a united or at least coordinated Arab world free of external domination and liberated from the last traces of territiorial occupation. The Palestine and Arab-Israeli questions, of course, are central among these all-Arab concerns. Part of the rationale for the Arab revolutions has been the achievement of these aims. One of the most effective revolutionary weapons against several of the *anciens régimes* was the charge that they had failed to shoulder their all-Arab responsibilities. The salience of these all-Arab concerns is high throughout the Arab world, including, as we have seen, the monarchies, especially Jordan. Among the republics, however, they are most important in the area where Arab nationalism first took root and where the Palestinian and Arab-Israeli drama is being played out. In this chapter I compare the political systems of the pan-Arab core: Egypt, Syria, Iraq, Lebanon, and the Palestinian movement. Here all-Arab concerns are ubiquitous and probably growing in intensity, and all regimes must take account of them. The centrality of these issues is both a potential legitimacy asset and a practical liability. In the following chapter I look at the republics of the periphery—newer, further from the heartland of Arabism, and somewhat less affected by all-Arab issues like Palestine in their search for legitimacy.

EGYPT

Despite its present weaknesses, Egypt is the preeminent country of the Arab world. Its population is over twice the size of the next biggest Arab states (the Sudan, Morocco, and Algeria). Its history of modernization is the longest, its industrial sector the most extensive, its educational and cultural institutions the most prolific, its military machine the biggest. Geographically and strategically the fulcrum of the Arab world, it was its political center as well during the regime of Gamal Abd al-Nasir, and any pan-Arab political integration or coordination is difficult to conceive of without a major Egyptian role.

Not only is social mobilization further advanced there than elsewhere in the region, the political sphere is more differentiated ideologically and structurally and has been so for a longer time. Nowhere else in the Arab countries (except for pre–civil war Lebanon) could one find such a diversity of opinions and political organizations: Islamic fundamentalists, liberal constitutionalists, varieties of Marxists, informal intellectual circles concerned with politics, influential bureaucracies, labor and student organizations, and, of course, the politicized military officers. To be sure, the Egyptian political system today faces a serious legitimacy problem, but as a society and political culture, Egypt, by virtue of its differentiated and elaborate structures and value patterns, is the most advanced in the Arab world. Accordingly, its experience in developing a revolutionary legitimacy is of interest not just because of

Egypt's intrinsic weight in Arab affairs but also for insights into the future of other systems in the region.

That experience has not been altogether a happy one. While it has been marked by dramatic successes, there have also been grave setbacks. The Nasir revolution, which became the model for many Arab and Third World reformists, appears to have been a tactical success but a strategic failure in terms of generating permanent system legitimacy. Through an extraordinary manipulation of anti-Western and pan-Arab values, the officers that made the revolution in 1952 set Egypt on a course toward relative stability, economic and social development, and regional and world political influence. Above and beyond all these accomplishments, the strong personal legitimacy that Gamal Abd al-Nasir generated was basic in molding a more integrated Egyptian political community and promoting what many observers called a new sense of dignity. The Nasir regime, however, conspicuously failed to legitimize itself or its successor in structural terms. To survive the incessant internal challenges and the external calamities which fell upon it at the end, it pursued heavy-handed and secretive procedures which repressed but could not dissipate opposition opinion. Just as it was unable to find structural legitimacy through institutionalized, open participation, it was also increasingly hard-pressed after 1967 to provide the social welfare to which the revolution was committed, and this insufficiency of capabilities, alluded to in chapter 6, has persisted into the new regime of President Muhammad Anwar al-Sadat. The Sadat regime, as I shall argue below, was not only the heir to the unsolved structural legitimacy problems of Nasirism, it also was weakened by problems that its predecessor had solved. The tempering of Egypt's pan-Arab and socialist commitments involved some loss of ideological legitimacy to important sectors of society, and the inability of President Sadat to generate the charisma of his heroic mentor further complicated the legitimacy problem.

Legitimacy Resources in Egyptian Political Culture

A glance back at the recent history of Egypt reveals some of the positive as well as negative characteristics of the legitimacy problem. It is, of course, one of the most homogeneous societies in the Arab world, displaying relatively little of the primordial kinship, ethnic, and religious tensions which exist in several other countries of the area. While it has had one of the longest periods of interaction with the Western world, it has also long been the intellectual center of gravity for the Islamic world. After the collapse of the Ottoman state, it was in Egypt that the most significant debate on the relation of Islam and

Western civilization took place. While on a philosophic level the efforts of the Islamic reformists to reconcile their creed with Western positivism and rationality have perhaps been inconclusive, as Kerr and others have suggested,[7] on the political level an uneasy accommodation has taken place.[8] To be sure, a certain ambivalence persists, and the currents of secularity and religiosity fluctuate, but it is perhaps an exaggeration to depict Islam and secularism or Islam and nationalism in Egypt as essentially irreconcilable.[9] On the whole, both Nasir and Sadat have exploited Islam effectively without embracing either fundamentalism or anticlericalism: Nasir's Islamic appeal (notwithstanding his regime's secularism) was far more than cosmetic, and Sadat has sought to appropriate the revival of orthodox piety to his own political purposes.

Egypt began to develop a modern national consciousness and modern structures from just after the middle of the nineteenth century, when most other Arab societies were under traditional local leaders. The historian Afaf Lutfi al-Sayyid divides the early period of Egyptian nationalism into two parts: the military-inspired unrest against Khedive Tawfiq which inspired the rebellion of Colonel Urabi which in turn led to the British occupation in 1882, and the "second nationalist movement," precipiated by Khedive Abbas against the British.[10] At the root of this development lay two factors. One was the officially generated movement toward bureaucratic rationality and economic mobilization undertaken at the beginning of the century by Muhammad Ali. Muhammad Ali and his successors, notably Khedive Isma'il, were explicit in their intention to modernize Egypt along European lines. The second factor was a byproduct of the first: when Khedive Isma'il's enthusiasm to modernize led to fiscal imprudence and bankruptcy, his European creditors were quick to exploit his vulnerability, as were his foreign and domestic enemies. European financial retaliation, the Turkish sultan's effort to bring his erstwhile vassal to heel, and internal dissatisfaction with Isma'il and his successor all created pressures for a constitution, representation, and limitations on the Khedive's power.[11]

7. Malcolm Kerr, *Islamic Reform*, op. cit.

8. An illuminating insight into the accommodation between organized religion and the revolutionary regime may be found in Daniel Crecelius, "Al-Azhar in the Revolution," *Middle East Journal*, 20, 1 (Winter 1966), pp. 31–49.

9. See, e.g., Nissim Rejwan, *Nasserist Ideology* (New York: Wiley, 1974) chap. 3.

10. Afaf Lutfi al-Sayyid, *Egypt and Cromer* (New York, Praeger, 1969) chaps. 1 and 7; p. 137.

11. On this period, and generally, see P. J. Vatikiotis, *The Modern History of Egypt* (London: Weidenfeld and Nicolson, 1969), Parts 1 and 2.

The principal nationalist figure of the early period came to be Mustafa Kamil, whose Hizb al-Watani (Nationalist party) succeeded, through its anti-British position, in mobilizing mass opinion, including the peasantry. But unlike the earlier nationalist group of Urabi Pasha, it was not made up predominantly of military officers. Having forcibly established its protectorate in 1882, Great Britain tried to undercut local hostility with modern administration. But Lord Cromer's economic and administrative reforms were not enough to quiet the nationalist outrage over his high-handed rule. One of the crucial events in the rise of Egyptian nationalism and the deterioration of Britain's position was the Denshwai crisis of 1906 in which the British carried out a brutal reprisal against the villagers allegedly involved in the death of a British soldier. But instead of teaching the natives the intended lesson, it accelerated the anti-British movement among the people by ten years, as Mustafa Kamil put it.[12]

The middle period of nationalist development involved the amalgamation of various nationalist groups into the broad-based movement for independence, symbolized by the Wafd, a delegation, led by Sa'd Zaghloul, which petitioned unsuccessfully to that effect in 1918. The Wafd, which later became the major independence movement, was far more broadly based than its predecessors and was able to mobilize enough popular pressure, through demonstrations and riots, against the British to extract a degree of independence by 1922. To appreciate the legitimizing potential of nationalism in Egypt today, it is important to note the intensified and broadened sense of Egyptian identity that has emerged since the 1880s. It is also instructive to observe the structural development that accompanied and nurtured this identity. In 1908, according to Lord Cromer, there were only 134,000 male adult Egyptians entitled to vote; of these only 34,000 registered, of whom only 1,500 voted.[13] By 1919 the masses throughout Egypt were demonstrating for a common goal. And even in the authoritarian Nasir and post-Nasir era, which in some respects marks a throwback in terms of curtailed political participation, there were still massive turnouts for the national plebiscites, the elections to the National Assembly, and the competition for local positions.

Internal corruption and regional turmoil became major issues in Egyptian politics in the post–World War I quasi-independence period. The relatively liberal era in Egyptian politics (1922–52) was marked

---

12. Cited in al-Sayyid, op. cit., p. 172. The incident is also described in some detail, pp. 169–75.
13. Cited by Jacob M. Landau, *Parliaments and Parties in Egypt* (New York, 1954), p. 50.

by the increasing corruption of parliamentary life, particularly within
the Wafd party; and it ended in a military coup not dissimilar to the
original Urabi coup. By the late 1940s King Farouk had become
profligate and ineffective. The wealthy landed and upper-bourgeois
elite was indifferent to Egypt's social and economic problems. The
party politicians were consumed with narrow self-interest. Radical
movements of the Left and Right were mobilizing themselves. The
army was neglected at a time when it was increasingly needed in the
struggle against the British presence. Thus it is hard to overestimate
the role of internal Egyptian grievances in stimulating Nasir and the
Free Officers to make their coup.

But at the same time regional pan-Arab concerns were gaining
salience in Egyptian politics. As far back as the early 1920s, there were
some intellectuals and officers, like Aziz Ali al-Misri, who for various
reasons preached an "Arab connection" for Egypt, but it was not
until the late 1930s that the affinity developed any mass support. The
Arab rebellion in Palestine, from 1936 to 1939, was a key event in
the development of an Arab consciousness in Egypt; and with the
signing of the Anglo-Egyptian Treaty of 1936, the idea of a major role
for Egypt in a postcolonial Arab world began to germinate in Egyptian
political and intellectual circles.[14] Palestine continued to work its
powerful spell from the middle-1940s onward, not just as a national
issue but also as an anticolonial and a religious cause. As an anti-
British cause it dovetailed with the driving force of the old Egyptian
nationalism; as a religious cause it enlisted the powerful Muslim
Brotherhood, perhaps the most formidable of the revolutionary-reform
movements challenging the decadent triumvirate of the monarchy, the
British, and the Wafd.[15]

The Nasirist Legitimacy Formula

The young military officers who seized power in 1952 were said to
be politically innocent—lacking a clear ideology, uncertain about
what to do or how to do it. To be sure, they were first and foremost a
closely-knit band of professional colleagues only peripherally connected
with the established parties and movements. In fact, however, they
proved to be consummate politicians. Indeed, no sooner were they in
power than they destroyed both the forces of the Left, such as the
Communists, and those of the Right, represented by the Muslim

14. Sylvia G. Haim, *Arab Nationalism: An Anthology* (Berkeley: University of California Press,
1964), p. 49.

15. On the brotherhood see Richard P. Mitchell, *The Society of the Muslim Brothers* (London:
Oxford University Press, 1969), esp. pp. 55–58 on Palestine.

Brotherhood. Even more important, they were able to fashion, in bits and pieces, a set of positions (not a well-articulated formal ideology) that preempted their rivals and touched a responsive chord in the Egyptian people.[16]

While transnationalist symbols ultimately came to bulk largest in the Nasirite legitimacy formula, the initial thrust of the Free Officers' appeals was domestic. The scandals of the royal regime, its corruption, and its lack of interest in facing demands for more socioeconomic equality were conditions readymade for political exploitation. The incompetence of the king and the Wafd in dealing with the British occupation was deeply felt. Yet domestic reform was uppermost in the concerns of the Officers at the time of the revolution, and the first major act of the new regime was the promulgation of a land reform law. This law and subsequent interventions in the economy served the dual purpose of advancing the Officers' strongly felt but undeveloped notions of social justice—a kind of radical populism—and also undercutting the influence base of the landed elite which had effectively dominated both the palace and the political parties. Subsequently, emphasis was placed on development rather than redistribution, as the state tried to cope with the problems of overpopulation, agricultural production, and employment. The Aswan High Dam scheme was not just an economic development project but an important legitimacy-building device, which explains in part Nasir's violent reaction to America's decision not to finance it.

The trend toward increasing government intervention which culminated in the socialist decrees of July 1961, according to participants, was not the result of a sudden ideological commitment to socialism, but only the pragmatic, incrementalist response of the regime to the unwillingness of the private sector to shoulder its development burdens. Nasirism had gradually emerged as a non-Marxist ideology of economic development and social justice, and by the end of the 1950s, it was apparent that an increase in governmental capabilities was essential to meet these commitments. Such was the rationale behind the establishment of Egypt's first five-year plan in 1960 and the socialist decrees of 1961. The first plan largely achieved its targets, but the mainly external setbacks from the middle 1960s onward, beginning with the cancellation of U.S. grain supplies, initiated a process of decay which inevitably began to erode Nasirist legitimacy in the domestic sphere.

16. A thorough study of Nasirite legitimacy is R. Hrair Dekmejian, *Egypt Under Nasir* (Albany: State University of New York Press, 1971). See esp. chaps. 6 and 13.

It was in the regional sphere, however, that Nasirism was to develop its deepest, strongest legitimacy for Egyptians and Arabs in general—a legitimacy which indeed has survived the passing of Nasir himself and continues to mobilize political movements in several Arab countries. By committing himself in the most dramatic way to the Arab nationalist and Palestinian causes, Nasir achieved a degree of greatness that undoubtedly will survive the bitterness of the enormous sacrifices and defeats which Egypt suffered in pursuit of those causes.

Palestine was unquestionably a formative experience in the revolutionary consciousness of the Free Officers. To be sure, as Nasir wrote in *The Philosophy of the Revolution*, the Palestine war of 1948 did not directly cause the Egyptian revolution of 1952.[17] But it is clear that Palestine was a significant, not just a peripheral, factor in galvanizing the Free Officers to act. Nasir actually fought in Palestine and indeed at one point had contacts with Israeli officers when the force he was leading was surrounded. For Nasir, fighting in Palestine was not fighting on foreign territory; it was "a duty imposed by self-defense" against imperialism. In Palestine he recalls

> a young girl of the same age as my daughter. I saw her rushing out, amidst danger and stray bullets and, bitten by the pangs of hunger and cold, looking for a crust of bread or a rag of cloth. I always said to myself, "This may happen to my daughter." I believe that what was happening in Palestine could happen and may still happen today, in any part of this region, as long as it resigns itself to the factors and the forces which dominate it now.[18]

Not only are those thoughts unhappily prophetic of what would happen in 1956 and 1967, they express a world view and an attitude that runs very deep in Egypt and North Africa, as well as the Arab east—one that has become increasingly fixed on the consciousness of the new elites throughout the Arab world.

Egypt's Arabism no doubt was accelerated by the events in Palestine, but its scope was far broader. Long the intellectual, cultural, and religious center of the Arab world, its leaders, especially after the Nasir revolution, saw a political role as well for Egypt throughout this area. Great Britain encouraged the formation of the League of Arab States, headquartered in Cairo, on the assumption that such a regional organization would enhance British interests and influence. But it was

17. Gamal Abdel Nasser, *The Philosophy of the Revolution* (Buffalo, N. Y.: Economica Books, 1959), p. 26.
18. Ibid., p. 65, and pp. 63–70 on Palestine.

an Egypt ruled by the bitterly anti-British Free Officers that came to dominate the League. Nasir used the League and many other instruments to project Egypt's influence from North Africa to Kuwait, and Egypt's hostility toward Britain was diffused to such sensitive areas as the British-controlled principalities of the Gulf and south Arabia.[19]

During the first two years of the revolution, it appeared that Egypt might turn inward and abjure a dynamic role in the area. But by the time of the Bandung conference of April 1955, President Nasir had decided to exploit the complementary themes of Arabism, anti-Westernism and nonalignment. Egypt pursued an active policy of fostering Arab unity involving diplomacy, propaganda, and insurgency aid throughout the Arab world. Nasir explained it to Jean Lacouture as follows:

> Listen to me: I have an exact knowledge of the frontiers of the Arab nation. I do not place it in the future for I think and I act as though it already existed. These frontiers end where my propaganda no longer arouses an echo. Beyond this point something else begins, a foreign world which does not concern me.[20]

Conservative, pro-Western Arab regimes saw the policy as Egyptian imperialism rather than national liberation, and Egyptian-sponsored antiregime activities occurred throughout the area during the Nasir era in Morocco, Tunisia, Libya, Lebanon, Syria, Iraq, Kuwait, Sa'udi Arabia, Yemen, and southern Arabia. In a diplomatic sense, these activities constituted external intervention in the internal affairs of sovereign states; but so palpable was the concept of an Arab community and the goal of Arab unity that significant segments of mass and elite opinion throughout the area, including the countries where the interference as taking place, supported the activity as legitimate and legitimizing for Egypt and for Nasir. Egypt won vast moral support from Egyptians and Arabs generally for championing the Algerian struggle against France begun in November 1954 and for supporting the movement to expel Britain from both its base at Aden and its protectorate in southern Arabia in the 1960s.

By identifying with pan-Arabism, antiimperialism, and Third World nonalignment, the revolutionary regime in Egypt was able to fashion for itself a legitimacy formula of considerable strength. The legitimacy mechanism employed was unusual in that it did not arise exclusively

---

19. Robert W. Macdonald, *The League of Arab States* (Princeton: Princeton University Press, 1965), pp. 105–18, and passim.
20. Jean Lacouture, *Nasser: A Political Biography* (New York: Knopf, 1973), p. 184.

from the domestic political arena. Instead, it was a "reflected legiti-macy," deriving its effect from behavior in the regional and interna-tional system. By winning approval in the Arab world outside and in the broader constituency of the Third World, the new Egyptian regime became even more legitimate in the eyes of Egyptians; indeed, by all accounts it gave Egyptians sense of dignity and some substantial psychic gratifications. One could only find this mechanism effective in a socially mobilized polity. Modernization thus provides new resources as well as new problems for regime legitimacy.

PERSONAL LEGITIMACY: THE CHARISMATIC NASIR

President Nasir died on September 28, 1970. There is a memorable photograph of his funeral in which the coffin seems to be bobbing like a little boat in a sea of Egyptian mourners—the last of many occasions when the *Ra'is* (the chief), as he was called, could mobilize millions seemingly by force of personality alone. He, along with Kings Abd al-Aziz, Muhammad V, and President Bourguiba, was one of the few indisputably charismatic leaders that the modern Arab world has produced. From the time of his nationalization of the Suez Canal Company in July 1956, Nasir exerted a hold over the Egyptian masses that may fairly be described as charismatic in the Weberian sense, that is, possessing an authority " . . . resting on devotion to the specific and exceptional sanctity, heroism or exemplary character of an individual person, and of the normative patterns or order revealed or ordained by him . . ."[21] Furthermore, Nasir's charisma served an important legitimizing function for the Egyptian political system by rendering compatible key traditional and revolutionary values and structures: Islam and secularism, Egyptian nationalism and Arabism, patriarchy and presidency. Indeed the fact that the traditional values and structures were only curbed rather than eliminated has raised doubts among some observers as to just how revolutionary Nasirism really was. Nevertheless, the chemistry of charisma was certainly effective in dissolving to some extent the antagonisms and cleavages in the modernizing Egyptian political culture. In a sense Nasir was the high priest of a new pan-Arab political religion.

But one could overstress the magical character of the Nasirist charisma, for it was very much derivative of the political context of the times. As Robert Tucker points out in his study of charisma in

21. Max Weber, *On Charisma and Institution Building, Selected Papers*, edited and with intro-duction by S. N. Eisenstadt (Chicago: University of Chicago Press, 1968), p. 46 (from his *The Theory of Economic and Social Organization*).

revolutionary situations, the charismatic leader often arises out of a movement for change or reform. Moreover, there has to be a widely felt longing for salvation in the society in question, or a crisis that demands immediate resolution.[22] Certainly the movement of the Free Officers long antedated Nasir's emergence as a charismatic hero, and Egypt's politically conscious sectors increasingly perceived Egypt's domination by Great Britain, the corruption and ineffectiveness of its domestic structures, and the humiliation of its army in Palestine as intolerable conditions. That Nasir addressed himself to these issues made him popular, not so much that he occasionally succeeded. Indeed, his failures far outweighed his successes, and yet he was never more popular than in defeat in June 1967. In addition to his charisma, Nasir, once in power, also benefited from a historical pattern of autocracy and bureaucratic control that enabled him to exercise power effectively; in this respect he was more fortunate than a number of other Arab military leaders, such as those in Syria and Iraq, who came to power under similar circumstances but who were soon crippled by the divisions within their countries and an insufficiency of control capabilities.

These considerations suggest that one should not overemphasize charisma in itself in accounting for legitimacy, even in the case of Egypt. This is not to suggest that Nasir was not a heroic figure; that he was extraordinarily able in manipulating the myths of legitimacy in Egypt and throughout the Arab world is undeniable. The Ra'is's popularity was compelling. As a small example, this writer recalls sitting on his balcony in Beirut on July evenings over a period of several years listening to Nasir's annual speech commemorating the revolution and the Suez Canal nationalization; one did not need to turn on one's own radio because the voice was audible from thousands of other balconies as well. The folksy humor, the Egyptian dialect, rather in the manner of Franklin D. Roosevelt's "fireside chats" to the Americans, clearly was effective. But to suppose that he could have maintained his charisma and legitimacy without exploiting those potent symbols and myths is doubtful. And so, upon reflection, it may not have been the man or the voice that beguiled people as much as the message itself, with its symbols of dignity, social justice, development, anti-imperialism, anti-Zionism, and pan-Arabism. As Jean Lacouture observes, "It was not he who took possession of Arabism, but Arabism which took possession of him. It was Arabism that

22. Robert C. Tucker, "The Theory of Charismatic Leadership," *Daedalus*, 97, 3 (Summer 1968), pp. 731–56; esp. pp. 737–39, 743–46.

invested him, and established him as its hero."[23] The years since Nasir's death reinforce this interpretation, for it would seem that, as Tucker puts it, his charisma "lives on after the charismatic individual is gone."[24] Nasir's successor, Anwar al-Sadat, was able to benefit from it and buy the time to consolidate his position and turn the Nasir legacy to his own purposes before attempting to deflate it. Nasirist movements (in some cases virtual cults) still have a significant hold on nationalist legitimacy in Lebanon, Syria, Iraq, and the Arabian peninsula; and in revolutionary Libya the president, Mu'ammar al-Qadhafi, has deliberately modeled himself along Nasirist lines and won considerable political success in so doing. But the legitimacy would seem to lie not so much in the man himself but in the particular legitimizing mythology that he has come to embody.

FLAWS IN THE NASIRIST FORMULA

The Nasir regime was one of the longest-lived, most stable, and popular governments in the modern Arab world. Astute ideological mythmaking and the emergence of a heroic leader account for most of its success in building an effective legitimacy formula. But there were also major weaknesses. Despite his awareness of the need to develop structural legitimacy, Nasir was essentially unable to do so, and his successor Sadat, who lacks Nasir's ideological and personal assets, has been left to deal with this increasingly serious problem. The rapid industrialization of the country and concomitant social changes complicated the regime's effort to arrogate to itself the legitimizing effects of economic development. A noted Egyptian journalist, in an interview with this writer in 1968, likened the growth of a more complex society, especially a new urban proletariat and skilled technocratic middle class, to a young girl bursting out of her (revolutionary) dress. That was putting the matter a bit euphemistically. The crux of the issue was the growing demand for political participation across the entire political spectrum which collided with the unwillingness of the Free Officers to provide it if it meant (as they thought it did) the return to the paralysis and chaos of the old regime.

From the beginning, at least from the time that General Muhammad Naguib was removed as titular leader of the revolution, the Officers had been chary of sharing power with any organized elements. The old political parties were banned. The Muslim Brothers were encouraged briefly and then crushed when they appeared to pose a

23. Lacouture, op. cit., p. 188.
24. Tucker, op. cit., pp. 753–54.

threat to the Officers' power. One of the first acts of coercion of the revolutionary regime was the crushing of a workers' strike. The Arab Socialist Union and its predecessor organizations for mobilizing and consolidating opinion were consistently unable to mobilize Egyptians behind the regime's domestic programs. Persecution of the Communist party in 1959 and repression of critics on the Right like the Amin brothers, prominent newspaper editors, in 1965, indicated the regime's lack of tolerance for independent political organizations and opinions.

Setbacks in the regional sphere also corroded Nasirist legitimacy. Egypt's pan-Arab foreign policy crested in 1958 with the establishment of the union with Syria, but the collapse of that union in September 1961 marked the beginning of its decline. Soon the rising Palestinian movement would become the symbol of revolutionary and nationalist legitimacy. Initially, Egypt's support for the republican revolution in northern Yemen restored a measure of positive momentum, which dwindled as the Egyptian expeditionary force became bogged down in a protracted mountain war between royalist tribesmen and the republican forces. Then, having been cynically taunted by both Jordan and Syria for abandoning his pan-Arab militance, Nasir gave Israel the pretext it so desperately needed to launch its devastating surprise attack of June 5, 1967.

The defeat in the June war, which Nasir survived mainly by virtue of his own charisma and by effective internal security, nonetheless exposed grave cracks in the legitimacy formula. By February 1968 both the regional and domestic implications of the disaster had sunk in, and the latent opposition forces had had the time to mobilize themselves. The widespread disturbances of that month, as described by two Egyptian Marxists writing under the pseudonym Mahmoud Hussein, pitted the "democratic" forces of workers, students, and the unemployed, as well as traditional elements from the old Wafd and the Muslim Brotherhood, against key figures of the regime like Anwar al-Sadat, Sha'rawi Goma's and Muhammad Hassanayn Haykal, editor of *Al-Ahram* newspaper.[25] In November yet another major outburst occurred. But in both cases the regime was able to restore control while it slowly rebuilt its armed forces for the next round with Israel and a victory that would restore an important component of regime legitimacy.

In fending off successive challenges from the radical religious Right, the Communist Left, and the liberal-bourgeois ancien régime, the

25. Mahmoud Hussein, *Class Conflict in Egypt 1945–1970* (New York: Monthly Review Press 1973) pp. 292–97, 311–16.

revolutionary government exerted a degree of repression that put an end to the climate of free expression, flawed though it was, that had developed under the parliamentary monarchy. This governmental behavior pattern illustrates the same problem that we have observed in the modernizing monarchies. The problem is that modernity generates increased demands for participation, indeed, opposition, as a condition of legitimacy. But the lack of institutionalized procedures for participation may lead to systemic instability if the demands are not met. The alternative is repression and at least short-term stability. It was this alternative that Nasir, whether by choice or his perception of political necessity, finally adopted. What is interesting is not that the regime chose the latter alternative but that it was able to carry it out. The reason that it was able to curb the opposition so effectively is that there was a sufficiently elaborate and capable governmental apparatus already in existence to exert the necessary controls. With the exception of Tunisia, no other Arab republican regime had been as successful as Egypt in maintaining stability over time. But unlike most of its revolutionary neighbors, Egypt had a massive governmental bureaucracy and a history of bureaucratic rule. To be sure, the civil and military bureaucracies were not known for their efficiency, but their presence was ubiquitous; and the security apparatus, particularly the mukhabarat (intelligence service), was relatively modern and professionalized. One American "crypto-diplomat," presumably specialized in such matters, pronounced Nasir's regime as virtually "coup-proof." [26]

In short, the race in Egypt between demands and capabilities was a close one which the Nasir regime barely won. Structural factors played only a limited role in this limited victory. Apart from the fact that governmental authority by and large was maintained—and even critics of the regime admit that there was little in the way of an overt police-state atmosphere—there is little evidence that governmental procedures were intrinsically valued as legitimate in themselves. One's impression rather is that most Egyptians displayed a mixture of resignation, cynicism, and humor toward their government. Nasir's legacy did not include a widespread new respect for procedures and institutions. His three attempts at building legitimate structures of interest aggregation—the Liberation Rally, the National Union, and the Arab Socialist Union—were not successful in mobilizing and integrating the national polity, even in the view of high officials of

26. Miles Copeland, *The Game of Nations* (London: Weidenfeld and Nicolson, 1969) p. 235, and chaps. 5 and 6.

these organizations. The problem of political participation, which requires a certain structural legitimacy for its solution, was not solved by the Nasir regime.

I cannot conclude, however, that the system lacked any structural legitimacy whatever: it was certainly not a praetorian state. The deep and widespread value attached to Nasir's ideology and Nasir's person were to some extent reinforced through the structures of the government. The regime was buttressed by a set of bureaucracies—the military, the civil service, and the ASU—with concrete interests and organic linkages to the center of power. These bureaucracies, although much maligned, accomplished important things. They fought battles for what were perceived as noble and vital causes, and ordinary soldiers at least were heroes even in defeat. The omnipresent civil bureaucracies actually did provide valued new services: free education, full employment, land redistribution, social insurance, rent control, and other tangible political goods. Even the ASU, although it fell short of its primary national tasks, proved effective at the local level in introducing a new dynamism and rationality to agricultural administration and rural development, as it operated in conjunction with the local government authorities.[27] While the Nasir regime failed to achieve structural legitimacy in the quintessential political sense—there was and still is no institutionalized process of collective choice making—it certainly possessed some structural linkages with the society and a degree of structural capability extending beyond the mere ability to repress dissent.

Sadat's Strategy and Problem

Legitimacy based mainly on an individual leader or certain highly valued symbols is inherently fragile and must constantly be renewed. President Sadat thus was confronted with major problems when he came to power after Nasir's unexpected death in 1970. He proved to be a shrewd and tough political fighter in the way that he consolidated his personal rule and put down the challenge of the radical group led by Ali Sabri. By the middle 1970s he had assembled a following which represented some of the principal politically relevant elements in the country. Two key figures in his entourage (each with sons married to his daughters) were Osman Ahmad Osman, a successful contractor whom Sadat placed in charge of reconstructing the Canal cities, and

27. Iliya Harik, "Mobilization Policy and Political Change in Rural Egypt," In Iliya Harik and Richard Antoun (eds.) *Rural Politics and Social Change in the Middle East* (Bloomington: Indiana University Press, 1972), pp. 287–314, esp. pp. 306–13.

Sayyid Marei, a wealthy landowner. With the premiership in the
hands of an ex-police official, Mamdouh Salem, and the vice-
presidency occupied by the former air force commander, Husni
Mubarak, two of the key military-security bureaucracies were also
represented in the president's inner circle.

But President Sadat was unable to exert the kind of personal
magnetism of his predecessor. Nor was he entirely successful in maintaining the ideological momentum of the Nasir regime. Saddled
with the bitter and seemingly permanent legacy of the 1967 Arab-
Israeli war and burdened by mounting economic problems, Egypt
seemed headed for a legitimacy crisis when Sadat and President Asad
of Syria launched the 1973 war against Israel. The successful crossing
of the Suez Canal and the considerable damage inflicted on Israel
constituted for Sadat a legitimacy bonanza.

Having thus effectively established his pan-Arab credentials, the
president was in a position to crystallize a legitimacy formula very
different from that of his predecessor. While steadfastly claiming to
have extended, indeed improved, the Nasir revolution, Sadat in
fact began to pull in another direction. "Egypt first" became the
emphasis in regime propaganda, and a related theme was the sacrifices
Egypt had made for the pan-Arab and Palestinian causes over the
years only to be ungratefully attacked by certain regimes and movements whose own sacrifices had been comparatively meager. Denuncia-
tions of the Palestinian movement could be heard among ordinary
people in Cairo in the middle 1970s and wishes for normalizing
relations with Israel were expressed in the educated, business-oriented
upper middle classes.

On the regional level, President Sadat began his regime by exploring
the idea of unity with Syria and Libya; but these collapsed in acrimony
after Egypt, under the tutelage of U.S. Secretary of State Kissinger,
made what was widely seen as a separate peace with Israel. On the
international level, Egypt accelerated its movement out of the Soviet
orbit and plunged into what it felt would be the warm embrace of the
Americans. Although it cannot be said that Egypt even under Nasir,
nor indeed most other regimes in the pan-Arab core, had ever exerted
their strongest efforts toward achieving all-Arab goals, President
Sadat's steps to minimize Egypt's commitment to Arabism were both
dramatic and significant. The leader of the most powerful Arab state
was in effect challenging some of the most sacred values in Arab
public opinion.

This shift was paralleled in the internal level by moves away from
state socialism. The huge public sector was blamed for the visible
deterioration of the Egyptian economy and infrastructure, and

cautious efforts were initiated to reintroduce a measure of free enterprise into the system. At the same time, President Sadat undertook a
dramatic "Opening" (infitah) of the Egyptian economy to foreign
capital. This relaxation of socialist austerity had tangible appeal for
many in the upper-middle-class business community who found new
opportunities for quick enrichment. While foreign investment in
productive activities was very slow in getting under way, there was a
sudden inflow of liquid funds in the form of grants and real estate
investments from the oil-rich kingdoms of the Gulf. Two years after
the "Crossing," (of the Canal) a limited, superficial prosperity was
evident in Cairo. Imported luxury goods were now available for those
who could pay for them; new European automobiles were more in
evidence than before; and, for the poorer people, there were even
some new buses to relieve the unbelievable congestion in urban public
transport.

Possibly the most significant aspect of President Sadat's strategy was
addressed to the critical question of political participation. The
spectrum of permissible opinion in the press was broadened. Egypt's
National Assembly, in the Nasir years little more than a rubber stamp
of the president and the Arab Socialist Union, was allowed greater
latitude in the discussion of government policies. One of the most
interesting developments was the creation in 1975 and 1976 of forums
(minabar) under the aegis of the Arab Socialist Union in the National
Assembly. The forums were groups of politicians sharing a common
orientation. Of the some forty groupings that initially identified
themselves, three were most important: one on the Right, one on the
Left, and one in the center. While a full return to political parties was
ruled out as premature, and perhaps too reminiscent of the pre-
revolutionary period for some, the forums were intended as a modest
step toward allowing more diverse input into the political process.
The three groupings roughly paralleled the reemerging cleavages in
the country as a whole, which found the Muslim Brotherhood and its
allies at one end of the spectrum and the Marxists at the other. In
the middle was the regime itself, giving (as one report put it) its full
weight to the forum headed by the prime minister and President Sadat's
brother-in-law, Mahmoud Abu Wafia.[28] Despite the skepticism
expressed by both rightists and leftists, the possibility could not be
excluded that President Sadat's cautious liberalization of organized
political participation might eventually enhance the structural
legitimacy of the political system.

The risks accompanying Sadat's strategy, however, were consider-

28. Thomas W. Lippman, in the *Washington Post*, July 18, 1976.

able. The cumulative decay of Egypt's economic and administrative infrastructure was unmistakably evident, and the need to enhance or at least maintain governmental capabilities was urgent. But as we have already observed in chapter 6, a solution to this problem was not immediately in prospect. Massive assistance from the Arab Gulf states and the United States, as well as foreign investment, were seen as an immediate necessity to avoid sociopolitical turmoil. Another problem was the reemergence of organized opposition at the right and left extremes of the political spectrum. The Muslim Brotherhood, long banned after its abortive challenge to Nasir in 1954, had never disappeared, and in the middle 1970s it came once more into public view. On the Left, a circle of intellectuals with connections in the civil and military bureaucracies, was circulating a Marxist critique of the regime, charging that it had sold out the populist, social welfare, egalitarian tenets of Nasirism to the small monied upper bourgeoisie. Many of those on the Left who had accused Nasir of distorting socialist and democratic ideals found Sadat's course even more reactionary, mitigated only by his liberalization of political expression. Knowledgeable Egyptians in the middle 1970s were divided over whether the left forum headed by Nasir's old Marxist comrade, Col. Khalid Moheiddine, would prove to be an effective input for leftist opinion. Finally, Sadat's turnaround on pan-Arabism and his moderation toward Israel represented the biggest gamble of all. It appeared to assume that Egyptian public opinion, fatigued by Nasir's activist Arab policies, would accept his redefinition of Egypt's goals and interests instead of viewing it as abandonment of the Arab cause.

In April 1974 an insurrection by a Muslim fundamentalist group at the Egyptian technical military academy was put down with violence and casualties, and early in 1975 riots and labor unrest resulting from low wages and a 25 percent inflation rate led to hundreds of arrests. The latter disturbances were said by the government to be inspired by left-wing or Communist elements. And in January 1977 Egypt experienced its worst riots in twenty-five years as thousands protested the government's attempt to reduce its huge food subsidy program; at least 80 people were killed and 1,500 arrested. Sadat was forced to rescind his decision hastily, a retreat that could only further weaken his position.

Lacking Nasir's overwhelming symbolic magic, Sadat was in no position to carry on in the same tradition. On the regional level, instead of leading like his predecessor, he was now subordinate to his Sa'udi benefactors and reduced to equality with Syria and Jordan. Therefore, his course of turning inward, relaxation, and liberalization was understandable as a legitimizing strategy. But it seemed likely that liberalization would rekindle the latent ideological polarities represented by the Islamic Right and the socialist Left and that the increasing distress within Egypt's substantial new industrial proletariat would feed both tendencies. Little progress was being made in coping with the economic crisis. Furthermore, a posture of moderation on the diplomatic front—as long as it did not yield substantial Israeli concessions—was costing Sadat heavily in terms of ideological legitimacy. Thus, despite Egypt's past success (compared to most of its sister revolutionary regimes), there were reasons to suspect that it would not be easy for Nasir's successor to construct an alternative legitimacy formula that would encompass the country's restless political forces as successfully as that of the Ra'is.

SYRIA

At the end of January 1958, the Syrian cabinet flew en masse to Cairo and persuaded President Nasir to allow Syria's fusion with Egypt. According to a distinguished Lebanese journalist, after the documents were signed the Syrian President, Shukri al-Quwatli, turned to the Ra'is and whispered how happy he was to be relieved of trying to rule over people each of whom considered himself an eminent politician: "Half claim the vocation of leader, a quarter believe they are prophets, and at least 10 percent take themselves for gods." Nasir is supposed to have replied dryly, "You waited until I signed before revealing all this." [29] In fact, Syria at the time was in the throes of a slow revolution, its political order irreversibly fractionated by incompatible ideologies; but even union with Egypt and the hero of Arabism could not resolve the difficulties.

It remained for the Ba'th, the Arab Socialist Renaissance party, to impose a degree of coherence on Syrian politics. The Ba'thists, who seized power in 1963 and who were still ruling in the middle 1970s, achieved a limited degree of success in establishing legitimacy. Ba'thist ideology articulated three of the most salient Arab values: unity, freedom, and socialism. Their leaders, while not charismatic or even universally popular, were at least capable politicians with the wariness and agility to maintain power. And while structural legitimacy in Syria lagged, as it has in almost all the other revolutionary republics, the Ba'thists were able to begin a significant degree of linkage building and even to open the political process somewhat for wider political participation. Notwithstanding these developments, however, the

29. Edouard Saab, *La Syrie ou la révolution dans la rancoeur* (Paris: Julliard, 1968), p. 92.

search for legitimacy in Syria was frustrated by two serious and related problems. One was the chronic and bitter factionalism within the Ba'th, which was due to personal rivalries and deep ideological differences. The other was the deviation of the ruling wing of Lt.-Gen. Hafiz al-Asad from the path of militant pan-Arabism originally expounded by the Ba'th itself toward the conservatism of Sa'udi Arabia, Jordan, and Sadat's Egypt. Motivated by internal tactical considerations and by external pressures flowing from the Arab-Israeli conflict, the Asad regime dealt serious blows to the Palestinian movement in Jordan in 1970 and in Lebanon in 1976, and in so doing appeared to align itself with the main enemies of revolutionary Arab nationalism and progressivism, Israel and the United States. As we shall see, Syria has played a historic role in the forefront of the Arab struggle; and for Syrians who value that role, the regime's behavior could not easily be accepted as legitimate.

Syria's reputation for instability is well deserved, as the event-data plot in the Appendix indicates. Major changes of government since independence have usually occurred through coups d'état or other irregular circumstances rather than according to normal constitutional procedures. Three military coups occurred in 1949 alone and the strongman of that period, Col. Adib Shishakly, was himself overthrown in 1954. A major assassination and various plots preceded the union with Egypt. The secession from the UAR at the end of 1961, although nearly bloodless, was accomplished through the direct threat of force. It was followed in half a year by another military coup which in turn paved the way for the decisive seizure of power by the Ba'th on March 8, 1963. Ba'thist rule to date has been marked by the militant "neo-Ba'th" coup of 1966 and the "corrective movement" of November 1970, which brought to predominance the present government of President Hafiz al-Asad, a regime generally regarded as less doctrinaire than its predecessor on domestic socialism, popular armed struggle, and relations with the capitalist powers of the West. Even though these upheavals (with the exception of the 1966 coup) have been largely free of widespread civil violence, compared, for example, to Iraq or Lebanon, they still support President Quwatli's observation on the problems of governing the country.

What cultural and historical conditions account for these problems? Why has it taken over two decades to carry out a revolution in Syria, with the end still not clearly in sight? The answer lies in the conjunction of four factors: serious and persisting subnational parochial identifications, a deep strain of Arabism that transcends the territorial boundaries of the republic, vulnerability to external regional and international political forces, and a high level and relatively long experience of social mobilization and elite politicization. Perhaps none of these loads on the system, considered individually, is decisive for explaining the fragmentation of Syrian politics; taken together, however, they add up to a formidable challenge. Syrian politics is often interpreted as hopelessly corrupt and praetorian,[30] but it is interesting to recall that Syria and the other former Turkish territories were considered under the League of Nations Covenant in 1919 to "have reached a stage of development where their existence as independent nations can be provisionally recognized ..."[31]

Parochial Identifications

In analyzing political culture in Syria, it is useful to consider the nature of collective identifications and the configuration of solidarity groupings. The first involves the classical distinction between primordial and interest-based relationships. As in most states in the region, the kinship nexus has bulked large in Syrian politics. Although less than 10 percent of Syrian society can be considered today as predominantly tribal, family and clan solidarity is still very much a feature of the agricultural and even the urban sectors. And while kinship loyalty was never strong enough to engender much enthusiasm for monarchy, as it has in several largely tribal polities which I have surveyed, it doubtless contributed to Syria's quasi-feudal agricultural order and the upper bourgeoisie, both of which were dominated by the notables of the best families. Thus Syrian politics was family politics, and even the first generation of nationalists who struggled to lift French control derived their influence from local family position: the Jabiris, Kikhias, and Qudsis of Aleppo; the Azms, Barazis, and Kaylanis of Hama; the Atasis of Homs; the Asalis, Haffars, Mardams, and Quwatlis of Damascus.[32] One of the reasons for the failure of these leaders to build a stable order after the French withdrawal in 1946 was the localized scope and particularist nature of their support bases. Consequently, they were unable either to compose their intraelite differences or to

---

30. See, e.g., Miles Copeland, *The Game of Nations* (London: Weidenfeld and Nicolson, 1969), pp. 37–46.

31. Article 22 of the League of Nations Covenant, 1919, reproduced in Stephen S. Longrigg, *Syria and Lebanon under French Mandate* (London: Oxford University Press, 1958), Appendix C.

32. On the great families, see Patrick Seale, *The Struggle for Syria* (London: Oxford University Press, 1965), chap. 4 passim, esp. pp. 28–29; Michael H. Van Dusen, "Intra- and Inter-Generational Conflict in the Syrian Army," Ph. D. dissertation, Johns Hopkins University, 1971, pp. 310 ff.; and Albert H. Hourani, *Syria and Lebanon: A Political Essay* (London: Oxford University Press, 1946), pp. 190–94 and passim.

build national associational constituencies, even in the face of a growing threat to their position as the ruling class. This threat was a function of Syria's social mobilization, the popularity of new nationalist and socialist ideologies, and the intolerable strain of defeat in the 1948 Palestine war. But the prevalence of primordial solidarities proved inhibiting as well to politicians and parties outside the establishment, such as the populist Akram Hourani, the early Ba'thists, and the Syrian nationalists. Ironically, the limited success of these groups in the 1940s and early 1950s may have been due more to their ability to exploit kinship, ethnic, sectarian, and regional solidarities than to overcome them as their ideologies preached.

The configuration of parochial loyalties also complicated the problem of governance in Syria. Compared to other Arab states, Syrian political culture is only moderately fragmented—less than Iraq but more than Egypt, for example. The vast majority of Syria's seven million people are Arabs. The principal ethnic minorities are Kurds (about 8 percent) and Armenians (3 percent) many of whom are conversant in Arabic. The principal religious minorities, the Alawites (who are concentrated in Lattakia Province), the Christians, and the Druze (located mainly in Southern Syria) together account for probably less than a quarter of the population, and all are Arabic-speaking. The Alawites, whose doctrine is discussed in chapter 3 above, are the largest minority in Syria, accounting perhaps for 10 percent of the population; the Christians are perhaps 8 percent and the Druze perhaps 2 percent. Nevertheless, there was a very high degree of separatist activity during the French mandate period, strongly abetted by the mandatory. It is true, as the nationalists emphasize, that Syria under Turkish administration was undivided: common rules and regulations prevailed throughout the area (with the qualified exception of Mount Lebanon) and one could travel unhindered by frontier or customs formalities. But this is not to say that it was a coherent political entity. The fact that the French considered a policy of divide-and-rule expedient is in itself an indication of the fissiparousness of Syrian politics, and a simple listing of the separate states which France imposed during its two-decade tenure reveals where the major cleavages were. Between the historic battle at Maysalun in July 1920, when French troops terminated the Hashimite Amir Faisal's Arab Kingdom of Syria, and 1925, on the eve of the bloody Druze-led nationalist uprising, the mandatory carved geographical Syria into five distinct political units: the Territory (later State) of the Alawites, the independent Government of Jabal Druze, the State of Aleppo, the State of Damascus, and last but far from least the State of Greater Lebanon substantially larger than the old semiautonomous Christian *sanjak* (district) of Mount Lebanon. Of these divisions only the last has persisted to the present day in the independent Republic of Lebanon. The others underwent various modifications after the 1925 uprising: the Damascus and Aleppo states were merged into the State of Syria, and the Alawite and Druze states were amalgamated in 1937 and then again, after a separatist lapse, in 1942.[33] There were, in addition, separatist rumblings in the fertile Jazira area of northeastern Syria in the late 1930s, where Kurds, Christians, and other minorities intermittently fought the nationalist centralizers in Damascus and each other. In assessing the relative strength of communal separatism and Syrian Arab nationalism during the mandate, it is well to recall the structural weaknesses of each tendency, which were turned to good advantage by the French administrators. Fears of oppression and jealousy could easily be stirred among the minorities, while the nationalists, though speaking for a huge theoretical majority were in fact a thin stratum of urban, educated, upper bourgeois notables. In any event, the seeds of separatism once sowed could not be quickly uprooted. Even after the Popular Front government of France concluded a treaty in 1936 (never ratified) to reintegrate Syria in accordance with moderate nationalist demands, there was a resurgence of particularist opposition which receded only after the fall of France and the liberation of the territories by the British and Free French. Brigadier Longrigg, whose study of the mandate is as cool to the French as to the nationalists, concludes:

> The failure to make good the 1936 decision in favour of unity in Syria was due to the strength of local autonomist feeling which, during sixteen years, an unhappy policy of planned fragmentation had allowed—or encouraged—to build up: to the resulting lack of confidence between these minorities and the main body of Syrian opinion: to the provocation on the spot by French officials with convinced localist preferences: and to the absence of firm French backing, at all levels, for the policy which their own new decisions and statutes implied. To these causes of failure must be added a lack of tact in the Syrian officials directly concerned.[34]

The difference between Syria of the mandate period and today is indeed striking; although there have been rumblings among Sunnis about disproportionate Alawite influence in the Ba'thist regimes since

33. Hourani, op. cit., pp. 172–73
34. Longrigg, op. cit., p. 247

1966, there was until the middle 1970s at least far less communal tension and far more national cohesion than there was before independence. The locus of Syria's identity problem has shifted from subnational dismemberment to the degree of the Syrian region's integration in the Arab world.

Pan-Arabism

If Arabism has been the main source of political legitimacy in modern Syria, it has also contributed significantly to its instability. The state's present boundaries have been scalloped out of the larger entity of geographical Syria by Western imperialism. Alexandretta province went to Turkey; the Tripoli plain, Biqa valley, and Litani river region went to Greater Lebanon; Transjordan went to the Hashimites; Palestine and now Golan have gone to Israel. Little wonder that the present territory of Syria inspires little satisfaction among pan-Arab nationalists. The supranational dimension would be less complicated were it not for Syria's historical involvement with Arab nationalism. I have already indicated in chapter 2 the high salience of the Ummayad Arab Empire of Damascus in Arab mythology. In the nationalist revival of the late nineteenth and early twentieth centuries, Syria emerges once again as the heartland of the Arab nation, and it was Damascus—not Baghdad, Jerusalem, Amman, Beirut, or Cairo— that was chosen as the seat of the first short-lived independent Arab state.

But the original Arab nationalism declined temporarily because of conflicting elite orientations and European imperialism. Several competing ideological and strategic variants emerged. One was the Syrian nationalism of Antun Sa'ada and his Syrian Social Nationalist party, which was established in 1932 and remained a threat to established regimes in Syria until 1955 and in Lebanon until 1962.[35] Against what they saw as the Islamic and linguistic bases of Arab nationalism, the SSNP ideologues advocated the establishment of a Syrian nation-state comprising the area from the Taurus mountains in the north to the Suez Canal in the south and from Cyprus and the Mediterranean in the west through Iraq and the Zagros mountains in the east.[36] The rationale for this entity was the alleged geographical and racial distinctiveness of the Syrian people. The reformist nature of the party's secular, antifeudal and state-directed modernization

35. The definitive work on the SSNP is Labib Zuwiyya Yamak, *The Syrian Social Nationalist Party: An Ideological Analysis*. Harvard Middle Eastern Monograph Series, 16 (Cambridge: Harvard University Press, 1966).

36. Ibid, p. 84

principles may account for its attraction to some of the area's most able young intellectuals—some of whom later abandoned it to take up Arab nationalism of Nasirite, Palestinian, or Marxist coloration. One reason for its demise in Syria in the middle 1950s was its reputed cooperation with the United States in opposing the Communist party and Ba'thist-Nasirite Arab nationalism.

The other principal transnational competitors to mainstream Arab nationalism were the Greater Syria plan, sponsored by the Hashimite Amir Abdalla of Transjordan, which embraced Transjordan, Syria, Lebanon, and Palestine; and the Fertile Crescent plan put forth by the Iraqi leader Nuri al-Sa'id, which would have linked Iraq to Greater Syria and, eventually, other Arab states as well. But by the end of World War II, both the Transjordanian and the Iraqi Hashimite kingdoms had forfeited the family's claim to be the standard-bearer of Arab nationalism: their suppression of more militant nationalist elements (both inside and outside the ruling establishments in each country) and their too obvious compliance with British interests drained their respective schemes of legitimacy. Nevertheless the Iraqi regime in particular was able to exert considerable influence in Syrian affairs and help keep the question of Syrian identity unsettled.

Despite these deviationist phenomena, the diffuse idea of pan-Arabism has remained perhaps the most widely and intensely held symbol of political identification in Syria since independence. The two principal manifestations of this Arabism—the Ba'th movement and Nasirism—have found in Syria a supportive environment. It may be surmised as well that this affinity with Arabism has been enormously strengthened by the Palestine problem and Syria's proximity to it. The Zionist assault may well have generated a commitment on the part of many Syrians who might otherwise have been only theoretically interested in Arabism for a collective Arab response.

It seems paradoxical that Syria should have been so often the object of the unity struggle and not the initiator. The answer to this puzzle lies both in its subnational divisions and instability and in the bitter rivalry among the supranationalist movements, most of which were supported by outside elements like the Hashimites who were seeking hegemony in the region. Thus the theoretical center of the Arab nation was a power vacuum. But since independence, and notwithstanding the chronic instability, there has been a diminution of separatist tendencies and a spreading of central authority, and since the consolidation of Ba'thist rule in the 1960s, Syria has developed enough structural solidity for it to play a more active regional role. One might also argue that there has been a tendency toward coherence on the supranational level as well. The Hashimite regimes were destroyed or weakened, their credentials as Arab nationalists were diminished and so perforce were their plans for Arab unity. The Syrian nationalists, who staked out a position strongly opposed to Arab nationalism, were virtually eliminated as a political force in Syria and Lebanon between 1949 and 1962.

Meanwhile the great wave of Nasirist Arab nationalism passed over Syria in the 1950s and 1960s and gradually receded, while the Ba'thists doggedly worked their way into power. By the late 1960s Ba'thist Syria had begun to play a dynamic role in regional affairs and was reasserting its old claim to leadership of the revolutionary nationalist forces. But the inability of the Ba'th National (i.e., pan-Arab) Command to control its Regional Commands in Iraq and Syria after the 1963 coups, and the tendency to unmanageable factionalism in each of the regional commands has clouded the claims of the present regimes in each country to embody the true Ba'thist Arabism. The coup of the militant neo-Ba'thists in Syria in February 1966 was denounced by the "historic chiefs" of the movement as a regionalist and isolationist deviation, and these charges were intensified against the Asad regime that carried out the "corrective movement" of November 1970 because of its crackdowns on the Palestinian movement and its opening to Western investment. Intraparty factionalism seems to account for the continuing friction rather than clear-cut ideological conflicts. Yet while such frictions sap the supranational (Arabism) legitimacy claims of the Syrian Ba'th (and the Iraqi Ba'th as well), it must also be recognized that both the neo-Ba'th and the Asad regimes immeasurably strengthened their Arabism credentials by involving Syria in war against Israel—the neo-Ba'th by encouraging Palestinian raids in the months prior to the Six-Day War and the Asad regime by coordinating with Eygpt in the war of October 1973. For Asad, like Sadat, the October war had opened up a virtual gold mine of pan-Arab legitimacy. Unfortunately, however, the leader who stakes his claim to legitimacy of this kind finds it difficult to maintain, for he becomes vulnerable to outbidding by his enemies as well as to the objective risks of pursuing these goals. As I shall show, by intervening against the Palestinians and the Lebanese left-wing in the Lebanese civil war in 1976, the Asad regime found its all-Arab legitimacy challenged.

External Intrusions

Implicit in the foregoing discussion is a third factor that has complicated Syria's search for revolutionary legitimacy: its vulnerability to external political interference. France's manipulation of minority groups, such as the Alawites, during its mandate was just an extension of the "rule by consuls" in nineteenth century Ottoman Syria. In the postindependence period, the United States helped destabilize the parliamentary nationalist civilian government, which was thought to be dangerously weak and thus open to penetration by others, and initiate the first of the long cycle of military-reformist coups.[37] In the 1950s Hashimite Iraq and Jordan, with their close British association, intervened in Syrian affairs to further their respective regional ambitions; and anti-Hashimite states like Egypt and Sa'udi Arabia engaged in similar activities in pursuit of their interests. The Soviet Union, when it began to play an active role in the area, projected its influence in Syria through supporting the small but venerable Syrian Communist party and, more importantly, by supplying arms to the restless armed forces. Even Turkey was induced to mass troops on Syria's northern frontier in 1957 as rumors spread of an imminent take-over by the forces of "international Communism" and American military attachés were expelled for plotting a coup. Small wonder that Syrian nationalists are often described as xenophobic.

But these examples are less important than the catalytic impact of France's occupation during the mandate and Israel's military and political threat since independence. Because they were traumatic these were nation-building experiences. Like the 1920 tribal uprising in Iraq, the Druze-initiated rebellion of 1925–27 ignited widespread resistance against the occupying power and as such became a landmark in nationalist mythology.[38] No doubt the uprising was less a coherent nationalist insurgency than an amalgam of various local factors; yet the fact of its persistence and its widespread manifestations as well as participation by a key nationalist leader, Dr. Abd al-Rahman Shahbandar, turned it into something far more significant than a local uprising. The crystallization of latent but widespread antipathy for the occupier was the first step toward a more coherent national feeling. The French bombardment of Damascus in 1945 only reinforced this national solidarity.

As for Palestine, its impact was major and was felt in many ways. The Syrian army's inept performance in 1948 revealed the real dimension of Zionist power and made the Palestine struggle more of an issue than it had been before independence. It also crystallized the animosity between the military and the new nationalist establishment. The military were bitter about the civilian politicians' misperception

37. Copeland, op. cit., chaps. 1 and 2 and passim.
38. On the nationalist dimension of the uprising, see Elizabeth P. MacCallum, *The Nationalist Crusade in Syria* (New York: Foreign Policy Association, 1928), chaps. 6–11.

of the Israeli threat and their failure to have built up the army. The civilian notables, who generally considered the army a lower-status social institution, were scathing in their criticism of corruption within the military after the debacle. And young nationalist ideologues, notably the leaders of the Ba'th, found ready adherents both inside and outside the military to their call for reconstruction of the entire political system.[39] Palestine in short became an explosive issue in Syria both as a local issue, catalyzing perceptions of the incompetence of the upper-bourgeois nationalist elite, and as a manifestation of the need for Arab unity; on both counts the Ba'th, at least until the middle 1970s, was the most successful of all the competing groups in exploiting this legitimacy resource.

Social Mobilization

Underlying the heightened sense of subnational and supranational identifications I have discussed has been Syria's long experience with social mobilization, dating to the Egyptian occupation of the 1830s and then the impact of foreign educators. The events of World War I and the mandate and the even more recent impact of formal education and mass communications would seem to have greatly enlarged the population (both elite and mass) that are, in Deutsch's term, available for politicization. It is useful to recall, for example, that in 1947, a year after the French evacuation, there were 8,855 primary school graduates while in 1970 the figure was 85,717; the corresponding figures for secondary school graduates (a level where politicization is significant) are 666 and 21,567.[40] Against the background of this kind of growth one can better understand President Quwatli's lament to President Nasir. One can also understand better the profusion and fragmentation of ideological political movements in the last years of the mandate and after independence. In the ideological realm, there was not only ferment over Syrian identity, there was also agitation for social and economic reform. Modernization as well as the "Syrian nation" was an important appeal of the SSNP. For many other

39. In his Ph. D. dissertation on the Syrian army, Michael Van Dusen found in his interviews that the Palestine debacle and the first military coup by Husni Za'im in 1949 were two key events in politicizing the military. Moreover, the first coup was itself an outgrowth of the Palestine defeat. He cites Adib Shishakly, the principal military strongman of the 1949–54 period, as believing that the Za'im coup "was the spontaneous and popular response to the situation in Syria, and in particular the Palestine war". Van Dusen, op. cit., p. 172, and passim pp. 167–73. See also Saab, pp. 38–41 and chap. 1 passim; and Seale, op. cit., pp. 41–45.

40. Syrian Arab Republic, Office of the Prime Minister, Central Bureau of Statistics, *Statistical Abstract*, 1971 (Damascus: Government Printing Press), p. 341.

intellectuals the Syrian Communist party, under the able leadership of Khalid Bakdash, was a more important vehicle for secularism and socialism than it was (in its somewhat equivocal way) for nationalism. In the structural realm, the military became the center of reformist, anti-Western, and nationalist ideas. And because of the greater mass availability for political participation, radical counter-elites had an important resource for challenging the old families' monopoly of power. In the long run the Ba'th proved the most effective in mobilizing this resource, but the Nasirite movement provided a more dramatic though short-lived example. Nasir produced such a ground swell of support among the poor that the divided Syrian establishment felt compelled to sign away Syrian sovereignty in its behalf in 1958; public opinion, although ill-formed, was by then a far more potent factor than in the period of the 1925 revolt.

The Ba'thist Synthesis

To many observers, contemporary Syria stands as a preeminent example of the praetorian state. Indeed, the cleavages and contradictions in Syrian political culture that I have sketched would seem to be reflected in a performance record that is unstable by almost any standard: the separatism of the mandate period; the incompetence of the older generation nationalist notables; the era of military coups and dictatorships from 1949 through 1954; the interregnum of chaotically free politics until the disappearance of sovereign Syria in the merger with Egypt in 1958; the secession and military revolt of 1961–62; the Ba'th coup of March 1963 and subsequent civil unrest; the neo-Ba'th coup of 1966; and most recently the counter-neo-Ba'th corrective movement of November 16, 1970, under the command of Lt.-Gen. Hafiz al-Asad. Yet a case can be made that Syria after more than a decade of Ba'thist rule had developed a significant degree of political coherence.[41] To be sure, the internal party coup of 1966 was unusually violent, and important tensions still exist both within the party in Syria and between the Syrian and Iraqi Ba'th regimes. The fact remains, however, that as of the middle 1970s Syria had been governed by a single ideology and party structure; and during that period it accomplished the final displacement of the older wealthy elite, expanded the capabilities of government, and diminished the influence which neighboring regimes could bring to bear on internal politics.

41. This is also the conclusion of Itamar Rabinovitch in his illuminating study, *Syria Under the Ba'th, 1963–1966. The Army-Party Symbiosis* (Jerusalem: Israel Universities Press, 1972), pp. 212–13.

How were these accomplishments achieved? In terms of Easton's three bases of legitimacy, the Ba'thist formula rested mainly upon ideology but increasingly upon structure as well. For all their alleged emotionalism, the Syrians have never submitted for long to a charismatic leader: legitimacy grounded in a strong personality has not manifested itself in Damascus as it has in Egypt, Tunisia, Sudan, Libya, and most of the traditional monarchies.

BA'THIST IDEOLOGY

Ba'thist ideology has been successful less by being revolutionary than by synthesizing a set of deeply held traditional values with ideas of modernity. Intraparty conflicts which on one level reflect factional power struggles also represent attempts by one or another element to change the mix of values in the legitimacy formula. One of the reasons for the party's durability and its considerable political success is the catholicity of its original ideological program. Although his political philosophy is sometimes criticized on intellectual grounds,[42] Michel Aflaq, founder of the party, was a superb ideologist: he laid down a set of principles that tapped the principal wellsprings of legitimacy in the Arab world—kinship, religion, history, nationalism, and modernity— and yet retained an overall dynamism. Diffuse rather than doctrinaire, Ba'thism had wide elite and mass appeal. Despite the acute factionalism and other problems of practical rule that have beset the Ba'th, the set of values articulated by Michel Aflaq has provided a viable formula to an important segment of the reformist elements in Syria and elsewhere in the Arab world.

Aflaq's starting point is an attack on the divisions in Arab society and its moral and political weakness; hence the call for unity (*wahda*) which in its fullest sense means not just the unification of existing states but the transformation (*inqilab*) of society itself. As a strategy for political integration, it is particularly interesting that the Ba'thist approach to these divisions is less than revolutionary. Aflaq does not wish to erase the slate of tradition in Rousseau-like or Communist fashion, instead he celebrates the Arab cultural heritage and calls for its renaissance (ba'th). This revolutionary doctrine is in fact remarkably accommodationist and as such it reflects political realism, given the cleavages present in the political culture of Syria, and even more so in other Arab countries like Iraq and Lebanon. The problem of primordial and particularist group identifications—kinship, ethnic, and sectarian—

---

42. See, e.g., Nabil M. Kaylani, "The Rise of the Syrian Ba'th 1940–1958: Political Success, Party Failure," *International Journal of Middle East Studies*, 3, 1 (January 1972), pp. 3–23; p. 22.

is attacked not with a call for complete assimilation but for reform and toleration of minorities within an overall Arab political framework. The close-knit Arab kinship values should remain but must no longer be exploited by the upper bourgeois and feudal families. Arab society is not to be restructured along impersonal mechanistic lines; it is instead an organism to be cured of its diseases through the application of love, faith, and brotherhood. The existence of ethnic and religious minorities is admitted, not deplored; and the problem of integrating them with a modernizing (centralizing) Arab nationalism is approached by guaranteeing their communal and cultural identity. Admitting the excesses of some fanatic movements of Arab or Islamic nationalism, Aflaq addresses himself specifically to the apprehensions of Christians, Kurds, Assyrians, Armenians, and Berbers, assuring them that Arab nationalism is "open, developing, and human."[43] The reason for this is that Ba'thist Arabism is also socialist, and socialism erases the hostility between groups and prevents monopoly or political domination by any group; thus, in the civic polity there will be no difference between Arab Muslims and Christians, Kurds, or Berbers, etc. But the granting of economic equality and equal opportunity is not to be taken as a demand for cultural assimilation. "Nobody denies that the Kurds should learn their language on condition that they obey the laws of the state and not present a danger to it."[44] Nor will anyone forbid the Christian denominations to practice their creed and to have a Christian education within the framework of a general Arab education. And to emphasize this liberal nature of Ba'thist Arabism, he contrasts it with the fanaticism of the Nazi and Nazilike parties in the Arab world which preach a doctrine of racial exclusivity, and with the communists whose internationalism obliterates the identity of peoples in an artificial materialist order. To be sure, this position has by no means eliminated the ethnic-religious tensions in Syria or especially Iraq which are, in Aflaq's view, significantly stimulated both by self-serving religious and ethnic group politicians and feudalists and by Western imperialism. But it has committed the party to an explicit tolerance and flexibility toward minorities, the existence of which in Syria and especially Iraq has complicated the problem of governance. Ironically, the disproportionate numbers of minority Alawites in Syria's Ba'thist regime has given rise to some discontent within the Sunnite majority.

But the most striking accommodation with traditional culture is

43. Michel Aflaq, *Fi Sabil al-Ba'th* (Beirut: Dar al-Tali'a, 1959, 1963, third edition), pp. 94–95.

44. Ibid., p. 98.

Aflaq's positive treatment of Islam, and his insistence not simply on
its compatibility with nationalism but also the symbiosis between
the two:

> Islam in its pure truth sprang up in the heart of Arabism and
> it gave the finest expression of the genius [of Arabism], and it
> marched with its history and it mixed with Arabism in its most
> glorious roles, so it is impossible for there to be a clash between
> them ... [45] Have no fear of a clash between nationalism and
> religion for nationalism is its likeness, springing from the heart
> and issuing from the will of God, and the two walk together
> embracing, especially if the religion represents the genius of
> nationalism and mixes with its nature.[46]

Nor, he asserts, is there any contradiction between religion and the
other two main Ba'thist symbols, liberty and socialism. It was left to
the Syrian nationalists and the Communists to assert a more clearly
secular and anticlerical position. Thus the idea, so common in progressive circles, that Islam is a serious impediment to development,[47]
is firmly rejected by the Ba'th; and if this rejection has made the
revolutionary claims of the party suspect to some, it has also enhanced
its legitimacy among many others and thus contributed to its political
success. From a politician's point of view, the Ba'th neatly (and on the
whole successfully) avoided the problem of too close an identification
with Islam, on the one hand, and of indifference or hostility toward it,
on the other, by revering it in its historical and cultural context. As
Michael Suleiman has succinctly put it, "For Aflaq, then, Islam *was*
Arab nationalism."[48]

Because of the Ba'th's accommodation toward particularist and
primordial identifications, its credentials as a progressive movement
are questionable to some. But this emphasis is counterbalanced on the
revolutionary side by its strong commitment to unify the Arab world
politically against the depredations of Western imperialism and its call
for a socialist system to cure the maladies of the Arab body politic.
There is little need to dwell further on the salience of Arab unity as a
legitimizing value except to remark that the movement for Arab
nationalism, weakened and dissipated in the mandate period, was

45. Ibid., p. 43.
46. Ibid., p. 46.
47. The antireligious critique has been formulated most strongly by Dr. Sadik Jalal al-Azm
in *Naqd al-Fikr al-Dini* (Beirut: Dar al-Tali'a, 1969).
48. Michael W. Suleiman, *Political Parties in Lebanon* (Ithaca: Cornell University Press, 1967),
p. 140.

resuscitated by the Ba'th and, more importantly, harnessed to a modern single-party structure. The unity principle gave the party a degree of legitimacy that helped compensate for its small size and lack of popularity as a political structure, and the party structure provided the security and durability for the Ba'th to survive its attackers and outlast its competitors, such as the Nasirite movement. And, as we have seen, the Palestine defeat intensified the salience of the unity goal, and the Ba'th took full advantage of this melancholy opportunity. As for the Ba'th's socialism, it was only vaguely formulated by Aflaq and Salah al-Din al-Bitar, but in the context of the 1940s and early 1950s, it was more radical and systematic than most rival ideologies. It was not until the 1960s that Ba'thist theoreticians had the chance to put their socialism into practice. It took the form of land reform and machine-tractor cooperatives, the nationalization of large businesses, and later the establishment of "popular organizations" of peasants, workers, and professionals. Although lacking the democracy and local worker autonomy so essential to an ideal socialist order, the Ba'th socialism was revolutionary by Arab standards in that it permanently eliminated the very rich landed and bourgeois elite from power. At the least, one must conclude that Ba'th's socialism is more than rhetoric. And one must conclude that the Ba'th ideology as a whole has been functional in the slow, painful, and incomplete process of building a coherent legitimacy formula for Syria and perhaps for the Arab world beyond.

STRUCTURE

Ideology alone, however, cannot account for the Ba'th's successes, limited though they are, in Syria and the Arab east; structure is also important. Four factors characterize the Ba'th's structural development. First was the merger in 1953 of the Ba'th with the Arab Socialist party of Akram Hourani. Hourani, the populist leader from Hama, enemy of the landed elite and friend of the nationalist-reformist military officers, brought to the merger a degree of proletarian orientation and a sense of political realities somewhat lacking in Aflaq and Bitar. He also brought some serious divisions into the party leadership.[49] Second, the party developed a coherent cellular structure well suited for the requirements of clandestineness and survival, although not so well suited for winning a direct mass following; and the attempts by the neo-Ba'th and the Asad regime to open up the system have

49. Kaylani, op. cit., p. 22.

been undertaken with understandable caution and not without risk.[50]
Third, the party developed a base both in the military and civilian
sectors; and while at times the party has been dominated by one or the
other, the cleavages have never been absolute nor have there been
corresponding clear-cut ideological divisions. Whether this "symbiosis
... of a relatively vigorous ideological party and a military cabal" (as
Rabinovitch describes it) is as exceptional as he suggests—for we see a
similar pattern in Iraq and perhaps Algeria—and whether it has led
to a virtual take-over of the party by the military, as he asserts, remains
to be seen.[51] The fourth and most recent development would seem to
imply the contrary. It was the development of institutions of elite-mass
linkage and participation. The growth of the mass organizations, such
as the Peasant Union, which are dominated by the Ba'th, was one
example of a structural trend away from praetorianism.[52] Another was
the reinstitution of elections at the local and national levels in 1972
and 1973. Another was the opening up in 1972 of the system through a
National Progressive Front, whose central leadership consisted of nine
Ba'thists and two each from four other progressive groups (the Union
of the Arab Socialist party, the Socialist Unionist Organization, the
Arab Socialist movement, and the Syrian Communist party), chaired
by the president of the Syrian Arab Republic and secretary general
of the Ba'th.[53]

The Challenge to Syria's Arabism

Having championed a legitimacy formula of progressive Arabism,
the Syrian Ba'thists found themselves in the mid-1970s taking positions
which could only erode that legitimacy. Compared to the doctrinaire
excesses of his neo-Ba'thist predecessor, Gen. Salah Jadid, President
Asad's limited economic relaxation was welcome to Western-oriented
businessmen and bureaucrats, but it was received with alarm by the
more militant socialists in the party and the country who favored the
Soviet and east European model of development. Even more potentially
delegitimizing was the dilemma posed for Syria in the ranks of Arabism
by the rise of the Palestinian national movement in the late 1960s and
the Lebanese civil war of 1975–76. The double-edged character of

50. An early description may be found in Kamal Abu Jaber, *The Arab Ba'th Socialist Party*
(Syracuse: Syracuse University Press, 1966), pp. 139–45; see also Rabinovitch, op. cit.

51. Rabinovitch, op. cit., p. 212.

52. This development is spelled out in an interesting paper by Raymond A. Hinnebusch, Jr.,
"Elite-Mass Linkage: The Role of the Mass Organizations in the Syrian Political System,"
delivered at the annual meeting of the Middle East Studies Association, Boston, November 1974.

53. The Ba'th Arab Socialist Party, National Leadership, "Covenant of the National Progressive Front," Damascus, March 7, 1972.

pan-Arabism as a legitimacy resource was never better illustrated than in Syria's response to the Palestinian national movement. During the formative period of that movement in the middle and late 1960s, Jadid's militant neo-Ba'thist regime nurtured and protected it from its numerous enemies inside and outside the Arab world. At the same time, the Syrian leadership sought to control the Palestinian organizations as much as possible, recognizing the political potential arising from their successful claim to embody the most important Arab cause, despite being vulnerable to exploitation by a variety of outside elements. By setting up al-Sa'iqa, a Palestinian organization obedient to Jadid, the Syrian strongman was trying not only to influence Palestinian affairs but also to exploit the strong Palestinian sympathy in Syrian public opinion for his own domestic purposes. The Palestinians thus became embroiled unintentionally in internal Syrian politics. When the Jordanian army in September 1970 moved to crush the growing Palestinian challenge to King Hussein, Jadid rushed Syrian-based Palestinian reinforcements into Jordan. But Jadid's rival Asad, commander of the Syrian air force, refused to provide the necessary air cover to support the initiative. Hussein's forces prevailed, the Palestinians in Jordan were defeated, and Jadid—weakened by the failure of his initiative—was shortly overthrown and jailed by his colleague Asad. All-Arab objectives had been sacrificed in favor of intra-Ba'th Syrian rivalries.

President Asad, as we have noted, restored his all-Arab legitimacy in 1973. But in 1976 Asad again moved to weaken, though not destroy, the Palestinian movement in Lebanon by intervening along side the mostly Maronite Christian right wing to thwart the possibility of an even more militant, revolutionary Arab nationalist, anti-Israel regime coming to power there. Unwilling to be outbid or threatened by such a regime, and undoubtedly worried about the Israeli response, President Asad again sacrificed all-Arab concerns for local interests. Significantly, however, his regime steadfastly reiterated its previous support of the Arab and Palestinian causes and insisted that its intervention in Lebanon was dictated only by a desire to preserve those causes from their misguided adherents. The question which Syrians, Palestinians, and all others concerned with the Arab-Israeli conflict were left to ponder was whether (or when) the Asad regime's seeming retreat on a core legitimizing issue would lead to a renewal of the internal instability of previous years.

IRAQ

The frequency of its political upheavals and the violence associated with them would seem to justify the opinion that Iraq is the least governable of the Arab countries. But it would be simplistic to interpret Iraqi politics as purely praetorian, with one group of opportunistic officers periodically seizing power from another. To do so not only overestimates the importance of the military—as some writers are wont to do—but it also implies that their politics is primarily a raw struggle for power and that legitimizing values are either nonexistent or of only marginal importance. While it is true that the various regimes that have come and gone have been short of support, it is also true that the issues of legitimacy have been at the very heart of the struggles that have taken place. Paradoxically it is the higher level of social development and political consciousness in Iraq that makes the loads on system legitimacy so great and complex. Subnational and supranational loyalties of a primordial character are not only incompatible with one another but also appear to have greater salience than affinities with state or regime. In such a deeply divided political culture, the effectiveness of a mobilizing ideology is limited; personal leadership as a source of legitimacy (in the Nasirite manner) is hard to develop, and the development of structures like the vanguard party is impeded. But as I shall show, it is in the area of structural development, with a strong emphasis on coercion and control, that the solution—if any is possible—for Iraq's legitimacy quagmire may lie.

The name Iraq is derived from an Arabic root meaning deep-rooted and venerable, fitting indeed for the land of the ancient civilizations of the Tigris-Euphrates valley. But the name mocks the political environment out of which the contemporary Iraqi republic has been so painfully fashioned: in fact, even after the state was designated Iraq in 1918, it was still known for a time as Mesopotamia, a geographical term.[54] Even today official Ba'thist publications rarely refer to the "Iraqi republic" as such, instead they speak of the "Iraqi region of the Arab homeland" or the "two rivers" (rafidayn) area. Politically, the territory, when it was a backwater of the Ottoman Empire, was divided into three separate districts of Basra, Baghdad, and Mosul; and the Arab nationalist currents out of which the anti-British independence movement grew were to be found as much outside Iraq proper—in Syria, the Hijaz, Beirut, and even Egypt and Libya—as inside it. The new state's boundaries were fixed through a long and somewhat ad hoc process which began with the British occupation in 1914 through the forced cession of Dayr al-Zur to the Arab government of Damascus at the end of 1919, and finally the

54. Philip Willard Ireland, *Iraq: A Study in Political Development* (London: Jonathan Cape, 1937), p. 21, n. 2.

awarding of oil-rich Mosul (claimed by Turkey) to British-ruled Iraq in 1925 by the International Court.[55] While Iraq's territorial boundaries are now clearly demarcated—although until 1975 there was a serious dispute with Iran over whether the Shatt-al-Arab river was wholly in Iraqi territory—the question of national identity remains unresolved. The pan-Arab origins of the nationalist movement never gave way entirely to a purely Iraqi nationalism, despite the establishment of an Iraqi monarchy, a military and civilian bureaucracy, and an elitist party system. Forty years later, during the 1960s, the question of Iraq's Arab orientation remained a principal axis of conflict between the monarchists and the nationalist military rebels, and then between the Ba'thists and Nasirists; and in the early 1970s observers puzzled over the consolidation of a new Ba'thist regime with a national (e.i., pan-Arab) as opposed to regional orientation and yet which remained isolated in Arab politics, with virtually no close allies. Although Iraq participated actively on behalf of Syria in the 1973 war with Israel, it remained regionalist enough not to participate in the Arab oil boycott that was imposed during the fighting.

While one cannot dismiss the unresolved problems of violence and identity, one should not allow them to obscure the enormous change that has occurred in Iraq's political culture since the mandate period. Today it may no longer be accurate to interpret Iraqi politics as mainly praetorian—an unending cycle of primordial parochial conflict. To put Iraq's current problems in proper perspective, it is necessary to compare the political culture of present Ba'thist state with that of the post-Ottoman period some fifty years ago.

New Monarchy in a Divided Society

The new Iraqi state, constructed so intrepidly by Sir Arnold Wilson, Gertrude Bell, Sir Percy Cox, and other British colonial officers, was implanted upon an area in which the principal social values were tribal and religious and group identifications were parochial in scope. Over half of the population was nomadic or seminomadic; in the north it was organized largely into three Sunni Muslim tribal confederations, the Anaza, the Shammar, and the Dulaym, while in the south there were some thirty-six tribes, mainly Shi'ite, of which the Muntafiq was

55. On these developments, see Ireland, op. cit., pp. 253 ff. It is interesting to note that in 1921 the Arab shaykh of Muhammara, the district adjacent to the Abadan refinery on the Shatt al-Arab river, which is now Iranian Khoramshahr, presented himself as a candidate for the kingship in Iraq. Ireland, op. cit., p. 306.

the principal confederation.[56] If the tribes shared a common way of life, they also shared rivalries and antipathies with one another and with the urban and settled sectors of society.[57] In addition to being divided by confession, tribal society was also marked by status divisions: peasants, marsh dwellers, the sheep people, and—at the highest level—the people of the camel. Furthermore, from the middle of the nineteenth century up through World War I the social cohesion of the tribes was further perturbed by external technological, economic, and administrative factors: river steam navigation, the telegraph, English commercial penetration, the opening of state schools, newspapers, and the attempts by Ottoman governors to break tribal autonomy through land ownership reforms. The British Mesopotamian expedition thus found the traditional tribal system in an advanced state of decay, but in resuscitating it for their own purpose, they failed to appreciate its capacity for dissidence and its functionalism for the new nationalism.[58]

Iraq was also distinctive among Arab states for the centrality in its national politics of the sectarian cleavage between orthodox and heterodox Islam. With a population divided perhaps equally between Sunni and Shi'ite, this cleavage assumed greater importance even than in Lebanon, where Sunni-Shi'ite differences have been subordinate to the deeper Muslim-Christian and sociopolitical divisions. Reinforcing this basically theological difference were regional and social cleavages: the Shi'ites were concentrated mainly in the south, and they were relatively more settled and poorer than the Sunnis. Moreover, their local social organization and religious leadership was also quite different from that of the Sunnis. Although a Shi'ite tribal landed elite flourished during the monarchy, it was Sunnis who were preponderant in the important governmental positions. In spite of these differences, however, Sunni-Shi'ite relations were not normally overtly hostile; there was rather an underlying tacit tension which only occasionally exploded into open conflict. In fact, there were important occasions of Sunni-Shi'ite collaboration, such as in the anti-British uprising of 1920.

56. Amal Vinogradov, "The 1920 Revolt in Iraq Reconsidered: The Role of Tribes in National Politics," *International Journal of Middle East Studies*, 3, 2 (April 1972), pp. 123–39; pp. 125–27, citing in part E. Dawson, *An Inquiry Into Land Tenure and Related Questions* (Baghdad, 1932).

57. On religious, ethnic, and class divisions in Iraq, I am indebted to Professor. Hanna Batatu of the American University of Beirut for allowing me to read parts of his manuscript, *The Old Social Forces and the Revolutionary Movements of Iraq*, forthcoming, Princeton University Press, 1978. I have also consulted Walid Khadduri, "Social Background of Modern Iraqi Politics," unpublished Ph. D. dissertation, The Johns Hopkins University, 1970.

58. Ireland, op. cit., pp. 95 and 174–75; and Vinogradov, op. cit., pp. 124–25 ff.

Ethnicity comprised yet another dimension of Iraq's fragmented political culture. The Kurdish question has been the most violent issue in modern Iraq and indeed one of the most serious communal conflicts in the entire Middle East. Frustrated by the nonimplementation of international commitments for a Kurdish state after World War I, the Kurds were understandably diffident if not hostile toward the new Arab Iraqi state's being constructed by Great Britain. The Arab orientation of Iraqi nationalism was viewed with apprehension by Kurdish nationalists, particularly when various schemes for Arab unity began to reemerge in the 1940s as European control faded. By the same token, the Kurds constituted a problem for Iraqi Arab unionists. The tensions inherent in Arab-Kurdish relations were exacerbated by the geophysical separateness and mountain defensibility of Iraqi Kurdistan and by the fabulous wealth of its oil fields. The Kurdish question has overshadowed all other communal cleavages in modern Iraq. Consequently, the collapse of the latest Kurdish rebellion in March 1975, following a diplomatic rapprochement between Iran and Iraq which involved the withdrawal of Iranian support for the Kurds, may have removed the most serious impediment to regime legitimacy. It should also be noted that there were numerous other small ethnic communities—notably Jews, Assyrians, Armenians, Iranians, Turkomans, Chaldeans, and Yazidis—whose corporate identities further complicated the development of an overall national sense of community.

These ancient divisions, however, are not the only significant features of Iraqi political culture. New and nonparochial nationalist values were also taking root in Iraq as education and exposure to modernity —particularly the example of political ferment elsewhere in the Arab world—spread among the relatively well-to-do. An external catalyst in the form of the British occupation set in motion demands for a new political order, and even though the identity and boundaries of that order were ill defined and remain so even today, the process of change was unstoppable. George Antonius, commenting bitterly on the imposition of the mandate system, notes that the Baghdad-Basra region of Iraq was one of the most politically developed and mature areas of the Arab world.[59] It was a diverse amalgam of political forces that rose up together in 1920 against the British occupation: the pious and secular, Sunni and Shi'ite, Kurd and Arab, tribesman and urban nationalist, traditionalist and modernist. The insurrection was not governed by a single coherent nationalism or group, and although it

59. George Antonius, *The Arab Awakening* (London: Hamish Hamilton, 1938), p. 249.

was crushed within a few months (at considerable cost to the British),
it created a myth of cooperation and resistance that has since become
enshrined in the history of Arab nationalism. As Hanna Batatu puts
it, "Nationalism did not displace old loyalties. Although it grew at
their expense, it existed side by side with them, corroding them, yes,
but at the same time absorbing some of their psychological elements
and expressing itself within the emotional and conceptual patterns of
the Islamic religion."[60]

Lacking a coherent national identity, having been created to further
British imperial interests, the new state was further burdened by the
imposition of an alien institution, kingship, and an alien ruling family,
the Hashimites of the Hijaz. Indeed, so fluid were political conditions
after Britain finally drove out the Turks that the nation-building
process, as described by Gertrude Bell and others, appears to have
been very much the work of a handful of British officials (assisted by an
appointed council of notables) acting with almost whimsical self-
assurance. Actually, the term "nation-building", a comparative politics
concept connoting the development of a coherent political culture, is
not fully applicable to this particular period of Iraqi development;
"king-making" would be better. And a mere list of candidates considered for the newly created throne illustrates the latitude which the
king-makers felt they could exercise: Prince Burhan al-Din (a Sunni
Turk), Abd al-Rahman al-Gailani (the Naqib of Baghdad), Sayyid
Talib Pasha (of Basra), the shaykh of Muhammara (Persia), Ibn Sa'ud
(of Najd, later Sa'udi Arabia), the Agha Khan, the Wali of Pusht-i-Kuh
(Persia), and even apparently Sir Percy Cox himself.[61] Faisal, son of
Hussein of the Hijaz, standard-bearer of the Arab revolt, instrument
of British policy, and lately ruler of the short-lived Arab Kingdom of
Syria, was selected by virtue of his nationalist credentials, his prophetic
lineage (making him more acceptable to Shi'ite opinion), his reputation
for tolerance and realism, and his cooperative attitude toward Great
Britain. Perhaps it is true, as some English writers have pointed out,
that the king was the only unifying element in the whole country; but
it is also true that the institution and the family were imposed upon a
political culture in which there were strong republican, nationalist,
and antiimperialist elements. Furthermore, the "development" of the
monarchy, if such it was, exacerbated social inequalities through the

60. Batatu, op. cit., book 1, chap. 1.

61. Stephen H. Longrigg, *Iraq, 1900 to 1950* (London: Oxford University Press, 1953),
pp. 126–31; Ireland, op. cit., pp. 303–11; Vinogradov, p. 134. See also Gerald de Gaury, *Three
Kings in Baghdad* (London: Hutchinson, 1961).

enrichment of a tribal landed elite. It systematically frustrated the nationalism and liberalism of the educated middle-class political parties and groups, such as the Ahali movement of the late 1930s. Unwilling and most probably unable to share power with the diverse opposition elements—pan-Arabists, socialists, military officers, and the leaders of various traditional constituencies—the palace kept a tight rein on opposition groups. The long-time master-manipulator of Iraqi politics, Nuri al-Sa'id, proved ultimately to have underestimated the strength of revolutionary ideas implacably hostile to the royal regime.

Revolutionary Iraq

On July 14, 1958, King Faisal II, Crown Prince Abd al-Illah and Nuri al-Sa'id were killed and a republican regime of nationalist military officers, led by Brigadier Abd al-Karim Qassim, was installed in Baghdad. It was not the first time that the Iraqi military had supported a coup; such was the praetorian character of the Hashimite system that as early as 1936 General Bakr Sidqi and a group of politicians inclined toward socialism had deposed a government, without however attacking the monarchy itself. Then in 1940 an anti-British military uprising in support of the nationalist government of Rashid Ali al-Gailani was put down by British forces hastily brought in from Palestine, Transjordan, and India. But the Qassim coup destroyed the old regime. It also brought Iraq into the ranks of the revolutionary polities by shifting the bases of system legitimacy from kinship and religion, buttressed by affinity with the West in the international system, to modern nationalism, social reform, and neutralism in Great Power rivalries. But neither the Qassim regime nor the Ba'thist and quasi-Nasirite regimes that followed it after Qassim's overthrow and murder in 1963 were able to articulate a legitimacy formula out of these resources that might diminish the Hobbesian character of Iraqi politics. These years were marked by unsuccessful efforts to deal with Communists, Nasirists, factions within the Ba'th, and particularly the Kurds. It was not until the Ba'thist coup of 1968 that the contours of a more cohesive legitimacy formula and a more stable order emerged.

The instability of revolutionary Iraq from 1958 through 1968 suggests that the mere invocation of nationalist and socialist symbols, no matter how popular, could not in itself generate authority and legitimacy. This problem, common to all of the region's revolutionary regimes, was all the more difficult for the Iraqi Ba'thists in view of the internal cleavages and the regional inter-Arab ferment which at once stimulated and frustrated the exploitation of pan-Arabism as a legitimacy resource. Overloaded with threats and pressures from various quarters and underequipped structurally to grasp the reins of power firmly, the successive regimes of this period were too insecure to permit any opening toward pluralism in the political process. The Qassim regime for a time successfully warded off Communist and Nasirite factions but it became increasingly isolated and vulnerable to overthrow. The short-lived Ba'th regime of February through November 1963 was divided between relatively conservative and radical factions. In addition to their leadership factionalism, the Ba'thists had not been able to develop their national guard militia sufficiently to ward off threats. Thus weakened, it was displaced by the Nasirite pan-Arabist Abd al-Salam Arif. Arif's civilian prime minister Abd al-Rahman al-Bazzaz tried to reach an accommodation with the Kurds and to liberalize domestic politics. He also attempted to ease Iraq's strained relations with Sa'udi Arabia, Turkey, and Iran. These initiatives aroused the opposition of Arab nationalist officers of various tendencies, who suspected that he was trying to weaken Iraqi solidarity with Egypt and Syria. But Bazzaz's fall and the return to a military prime minister did nothing to enhance regime legitimacy, and after the Arab defeat by Israel in 1967 it was further eroded. The revolutionaries have been unable to guide Iraq toward either a reconciliation type of polity or to mold it into a mobilization system by turning Arabism and socialism into a political religion and developing a pervasive single-party control apparatus.

The Ba'thist Approach

In July 1968 the Ba'th returned to power in yet another coup, determined to achieve legitimacy through a mobilization strategy. Eight years later it was still in power—a longevity record for postrevolutionary Iraq—and by most accounts more firmly entrenched than ever. It seems appropriate therefore for an observer of Iraq in the middle 1970s to ask whether the Ba'th's transformationist strategy has begun to pull the country out of its legitimacy crisis. The answer has import beyond Iraq itself because this polity, one of the most fragmented in the Arab world if not in the entire Third World, is the archetypical overloaded political system. Social mobilization is rapid, economic development is uneven, internal primordial cleavages are deep, and external threats are numerous. Moreover, as I have shown, the history of government itself has been grim—hardly conducive to present or future system legitimacy. In his conceptualization of authority, identity, and equality as the building blocks of the modern nation-state (which I discussed in chapter 1), Rustow suggests that the achievement of authority usually precedes the other two.[62] Without suggesting that the achievement is complete, it appears that the Iraqi Ba'th has succeeded since 1968 in establishing itself as an all-pervasive control structure. General membership is estimated by some observers at perhaps a half million, with a hard core of 20,000. The militancy of Ba'th cadres and the party's tight organization has made it far less likely to succumb to the kinds of coups through which it overthrew the monarchy in 1958 or even through which it came to power itself in 1963 and 1968. Saddam Hussein, the party's assistant general secretary and vice-chairman of the Revolutionary Command Council, told a British journalist in 1971, "With our party methods, there is no chance for anyone who disagrees with us to jump on a couple of tanks and overthrow the government. These methods have gone."[63] That this was no idle claim has been demonstrated by the party's successful suppression of organized putschs, such as those of 1970 and 1973, and of individual Iraqis who were seen as a threat. The Ba'th has penetrated all the major organized associations in Iraqi society—the unions, businesses, agricultural cooperatives, universities, professional associations, the civil service, and (not least important) the army. To compare this apparatus with the tribal-religious-feudal-bourgeois power-holding notables of the British-Hashimite era is to appreciate the structural revolution which has taken place in Iraqi politics.

Control there may be, and there are few in Iraq today that would question the party's authority. At least it may be said that the party's development has bought time for other problems to be tackled. But observers are more divided on the question of whether this important structural development is being accompanied by a parallel growth in system legitimacy. The evidence is mixed. On the positive side, Ba'thist Iraq has taken advantage of its harshly won stability to enhance its identification with the powerful legitimizing symbols of nationalism and socialism. The Iraqi Ba'th still represents itself as the faction most faithful to the original national (i.e., pan-Arab) orientation of the party and its founder, Michel Aflaq. In fact, Aflaq was invited to Baghdad after the 1968 coup to certify the genuineness of the Iraqi branch as compared to the deviationist-regionalist faction ruling in Syria since 1966. On the Palestine conflict, that touchstone of Arabism, Iraq remained the most militant of the Arab states, in principle, by

62. Dankwart A. Rustow, *A World of Nations* (Washington: Brookings Institution, 1967), p. 125.
63. David Hirst of the *Guardian*, in the *Washington Post*, November 28, 1971. Saddam and several key colleagues come from the same town, Tikrit, which lends clan solidarity to the party command.

refusing to encourage the peacemaking initiatives of the UN and the big powers. It has supported the militant elements in the Palestine national movement such as the Popular Front for the Liberation of Palestine which is the present day incarnation of the post-1948 Arab Nationalist Movement. In the 1973 war the Iraqi Ba'th leadership temporarily buried its differences with Ba'thist Syria and played an important role in helping blunt the Israeli advance. And in that shadowy, sometimes sinister, arena of inter-Arab politics, Iraqi influence has been brought to bear against regimes and politicians deemed reactionary. Iraq has supported progressive elements in several Arab countries.

On the internal level, the regime's nationalist and socialist credentials were greatly enhanced by its nationalization of the Iraq Petroleum Company in June 1972. The IPC had long been a symbol of imperialist exploitation to various nationalist groups and governments, and its leverage over production quotas and marketing contributed to Iraq's comparatively low economic growth in the postmonarchy period. But an event not of the regime's making—the fourfold increase in world oil prices of the early 1970s—is already having far more tangible effects in enhancing national development and regime capabilities. The richness of Iraq's mineral, agricultural, and manpower resources has generally been obscured in Western minds by its political violence and instability. But in the new age of petro-money Iraq has moved dramatically to try and make good on some of the basic promises of Ba'thist ideology. As noted in chapter 6, comprehensive social welfare programs and central planning are now comparatively well developed. The expropriation of the enormous landholdings of the fifty or so largest families is an accomplished fact, as is the gradual redistribution of lands and the lifting of indebtedness from peasants. Agriculture has been given first priority in investment allocation in the recent development plans. A new agricultural reform law promulgated in 1970 calling for the establishment of cooperatives and collective and state farms is an attempt to straighten out the efforts of the previous military regimes in this field. But the enormity of the task may be gauged by an estimate that in mid-1971 only 10 percent of Iraq's peasants were members of cooperatives and thus accessible to government credit facilities. Expanded social security and a wide variety of welfare services for all state employees have been achieved. For example, a government employee has the right to a piece of property; civil servants and retired military officers have been able to construct houses virtually at government expense with interests free loans in amounts equivalent to eighty months of salary. Moreover, the rapidly expanding government sector includes much of the former private sector following the nationalization of major industries, banks, insurance companies, and large commercial establishments. From a political standpoint, government employees make up a relatively privileged and not inconsiderable constituency for the party. Iraq has been among the most active of the Arab oil-exporting countries to solicit development assistance, not only from the Soviet bloc but also through the recruiting of trained Arab manpower from Western and other Arab countries in a kind of reverse brain drain. In short, while staving off the instability associated with excessive loads on the system (often through Draconian methods), the regime has enhanced its capabilities for governing. It has also had some success in embodying salient legitimacy symbols, like Arab and Iraqi nationalism and socialist egalitarianism. Its behavior seems to support Rustow's observations about the sequence of "problem solving" in modernizing societies.

But there is a negative side as well to the Iraqi Ba'th's attempt to build a viable legitimacy formula, which makes it difficult to say with confidence whether such a formula will take root. Judging by the persisting insecurity of the regime, there is still a long way to go. First, the control that has been achieved is based to a substantial degree upon fear and intimidation; such is the impression of foreign observers, most of whom are strongly biased against the regime, but it is also admitted by loyal and responsible party members. As one of them put it to this writer in a 1972 interview, "Politics in Iraq is no longer an avocation for gentlemen." But if the party is excessively repressive one must remember the number of enemies it has. Given this high coercion factor, the question arises as to what extent obedience is merely compelled. To what extent is rule regarded not just as effective but as legitimate? Even discounting for exaggeration, the accounts of the brutality and torture inflicted upon suspected regime opponents by the late chief of security, Nazim Kazzar, are chilling. In 1973 this "Beria of Baghdad" (as Eric Rouleau called him) masterminded a plot to assassinate President Bakr and Saddam Hussein, among others. Its near success indicated that intraparty rivalries at the highest levels might comprise a threat to the regime more serious than the subversion from external forces which the leadership was combatting so assiduously.[64] Legitimacy would seem to be as much a problem within the party as outside it.

A second problem is the still unresolved ambiguity of national

64. The plot is described by Eric Rouleau in a series of articles in *Le Monde*, July 21, 22, and 24, 1973.

identity. The roots of Iraqi identity are partly supranational and partly subnational. Nasirite pan-Arabism was one of the inspirations for the antimonarchy coup of 1958 and it was highly attractive to certain military and civilian politicians in the 1960s, notably Abd al-Salam Arif. But pan-Arabism is less popular among Iraqi Shi'ites than the politically dominant Sunnis. Even more serious is the subnational identity problem of the Kurds, who until the spring of 1975 comprised the only center of power in the country not subdued by the Ba'th. Although the Kurds' loss of Iranian support terminated their military threat, Kurdish communal identity still poses a philosophical problem for the Ba'thist regime. The kind of integration that develops depends on whether the mythic substructure of Ba'thism is sufficiently liberal to accommodate a non-Arab community without insisting on full assimilation. It also depends on the political environment: an insecure Ba'thist elite is likely to perceive a narrower range of options vis à vis the Kurds than one whose legitimacy is widely accepted. A positive sign is that Iraqi Ba'th party statements, such as the National Action Pact of 1972, speak of *wataniyya* (local patriotism) as well as *qawmiyya* (volk, i.e., Arab nationalism) in referring to loyalty to Iraq, as if to make special provision for the Kurdish and other non-Arab minorities.[65] This position is consistent with the relatively tolerant position of Michel Aflaq on minorities discussed above in the analysis of Syria. Closely related to the continuing identity problem is the problem of legitimizing the internal political order. Because of its relatively long history of independence, social mobilization, and quasi-autonomous politics, there remains a diversity of views even among progressives as to how power should be used and limited. The Ba'thists were ruthless in their suppression of Communists until quite recently, when the regime's increased dependence on the Soviet Union may have stimulated a moderating influence. Its exclusivism alienated or frightened prominent liberals or social democrats who had long opposed the British and the Hashimites such as Kamal Chaderji of the old National Democratic party.

The fourth problem standing in the way of regime legitimacy is the isolation of Iraq in the regional system. We have already observed other cases of legitimacy from external origins; it is a condition particularly noticeable in the states of the pan-Arab core. It is a paradox that Iraq, as the vanguard state of Arab unity, was the only major Arab exporter not to participate in the boycott of 1973–74. A pariah

---

65. *National Action Pact (Mithaq al-Amal al-Watani) and Internal System and Bases for Action in the Progressive National Front* (Baghdad: Ministry of Information, Document Series, No. 29, 1973), pp. 23–35.

from the times of Nuri al-Sa'id and the Baghdad Pact, even the post-revolutionary Iraqi regimes have been hard pressed to find friends, much less partners. Issues of power sharing and national priorities have separated it from the other mainstream countries of Arab unity such as Egypt and Syria; issues of political philosophy and socialism have separated it from its more conservative neighbors in the Arabian peninsula. And in the northeast, imperial Iran challenges Iraqi influence on the Arab side of the Gulf and possesses a superior military capability. Iraq's position as heir to the original Ba'th impulse to progressive Arab unity endows it with all the special legitimizing strengths and weaknesses associated with this cause. When Syria intervened against the left-wing forces (including Iraqi-oriented Ba'thists) and the Palestinian organizations in the Lebanese civil war in 1976, the Iraqi Ba'thists found themselves with an extremely potent ideological weapon to use against the hated Asad regime in Damascus. All of the considerable propaganda instruments of the state were mobilized to attack the Syrians for treason to the Arab cause. But just as the Palestinians in Jordan in 1970 had waited in vain for the Iraqi troops based in the country to assist them against the king's army, so again they waited with their Lebanese allies in 1976 for decisive military help above and beyond propaganda and material aid in their losing battle against the Lebanese Right and the Syrians. Would Iraq's failure to match words with deeds ultimately lead to significant public disenchantment over its own all-Arab credentials?

These four problems notwithstanding, the Iraqi political system by the middle of the 1970s had taken on considerable institutional and ideological coherence. Its economic and social future was possibly the brightest in the Arab world, owing to its felicitous combination of petroleum, agricultural and manpower resources. Despite the regime's prudence in backing its militant Arabism with open intervention to help its friends, it appeared that it could continue to present itself effectively as the best guardian and strongest arsenal for all-Arab concerns among the states in the area, particularly in light of Egyptian and Syrian behavior after the October war.

On the domestic front, there was also a palpable relaxation of regime insecurity from the time of the abortive Kazzar coup. In July 1973 the Ba'th and Iraqi Communist party, long bitter rivals, concluded a National Action Pact. Subsequently a National Progressive Front was established, including the Kurdistan Democratic party as well. Ba'thists, however, continued to dominate the government. The regime also offered a new plan of limited regional autonomy for the Kurds which was more favorable than anything previously proposed by Baghdad. After the Kurdish leader Mulla Mustafa al-Barzani rejected the plan in March 1974, the Iraqi army opened a new offensive against them. A year later, in exchange for the concessions on the Shatt al-Arab boundary, Iran withdrew its support for the Kurds, thus relieving Baghdad of a major problem. The agreement with Iran also reduced at least for a time the rivalry of these two major regional powers for hegemony in the Gulf. In a further demonstration of regional détente, Iraq moved to improve its relations with Egypt and some of the traditional Arabian peninsula regimes. And pursuing the pragmatic course pioneered by radical Algeria in its international relationships —the separation of ideology and state interests—Iraq also began to encourage American investment and to seek ways of reducing its dependence on the Soviet Union. In short, this regime began to undergo a discernible relaxation in the middle 1970s. Buttressed by new oil revenues and the collapse of the Kurdish insurgency, relieved to some extent of the Iranian threat, the Ba'thist government appeared ready to make some cautious moves toward sharing power with other progressive groups. By encouraging limited participation it may have hoped to develop a legitimacy formula that went beyond the largely repressive base of the early years of the regime.

LEBANON

My analysis of Lebanese politics published in 1968 concluded with the following question and answer:

> Are the loads on this system increasing even faster than its capabilities? The evidence presented here, although incomplete, suggests that they are. Lebanon's historic problems are not disappearing: Parochialism if anything is aggravated by social change. The prospects for domestic prosperity and tranquility are dubious in the light of demographic trends and a weak productive sector. Radicalism, partially a function of continuing ferment in the Arab world as a whole, finds no legitimate place in Lebanese politics; and the system has failed to develop a responsible leftist opposition. Despite the National Pact, Arab nationalism and regional rivalries continue to pose a certain threat to the Lebanese entity, and Great Power competition continues to involve the people in the area. Lebanon is too strategically situated to escape embroilment in these conflicts. At the risk of underestimating Lebanese ingenuity, it must be concluded that the Republic's political future will be stormy.[66]

66. Michael C. Hudson, *The Precarious Republic: Political Modernization In Lebanon* (New York: Random House, 1968), p. 300.

Eight years later Lebanon was in the throes of one of the bitterest, most destructive civil wars of modern times. When the nineteen months of heavy fighting came to an end in November 1976, upwards of 60,000 people were thought to have been killed and 200,000 wounded, mostly uninvolved civilians cut down by heavy battlefield weapons indiscriminately fired. Physical damage was placed at $3 billion. A cascade of disasters, domestic and regional, proved too much for such "Lebanese ingenuity" as remained during the regime of President Suleiman Frangieh and for the political system itself, a mechanism ill equipped to cope with social and political change.

The old system had succumbed to a crisis of legitimacy. Its people lacked any minimum, cohesive national identity; its government could not maintain authority; its establishment was insensitive to the egalitarian demands of a burgeoning politicized population. But the old system had been remarkably successful in many ways, and it represented a unique approach to some of the basic problems of Arab politics. Lebanon was not a revolutionary republic in the conventional Arab sense, although it had emerged from a struggle with a colonial power, France. Unlike the monolithic and autocratic systems around it, the Lebanese system was relatively pluralistic, and although its politics were dominated by a small, multisectarian, landed commercial elite, it was for over thirty years the closest approximation of a liberal democracy in the Arab world. As such, and whether or not it can be restored, it merits scrutiny.

Modern Lebanon is not a nation but an uneasy association of communities and classes, and Lebanese politics during the period of the liberal republic was primarily concerned with holding this association together. Because so much political energy was expended for this elemental purpose, opportunity costs were incurred in other domains. Governmental capabilities were retarded by the immobilism which the consociational conflict-management system known as confessionalism engendered. Because Lebanon had experienced acute modernization—a trend further exacerbated in the middle 1970s by the flood of new petro-money—it was subjected to unprecedented administrative and political pressures which the confessional system was not designed to cope with. An additional source of strain originated in the regional and international political systems. Always delicately balanced between the West and the Arab hinterland, Lebanon suffered from Cold War rivalries and the revolutionary ferment in the Arab world, with its anti-Western characteristics. From the mid-1960s this little country was sucked into the vortex of the reactivated Arab-Israeli conflict, suffering not only the direct armed assaults of its enemy

Israel but also serious internal disorders precipitated by the growth of Palestinian resistance.

Until the civil war, Lebanon had the only liberal, competitive parliamentary system remaining in the Arab world. Ever since its independence in 1943 it had held regular elections; its press was by far the freest in the Arab world; it had not experienced a successful coup d'état (though there had been at least two major attempts); it had not fallen under military rule, except for brief emergency periods. Lebanon's political success was facilitated by generally favorable economic conditions. At the same time political stability encouraged economic development. The "penalties" of immobilism and inefficiency were heavy, but until the early 1970s they had not bred enough chaos to prevent the country from achieving an impressive degree of economic and financial growth. In addition to its internal economic capabilities, Lebanon benefited as the banker and merchant to the fast-development Arab hinterland. The impact of Arab oil money was evident in a hundred ways, as in the forests of luxury high-rise apartment buildings in the Beirut area. The neighboring Arab states generally recognized Lebanon's delicate internal situation and appreciated the useful function it served as a linkage with the West and a kind of political free zone—a meeting place and forum for opinion makers, intellectuals, and politicians. External actors, therefore, bestowed a degree of legitimacy and stability upon Lebanon even though they also caused trouble for it. These were considerable accomplishments in light of the prevailing political conditions and trends in the region and all the more remarkable considering the fragmentation of Lebanese political culture. This fragmentation was both an obstacle to legitimacy and stability, and the raison d'être of Lebanese pluralism.

Political Culture Fragmentation

Appearances of modernity notwithstanding, Lebanon's political culture is basically traditional. Sectarian and clan affiliations define the parameters of political behavior. The unusual attention to religion in Lebanese political life is a function of the country's multisectarian population and its history as a place of refuge for religious minorities. Officially, according to a census taken by the French in 1932, the Christians hold a slight majority over the non-Christians—Sunnis, Shi'ites, and Druze. Among the Christians, the Catholic Maronites are the largest single sect, outnumbering the next largest, the Greek Orthodox, by nearly three to one and the Greek Catholic by four to one. Among the non-Christians, the Sunnis are said to hold a slight edge over the Shi'ites and both are around two and a half times the size of the smaller but influential Druze community. The Maronites are thought (officially) to constitute the country's largest sect, with about 30 percent of the population, followed in rank order by the Sunnis, Shi'ites, Greek Orthodox, Greek Catholics, and Druze. There are, in addition, more than eight other sects. Even before the civil war, there was a certain tension between Christians and non-Christians, but it was normally suppressed by tacit agreement within the ruling elite. Moreover, each sect was jealous of its particular interests. Herein lies what most observers saw as the fundamental problem of governance in Lebanon.

What accounted for Lebanon's sectarian insecurity and just how religiously based was it? In the modern history of Lebanon there is little substantial evidence of strife that was intrinsically sectarian in origin: the most important recent example was the turmoil of the period 1840 to 1860, which culminated in the massacre of Christians by Druzes; but this conflict, as Malcolm Kerr and others have shown, was socioeconomic as well as religious in its origins and was exacerbated by the maneuverings of the French and British consuls in the area and the Ottoman government, to whom the amirs of Mount Lebanon were subject.[67] Even the widespread turmoil that occurred in the summer by 1958 was not a religious war, and serious sectarian violence occurred only briefly after several months of disorders. The salience of the sectarian cleavage must rather be accounted for by three factors other than religion per se. First was the interrelatedness of religious and national identity among the Maronite Christians. I have already noted the peculiar religious content of national identities in Islam. The same is true for Middle Eastern Christianity and particularly so because of the minority character of Christianity. Among the Maronite Catholics, lodged since the seventh century in their mountain retreats, the sense of communal cohesion and isolation from the world of Arab Islam to the east was especially strong and was institutionalized through the Maronite clergy, as Iliya Harik has noted.[68] In the process of successfully resisting direct Muslim control, be it from the Ummayads, Abbasids, or Mamluks, the Maronites developed a sense of cultural as well as religious separateness, and in modern times this separatism was transformed into a kind of proto-nationalism and an ideology asserting the non-Arab Phoenician origins of the nation.

67. Malcolm Kerr, *Lebanon in the Last Years of Feudalism, 1840–1868: A Contemporary Account by Antun Dahir Al-'Aqiqi, and Other Documents* (Beirut: American University of Beirut, Faculty of Arts and Sciences, Oriental Series, no. 33, 1959).

68. Iliya Harik, *Politics and Change in a Traditional Society: Lebanon, 1711–1845* (Princeton: Princeton University Press, 1968), chaps. 4–6.

The second factor was the Maronite linkage with European Christianity, culture, and politics. The tough Maronite peasants cooperated with the Crusaders. The Maronite Church united with Rome around 1180 and sent its clergy to Europe for training.[69] From the middle of the sixteenth century, France developed special relationships with the Maronites, by proclaiming itself protector of the Catholics in the Ottoman Empire. France played a decisive role when it cooperated with Maronite leaders in the aftermath of the Ottoman defeat in World War I to establish a Maronite-dominated state of Lebanon, embracing the predominantly Muslim coast and Biqa valley in addition to the traditionally Christian and Druze mountains. The Maronites' Western connection became a source of conflict with the Islamic communities, just as the persistent convulsions of pan-Arab nationalism, uniting the mostly Muslim-Arab states around Lebanon, awakened primordial memories of an Islamic threat.

The third factor that exacerbated sectarian cleavages was the severe maldistribution of income in Lebanon. It is true that, since the Muslim notables were finally coaxed into participating in the new state's affairs toward the end of the French mandate in the late 1930s, an affluent and influential Muslim upper class has developed. Nevertheless, most observers and at least one comprehensive Lebanese government study agree that the largely non-Christian regions of the north, south, and Biqa were much poorer than Beirut and Mount Lebanon[70] and that the poorest sections of the Beirut area were, by and large, non-Christian. Some Muslim elements, particularly the Shi'ites, chafed under what seemed increasingly to be an arbitrary and anachronistic proportional rule which assured Christian predominance; and others, particularly the Sunnis, remembered that until 1920 they were the privileged religious community and that Lebanon was under the Ottoman sultan's administration (subject to certain European restrictions).[71] In sum, one must look beyond intrinsic doctrinal or theological differences to explain the importance of the religious issue in the problem of Lebanese legitimacy.

69. Kamal S. Salibi, *The Modern History of Lebanon* (London: Weidenfeld and Nicolson, 1965), p. 12.

70. See Lebanon, Ministry of General Planning, *Besoins et Possibilités de Développement du Liban*, A study made by the Institut International de Recherche et de Formation en Vue de Développement (IRFED), 2 volumes (Beirut, 1961). The report and its political implications are discussed in Hudson, op. cit., chaps. 2 and 8.

71. The Sunni position is carefully explored in Najla Wadih Atiyah, "The Attitude of the Lebanese Sunnis Towards the State of Lebanon," Ph. D. dissertation, University of London, 1973.

Important as it is, sectarianism was not the only characteristic affecting and complicating the problem of political legitimacy in Lebanon. The commanding heights of political influence were held tenaciously by several prominent families and clans, whose traditional patron-client relationships in their respective regions were reinforced in recent decades by their growing commercial and financial wealth. In Lebanon the institution known as wasita, which as I have noted is present throughout Arab politics, has perhaps attained its most perfect form. Wasita technically is "a procedure of mediation consistent with the segmentary organization of kin groups within the clan." [72] But in Lebanon it conventionally refers to a much larger arena—the entire political process—and denotes a particular means of influence or pull which is usually, but not always, kinship based. A contractor may tell a prospective customer that he has a wasita through his cousin employed in the Ministry of National Economy and can thus obtain the desired license or permit. Or a south Lebanon farmer involved in a property dispute with a neighbor may arrange through the patron or za'im (leader) of his area to obtain a favorable out-of-court settlement. [73] In return, the za'im, like a mafia godfather, may expect to call upon his client for unspecified (often political) support in the future. The norms of family solidarity and mutual obligation in Lebanon were such that the legitimacy of the principal actors, the za'ims, was largely a function of kinship.

But even though heavily influenced by kinship structures, the political system itself was not strongly legitimized by kinship in the way, for example, that the paramount reputation of the Sa'ud family legitimizes the Sa'udi Arabian system. This is because the Lebanese system was a well-structured process of coalition building and maneuvering among quasi-autonomous clan leaders. The legitimacy of this process depended rather upon highly rationalistic calculations about its results.

The Liberal Solution

To accommodate a political culture so crisscrossed with primordial cleavages—sectarian, ethnic, kinship, and regional—the founding fathers of Lebanon, notably Michel Chiha, designed a political order based on representation of all the major notables and factions. The

72. Victor F. Ayoub, "Conflict Resolution and Social Reorganization in a Lebanese Village," in Louise Sweet (ed.), *Peoples and Cultures of the Middle East* (New York: Natural History Press, 1970), pp. 137–154; p. 142.
73. Laura Nader, "Communication between Village and City in the Modern Middle East," *Human Organization*, 24 (1965), pp. 18–24.

Lebanese constitution of 1926 stipulated a parliamentary form of government. Full Muslim participation, however, was not secured until the eve of independence in 1943, when the National Pact was concluded. This covenant consisted of correspondence between the leading Sunni and Maronite politicians of the day, Riyadh al-Sulh and Bishara al-Khuri. It was agreed that the president of the republic be a Maronite Christian, the prime minister a Sunni Muslim, and the president of the Chamber of Deputies a Shi'ite Muslim. It also stipulated that neither community should ally itself with external forces, meaning that the Christians should not seek to restore European protection and the Muslims should give up their goal of reattaching the Muslim parts of Greater Lebanon back to Syria.

The principle of fixed proportional sectarian representation, known in Lebanon as confessionalism, applied not only to the highest offices but also extended throughout the political system. Posts in the civil service, the judiciary, the military, and seats in the parliament itself were allocated according to the sectarian distributions reported in the 1932 census. On that basis, the ninety-nine-member Chamber of Deputies allocated fifty-four seats to Christians and forty-five to non-Christians (Muslim and Druze). Since neither the Christian nor non-Christian sides were doctrinally homogeneous, each major sect was also jealous of its proper representation. Table 8.1 shows what each of them was allocated.

TABLE 8.1

Allocation of Seats in the Lebanese Chamber of Deputies,
According to Religious Sect

Christians (54)		*Non-Christians (45)*	
Maronites	20	Sunni Muslims	20
Greek Orthodox	11	Shi'ite Muslims	19
Greek Catholic	6	Druze	6
Armenian Orthodox	4		
Minorities	3		

Source: Michael C. Hudson, *The Precarious Republic: Political Modernization in Lebanon* (New York: Random House, 1968), p. 23.

Positions within the state bureaucracy were allocated along similar lines, with sect taking priority over merit as a criterion of employment from the highest to the lowest levels. The most sensitive and influential of the high posts, in addition to that of the president himself, notably in the armed forces, were also reserved for Christians.

Confessionalism served a number of the conflict-management functions which have been proposed by Eric Nordlinger as vital for deeply divided societies.[74] It facilitated what he calls "purposive depoliticization,"[75] wherein a potentially uncontrollable issue is removed from the day-to-day political arena. It accomplished this end by ensuring to all the sects that the normal competition for power and influence would not lead to unacceptable domination by any one of them. This mutual security condition was implemented through the fixed proportionality mechanism that pertained to all structures in the system and through the implicit mutual veto which any major sect could resort to in extreme crises. It encouraged leaders of the various sects to compromise in order to maintain the stability which confers prosperity and various other political "goods" on all the sects. The structure of confessionalism also promoted, for better or worse, another of Nordlinger's conditions, the maintenance of a stable coalition. In the Lebanese case, the confessionalist electoral laws by and large favored the traditional leaders, whose family status, wealth, and claims to sectarian leadership made them indispensable for the building of a winning list. Candidates who worked against or outside the system found that they lacked the patronage, the influence (wasitas) to compete with the cross-sectarian elite. No political party, regardless of ideology, was able to challenge this establishment. Even the biggest and best organized, the right-wing Kata'ib (or Phalanges), could win only nine seats in the ninety-nine-man Chamber in 1968, and seven in 1972; and this party itself was rooted in the Maronite community. In fact, the one significant party most clearly opposed to confessionalism, the Progressive Socialist party, derived substantial influence from the Druze community and its leader, Kamal Jumblat, who—ideology notwithstanding—was very much a traditional za'im.

The principal actors in the Lebanese liberal republic, therefore, were notables, each with a parochial, particularist constituency. Their support bases were relatively secure by virtue of the primordial character of allegiances and the socioeconomic leverage they could exert over their clienteles. Consequently, the Lebanese political process

---

74. Eric A. Nordlinger, "Conflict Regulation in Divided Societies," Harvard University, Center for International Affairs, *Occasional Papers in International Affairs*, no. 29, January 1972; esp. chap. 2.

75. Ibid., p. 26.

consisted mainly of the competition within the elite for relative prestige and material advantage.

Challenges to Legitimacy

Like many strong medicines, confessionalism had some negative side effects. It was a peculiarly static solution, depending upon continued acceptance of the validity of the original proportions. Although in an important way it neutralized sectarian competition, it also institutionalized sectarian structures and perpetuated sectarian identifications. The requirements of proportionality introduced additional administrative inefficiency, compared to a system of appointment by merit. Nor did the system appear to be responsive or structurally flexible in the face of modernization and its attendant governmental problems, the spread of new radical ideologies and the growth of new organizations and counter-elites.[76] In short, the confessional solution worked well when there was not very much for government to do.

The Lebanese elite attempted to bridge the gap between its essentially traditional legitimacy bases and the modern demands of nationalism and modernism through its efficacy in achieving minimal goals. But one of the effects of rapid modernization is an expansion of popular expectations about government performance. Based as it was on particularist and parochial values, the system increasingly came under attack as the demands of the younger and the disadvantaged sectors for a modern state, for more democracy, for more social justice, and for more responsible fulfillment of Lebanon's responsibilities to the Arab world also increased. Modernization has brought unexampled aggregate prosperity, but it has also added a number of new complications to the system's legitimacy formula.[77] For one thing, the demographic growth since 1932 has led most knowledgeable observers to conclude that non-Christians outnumber Christians because of suspected higher Muslim birthrates and higher Christian emigration; furthermore, the large resident populations of mostly Muslim laborers from Syria and refugees from Palestine were thought to number perhaps 800,000 compared to the 2 million or more resident Lebanese.[78]

76. Some Lebanese scholars like the sociologists Halim Barakat and Samih Farsoun have strongly criticized the confessionalist "solution," which they see as not a real solution at all. See, e.g. Halim Barakat, "Social and Political Integration in Lebanon: A Case of Social Mosaic," *Middle East Journal*, 27, 3 (Summer 1973), pp. 301–18; Samih Farsoun, "Students Protests and the Coming Crisis in Lebanon," *MERIP Reports*, no. 19, August, 1973, pp. 3–14.

77. Such is the view developed in Hudson, op. cit., chap. 3.

78. For recent estimates and a general assessment, see Michael Wall, "The Tightrope Country: A survey of Lebanon," *The Economist* (London), January 26, 1974.

These people were not citizens, but they exerted political influence, particularly the Palestinians, whose national revival in the middle 1960s, which I discuss in the next section, created the most serious strains on internal political and national security.

Another potentially disruptive aspect of the demographic challenge was that the Muslim Shi'ite community, according to some observers, may now have surpassed both the Maronites and the Sunnis as the largest single sect.[79] The National Pact had been drawn up by a Sunni and a Maronite and served basically as an entente between those communities, and to some extent it divided Lebanon into two spheres of influence. By contrast, the Shi'ites were the poorest and most deprived of all the main sects: their region in the hill country of the south and in parts of the Biqa was the least developed in the country. Until the last few years it was largely ignored by the government, except for some "pork barrel" projects which the local Shi'ite za'ims extracted to distribute as patronage. Shi'ites began migrating in large numbers into the Beirut areas, driven out in part by Israeli reprisal attacks on Palestinian guerrilla bases and refugee camps in the south. Their increasingly serious plight and their claim under the principle of proportionality to a far bigger share of power gave the Shi'ites a sense of sectarian identity and activism hitherto absent. A dynamic imam, Musa al-Sadr, challenged one of the traditional establishment leaders and proved to have strong popularity and influence, showing the characteristic independence from worldly governmental authority that Shi'ites have historically displayed.

The Lebanese system was not entirely unresponsive to pressures for changing the proportionality formula. An important outcome of the 1958 civil war was a move to upgrade the non-Christian quota of high civil service commissions to full equality. The influence of the Sunni and Druze communities as strengthened by the creation of community councils under Lebanese law in 1955 and 1962, respectively, and in 1969 a Higher Shi'ite Council was established to ensure that growing Shi'ite demands would be articulated within the system. At the highest level, however, the Maronites maintained their occupancy of the presidency—by tradition, not the constitution—and retained the key military, security, and foreign policy posts. The deepening troubles of the early 1970s brought increasing demands, largely on the part of the Left, for an end to confessionalism entirely, or failing that, the election of a non-Maronite president and the upgrading of the power of the Sunni and Shi'ite top offices.

79. Ibid., p. 14.

A second challenge of modernization to Lebanon's legitimacy formula was growing class-consciousness and unrest. Outside of Mount Lebanon, where there was a tradition of small landholders and independent farmers, the tenant farmers and day laborers were being increasingly squeezed by an archaic quasi-feudal order and agricultural mechanization; this push off the land accounts in part for the heavy migration to Beirut. Many of those who remained were largely integrated into the system, as indicated by very high voter turnouts in the electoral contests between traditional rural bosses. But in recent years a sizeable protest vote for nonestablishment candidates has developed; Communists and radical socialist-nationalist parties have found support from this constituency. The industrial proletariat and the urban unemployed constituted another sector which has traditionally mustered only marginal influence. Included here were large numbers of Syrian, Kurdish, and Palestinian laborers who were formally excluded from the political system. The labor movement, while stronger and older in Lebanon than in most Arab countries, still had not developed substantial independence, although a federation of Communist-supported unions did exist. Like their rural counterparts, much of the urban labor force appeared to have been integrated into the traditional system of local notables who dispense jobs, security, and other assistance. A landmark social security bill passed during the regime of General Fu'ad Chehab (1958–64) has begun to alleviate some of the problems of some of the laborers. But there was also labor unrest, and in the middle 1960s the coalition of left-wing groups under the nominal leadership of Jumblat was able to mobilize substantial labor support. Up to the eve of the civil war, observers continued to doubt whether the state's administrative and political structures were sufficient to handle the growing demands of the urban masses.

The student population of Lebanon, always politically active, also became a volatile force on the local political scene in the early 1970s lending its weight generally to the progressive movements. A major intellectual center of the entire area, quantitatively as well as qualitatively, Lebanon found its traditional legitimacy constantly under bitter attack from student groups in universities and increasingly in the high schools. Here the radical critique of the Lebanese system as oligarchic, repressive, irresponsible, and delinquent in its obligations to "the people" and "the Arab nation" was forcibly articulated. Thus, from many quarters, the elitist-pluralist legitimacy formula of Lebanon came under attack.

As the ruinous civil war of 1975–76 unfolded, it was poignant to recall how close Lebanon's politicians had come toward serious reforms only a decade earlier. The late General Chehab, the army commander who had resolved the 1958 crisis, recognized explicitly the need for political and administrative modernization. During his regime (1958–64), important achievements were made in the fields of social security, civil service reform, agricultural development, and planning. Among his staunchest supporters were Kamal Jumblat's Progressive Socialist party, which was the system's only tenuous link with the growing nonestablishment Left, and the Kata'ib party (Phalanges) of Pierre Gemayel, the best-organized group representing the Maronite community. At that time, as John Entelis has shown, an important part of the Kata'ib leadership was committed to modernizing the Lebanese state in hopes of forestalling further social problems which would in time threaten Lebanon's national cohesion.[80] Modernization of the state was something which important components of conservative Maronite and progressive non-Maronite opinion could agree about, even though their respective national identity orientations remained fundamentally different; and for a time Chehab was able to exploit this parallelism. It constituted the system's only hope, albeit a slim one, for escaping further turmoil. But Chehab was unable to effect lasting changes in the system, which, because of its immobilizing proportionalism and its contrived traditional elitism, proved to be immune to reform by evolutionary means.[81]

The Civil War

In their determination to modernize, General Chehab and his military-technocratic constituency met with widespread opposition, direct and indirect, from the interlocked traditional politicians, businessmen, and bureaucrats, each with their privileges and patronage networks. The regime then deployed the Deuxième Bureau—the intelligence and security branch of the army—to threaten and, if necessary, coerce recalcitrant politicians into conformity; and, some were severely maltreated. These official acts of terror and repression violated the norms of Lebanon's free-wheeling, relatively open parliamentary system; and the traditional leaders began to resist the excesses of "Chehabism." Although the Chehabists themselves had allies in some traditional quarters and enjoyed a degree of diffuse support from the Muslim populace oriented toward Arab nationalism, they

80. John P. Entelis, *Pluralism and Party Transformation in Lebanon; Al-Kata'ib 1936–1970* (Leiden: E. J. Brill, 1974).

81. For a different interpretation, see Elie A. Salem, *Modernization Without Revolution: Lebanon's Experience* (Bloomington: Indiana University Press, 1973), esp. chap. 6.

were unable to overcome the systemic obstacles. General Chehab, unlike his two traditionalist predecessors in the presidency, observed the constitution's prohibition of a second successive term, and so his movement lost an important symbol of personal legitimacy. His protegé, Charles Helou, was unable to maintain the reform movement during his presidency (1964–70), and immobilism began to set in once again. The election of President Suleiman Frangieh, a parochial mountain politician who saw little need for presidential initiative in modernization, accelerated the deterioration.

Protracted turmoil in the pan-Arab core region was the final factor contributing to Lebanon's political undoing. Even if the Lebanese system were situated, for example, in Bahrain or Tunisia, one might reasonably have predicted a "stormy political future." But located as it was in the zone where the Palestinian and Arab-Israeli issues began to fester with new virulence in the middle 1960s, it was unable to cope with the ideological cross-pressures. The external dimension of the National Pact was an agreement that Lebanon's foreign policy should not become unduly aligned with the Christian West or the Islamic Arab world. It had not been easy, but Lebanese policy makers in the past had generally succeeded in walking this tightrope. Traditionally, they had managed to excuse their country from anything but passive participation in the Arab-Israel conflict on the plausible if not very honorable grounds that it was too weak and divided. That stratagem worked until the middle 1960s when the Palestinian resistance movement began to develop. Ever since they were driven out of Palestine in 1948, the Palestinians have comprised a large and significant community in Lebanon—today numbering perhaps 400,000—not just in the refugee camps but also in the main cities where many of them prospered. Although Lebanon was spared during the 1967 war, it became the object of fierce attacks as the resistance groups began to undertake sabotage and armed attacks inside Israel. As a result, much of south Lebanon was depopulated and devastated by repeated Israeli raids. A major aim of the Israeli attacks was to turn the Lebanese against the Palestinians and destroy their capacity for attacking Israel. In fact, however, solidarity between the Palestinian resistance and the Lebanese Arab-Muslim nationalist groups grew, and it appears that the Palestinians, without directly involving themselves, served as a catalyst for Muslim nationalist discontent and as a model for organizing it. A grimmer consequence was further erosion in the legitimacy of Lebanon's political institutions. For some five years the Lebanese state suffered constant humiliation, not to mention material devastation, from the Israelis who could strike with complete impunity. By spring 1973 there were clear signs of a Palestinian-Christian right-wing confrontation in the making, as the followers of Camille Chamoun, Father Cherbel Kassis, the Kata'ib, President Frangieh, and Christian army officers like Col. Antoine Barakat began to coerce the Palestinians and try to reduce the power of the Lebanese Muslim elite.

As the crisis boiled up in 1975 into full-scale chaos, a Lebanese political scientist told a friend that he now knew how Hobbes had felt. The pillars of the consociational-confessional system had been eroded. The different elites were in open conflict with one another; instead of restraining their untutored flocks, their leaders were inciting them. On the mostly Muslim Left (the label is even more oversimplified than the term, "mostly Maronite-right"), the control of traditional elites over their constituencies was being seriously challenged by radical socialist and Arab nationalist groups and militias. Popular acceptance of the old elitist prerogative to manage conflict had evaporated. The military was now perceived as a party to the conflict, not an impartial balancer. The presidency, which under Chehab almost became a modernizing instrument because it was supported by Muslims, was now illegitimate in the eyes of Muslims. The "external threats" posed by Israel and the radical Muslim-Arab world to the two sides now tended to exacerbate rather than moderate the internal Lebanese conflict.

The civil war marked the failure of the Lebanese experiment. Did this failure indicate the impossibility or irrelevance of a pluralist political process in the Arab world generally? Not at all. On the contrary, the relative openness and tolerance of the liberal republic had not only helped maintain the long period of stability in a highly fragmented and volatile political culture, it had also served as a kind of incubator for the free and serious political debate without which the development of genuine structural legitimacy is impossible. In this respect, Lebanon served the entire Arab world even better than it served itself. The Lebanese system foundered not from an excess of liberalism but from a shortage of it. Had it proved to be more flexible in admitting the numerous and increasingly important elements which had been systematically excluded from political participation, it might have avoided the disaster.

Did its failure indicate the impossibility of a secular polity in the Arab world? Again, the answer is firmly negative. Although liberal, the old Lebanese republic was anything but secular; in fact, religion was built in to the very fiber of the system. Even though social change was demonstrably eroding religious parochialism,[82] the political structures virtually perpetuated a sectarian orientation, particularly among the predominant Maronites. In good times these orientations were submerged, but in the inevitable crisis periods, they were like mines which would eventually explode under enough pressure. Secularism, far from being the problem, was in fact the solution. To be sure, in light of the war's barbaric violence, in which religious symbols were all too evident, the idea of a secular state might now seem utopian. But in the previous decade the idea of secular reforms had been freely debated and widely supported, except by some of the conservative ruling politicians. Unfortunately, the grimmest nightmares of these people became self-fulfilling prophecies as they acted on the basis of their worst assumptions. There is little doubt that the feasibility of secular reform was seriously undermined by the mindless fanaticism of the long war itself.

The Syrian regime dispatched 30,000 troops to end the fighting and prevent a leftist and Palestinian victory, but Damascus would not find it easy to restore Lebanon's political legitimacy. Certainly, economic factors and the need for regional security were good arguments for preserving Lebanon's unity. Moreover, if the underlying socioeconomic causes of the war were to be effectively dealt with, a program of administrative development and reform, along with a more equitable sectarian distribution of power which might pave the way to eventual secularization, was surely needed. This was essentially the program of the Left. But some voices on the Right were calling for cantonization, if not outright partition, and there was little disposition among the Maronites in general to make concessions as long as Syria was supporting them. What the tragedy also indicated, was that the ongoing unresolved Palestinian and Arab-Israeli problems posed virtually insuperable obstacles for the development of any kind of systemic legitimacy in Lebanon, just as they generated permanent tension and frequent instability in the other states of the pan-Arab core and beyond. It is true, as we have seen, that particular leaders, regimes, or groups could regularly exploit the legitimacy of being in the vanguard of all-Arab causes, but there were always competitors who could promise even more. In Lebanon where a resistance movement took root among Palestinians themselves, the legitimacy crisis of the Arabs took on its ultimate tragic form.

---

82. See, for example, the opinion survey data reported by David and Audrey Smock, *The Politics of Pluralism: A Comparative Study of Lebanon and Ghana* (New York: Elsevier, 1975), esp. pp. 152–72 and 335–37.

THE PALESTINIAN MOVEMENT

The area of greatest all-Arab concern is Palestine and the Arab-Israeli conflict. As I noted in chapter 5, the implantation of the Zionist entity in Palestine after World War I traumatized Arab politics. It continues to do so. While the issue has on occasion inspired the greatest feats of Arab unity, as in the 1973 war and boycott, it has more often been the cause of inter-Arab divisions and internal conflict because it is intolerable and insoluble. Consequently, it has constituted the principal drain on political legitimacy, especially in the pan-Arab core, and has generated chronic efforts at outbidding on the part of domestic oppositions and rival regimes.

By the middle of the 1970s the Palestinians had not yet formed a republic, but their impact on the internal and regional politics of the Arab world had already been profound, for they had succeeded in presenting themselves as the most legitimate expression of this most important all-Arab concern. Rising in the wake of the 1967 Arab-Israeli war when all the front-line Arab regimes were in disgrace, the Palestinian resistance movement (*al-muqawama al-falistiniyya*) made its own revolution in Palestinian politics and at the same time projected itself as a new force throughout the Arab world—the successor to Nasirism and other revolutionary movements.[83] The muqawama called for popular armed struggle to achieve a democratic and secular state in Palestine—an ideology dynamic and yet diffuse enough to mobilize radicals and conservatives in the Palestinian community and throughout the Arab world. In spite of persistent factionalism, it developed a degree of structural coherence through the main political-military organization, Fatah, and the umbrella institution, the Palestine Liberation Organization, with its executive committee and constituent assembly, the Palestine National Council. Its leaders, too, came to enjoy wide respect, certainly in comparison to the previous generation of Palestinian leadership. The Fatah leader and PLO chairman, Yasir Arafat, was not a hero of Nasir's stature, but his reputation as a low-key, dedicated leader was well established among Palestinians. And George Habash, the principal leader of the militant opposition, was respected even by those who did not accept his Marxism. Unlike most of the established regimes, the government of the Palestinians

83. Michael C. Hudson, "The Palestinian Arab Resistance Movement: Its Significance in the Middle East Crisis," *Middle East Journal*, 23, 3 (Summer 1969), pp. 291–320; and Michael C. Hudson, "Developments and Setbacks in the Palestinian Resistance Movement, 1967–1971," in W. E. Beling (ed.), *The Middle East: Quest for An American Policy* (Albany: State University of New York Press, 1973), pp. 101–25.

rested not on its coercive capabilities, which were very limited, but on the legitimacy which most Palestinians freely accorded it. The formal legitimacy accorded to the PLO in October 1974 by the UN General Assembly only reflected its evident authenticity as the representative of the Palestinian people. Winning legitimacy, however, did not by any means guarantee success for the PLO in fighting for the Palestinian cause. Indeed, its legitimacy victory only stimulated the campaign by its enemies to destroy it. Israel, seeing in the PLO not just a threat to its security but implicitly to its own legitimacy, deployed its full military, subversive, diplomatic, and propaganda resources against it.

But the emergence of a coherent, authoritative Palestinian movement was also seen increasingly as a challenge to the sovereignty of the main host Arab countries—Jordan, Lebanon, and Syria. Were the Palestinians to be considered just as guests in these countries, enjoying certain privileges conferred by the host governments? Or were they brother Arabs, equal in status yet possessed of the special right to organize themselves to recover their homeland? Were the host governments, by virtue of their commitments to the Palestine cause, obligated merely to provide minimum facilities for refugees or to support the Palestinian movement for national liberation, even if this meant giving up sovereignty to a limited extent and suffering Israeli reprisals? The dilemma of the Arab legitimacy problem was never more cruelly apparent than when the general Arab national principle conflicted with particular state and regime interests.

The Basic Issue

The roots of the Palestinian problem, as noted in chapter 5, go back to World War I and Britain's multiple and contradictory promises over the future of Palestine. Once the Balfour Declaration became known in the Arab world there were intense protests. Not only did the Arabs consider Palestine an integral part of the Arab nation, they also felt, with justification, that it had been included within the territory of the independent Arab state which Britain had promised to support in return for the Arabs' revolt against the Turks. Aided by the fact that the Balfour Declaration had been written into the British mandate document, the Zionist movement was able to expand and organize the Jewish community into an effective political entity. The Palestinian Arabs repeatedly protested the establishment of the Jewish national homeland. Their political structures during the mandate had been essentially parochial and traditional, consisting of clan and religious notables like the Husseinis and the Nashashibis.[84] Although influenced somewhat by the modern nationalist currents in Syria and Iraq, the Palestinian leaders proved incapable of combating the structurally developed Jewish organizations—the Jewish Agency, the parties, the kibbutzim, the Histadrut, and the Haganah. Serious rioting broke out in 1921 and 1929, and finally in 1936–39 there was a massive general strike and armed rebellion. All this failed either to reverse or contain the Zionist state-building process.

But the event which cast the struggle into its present form and turned it into a permanent crisis both for the Arabs and the rest of the world was the strife of 1947–49 which led to the forced expulsion of some 770,000 to 780,000 Palestinian Arabs from their homes in Palestine.[85] An indigenous Arab population and culture comprising some 90 percent of the population of Palestine on the eve of World War I had been driven out by a predominantly European Jewish settler movement.[86] By 1949 the Jews comprised some 90 percent of the part of Palestine occupied by Israel. If there had been a genuine settlement at the end of the 1948 war under which the refugees could have returned to their homes, instead of merely an armistice, the course of Israeli and Arab politics would have been very different. As it happened, however, no effective steps were taken by the parties directly involved or by the international community to break the impasse. What had been envisioned as temporary UN efforts to relieve refugee suffering became a permanent administration. The Palestinians, one of the most educated and industrious of the Arab peoples, had looked forward to self-rule in Palestine after the defeat of the Turks; but thirty years later they were dispossessed and landless, regarded by the world only as refugees, not as a society or a political community. And, in truth, their political strength was by then virtually nil. The militant leadership of the 1930s had been broken up; after 1948, with the

84. On Palestinian politics during the mandate see Ann Mosely Lesch, "The Palestine Arab Nationalist Movement Under the Mandate" in William B. Quandt, Fuad Jabber, and Ann Mosely Lesch, *The Politics of Palestinian Nationalism* (Berkeley: University of California Press, 1973), pp. 5–42. See also John Marlowe, *The Seat of Pilate* (London: Cresset, 1959).

85. Janet Abu-Lughod, "The Demographic Transformation of Palestine," chap. 5 in Ibrahim Abu-Lughod (ed.), *The Transformation of Palestine* (Evanston: Northwestern University Press, 1971), p. 161 and pp. 153–61.

86. The myth that the Palestinians somehow willingly left their homes has been refuted by Erskine Childers, "The Wordless Wish: From Citizens to Refugees," in I. Abu-Lughod, op. cit., pp. 165–201, and Erskine Childers, "The Other Exodus," *The Spectator* (London), May 12, 1961, and the subsequent debate.

community so dispersed, lacking a territorial base, and faced with a vastly superior enemy, the Palestinians were only nominally represented by Hajj Amin al-Husseini and the Arab Higher Committee in exile in Beirut.

The Contradictory Arab Responses to the Palestinians

The ambivalent responses in the Arab world to the Palestinians and their plight tell a great deal about the legitimacy problem of the Arab regimes and the ongoing survival problem of the Palestinians. Without exaggeration, it may be said that the disaster, as Constantine Zurayk described it in a well-known book, aroused the deepest indignation throughout the Arab world. Palestine was now the pre-eminent Arab concern, and the recovery of Palestine became, and remains, the principal rallying cry of Arab nationalists of diverse ideological tendencies. At the same time, Palestine became an internal political issue of great salience, particularly in the pan-Arab core states. Leaders vied with one another in expressing their fidelity to the cause. Authentic as this support undoubtedly was, it remained diffuse and peculiarly resistant to transformation into effective policy.

The Arab regimes had to look at Palestine as a policy problem. Their structural underdevelopment and lack of unity in the late 1940s had substantially contributed to the disaster. As the noted Palestinian liberal, Musa al-Alami put it in 1949:

> In the face of the enemy the Arabs were not a state, but petty states; groups, not a nation; each fearing and anxiously watching the other and intriguing against it . . . The structure of the Arab governments was old-fashioned and sterile. The regimes did not even understand the situation, or the importance and danger of the hour, or the course of events. They did nothing positive in accordance with the exigencies of the situation.[87]

Unfortunately, there was little improvement in Arab state policy in the following two decades. Jordan, which had fought most effectively to preserve the West Bank from the Zionists, immediately annexed it and sought to bring the great influx of Palestinian refugees, including the skilled and educated, under Hashimite authority. Egypt, both before and after the Nasir revolution, vied with the Hashimites for influence, and sought to use Palestine, and the 300,000 Palestinians under its jurisdiction in Gaza, for its own purposes. As we have seen, Nasir projected himself as a major regional leader through his successful

---

87. Musa al-Alami, "The Lesson of Palestine," *Middle East Journal*, 3 (1949), pp. 373–405.

championing of the cause. In Syria, where the trauma of defeat had been further poisoned by revelations of corruption during the war, regimes rose and fell in rapid succession, union with Egypt was tried and rejected, and finally the radical nationalist Ba'th emerged only to have to face again the consequences of a military encounter with Israel. Iraq, under the Hashimites and Nuri al-Sa'id, sought a Palestine solution by cooperating with the West in the Baghdad Pact, but that regime fell to rampaging mobs in 1958. Lebanese leaders paid lip service to the cause but took pains to remain as passive as possible, and they were very strict in suppressing political activity in the refugee camps. The yawning gap between words and deeds in all these regimes over these years did not go unnoticed either among the people of those countries or among Palestinians. Moreover, when Israel seized the opportunities in 1956 and 1967 to silence these bellicose Arab voices, it again exposed Arab government incapabilities and deepened the frustration in Arab politics. Yet in the process, Israel ironically helped further to Arabize the Palestinian problem, and the disaster of 1948 now had meaning and echoes well beyond the Palestinian community.

It is not surprising, on balance, that younger, socially mobilized Palestinians, already disenchanted with their own old leadership, should have become convinced that the Arab regimes would, in all probability, be unable to make the requisite effort in their behalf. They could see that no matter how sincere Arab public opinion was about the legitimacy of their cause, Arab leaders were constrained, first, by the instability and incapacity of their own regimes, and second, by the lack of interstate trust and coordination. It was these perceptions that stimulated a new group of leaders to reactivate the Palestinian political community.

The Challenge of the Palestinians

As early as 1955 small groups of Palestinian activists, dissatisfied with the Arab governments' activities in their behalf, began to mobilize for armed struggle against Israel. Among them was Yasir Arafat and his comrades who founded Fatah, the Palestine Liberation movement. A decade later Fatah and other guerrilla groups began staging raids into Israel. The Arab governments, too, became seized with the seriousness of the Palestine issue and in 1963 proposed the creation of a Palestine Liberation Organization. The PLO was formally established in May 1964 when the first Palestine National Council, consisting of some 400 prominent Palestinians, met in Jerusalem, Jordan. Under its first chairman, Ahmad Shuqayri, the PLO confined its activities mainly to propaganda and building a small Palestine Liberation army in the Egyptian-administered Gaza Strip. An important cause of the 1967 Arab-Israeli war was the series of Palestinian guerrilla raids launched mainly from Syria and the massive Israeli reprisals to them. After the humiliating defeats suffered by the Arab governments in the 1967 war, the Palestinian guerrilla organizations won vast new popular support, and in February 1969 Yasir Arafat of Fatah was elected chairman of the PLO.

Beginning in the late 1960s, the PLO began to develop national social and political institutions.[88] The most important are the 180-member Palestine National Council, which serves as the constituent assembly of the Palestinian people, and the PLO Executive Committee, the principal decision-making body, which has been dominated by the guerrilla groups. In addition to Fatah and the PLA, the major fighting organizations are the Popular Liberation Forces, the Sa'iqa (backed by Syria), the Popular Front for the Liberation of Palestine (PFLP), the Popular Democratic Front for the Liberation of Palestine (a radical offshoot of the PFLP), the PFLP General Command (another PFLP splinter group), and the Arab Liberation Front (backed by Iraq). The PLO also includes fourteen popular organizations which are distinct from the guerrilla groups and include students, teachers, labor, women, doctors, and lawyers, among others. Just before the 1973 war a clandestine resistance organization known as the Palestine National Front was established inside the occupied territories and Israel itself.

By the early 1970s the PLO was widely acknowledged as the sole legitimate voice of the Palestinian people. At the Arab summit meeting in Rabat in October 1974, King Hussein renounced Jordan's claims to represent the Palestinians of the West Bank. The following month the UN General Assembly conferred observer status on the PLO and passed a resolution reaffirming "the inalienable rights of the Palestinian people of Palestine," including "the right of self-determination without external interference" and "the right to national independence and sovereignty." In his historic address to the General Assembly, Yasir Arafat expounded his dream of a secular, democratic state of Palestine in which Arabs and Jews could live together. The Israeli representative denounced the PLO and declared that the PLO's intention was to destroy Israel.[89]

---

88. The most systematic treatment of the resistance movement is Quandt, et al., op. cit. The best general treatment of Palestinian society, culture, and politics is John K. Cooley, *Green March, Black September* (London: Frank Cass, 1973). One of the most articulate Palestinian analyses of the Palestine question is Hisham Sharabi, *Palestine and Israel: The Lethal Dilemma* (New York: Pegasus, 1969).

89. The texts of the speeches will be found in *The New York Times*, November 14, 1974.

Part of the reason for the PLO's success in achieving international legitimacy for its cause and for itself was its success in establishing itself as authoritative within the far-flung Palestinian community itself. Despite continual factional bickering within the movement, the leadership remained remarkably intact. William Quandt finds it "remarkable" that seven key leaders of Fatah in 1957–60 were still in command in 1971–72; they were still in place save for two murdered in Beirut by Israeli commandos four years later.[90] These men and other leaders outside Fatah like George Habash of the PFLP and Nayif Hawatma of the Popular Democratic Front, managed to keep relatively close to their constituencies and avoid the remoteness and isolation which has afflicted so much Arab leadership. They also remained remarkably untainted by corruption, personal vanity, and vindictiveness. As of the middle 1970s, one might hear sharp rank-and-file criticism of decisions made by these leaders but almost none about their basic integrity. Considering the repeated setbacks to the movement as a whole, as well as bureaucratic problems of structural growth, the leaders imparted to the movement an impressive degree of personal legitimacy.

Basically, however, it was the appeal of the resistance ideology, more than structural or personal legitimacy, that accounted for its considerable impact. The resistance had risen when the established vanguard regimes of Arabism had been defeated. Not only would Palestinians now step to the forefront of the struggle in a dynamic way, they would also restore the honor and further the aspirations of the Arabs as a whole. The core concept in resistance ideology was a simple yet vague evocation for the recovery of the lost land of Palestine. Recovery meant returning the refugees to the homeland and expunging the last remnants of Western colonialism from the Arab world. It meant self-determination, winning back the Muslim and Christian Holy Places, and reuniting of the eastern and western parts of the Arab world. This core concept, in short, evoked the most important symbols in modern Arab political culture. These were symbols of universal appeal, sacred both to conservatives and progressives. Left-wing critics charged that Fatah's and the PLO's programs lacked socialist content and were vague about the principles of social equality and democracy. They were suspicious of the middle-class biases of the resistance leadership. It appears, however, that this leadership preferred to adhere to a centrist position in order to generate much-needed support from the conservative as well as the progressive regimes. The formula of a Palestine state which would be secular and democratic, that is, in which

90. Quandt, op. cit., p. 84.

Arabs and Jews (including the European settlers) would live together under elected, representative governments, marked a considerable extension and liberalization of core Arab goals but was still considered insufficient by many on the Left. The question of how to achieve these goals was equally sensitive in terms of resistance political strategy, and the solution of armed struggle was equally vague. In the context of the 1967 defeat of Arab conventional armed forces, the idea of popular guerrilla warfare had obvious attractions, but there were drawbacks as well. Guerrilla warfare against Israel was impractical for achieving the stated goals; its main political benefits were to keep Arab support mobilized and to force the Palestinian issue into the calculations of the Great Powers. Far more serious were the reprisals which the Israelis mounted, with great efficiency, against the Arab host governments in Jordan and Lebanon. While some Palestinians felt that the reprisals would radicalize those regimes, more sober analysts feared that eventually they would turn the host countries against the resistance.

All things considered, it was a delicate ideological line that the Palestinians had to follow. One of the reasons that they followed it as successfully as they did was the very pluralism of the movement, which most observers have seen as a weakness. While the cleavages in the movement, as I shall argue, were a problem, they had the positive effect of broadening ideological support and diffusing responsibility from the mainstream for particular positions or actions. A variety of ideological movements in the Arab world, ranging from the Muslim Brothers to the Syrian Nationalists to the Communists of varying tendency, could and did find a place in the Palestinian revolution. In its formative stages, such aggregation of support was probably worth the price of factionalism.

For a brief period, from March 1968 to September 1970, the Palestinians appeared to have seized the moral leadership and attained enormous influence over almost the entire Arab world—despite the fact that they still lacked a secure territorial base and possessed only minuscule fighting forces (not more than 15,000 guerrillas) and rudimentary political infrastructure. Syria provided sanctuary; Egypt provided diplomatic support; Algeria supplied training and material; Sa'udi Arabia and the Gulf states provided money; Jordan and Lebanon almost provided a state.

The Challenge to the Palestinians

Compared to many of the Arab systems, the Palestinian polity did not have a serious legitimacy problem. During its first decade, it had won the loyalty of virtually all Palestinians, no matter under what regime they lived, under exceedingly difficult conditions. To be sure, as of the middle 1970s, it only ruled directly over Palestinians in Lebanon, but it is highly probable that Palestinians under the rule of Israel, Jordan, Syria, and other Arab countries would have accorded their support to the PLO had they been given the opportunity to express themselves freely. There was controversy, debate, and sometimes bitter conflict among various Palestinian parties and factions, yet there remained basic structural coherence based on shared beliefs and rules of the game.

Some of this coherence could be ascribed to a common awareness of the perils on all sides, and some was also due to the continual postponing by the leadership of hard decisions about future strategy. The legitimacy of the first decade was genuine but not enough to guarantee the Palestinians a political future.

There were three main challenges to the Palestinian movement. The most direct was from Israel. The Israelis had two types of leverage. As a successful functioning polity, Israel had the opportunity during its first quarter-century to assimilate the 10 to 15 percent of its population that was Arab and to convince the neighboring Arab states of its legitimacy. It was unable effectively to assimilate either its Arab subjects or to assimilate itself into the regional political order. The Arabs in Israel, although many of them enjoyed living standards higher than Arabs elsewhere, kept their own cultural identity and became increasingly politicized during the 1960s. This was due in part to their restrictive and prejudicial legal status. Even though military rule over certain Arab districts ended in 1966, the State of Israel, acting under the emergency and defense laws promulgated originally by the British mandate authorities, was given wide discretion to apply military rule, to detain or expel individuals, and to confiscate or destroy their property.[91] In the process of establishing itself, Israel had taken over or destroyed some 380 Arab villages and appropriated millions of dollars worth of Arab property. There was, on the whole, little social integration with the Jewish communities. The Israeli political scientist, Jacob Landau, concluded a 1969 study of the Arabs in Israel by noting that "their dual role as part of the larger Arab nation" and citizens of Israel "has imposed a tremendous emotional strain on them."[92] He discovered a wide range of attitudes, from

91. A critical analysis by a Palestinian lawyer then living in Israel is Sabri Jiryis, *The Arabs in Israel*, second edition (New York: Monthly Review Press, 1976).
92. Jacob M. Landau, *The Arabs in Israel* (London: Oxford University Press, 1969), p. 220.

moderate to extremist, with the younger and better educated tending
"to be more demanding and outspoken." Although he saw signs of
acceptance and assimilation that could be nurtured "by vigorous
activity by the Jewish majority on behalf of the Arab minority," it
would seem from the development of anti-Israel and pro-PLO sentiment in the occupied territories during the 1970s, and especially
after Arafat's UN speech, that the trend was running in the other
direction. The widespread anti-Israel rioting on the West Bank in the
spring of 1976 indicated the growth of more militant Palestinian Arab
nationalism. As for the use of foreign policy to help legitimize the state
in the eyes of the Arab world, the record was also one of failure. In
his exhaustive study of Israeli foreign policy, Michael Brecher writes
that while he feels that "Arab intransigence" was the main cause of
the continuing tension, Israeli policy did not contribute "to an easing
of that psychological block."[93] Thus despite a few notable efforts to
provide some economic, social, and legal benefits for the Israeli Arabs,
to administer a "liberal" occupation of the territories occupied in
1967, and to make certain limited accommodations in foreign policy
(such as with Jordan), Israel on balance was not successful in per-
suading the Palestinians to abandon their cause and accept the
Zionist state.

The second type of leverage available to Israel was coercive. With
formidable efficiency, the Israel Defense Force frustrated most of the
border raids and internal sabotage missions carried out by Palestinian
guerrillas. Guerrilla activity over the border was most intense in late
1967 and from October 1969 until Black September 1970. The state
of insurrection in Gaza lasted from 1968 through the summer of 1972.
By that time, apart from sporadic bombings, Israel had effectively
contained the modest military threat posed by the guerrilla movement.
More important, the Israeli military applied offensive pressure against
the guerrillas by attacking their sanctuaries in Jordan and Lebanon,
trying thus to turn the government and local people against them. It
also carried out commando assaults into Beirut and other Lebanese
towns and in one incident killed three top PLO leaders in their
Beirut apartments. Israel was also quite successful in combating
Palestinian terrorism against Israeli citizens abroad. Doubtless, the
power and effectiveness of the Israeli military and intelligence organizations was a constant morale burden on the Palestinian resistance.

The second principal challenge to the Palestinian resistance came

93. Michael Brecher, *The Foreign Policy System of Israel* (New Haven: Yale University Press,
1972), p. 562.

from the Arab states and the Arab state system. I have already re-marked on their contradictory responses to the Palestinians and their problem. These contradictions were only heightened by the emergence of the resistance. For King Hussein of Jordan, 65 percent of whose subjects were Palestinian, the resistance represented a threat to the integrity of his kingdom, on the East Bank as well as the West Bank. In August 1970 it was perfectly evident to a visitor to Jordan that the guerrilla movement was in the process of supplanting royal authority in the capital and elsewhere. Then, in what came to be known as Black September, King Hussein's army attacked the guerrillas and drove them out of Amman. Conservative estimates put the casualties, mostly civilians in the main refugee camps, at 4,000. But Syria and Iraq, the regimes most committed to the resistance, offered little help in the Jordanian crisis. Syria released tanks of the Palestine Liberation army under its control to intervene in northern Jordan, but Hafiz al-Asad, commander of the Syrian air force, refused to provide the necessary air support. An Iraqi force entered Jordan but remained strictly neutral, much to the embitterment of the Palestinians. Egypt's President Nasir, who had just accepted a U. S.-sponsored truce in the Suez Canal "war of attrition" with Israel, was also evidently cool to the Palestinian idea of armed struggle, and offered only mediation rather than tangible support to the guerrillas in the Jordan crisis. In the subsequent months, the guerrillas were pushed entirely out of Jordan and found themselves with freedom of action only in Lebanon. Syria, while continuing to provide some moral and material support, was clearly trying to keep the closest possible control over Palestinian activities. In the 1973 war, the Palestinians played a secondary role compared to the Arab states, but in the aftermath they succeeded in enlarging their international legitimacy and consolidating their position in Lebanon.

The Lebanese government, reflecting as it did the divisions in Lebanese society, was too weak either to support or control the Palestinian movement. But after an Israeli commando raid destroyed thirteen civilian airliners at Beirut's airport on December 28, 1968, it became clear that Lebanon would no longer be also to avoid involve-ment in Arab-Israeli fighting. The first of periodic clashes between Palestine commandos and Lebanese army units took place in the spring of 1969 and led to political violence in Beirut, Saida, Tyre, and Tripoli.[94] More Israeli raids and more internal turmoil led to a

94. Michael C. Hudson, "Fedayeen Are Forcing Lebanon's Hand," *Mid East*, February 1970, pp. 7–14.

seven-month cabinet crisis which was ended by the Cairo Agreement of November 1969, under which the resistance was allowed to administer the refugee camps and hold transit routes and certain positions in southern Lebanon in return for respecting Lebanese sovereignty. The expulsion of the resistance movement from Jordan did not lead to its destruction, as many had expected, but instead accelerated its development in Lebanon. In the camps and around the main Lebanese cities, it developed its political infrastructure; in the Arqub region of southern Lebanon, adjacent to the Israeli border, it developed its guerrilla bases. Friction with the Lebanese continued, despite the Cairo Agreement. The Lebanese army, urged on by President Suleiman Frangieh, failed in a major attempt to curb Palestinian activities in the spring of 1973. At about this time too, left-wing, Arab nationalist, and pro-Palestinian elements which were predominant in Lebanon's Sunni and Shi'ite Muslim communities and in the large Greek Orthodox Christian sect, were becoming increasingly disenchanted with the Frangieh regime's identification with the most right-wing, anti-Arab, and anti-Palestinian currents in the Maronite Christian community. In response to what they saw as growing and inevitable collusion between the Palestinian organizations (especially those of the Left) and the various Lebanese groups opposed to Maronite hegemony and right-wing isolationist policies, the right-wing groups and the regime became alarmed about a reformist, even revolutionary, threat to the Lebanon they revered—and controlled. With polarization feeding upon itself, only the 1973 Arab-Israeli war and the short-lived postwar euphoria could delay a new confrontation.

The precipitating events of the Lebanese civil war took place early in 1975 when a popular left-wing, pro-Palestinian Lebanese Sunni leader from Saida, Ma'rouf Sa'd, was killed in a clash with the army, and when Kata'ib gunmen ambushed a bus carrying Palestinian refugees, killing twenty-seven. The mainstream Palestinian leadership, which had always tried to avoid becoming embroiled in Lebanese politics, was sucked into the debilitating civil war and diverted from the struggle against Israel. Just as the Lebanese right-wing had understandable fears about the future of "its" Lebanon, the Palestinians could justifiably claim that their alliance with the Lebanese left-wing was dictated by self-defense. The resistance movement thus found itself maneuvered into armed struggle against the wrong enemy in the wrong place at the wrong time. It was forced to gamble that it would be on the winning side in a conflict whose outcome was at best uncertain. Palestinian fortunes were hostage to big power interests, Syrian policy, and a Maronite right-wing enemy which by the middle of 1976 was being openly supported by Israel. The same Arab regimes which heavily depended for their legitimacy on their loyalty to the Palestinian cause in principle found that any organized, concrete manifestation of that cause confronted them with agonizing dilemmas. In resolving these dilemmas the structure of the Arab state system defined the situation in such a way that rationality impelled them to put their own security particular interests ahead of those of the Palestinian movement.

The third challenge to the resistance movement came from within. While we have argued that the Palestinians were relatively successful in establishing legitimate political structures, we cannot ignore that their highly unfavorable operational environment imposed constant divisive pressures. Without describing the numerous and complex organizational changes which occurred during the first years of the movement,[95] it may be noted that the principal cleavage pitted radical groups like the Popular Front for the Liberation of Palestine (PFLP), the PFLP General Command, and the Iraqi-supported Arab Liberation Front against the pragmatic groups of which Fatah was by far the largest. The mainstream of the movement, PLO, dominated by Fatah and prominent Palestinians outside the guerrilla groups, thus fell into the pragmatic camp. Fatah and the PLO consistently opposed the PFLP's hostile stand toward the conservative Arab regimes, which were ready to support the Palestinians as long as they directed their frustrations exclusively toward Israel. The pragmatists also opposed the airplane hijackings and terrorist atrocities which the PFLP committed in the early phase of its existence and which other small groups continued to perpetrate. The pragmatists in the middle 1970s were prepared to adopt a flexible approach on a negotiated settlement of the Arab-Israeli conflict, involving creation of a small Palestinian state on the West Bank and Gaza, while the radicals refused to contemplate such a course. The radicals, who called themselves "the refusal front," suspected that anything less than militance would lead to a closing of the Palestine issue on terms so far short of their sacred goal as to be completely unacceptable.

A closely related internal problem was the role of various Arab states in sponsoring or controlling Palestinian organizations within the resistance movement as a whole. In an ideological sense, this problem reflected the delicate relationship between Palestinian nationalism and Arab nationalism as a whole. The Palestinians as a people were probably more committed to pan-Arabism than most

95. On this, see Quandt, op. cit., chap. 2, and esp. fig. 2, p. 61.

other Arabs, but for reasons which I have discussed, they were impelled
to reorganize themselves as a particular community with the Arab
nation. Accordingly, Palestinians in the movement felt both a need
for autonomy and for solidarity with the Arab world. It was Yasir
Arafat's task to walk a fine line, trying to generate all-Arab support
without falling completely under the influence of a particular regime or
ideological tendency. On the whole he was successful, at least up
until the Lebanese civil war. Fatah was able to pursue a reasonably
autonomous course and still receive vital aid from the monarchies of
the Gulf and the radical republics. But the existence of particular
guerrilla organizations such as the large Sa'iqa force controlled by
Damascus or the smaller ALF controlled by Baghdad posed a threat
to the internal coherence of the movement. Were the movement to
be "captured" by a particular Arab government, it would risk both
its freedom of action and its claim to speak legitimately for the Palestinian people and their rights.

The Palestinians were estimated to number nearly 3 million in
the early 1970s. Most were in Jordan (1.1 million), the West Bank
and Jerusalem (716,000), pre-1967 Israel (400,000), Gaza (357,000),
Lebanon (240,000), Syria (187,000), and Kuwait (147,000). Smaller
but strategically placed concentrations were located in Egypt (33,000),
Sa'udi Arabia (32,000), Iraq (16,000), the Arab Gulf states (15,000),
and Libya (5,000). There were also at least 25,000 Palestinian Arabs
in the United States.[96] Psychologically their political identity was
restored, but in actuality it was still unfulfilled. Their experiences at
the hands of the Zionists, the Great Powers, and the Arab regimes
would not easily be forgiven or forgotten. Their movement, symbolized
by the PLO, had largely succeeded in embodying what is perhaps
the central theme in modern Arabism. Beyond its Arab nationalist
dimension, their movement had also, for a time at least, presented
itself as a different type of political order from the established Arab
regimes—a revolutionary improvement over both the monarchies and
the new republics. During its growth periods, the movement embodied
a degree of voluntarism and participation from "the bottom up"
which has only rarely been seen in modern Arab politics.

But as the institutionalized conscience of the Arab world, the resistance inevitably attracted opposition from most of the established
regimes, even those that were in basic support of the Palestine cause.

---

96. According to figures from the Institute of Palestine Studies published in *Al-Nahar* (Beirut),
July 30, 1974, and from A. B. Zahlan and Edward Hagopian, "Palestine's Arab Population,"
Journal of Palestine Studies, 3, 4 (Summer 1974), pp. 32–73; pp. 52–54.

The resistance and these governments found themselves in a vicious circle of illegitimacy. Regimes which saw this challenge as a threat to their own claims to legitimacy through the Palestine cause only weakened themselves as they sought to curb or destroy the challenger. But the Palestinian leaders could gain little comfort from the turmoil they were causing because they needed Arab assistance. The movement could not develop simply on the basis of the diffuse support it enjoyed in Arab public opinion; and if it could not continue to develop, it would risk the erosion of its own claims to legitimacy and perforce its political and diplomatic strength as well. To face the hostility and the power of Israel and the United States, it clearly needed to have the Arab world and the Arab regimes mobilized behind it. It needed financial and diplomatic support from the conservatives and military-strategic support from the republicans. But as long as the Arab regimes were bitterly divided among themselves on how to deal with the Palestine problem, it would not be easy for the Palestinian national movement, no matter how internally coherent it might be, to continue to grow; indeed, mere survival might be a difficult task. To begin to exploit the Arab world's basic long-term advantages over Israel, the resistance needed unified pro-Palestinian solidarity among the Arab states, but owing to the nature of the Arab state system, the bigger the resistance became the more anti-Palestinian behavior it generated. To the extent that there was unity among the Arab states, it was unity in opposition to an autonomous role for the resistance. Withal, it was still conceivable that the Palestinians might have the last word because the opponents of the regimes would, as always, be able to accuse the incumbents of selling out on Palestine.

9

The Republics of the Periphery

The republics on the periphery of the Arab nation, as independent political entities, are newer than those that I have examined in the pan-Arab core. Generally speaking, the salience of Arab unity and the concern with Palestine are less fundamental issues, although still important, and local collective identities are stronger. They all share certain basic features of their core republic neighbors, however. The myths of revolution against a corrupt ancien régime and of socialist transformation remain cardinal legitimizing principles. The perceived threat of neo-colonialism is still, though in varying degree, a cohesive force for building political community. As in the other republics, the myth of rule by the people coexists with the reality of increasingly centralized government control. As a group the peripheral republics are even less "settled" institutionally than those of the pan-Arab core. Without suggesting that the core republics have achieved overmuch in the way of established order, it appears that the peripheral republics —with the qualified exception of Tunisia—are even less stable, lacking even institutionalized despotism and plagued with growing tensions between a variety of traditional and modern social groups. Personalist leadership is strikingly evident everywhere, with the possible exception of the PDRY. Intraelite conflict involving liberals and Marxists, secularists, the pious educated, technocrats, and efficiency-minded military officers is virtually ubiquitous.

Yet there is also considerable diversity within the peripheral republics as a group. Tunisia and Algeria possess a more elaborate social and physical infrastructure than the other states; and the Sudan too, although now very underdeveloped, is advanced enough to export trained manpower and skilled civil servants to the neighboring Arabian petro-kingdoms and north Yemen. Libya and the two Yemens, however, are only beginning to develop their human resources. Government and ancillary political structures, accordingly, are larger and more capable in the two former French-ruled territories.

In strictly political terms, the peripheral states have adopted a variety of pathways to legitimacy within the overall constraints I have noted. Libya, under the officers' republic, has consciously sought to be a part of the pan-Arab core, and the regime has staked its legitimacy to a very large extent on the causes of Palestine and Arab unity. It has, however, thus far been rebuffed in its attempts to merge with this theoretical core, and it has been hindered by the more parochial features of Libyan political culture. The Sudan, too, borders on the pan-Arab core and at times, both before and after independence, has had or has sought closer relationships with Egypt. But to an even greater extent than in Libya, local Sudanese conditions and an extraordinarily diverse political culture have cast it in another direction. Indeed, so complex and divided is the Sudan, politics under the Numayri regime have evolved (if that is the word) in a highly praetorian fashion, in which the strongman, through the adroit manipulation of symbols and coercion, manages to thwart challenge after challenge yet fails to develop lasting legitimacy for himself or for government in general. The case of north Yemen (the Yemen Arab Republic) is similar in some respects but not all. Since 1974, a non-radical military officer, Colonel Ibrahim al-Hamdi, has ruled in Sana, having replaced a moderate civilian republican regime which had failed to exert sufficient authority over Yemen's semiautonomous tribes. North Yemen too has had its encounters with Arabism via Nasir's support for the 1962 revolution, and I have noted above the all-Arab content in Yemeni school books. But in the 1970s Arabism for Yemen must be mediated through Sa'udi Arabia, and socialist transformation must confront the realities of underdevelopment and capital availability, which again is influenced heavily by Riyadh.

Unity talks between north and south Yemen have been in progress for years, but there could hardly be greater dissimilarity between their two systems of government. Perhaps alone in the Arab world, the PDRY has made a serious effort to transcend both patriarchal despotism and conventional centralized, statist revolutionary forms. While information about the PDRY is far from adequate, it suggests that there has been more radical social change and more local participation within the framework of a Marxist-inspired single-party regime than anywhere else in the Arab world. Only Iraq and Algeria seem to approach the transformationist goals which all the revolutionary regimes espouse, but even these political systems, as I have shown in Iraq and will show in Algeria, have reverted to a degree of centralized autocracy which ill accords with either the claims of ideology or the objective demands for participation generated by social modernization. The rulers of the PDRY, however, have also come under a variety of pressures from conservative Sa'udi Arabia which are not easy for a small impoverished country, with strong conservative elements in its own political culture, to resist. The revolutionary regime of Algeria is the self-proclaimed leader of Third World socialist nonalignment. Its support for liberation movements in the Arab world and Africa has been generous. The trauma of a particularly disruptive war of independence has given the myth of the revolution unusually potent legitimacy. Yet, as in most of the other Arab republics, political coherence in Algeria is deeply flawed. The single-party as an instrument for legitimation appears to have failed. The cleavage at the mass level between the Arab and Berber subcultures is managed but not reduced; and at the elite level, the tension between revolutionaries who are Francophone and secular and others who are Arabophone and Muslim adds a certain instability to Algerian political life. The Algerian solution has been to undertake vast, centrally directed social and economic development programs and to inculate the ideology of the socialist revolution in order to transcend political culture contradictions. As elsewhere, however, the issue of popular participation has not as yet been adequately addressed. Finally, I examine the republic of Tunisia. If Tunisia appears to be the most successfully legitimated of all the Arab republics, it may be because the political system—not just the leader or the regime—developed a relative balance of personal, ideological, and structural legitimacy. No doubt aided by the natural advantages of a homogeneous political culture, a comparatively benign colonial experience, few regional complications, and evenly distributed modernization, Bourguiba's republic, though authoritarian, appears to have the deep-rooted respect of most Tunisians. Yet even in this instance, participation has become increasingly an issue once open structures have become restrictive, and the political coherence of the republic after the disappearance of its gifted founding father thus becomes open to question.

THE LIBYAN ARAB REPUBLIC

Like Egypt, Syria, and Iraq, Libya is a revolutionary nationalist polity. Ideology is the principal source of system legitimacy. But the Libyan Arab Republic, which was created in a military coup on September 1, 1969, has evolved a distinctive strategy of legitimacy that sets it somewhat apart from its pan-Arab core precursors. It differs substantially even from Nasirist Egypt, which the Libyan leaders have consciously taken as a model for their own revolution. Fundamentally pan-Arabist, the Libyan revolution is also unabashedly Islamic. As such it differs from Algeria, in which Arab unity is relatively muted, and from the Ba'thist regimes in Syria and Iraq, which are at best ambivalent on the place of Islam in politics. On this score Libya is even more sharply at variance with the People's Democratic Republic of Yemen, the most unequivocally secular and Marxist of the revolutionary regimes. In a broader context, however, Libya and the PDRY are similar in the intense radicalism of their respective ideologies; both share a certain puritanical fundamentalism and a commitment to a comprehensive social and moral transformation.

Libya is distinctive not only for its emphasis on Islam but also for a structural experiment that bears a certain resemblance to Mao Tse-Tung's cultural revolution in China. The "Popular Revolution" of 1973 called for the spontaneous establishment of "People's Committees" (*lijan al-sha'biyya*) throughout Libyan society—in the schools, factories, companies and government departments—to carry out the principles of the revolution. This is an innovation intended to correct a weakness which the young Libyan officers perceived in other Arab revolutionary regimes. Although he is Nasir's most fervent disciple, Col. Mu'ammar al-Qadhafi has publicly criticized the Egyptian revolution for having failed to mobilize the masses. It is relatively easy, he said in a Beirut newspaper interview, for a new leadership to dictate changes from above, but no revolutionary purpose can be accomplished if the masses remain passive and unenthusiastic about mobilization for higher goals.[1] The Libyan leaders, notwithstanding their publicized rejection of Communism, seemed quite prepared to borrow selectively from its operational procedures in order to address this problem. In this respect too the Libyan approach to building political community was not unlike the officially encouraged local peasant uprisings that have occurred in the PDRY.

The eclectic radicalism of the Libyan pathway to legitimacy has inspired no small amount of outrage and ridicule both inside and outside the Arab world. What the critics sometimes overlook is the remarkable success of the Libyan formula. The few known plots to overthrow the regime have been swiftly put down, and the continuity of the original officers' movement has been largely maintained. The survival, indeed the vitality, of the Libyan Arab Republic during it first five years—in the face of constant regional and Western hostility—suggests that the regime has managed to generate significant legitimacy. This success may be due to the congruence of official ideology with fundamental values in Libyan political culture. It may also be the product of multiple systemic sources of legitimacy. Ideology, I would reiterate, has generated considerable support; but the strong personal leadership of Colonel Qadhafi has also been a factor. It is

1. *Al Nahar* (Beirut), May 24 and 25, 1973.

also probable but less certain that the Libyan Arab Socialist Union and, more recently, the above-mentioned People's Committees are contributing a degree of structural legitimacy to the system. In order to explore these propositions, I shall discuss first the traditional foundations in Libyan political culture, with particular attention to kinship, religion, and the historical legacy of Italian settler colonialism. I shall then turn my attention to the 1969 revolution and the ideological, leadership and structural developments that it has generated.

Foundations of Libyan Political Culture

Until very recently, Libya was a particularist political culture—or, more precisely, a collection of Muslim tribal political cultures. To be sure, the Ottoman conquest of the mid-sixteenth century had imposed a degree of coherence, but it was confined mainly to the coastal areas; and the Karamanli dynasty (1711–1835) had brought a certain degree of autonomy. But it was the spread of the Sanusi religious brotherhood from the mid-nineteenth century and its resistance to the Italian invasions of the twentieth century that were the crucial events contributing to the creation of a kind of tribal-religious proto-nationalism in Libya. After World War II, the United Nations, various interested powers, and Libyan notables and groups established an independent federal Libyan state—a monarchy—to be ruled by the Sanusi leader Muhammad Idriss. The process of state-building, which has been meticulously described by UN Commissioner Adrian Pelt, revealed just how salient the particularist and primordial identifications within this vast 685,000 square-mile land still were.[2] The beginnings of social mobilization in Libya after independence in 1951, which were vastly accelerated by the oil discoveries of the 1960s, coincided with the rise of pan-Arabism as a mass phenomenon throughout the Arab world. These events appear not to have destroyed the parochial kinship and religious orientations of Libyans but rather to have enlarged their boundaries, so to speak; so that the Arab nationalism of the 1969 revolutionaries could (and did) fuse with tribal asabiyya and Islam.

Tribalism and Royal Authority

Kinship group identifications are relevant to system legitimacy in two ways. First, kinship as a value in itself can be an instrument for

---

2. Adrian Pelt, *Libyan Independence and the United Nations: A Case of Planned Decolonization*, published for the Carnegie Endowment for International Peace (New Haven: Yale University Press, 1970), esp. chaps. 2, 6, and 8.

winning the consent of others if somehow the leader can present himself as the real or symbolic father of a people on the basis of blood solidarity. Ibn Khaldun, it will be recalled, asserted that royal authority results from the successful exploitation of group feeling (asabiyya) by a tribal chieftain. Second, the scope of kinship loyalties is parochial, conforming to the mosaic of family, clan, tribe, and tribal-ethnic structures. E. E. Evans-Pritchard, in his masterly study of Cyrenaica, makes the point succinctly:

> The tribal system, typical of segmentary structures everywhere, is a system of balanced opposition between tribes ... Authority is distributed at every point of the tribal structure and political leadership is limited to situations in which a tribe or a segment of it acts corporately ... Consequently the exact status of a Shaikh can only be defined in terms of a complicated network of kinship ties and structural relations ...[3]

Such complex cleavages pose a challenge to centralizing, modernizing leadership. In Libya under the monarchy, the double-edged character of kinship was easily apparent. Tribal solidarity was an important resource for the Sanusi king. He derived his royal authority in large part from his status as a tribal chieftain of Cyrenaica. By virtue of his being the leader of one group of tribes, he was also able to command a measure of respect from other tribes. On the other hand, internal tribal-regional fragmentation, and the concomitant insistence on local autonomy hindered the establishment of the independent state itself in 1950–51, and thereafter it slowed the growth of authority and capability of the monarchy. Ultimately, therefore, during the oil boom of the 1960s the regime was unable to respond effectively to the new challenges and opportunities; instead, it allowed corruption and profiteering among a very small circle close to the throne to escalate to intolerable proportions. All the while it was afflicted with an inability to comprehend the radical political developments occurring elsewhere in the Arab world and among some young politicized Libyans as well. Since the republican revolution, tribalism has continued to exert contradictory effects on regime legitimacy. The new leaders are unequivocally hostile to it, seeing it as a source of subversion; but insofar as it is congruent with a larger ethnic Arabism, it may still enhance national solidarity.

3. E. E. Evans-Pritchard, *The Sanusi of Cyrenaica* (London: Oxford University Press, 1949), p. 59.

Sanusi Islam

But kinship was by no means the entire base of King Idriss's authority and does not explain his role as first among equals among the tribal leaders of Cyrenaica, a position that made it possible for him to be made amir of Cyrenaica after the first Italian war and king of Libya in 1951. Muhammad Idriss was also a sayyid, a title of special respect rooted in religion. Most important, he was head of the Sanusiyya, a religious brotherhood, with zawiyas located throughout Cyrenaica and closely linked to the tribal structure and values.[4] Although ignorant of Islamic doctrine and lax in observance, the bedouin nevertheless displayed a deep-rooted Islamic identity, and their commitment to the Sanusiyya Brotherhood was mediated by their belief in the saintliness of the Grand Sanusi and his family. The Grand Sanusi was a marabout possessing baraka. Thus a symbiosis of religion and kinship gave coherence and dynamism to an order which transcended in scope the tribal society per se and permitted a degree of centralized and hierarchical authority. Although severely reduced as a political structure during the Italian occupation, it remained a positive and significant force in the state-building process of 1950–51.[5] And so the universalist character of Islam and its unique assimilation with tribalism through the Sanusiyya Brotherhood facilitated the integration of Libya's political culture. Although the revolutionary leaders of republican Libya reject tribalism and Sanusi Islam as reactionary, they reflect these values to some extent themselves and, indeed, benefit politically from their identification with them: we are reminded of Colonel Qadhafi's bedouin origins and his own intense religiosity.

Italian Colonialism

The traumatic experience of the Italian wars and colonization was another factor facilitating the development of a Libyan Arab identity broader in scope than particularist tribal solidarity. In Libya as elsewhere in the Arab world, internal political identity and coherence was significantly affected by external threats and interventions. The Italian domination of Libya was marked by two wars, 1911–17 and 1923–32, and a decade of exploitation that endured until British forces defeated the Italians in World War II. Its negative effects were not unlike those of France in Algeria, involving the seizure of choice lands and the dislocation of nomads and peasants; but it lacked the com-

4. Ibid., chap. 3, esp. p. 84.
5. Pelt, chap. 1 passim, and pp. 51, 56, 164, and 619.

pensating advantages, such as they were, of a *mission civilisatrice*. As such its politicizing effects were particularly acute: the heavy-handed violence and inequity stimulated resistance while the failure to socialize an Italianized indigenous elite made the subsequent Libyan Arabism "purer" and less complicated than the nationalisms that emerged in the French Middle Eastern territories.[6] In the first war, the Turks and Libyans—principally the Sanusiyya—formed a common bond as Muslims against the Christian imperialists; but by the time of the second, Turkey was no longer an actor and the Sanusiyya resistance had taken on a more specifically Libyan character. Indeed, from 1922 the Sanusi amir of Cyrenaica was recognized as ruler by the notables of Tripolitania as well. The partition lines of the other imperialist powers, France in Algeria and Tunisia and Great Britain in Egypt, also contributed to defining the boundaries of Libyan Arab consciousness.[7]

The Collapse of the Monarchy

The establishment of the federal Kingdom of Libya was something of a milestone in the annals of state-building inasmuch as it drew together three socially and geographically disparate regions. Cyrenaica and the Fezzan were conservative tribal societies; Tripolitania, more cosmopolitan, was dominated by a number of wealthy, high-status families. The lynchpin of the system was the hereditary monarchy. The Sanusi dynasty was more generously endowed with traditional kinship and religious legitimacy than any other structure. Moreover, it capitalized initially at least upon its record of resistance to the Italians. The king himself, though not a strong leader, was respected for his piety and rectitude. Had Libya remained politically tranquil, the monarchy might have survived beyond its seventeen years.

Neither of these conditions continued. The politicization of the region, accelerated by the anti-French and anti-British struggles on either side of Libya, the Palestine conflict, the spread of Nasirist and Ba'thist pan-Arabism, and the antiroyalist movements elsewhere in the Arab world were hardly propitious for the so-called political development of the Sanusi monarchy. A regime whose principal income was derived from American and British bases was quick to lose whatever anti-imperialist credit it may have once enjoyed—at least among the politicized youth. Similarly, its brief monopoly of the legitimizing value of nationalism, associated with the achievement of

6. Frank Ralph Golino, "Patterns of Libyan National Identity," *Middle East Journal*, 24, 3 (Summer 1970), pp. 338–52; p. 344.

7. Ibid., p. 348.

independence, was soon challenged from inside by the Tripolitanian National Congress party with its pan-Arab inclinations and from outside by the pan-Arab movements themselves. The discovery of major oil deposits in 1959, instead of providing a security cushion for the regime, appears only to have accelerated plotting against it from several quarters. The increasingly visible corruption of a small circle of businessmen and advisers close to the throne—men like the Shalhi brothers who were reaping personal windfalls from the new oil flow— was one of the factors that precipitated the movement of the Unitary Free Officers.[8] Conceivably, some of these threats to the system could have been perceived and dealt with had greater political participation been allowed. Geared as it was, however, to the maintenance of the traditional elite and the management of conflict within it, the leadership proved to be intolerant of autonomous political activity. It immediately banned the country's major party, the National Congress party of Tripolitania, and exiled its leader Bashir al-Sa'dawi. Although several elections subsequently were held, all parties henceforth were outlawed. In 1961 and 1968, respectively, Ba'thist and Arab nationalist activities were discovered and repressed; significantly, in each case the names of younger men from prominent families were linked with the forbidden organizations.

It cannot be said that the monarchy experienced a crisis of legitimacy in the sense of overt demonstrations of hostility against it. Public opinion hardly existed; subversion and governmental repression were not abnormally severe by Arab political standards. The bitter popular violence that broke out at the time of the 1967 Arab-Israeli war might have indicated the intensity of nationalist feeling beneath the surface. But when this writer visited Libya a year before the revolution, the prevailing mood was relaxed. A young and relatively liberal prime minister, Abd al-Hamid Bakkush, was attempting to prod the regime toward more effective planning and administration. There was a sense of relief in some quarters that the defeat of Nasir would reduce Egyptian influence in Libyan affairs, and there was talk of emphasizing a new Libyan (as opposed to pan-Arab) "personality." At the same time, however, it was noted that the king was nearly eighty years old and increasingly reclusive; Bakkush was shortly to be replaced, reportedly for having been too progressive for some elements; and corruption was rampant. According to one Libyan source, votes in the 1968 election had been sold for up to thirty Libyan pounds apiece (around eighty-

8. On Umar al-Shalhi and the atmosphere of the ancien régime see Patrick Seale and Maureen McConville, *The Hilton Assignment* (New York: Praeger, 1973), chap. 3.

four dollars). When the coup came, the regime did not fall under a wave of public disapproval so much as by its own accumulated incompetence. Indeed, the coup itself—an operation requiring close coordination over vast distances—succeeded because the technical expertise of the young officers, notably in radio communications, was superior to that of the regime.[9]

Republican Libya: A New Ideology

A few days after the revolution, speaking at a ceremony commemorating the martyrdom of Umar al-Mukhtar who led the anti-Italian resistance, Col. Mu'ammar al-Qadhafi stated the main goals of the new regime:

> The Revolution, dear Brethren, was staged in response to the appeal of the masses of our people. It was therefore a sincere rise by the armed forces, the vanguard of this people . . . The revolution . . . aims at freedom, socialism and unity. The freedom we mean is the freedom of both the country and the citizen; the freedom of the individual and of the Arab man in Libya . . . Our socialism . . . lies in our collective participation in production and work, and in the distribution of production with justice and equality. Our socialism, is the socialism of Islam, the noble religion; it stems from the heritage of this people, its beliefs, and the glorious events in its great history. . . . As for unity . . . it is a precious hope which has been cherished by the Arab people for centuries . . . it is the decisive historical answer to the challenges of both imperialism and Zionism . . . The road to Palestine is the unity of all the Arabs to strike one blow and liquidate the intruder's existence supported by imperialism . . . [10]

We see the principal symbols of Arabism, echoes of Ba'thism and Nasirism: freedom, socialism, and unity. Imperialism and Zionism are strongly attacked. The change is indeed revolutionary both in substance and in tone. Yet at the same time there is an invocation of the traditional values, especially Islam, and of the Libyan historical heritage. Legitimacy resources that served the old regime are also mobilized to serve the new one but they have been given a new context and different emphasis. Brotherhood there is, but the identification is

9. On the coup see John K. Cooley, in the *Christian Science Monitor*, October 25, 1969, and an anecdotal account by Frederick Muscat, *My President My Son* (Malta: Adam Press, 1974). The best study of the new regime is Ruth First, *Libya: the Elusive Revolution* (New York: Africana, 1975).

10. Meredith O. Ansell and Ibrahim M. al-Arif (eds.), *The Libyan Revolution: A Sourcebook of Legal and Historical Documents* (Stoughton, Wisc.: The Oleander Press, 1972), pp. 63–69.

not narrow tribal asabiyya but solidarity with a larger Arab community. Religion is repeatedly invoked, but it is not transcendental Sanusi maraboutism; instead it is the orthodox doctrine of right rule and social justice. History as before is invoked to mobilize support, but along with the heroic struggle against Italian imperialism, newer experiences are recalled: the corruption of the palace and its collaboration with world imperialism, the same malevolent force that oppresses Palestine and the Palestinians, and the revolution as a victory in the struggle against it. Underlying this reinterpretation of old symbols is an emphasis on populism: the people have risen up and the people are the source of legitimacy; all the people must be given a share of wealth and political responsibility. These principles were given concrete legal expression in the constitutional declaration of December 11, 1969. Among other things the declaration stated that Islam was the state religion; that the state is part of the Arab nation and the African continent; that the family is the core of society whose pillars are religion, morals, and patriotism; that the state shall try to realize socialism through social justice and the peaceful dissolution of class differences; that public ownership is the basis for social development (though nonexploiting private ownership would be safeguarded in the immediate future); and that freedom of expression is guaranteed "within the framework of the people's interest and the Revolution's principles".[11]

Libyan revolutionary ideology has been further elaborated and formalized since 1972–73 into a set of principles known as the Third International Theory. The Third Theory is intended as an alternative to the degenerate ideologies of capitalism and Communism. It is built on Islam. As an official publication puts it: "Practically, our ideology is Islam: Islam which is applied in a way that suits modernism."[12] Passages from the Qur'an are cited to support the various precepts of the Third Theory much like Marx is quoted in modern Communist ideological programs. The Third Theory is comprehensive in that it addresses all aspects of life: political, economic, metaphysical, and social. Within these categories, the Libyan ideology calls for positive neutralism and peaceful coexistence, direct democracy through People's Committees, an Islamic socialism based on the abolition of

11. Libyan Arab Republic, Ministry of Information and Culture, "The Revolutionary March," Tripoli: September 1974, pp. 13 and 14.

12. Libyan Arab Republic, Ministry of Information and Culture, "The Fundamentals of the Third International Theory," Tripoli: February 1974, 27 pp. The most recent and authoritative distillation of the Revolution's ideology is Mu'ammar al-Qadhafi, *The Green Book* (London: Martin Brian and O'Keeffe, 1976, 1978).

exploitation and the peaceful liquidation of class differences, the omnipotence of God, and a social order founded on Islam and the humanistic Arab nationalism in which the fundamental source of law is religion. According to the Third Theory, there is a struggle between truth and falsehood, but divine destiny is inevitable.

Some Western observers have dismissed the Libyan Third International Theory as superficial and eclectic. Whatever its intellectual weaknesses may be, they should not obsure its political effectiveness. As an instrument for generating legitimacy—and it seems to have been specifically designed as such—it is notable for its emphasis on pure absolutes. Its authors appear to have proceeded from an assumption that Libyan and Arab public opinion is concentrated at the extreme of Left and Right, not in the moderate center as is the case in certain Western civic cultures. The Libyan regime presents itself as *more* Islamic, *more* pan-Arab, and *more* democratic than any other regime; as long as it can credibly do so, it is in the strategically advantageous position of being able to outbid its internal and regional rivals. If its image of Arab public opinion and political culture is accurate, as it may well be, then this regime's ideology—which so forthrightly combines the sacred and the progressive—must be given credit for rationality and effectiveness. Moreover, the performance of the regime, however erratic it may appear, has in fact been quite consistent with its stated goals.

Personal and Structural Legitimacy

Colonel Mu'ammar al-Qadhafi, the handsome and youthful leader of the coup born of poor bedouin parents in 1942, has come to personify the Libyan revolution. No leader since Nasir has exerted such charisma among ordinary Arabs. Indeed, Qadhafi appears to have inherited the affection of the Nasirist constituency—the poor urban laboring classes and the unemployed. Even those who are repulsed by ideology and frustrated by his flamboyance and moodiness admit to a certain admiration for what they see as his dedication, candor, and dynamism. Even American journalists feel the spell: " . . . Perhaps because Colonel Qadhafi's sincerity and zeal were so evident I did not feel it suitable to interrupt him often. Indeed, I sometimes felt that I was in the presence of a holy man, a Koranic teacher in one of the great mosques of Cairo or Damascus. During the discussion, Qadhafi quoted the Koran no less than 40 times . . ."[13] He forcibly projects an image of religious rectitude and authority by invoking Islamic scriptures and symbols. Similarly,

13. Edward R. F. Sheehan, "Colonel Qadhafi: Libya's Mystical Revolutionary," *The New York Times Magazine*, February 6, 1972, p. 68.

he has astutely identified himself with the most salient symbol of modern Arab nationalism—Nasir. A visitor to Tripoli in 1975 observed that the "strongest cult of the personality devolves not on Gadafy but on Nasser, newsreels of whom are shown as if he were still alive. Nasser's photograph is everywhere and on a recent television programme, a mixed chorus sang the repeated praises of the saga of 'Abdul Nasser, Abdul Nasser' such as never have been seen on Cairo television."[14] This leader has thus succeeded in arrogating to himself the most potent symbols of traditional revolution and modern revolutionary nationalism.

But heroic leader that he is, Qadhafi apparently does not wish to dominate the Libyan system the way Nasir did in Egypt. Colonel Qadhafi, while officially head of state, is still only the chairman of the Revolutionary Command Council, first among equals in a collegial executive body of military officers which appoints the government and determines basic policy. Qadhafi has occasionally dropped out of sight temporarily, but government goes on; and much of the day-to-day ruling power has fallen to Major Abd al-Salam Jalloud, the premier. In 1974 Colonel Qadhafi was not even a member of the Council of Ministers. He frequently threatens to retire completely and never tires of insisting that Libyans must learn to govern themselves rather than relying on any particular leader or the bureaucracy.

But government by the people, as we have seen, is no easy matter in the Arab world. Like the other revolutionary regimes, the Libyan officers were confronted with a participation dilemma: how to generate popular support, as ideology required, without exposing the system to counter-revolutionary elements and immobility. At first they followed the Egyptian example and established an Arab Socialist Union in 1971. The ASU is described officially as "the popular organization that comprises within its framework all working forces of the people, defends all revolutionary achievements and guides the masses who have the real interest in revolution."[15] Organized on the national, governorate, and basic levels into some 366 units, ASU membership was open to all and in 1972 was estimated at around 320,000.[16] But it was not regarded as having much power, and apparently the ruling Revolutionary Command Council (RCC) was not satisfied that it was

---

14. T. D. Allman, "All out of step but Gadafy?" *The Guardian*, February 15, 1975.

15. Libyan Arab Republic, Ministry of Information and Culture, *The First of September Revolution Achievements, 1969–74* (Tripoli, 1974), p. 4.

16. Richard F. Nyrop, et al., *Area Handbook for Libya*, Second Edition (Washington: U.S. Government Printing Office, 1973), pp. 171–74.

performing its mobilization function properly.[17] Accordingly, on April 15, 1973, the regime initiated the Popular Revolution. This movement, as I have indicated, was intended to introduce a degree of grass-roots spontaneity, voluntarism, and direct democracy which the bureaucratically conceived ASU was not generating. It was a revolution against (1) "all reactionary laws," (2) "social diseases (the negativistic and passive attitudes which obstruct change and construction)," (3) "distorted meanings of freedom", and (4) "bureaucracy and administrative corruption." Fifth, there was to be a cultural revolution to stop "the ever-constant infiltration of corrupted foreign ideas and concepts."[18] The structural instrument of the revolution was the People's Committees. The people were enjoined to establish committees in all organizations throughout society—in villages, factories, universities, government offices, etc. By late 1973 over 2,000 People's Committees reportedly had been formed.[19] The committees monitored the conventional administrative structures. For example, the committee in a girls' high school ousted the headmistress because she was not seriously inculcating revolutionary principles among the students; and at the University, a People's Committee (including students, faculty, and administrators) vetoed the application of a foreign professor to visit the campus. Coordinating the work of the People's Committees at the national level was the General People's Congress, which reportedly was given some marginal executive powers by Colonel Qadhafi.

In theory at least, Qadhafi's attempt to build structural legitimacy was novel, compared to most other Arab revolutionary regimes; clearly he was trying to use all the power available to him at the top to transform society from the bottom up. In practice, however, there were some indications by 1975 that his goals would not be achieved easily. The former RCC member and planning minister, Umar al-Muhayshi, who had led an abortive coup in August 1975, continued to organize opposition to Qadhafi from his sanctuary in Cairo, with the full support of the Egyptian authorities. Late in 1975 the foreign minister, Abd al-Mun'im al-Hawni, also fled the country and took refuge in Egypt. Serious student rioting at the Libyan University campus in Benghazi on New Year's Day 1976 resulted in the death of at least ten students, and Libyan students occupied their embassies in several countries in

---

17. Ibid., p. 173.

18. Libyan Arab Republic, Ministry of Information and Culture, "The Popular Revolution: Fundamentals and Objectives," (Tripoli: Modern Press, January 1973), 39 pp.

19. According to *Africa Contemporary Record*, 5 (New York, 1973), p. 59, as quoted in Carole Collins, "Inperialism and Revolution in Libya," *MERIP Reports*, 27, (April 1974), p. 20.

support of the demonstrators. In April 1976 it was reported from Tunis that several persons had been killed and some 200 injured in clashes between army units and civilians.

Supplementing the regime's messianic domestic legitimacy strategy has been a vigorous foreign policy, another reflection of the Nasirist model. Libya has taken the lead in challenging the Western oil companies and governments and has played a vanguard role in the oil-price escalation of the early 1970s. Its insistence on Arab unity has led it into spectacular but abortive efforts to join with Egypt and Syria in the Confederation of Arab Republics. It has undertaken an immense expansion of its armed forces, buying French or Soviet weapons. And its well-publicized support for the Palestinian resistance movement, especially the more militant elements, has further enhanced its nationalist reputation. By the middle 1970s the regime was, if anything, intensifying its efforts in behalf of revolutionary movements. It was implicated in an assassination attempt against the prime minister of Tunisia. It had applauded the efforts to assassinate King Hassan of Morocco and, along with Algeria, had bitterly opposed Morocco's annexation of Spanish Sahara. It was helping the enemies of Colonel Numayri's regime in the Sudan. It was providing assistance to the Lebanese left-wing forces and Palestinians in Lebanon's civil war. Even beyond the Arab world, it was said to be supporting the Irish Republican army, Philippine Muslim insurgents, the Eritrean Liberation Front, and a rebellion in neighboring Chad. Israeli and other intelligence sources accused Libya of aiding and abetting a variety of terrorist activities, including the hijacking of an Air France plane to Entebbe, Uganda, in July 1976.

Libya remains vulnerable, however, to interference from external powers by virtue of its size and its still thinly developed infrastructure. Its wealth and strategic position make it an attractive target, too. Internally, it is far from clear whether the ASU and People's Committees will succeed in institutionalizing the revolution. Beyond the recent defections, little is known about the politics within the Revolutionary Command Council. Faced with burgeoning socioeconomic growth and suffering from a shortage of professional manpower, the RCC's governing capabilities are strained to the utmost extent. Whatever its future, however, the neo-Nasirist experiment in republican Libya is a significant test of the relevance of the dominant revolutionary legitimacy strategy of the 1950s to the much different Arab circumstances of the 1970s. In many ways these new circumstances are less propitious than the old ones. Libya's Arab regional policies have met with many frustrations. Not only have its unity efforts with Egypt, Sudan, Syria, and Tunisia been rebuffed, it has generated such widespread Arab regime hostility that its leaders rightly feel on the defensive. By 1976 there were reports that Egypt, Sa'udi Arabia, and Sudan had undertaken a coordinated effort to topple the Qadhafi regime. The question of Qadhafi's mass support, however, is more difficult to assess. Nasirism, though in eclipse, is by no means dead, and there is reason to suspect, if the analysis in earlier chapters is correct, that the salience of goals upon which Qadhafi has staked a strong claim remains high. If his regime, which lacks weight and internal structural development, survives the immediate internal and external assaults upon it, it may prove in the long run to possess stronger mass legitimacy than its moderate neighbors.

THE SUDAN

The Sudan, largest country in Africa, has the potential in terms of arable land and favorable climate to become the "bread basket" of the Arab world. But apart from its very low level of economic development, its political legitimacy problem casts a shadow over what could be a bright future. If one were to rank the countries of the Arab world in terms of political culture fragmentation, the Sudan would fall among the most divided polities. It is the only state whose basic ethnic-national identity is divided almost equally between an Arab and an African culture. The other states of the area seriously divided along ethnolinguistic lines—Iraq, Morocco, and Algeria—still possess a clear majority of one type along with (in most cases) some other common Arab cultural ties, notably Islam, or a fair degree of cultural intermixture. But in the Sudan, the Arab-African racial-cultural cleavage is also reinforced by a Muslim–non-Muslim cleavage; only Lebanon displays as important a religious bifurcation. To add to the problem, the Sudan's north-south cleavage was for many years systematically widened by British colonial policy. Hardly less important are the primordial and parochial subdivisions within both the north and the south; and in the north (long the arena of national politics) the rivalry between the Ansar and Khatmiyya tribal-based religious brotherhoods lent a distinctly communal cast to party structure and the competition for leadership. Finally, the Sudan's low level and, until recently, its slow rate of economic growth have made it difficult to generate sufficient administrative capabilities and material satisfactions to mute the demands of the urban sector. Indeed, the complexity of political structures and ideologies in the Sudan's independence period (since

1956)—somewhat surprising perhaps for so poor and divided a country
—attests to the strength and the unevenness of the social mobilization
that has set in.

I call the Sudan a revolutionary republic, but I do so advisedly, for
as Peter Bechtold has suggested, even a revolutionary regime has to
make some accommodation to deeply rooted traditional forces.[20] In
much the same spirit, I treat the Yemen Arab Republic—the next
case—as a revolutionary polity even though its sociopolitical structures
are suffused with primordial loyalties. As in Yemen, the traditional
structures of the Sudan today exert important but far from controlling
effects on political life, particularly in the Numayri regime. Unlike
Yemen, however, the modern Sudan has undergone comparatively
greater political structure development, as indicated by its well-
organized movements and multiparty system, which have exerted
autonomous influence, paralleling and rivaling the traditional patterns.

Yet the erratic course of Sudanese politics since independence indicates the seriousness of its political culture cleavages. Apart from
Yemen, most of the other traditional Arab states—notwithstanding
their unresolved identity problems—have made greater progress toward consensus and structural capabilities in the last quarter-century
than has the Sudan; even the most divided, like Iraq, have attained a
not inconsiderable ideological coherence and structural development.
But by the middle 1970s, it was not clear that the Sudan's body politic
had made similar progress, although there were some positive signs.
Thus far, the process of political change in the Sudan has a praetorian
quality: it is evident in the oscillation between civilian and military
rule, the suppression and regeneration of traditional political structures, the ideological zigzagging of the leadership between Left and
Right, Arabism and Sudanese separatism, the West and the Communist world. There is a resemblence between the Sudan's performance
and that of Egypt, but there is also a crucial difference: Egypt under
Nasir developed a more coherent and widely supported ideology of
Arabism, development, and socialism and more complex and capable
structures in a political culture that was basically less divided along
primordial lines.

The Legitimacy Problem in the Independent Sudan

The first period of the Sudan's experience as a modern state began
in 1953, three years before actual independence, when the first legis-

20. Peter K. Bechtold, "Military Rule in the Sudan: The First Five Years of Ja'afar Numayri,"
Middle East Journal, 29, 1 (Winter 1975), pp. 16–32; pp. 30–31. See also Peter K. Bechtold,
Politics in the Sudan (New York: Praeger, 1976).

lative elections were held. But the free, multiparty parliamentary system was overturned in 1958 by a military coup led by Gen. Ibrahim Abboud. Civilian government had been immobilized by an overload of problems. Traditional divisions between the Ansar and Khatmiyya brotherhoods (*tariqas*) were reflected—even magnified—by the problem of relations with Egypt. Administrative incompetence and an economic slump aggravated the situation, while beneath lay the smoldering "southern question" (discussed above in chapter 3). The military administration was equally unsuccessful in establishing itself as a legitimate form of government because its positions on Arabism, democracy, development, and especially the southern question were either too ambiguous or unsatisfactory to attract the potential constituency that existed on each one of them. And so in 1964, during another economic slump and after an unsuccessful effort to solve the southern question by bloody repression, General Abboud's government collapsed. Paralyzed by a general strike, alienated from the principal organized groups in society—civil service, labor, students and teachers —and divided by officer corps factionalism, the military regime was forced to turn over power to a transitional government.

But the return of open and participant politics also meant the return of the same problems that had beset the first civilian government. This time the spectrum of active participants was wider, with the Communists on one extreme and religious conservatives like the Muslim Brotherhood on the other; and the rivalries among the principal parties and leaders were more numerous and intense, as indicated by increased intraparty factionalism and coalition instability. Between 1964 and 1969 there were two general elections and five governments of which three were headed by a conservative Umma party politician, Muhammad Ahmad Mahgoub. Although the politicians were skillful in forming coalitions, they were not so successful in holding them together or in directing them toward the tasks of government. Thus, Mahgoub's third government was composed of Democratic Unionists (a party formed through the merger of the National Unionist party, composed of urban, merchant, and civil service elements, and the People's Democratic party, which represented the Khatmiyya Brotherhood) and the conservative faction of the Umma party, which represented the Ansar Brotherhood. But it lasted only one year and was paralyzed by the deep differences within the coalition. The Democratic Unionists represented relatively secular, pro–Arab-Egyptian and progressive opinions, while the Umma, especially the coalition faction led by Imam al-Hadi, was heir to the Mahdist tradition of Islamic fundamentalism, anti-Egyptian, "Sudan first" orientations. On May 25, 1969, a group of officers led by Colonel Ja'far al-Numayri, impatient with what they considered the bickering and incompetence of the civilian politicians, carried out the Sudan's second military coup, and seven years later Numayri was still in power.

The Numayri regime during those years proved less unstable than its predecessors, but neither did it develop a distinctively stronger legitimacy formula. The structures of participation are still meager for a country whose elite has placed a high priority on representation and free expression and whose political culture is pluralist both in the traditional and modern sense of the term. Although Numayri emulated Nasir in his socialist-nationalist and antiimperialist ideology, he could not succeed to the extent that Nasir did in building a myth of political community because the Sudan is too divided along primordial lines. He was more successful in pursuing the Nasirite tactic of suppressing his erstwhile allies on the conservative and then the progressive ends of the ideological spectrum, although the Egyptian regime's control capabilities were still superior to those of the Sudanese. The oscillation on the question of Sudanese identity thus continued into the mid-1970s, and the regime still searched for a permanent support coalition. Except for the important southern question, the problems of governance imposed by the Sudan's fragmented and differentially mobilized society remain. In order to understand these problems better, I must examine more closely the value and structural bases of political legitimacy in the Sudan and how they have evolved since the late nineteenth century under the impact of Western imperialism and modernization.

Kinship and Religious Identification

Compared to the Arab countries as a group the Sudan's political culture is deeply etched with parochial and primordial identifications and perspectives. Tribalism and religion figure so prominently as politically relevant values that any regime trying to modernize or secularize this vast country—the largest in Africa—faces a massive task. Like the other Arab-Islamic countries of Africa, notably pre-revolutionary Libya, both tribalism and religion have been uniquely manifested in the structure of the religious brotherhoods. Two of these tariqas, the Khatmiyya and the Ansar, have dominated the politics of the Muslim Sudan, the former based in the north and east, the latter in the western parts.[21] Founded early in the nineteenth century, the Khatmiyya (or Mirghaniyya) was a reformist brotherhood of tribes and families loyal to a particular saintlike leader, Uthman al-Mirghani

---

21. See P. M. Holt, *The Mahdist State in the Sudan, 1881–1898* (Oxford: Clarendon Press, 1958), chaps. 1 and 2.

and his descendants. During the first period of Egyptian rule (1821–85), the Khatmiyya shaykhs were favored as local agents of the Khedive Muhammad Ali and his successors, and this orientation has persisted through all the subsequent transformations in Sudanese and Egyptian politics. Thus in the independence period, the brotherhood functioned as the traditional structural base for a modern political party, the People's Democratic party (PDP) and has viewed proximity with Egypt as a means for combating British and other Western encroachments on the Sudan's independence and development. According to Holt, the Khatmiyya (like many other similar orders) began as an Islamic reform movement but eventually lapsed into orthodoxy and compliance with customary practices.[22] The Ansar, named after the disciples of the Prophet Muhammad, were the followers of the Mahdi of the Sudan, Muhammad Ahmad. Arising out of the turbulent sociopolitical conditions of the late nineteenth century, the Mahdist order, like the other brotherhoods, preached Islamic reform; and like the Khatmiyya it persisted long after the destruction of the Mahdist state and became woven into the modern Sudanese political system through the Umma party. But in other respects, the Mahdists were distinctive, if not unique. The ideology of Mahdism was ascetic and austere in its fundamentalist piety, far more so than conventional Islam in the Sudan, reflecting the Sufi influence in the Mahdi's upbringing.

Personal Legitimacy: The Mahdi

The emergence of the Mahdi is certainly not the only example in the modern Arab world of the efficacy of personal legitimacy in building a coherent political order in a fragmented society—one thinks of other nation-builders like Muhammad V, Bourguiba, Ibn Sa'ud, and Nasir—but the Sudanese case may well be the most dramatic. Here we see a traditional religious culture, crisscrossed with parochial kinship cleavages and deeply disturbed by the intrusion of external political forces suddenly molded into an integrated mobilization system by a leader emanating sacred authority. The Mahdi is a charismatic leader in the literal, that is, religious, sense of Weber's meaning.[23] He approaches most closely the ideal type of heroic leader who succeeds in embodying widely held primordial values and transforming them into a political resource; in our own time we see elements of Mahdist

---

22. Ibid., p. 20.
23. For an interesting discussion of the Mahdi's charisma, see R. H. Dekmejian and M. J. Wyszomirski, "Charismatic Leadership in Islam: The Mahdi of the Sudan," *Comparative Studies in Society and History*, 14, 2 (March 1972), pp. 193–214.

charisma in the leadership of a Nasir or Qadhafi and some lesser figures. To be sure, the value base in these cases is modern Arabism and socialism; yet one cannot but remark on the sacred character of these myths and (in varying degrees) their Islamic coloration. The Mahdi not only convinced an ever-widening circle of notables, tribes, and slave-traders of his saintliness and his ability to communicate with God; he also mobilized these elements into a viable, legitimate polity. Such was the strength of the Mahdi's legitimacy and political-military acumen that he was able to dislodge the Egyptian administration, humiliate the British through the extermination of the Hicks and Gordon expeditions, and through his successor, hold the Anglo-Egyptian forces at bay for fourteen years. Although the Mahdi died only a few months after his capture of Khartoum in 1885, he passed along to his successor, the Khalifa Abdallahi, the rudiments of a coherent polity; and the Khalifa succeeded in maintaining it under increasingly unfavorable conditions.[24] The Mahdiyya was shaken by the death of the supposedly immortal Mahdi, but it did not disintegrate. Such was the faith of the followers and so skillful had been the modeling of the movement on the original development of Islam under Muhammad and his successors —the brilliant exploitation of historical myth for legitimizing purposes —that the Mahdi's charismatic authority could be passed on. And although the Khalifa appears to have lacked the singular intensity of the Mahdi's charisma, he inherited sufficient legitimacy to permit some institutionalization of government, and thus he was able to strengthen his control and support base. Ultimately of course the Mahdist state collapsed under Kitchener's guns at Omdurman and Khartoum. Britain's imperial urge and its yearning for revenge were thus satisfied. But even its destruction exemplified the commitment of its defenders, as one gathers from this eyewitness account by an English journalist:

> No white troops would have faced that torrent of death for five minutes, but the Baggara and the blacks came on. The torrent swept into them and hurled them down in whole companies. You saw a rigid line father itself up and rush on evenly; then before a shrapnel shell or a Maxim the line suddenly quivered and stopped. The line was yet unbroken, but it was quite still. But other lines gathered up again, again, and yet again; they went down and yet others rushed on. . . . It was the last day of Mahdism and the greatest. . . . By now the ground before us was all white with dead men's drapery. Rifles grew red-hot; the soldiers seized them by

24. Holt, op. cit., esp. chaps. 5 and 13.

the slings and dragged them back to the reserve to change for cool ones. It was not a battle, but an execution.[25]

The political power of Islam, vastly intensified by the perception of the infidel threat, has never been so dramatically demonstrated; not only was it enough to weld together a deeply divided society, it also created a new and important strand in the idea of Sudanese nationalism.

Liberal Nationalism

If Mahdism represents the sacred-charismatic version of Sudanese political identity, another historical experience, the Anglo-Egyptian condominium and the rise of an educated urban elite, represents what might be called the liberal-nationalist version. The Egyptian conquest of 1820 marks the beginning of a more-than-rudimentary education system of a socially mobilized elite in the Sudan, just as it did in Syria and Lebanon.[26] At the same time the country, especially the South, was opened up to European Christian missionaries. Britain's influence in the Sudan expanded dramatically after it occupied Egypt in 1882 and even more so after it destroyed the Mahdist regime in 1898. But as its influence increased so did the resistance of the various politicized elements in the country. This resistance arose not only out of cultural xenophobia—exemplified by the Mahdiyya—but also ironically from the liberal policies of the colonial administration, such as the establishment of Gordon Memorial College in 1902. The rise of Egyptian nationalism toward the end of the nineteenth century also had an impact in the Sudan. As a result of the original Egyptian conquest and then of the Anglo-Egyptian condominium, many Sudanese went to Cairo for education or employment; and many came back sympathizing with the Egyptian cause in itself and also as an example for the Sudan. The educated, politicized elite began to acquire some political structure when the Graduates' club (of Gordon College alumni) was established in 1918. A highly significant political development was the establishment in 1938 of the Graduates' General Congress, modeled on the Indian Congress and consisting of educated Sudanese from Gordon College, the American University of Beirut, and the Graduates' club.[27]

---

25. G. W. Steevens, *With Kitchener to Khartum* (New York: Dodd, Mead & Company, 1899), p. 264.

26. Mohamed Omer Beshir, *Educational Development in the Sudan, 1898–1956* (Oxford: Clarendon Press, 1969), pp. 12–21.

27. Muddathir 'Abd al-Rahim, *Imperialism and Nationalism in the Sudan* (Oxford: Clarendon Press, 1969), chap. 4, esp. pp. 94–125.

It was this association that would spearhead Sudanese demands for more meaningful representation, an end to the separatist "southern policy," and eventual independence from foreign, mainly British, tutelage.

The conflict between the British and the Sudanese rose out of the imposed external power relationship as well as deep cultural differences. On the popular level, the xenophobia of Sudanese religious militants was matched by that of British publicists such as the journalist quoted above ("It is not a country; it has nothing that makes a country. Some brutish institutions it has and some bloodthirsty chivalry . . .").[28] It led to periodic open hostility, such as the anti-British violence of 1924 surrounding the assassination in Cairo of the governor-general of the Sudan, Sir Lee Stack. On the elite level, the British attitude was paternalistic, as one can see by perusing the dialogue between Sir Douglas Newbold, the civil secretary from 1939 to 1945, and the Graduates' Congress which was petitioning for liberalization measures.[29] In denying the authority of what he considered a self-appointed, unrepresentative, and very small educated minority to speak for the Sudanese nation, Newbold counseled gradualism, questioned whether the educated classes sufficiently understood self-government, and refused to allow the newly formed Advisory Council more than token participation in government. Although British control was liberalized in its last years and the transition to self-government was accomplished relatively gracefully, the net effect of the colonial presence was to crystallize a tangible if ill-defined sense of Sudanese nationalism.

But the Sudan, like all the other ex-colonial revolutionary regimes in the Arab world, could not evade the dilemma of legitimacy in post-traditional polities: the colonialism which, despite itself, helps crystallize a vital national (and anticolonial) mythology also stimulates other values, such as participation, national development, and social equality, which the new indigenous leadership is hard-pressed to satisfy. In the Sudan as elsewhere, the liberal structures of the immediate postindependence period collapsed because of low capabilities, corruption, and irreconcilable subnational cleavages. The three principal structures of that period—the Umma party representing the Ansar, the PDP representing the Khatmiyya, and the National Unionist party representing the educated urban elements—were unable to form coalitions that could actually govern; and a fourth

28. Steevens, op. cit., p. 324.
29. K. D. D. Henderson, *The Making of the Modern Sudan: The Life and Letters of Sir Douglas Newbold, K. B. E.* (London: Faber and Faber, 1953), esp. Part 2, chap. 5.

element—the various southern leaders—was able only to add an additional (and ultimately intolerable) load to the system. The first military regime of General Abboud was virtually invited to take over from civilian politicians who were aware of their own inadequacy, yet it too was unable to knit together a durable legitimacy formula with viable supporting structures. What, then, of the second military regime, that of Colonel Numayri?

Numayri's Legitimacy Base

The Numayri regime has greatly strengthened its legitimacy by bringing the long-festering southern rebellion to a peaceful and seemingly permanent solution. In doing so it has removed a load on the system that taxed the legitimacy of every preceding government. But many serious problems remain. By the mid-1970s little progress had been made in institutionalizing support-building structures or integrating the various ideologically diverse and structurally coherent elements of Sudanese politics. The regime has been subjected to persistent challenges in the form of plots and civil disorder, and it has been forced into a course of ideological zigzagging and a heavy reliance on the president's personalist rule. As a matter of practical politics, this behavior may have been necessitated by the ideological fission in Sudanese politics since independence. On the one hand, the liberal center—the old nationalist parties—were discredited, leaving a vaccuum in moderate opinion. On the other hand, the organized forces of the Left grew ever stronger. The Sudanese Communist party and allied groups, for example, were thought to number some 80,000 active members on the eve of the July 1971 coup[30]—the strongest in the Arab world. The organized Left also included other progressive elements, the Labor Union, the Youth Organization, the Students' Union, the Women's Union, and parts of the officer corps. Furthermore, although the religious traditionalists on the extreme Right, such as the Ansar and the Muslim Brotherhood, had suffered some reverses, they were still very much in existence. As I have shown, there is a pronounced conservative constituency in the Sudan, and it is doubtful that the Ansar, for example, could have been completely destroyed in their violent confrontation with the regime in April 1970. Moreover, they were extremely apprehensive and hostile to the rise of the Left. As if these internal conditions were not sufficiently problematical for Numayri, there was also the regional and international situation to

---

30. Fu'ad Matar, *The Sudanese Communist Party: Executed or Suicide?* (Beirut: Dar al-Nahar lil-Nashr, 1971, in Arabic), p. 44.

consider. The salience of Arabism was high, especially in the wake of the 1967 war, but its substantial legitimizing power was offset to a significant degree by the opposition both from the religious Right of the Ansar (anti-Egypt) persuasion and from the Communists, who were all too aware of the repression which Communists had suffered under Nasir in Egypt and in other Arab nationalist regimes. With the United States tainted by its support of Israel, there were both political and material benefits to be won from courting the Soviet Union, but here too there were predictable negative reactions to be expected. In short, it was a deeply divided polity that Ja'far al-Numayri had to govern.

As a result, Numayri's rule was characterized by a series of tactical maneuvers designed to keep extremist tendencies, Left and Right, off balance. By temperament an activist rather than a theoretician, Numayri (trained at the U.S. army's Fort Leavenworth) had also acquired the talent of political maneuver and conspiracy through a long-time involvement in politics—an involvement that had included participation in the coup against General Abboud in 1964 and possibly three earlier aborted plots. He came to power invoking the symbols of Arabism, socialism, and reform—values with comparatively widespread salience which would facilitate regional legitimation from President Nasir. In December 1969 Numayri proposed that Sudan join the projected Federation of Arab Republics. But shortly thereafter he curbed the pro-Egyptian and socialist elements in his government. Then, in April 1970, he broke an uprising of the Ansar at Aba Island in the White Nile, the spot where the Mahdi had embarked upon his religious and political mission nearly a century before. During the bloody confrontation, the leader of the conservative wing of the Umma party, Imam al-Hadi, was killed. But it was the forces of the Left that still posed the strongest challenge, and so in November 1970 he purged three Communist sympathizing officers from his cabinet: Major Hashim al-Atta, Lt. Col. Babakir al-Nur, and Major Farouk Uthman Hamadalla. It was Atta and his colleagues, along with the secretary-general of the Communist party, Abd al-Khaliq Mahgoub, who then emerged as leaders in the coup of July 19, 1971.[31] The coup was violent—some thirty officers loyal to Numayri were reportedly massacred—and so was Numayri's countercoup three days later. Pro-Numayri forces, using tanks from the Egyptian military college in Khartoum, broke the rebellion, and all the leaders were executed. Numayri also received windfall assistance from anti-Communist Libya, which forced down a British airliner carrying two of the coup leaders

31. On the coup and the Communist party generally, see Matar, op. cit., pp. 32–71.

and delivered them to Numayri. An Iraqi plane carrying Ba'thist supporters and well-wishers to the leftist government disappeared mysteriously over Sa'udi Arabia. The coup was considered a serious embarrassment to the Soviet Union, which was particularly outraged over the execution of the widely respected Abd al-Khaliq Mahgoub, and thus an indirect gain for American diplomacy. It was also a blow to the Iraqi Ba'thists, who had emerged as important supporters of the progressive forces in the Sudan, and a relative gain for the primarily Arab nationalist regimes of Egypt, Libya, and Syria. Numayri reaped important benefits from his successful countercoup. As Fu'ad Matar has observed, his destruction of the Right in 1970 had won him important support from the Soviet Union and the well-organized Sudanese Left; his destruction of the Left in 1971 would win back a great deal of the latent but conveniently weakened conservative and older centrist support.[32] The countercoup also opened the way for a peaceful settlement of the southern problem—ironically so, in view of the Left's consistent support for peaceful settlement over and against Numayri's old policy of a solution through force. By tilting away from the Soviet Union, the Left, and radical liberation ideology, Numayri succeeded in drawing away internal rightist support for the southerners and external Western support for it as well. And by cutting back his own support for the Eritrean liberation movement he won the influence of Ethiopia in helping mediate the solution. That solution was finally reached on March 3, 1972, and it appears likely to endure. If so, it is unquestionably the major accomplishment of the Numayri government, for it sealed the legitimacy hemorrhage that had contributed so significantly to the Sudan's postindependence malaise. It also freed scarce national resources for reconstruction and development, thus easing other burdens on the system, and it opened up possibilities for better relations with its African neighbors.

Another bitter irony for the progressives was Numayri's shift away from federation with Egypt, Syria, and Libya—a shift that they had long advocated. But the shift was a matter of degree rather than a change in direction, and its costs—the anger of Colonel Qadhafi and the disenchantment of Arab nationalist elements generally—was perhaps outweighed by the support of Sudan first sentiment at home and the warming of relationships with the traditional Arab oil states and the United States. In the short term, therefore, President Numayri had emerged from a host of difficulties in a strengthened position.

The long term situation is another matter. As I have observed, the Sudan's agricultural development potential is enormous. Wealthy

32. Ibid., pp. 61–62.

Arab states like Kuwait, Sa'udi Arabia, and the UAE have recognized this potential and have recently prepared a $5.7 billion investment program. If there is enough political stability to implement it, this development could eventually have a positive effect on political system legitimacy. But the legitimacy of this system remains extremely limited. Having reversed his ideological field so often, the president bears the stigma of opportunism, which complicates the development of a new consensus. Having wreaked so much havoc on existing political structures, traditional and progressive, he faces a difficult task in building new ones that will command genuine respect. In a country as vast and sprawling as the Sudan, it is hard for any government in Khartoum, given the existing infrastructure, to exert a high degree of coercive control; and it is most unlikely that the radicals of either the religious-feudal Right or the progressive labor and agricultural Left are destroyed for good. Arab analysts frequently classify the Numayri regime as conforming to the Nasirist model. The comparison is fruitful, both for the similarities and the differences.[33] The strong personalist leader dominates the system, propagating an ideology of nationalism, neutralism, and a state capitalism called socialism; and he tries to institutionalize his rule from the top through a government-sponsored single-party and related mass organizations, plus the civilian and military bureaucracies. Numayri succeeded in establishing himself as a strongman, but he is far from being a sacred, charismatic leader like the Mahdi—not that he or any leader in the contemporary Sudan would emulate that model. Even with his triumphant Southern settlement, it is doubtful that he has become a hero of Nasir's stature. As for the ideological component of the regime's legitimacy, by the middle-1970s it placed highest priority on a state-directed development effort known as Sudanese socialism. In Numayri's words,

> In such a Socialist system, it is the duty and the privilege of the state to develop and to modernize society through scientific planning and the promotion of skills, scientific research, vocational training, and wide-ranging fields of study. The Sudanese state owns and manages the fundamental means of production, while at the same time recognizing the right of private ownership and encouraging the private sector to play a positive and active role in the national economy.[34]

33. See, e.g., Samir Frangié in *L'Orient-Le Jour* (Beirut), July 22, 1971.

34. Quoted in an interview with the *Review of International Affairs* (Belgrade), July 20, 1974; reprinted in the *Daily Star* (Beirut), August 23, 1974.

It is not certain whether this formula will in the long run win the acquiescence of either the old capitalist, landed, and clerical elite out of which the earlier nationalist groups emerged or of the now-suppressed elements of the Left in the Communist party, the labor unions, the peasantry, the students, and even the military. Nor is it clear that Numayri's moderate Arabism and his effort to strike a harmonious balance between the Sudan's Arab and African identity will win wide support. Unlike Nasir as the voice of Arabism, Numayri is unable to personify a deeply held Sudanese identity because the Sudan has a more fragmented political culture than Egypt. In terms of structural development, the Numayri regime has instituted its own Sudanese Socialist Union, National Guard, and youth and women's organizations, but it must be doubted whether these approach very closely their Egyptian, Tunisian, Syrian, or Iraqi counterparts in terms of size, complexity, capability, and control and information capacity. One concludes therefore that there are important praetorian characteristics in the Sudanese system which will continue to test political skills. Indeed, the government was forced to declare a state of emergency following student and labor unrest in September 1973, and a new military plot was uncovered in October 1974. In September 1975 Lt. Col. Hassan Osman led a brief abortive coup, which was said to have been supported by a combination of Communist, right-wing and Muslim Brotherhood elements. And in July 1976 there was a more serious attempt to overthrow Numayri, engineered by the able former prime minister and leader of the liberal wing of the old Umma party, Sadiq al-Mahdi. The plot was foiled and President Numayri accused his one-time ally, Colonel Qadhafi of Libya, of directly supporting it with the possible help of the Soviet Union and Britain. Ninety-eight of the conspirators were executed.

THE YEMEN ARAB REPUBLIC

One of the last remaining strongholds of traditional Arab-Islamic culture is to be found in Yemen. Its folkways, so infused with kinship and religious values, are among the most intact and vital in the Arab world. Located in the mountainous southern corner of the Arabian peninsula, Yemen is the Arabia Felix of old, with a documented history dating from the Kingdom of Sheba ten centuries before Christ and sixteen centuries before Islam. But Yemen's political culture and political system can no longer be called strictly traditional, for the overthrow of the imamate of 1962 and the subsequent civil war that lasted until the spring of 1970 jolted this medieval polity across the revolutionary divide, and the Yemen Arab Republic came into being.

Yet because Yemeni society had been relatively untouched by modernization, economic development, or Western influence prior to the
revolution—less so than any other country in the area save Oman—
there has remained a set of coherent, widespread, and deeply rooted
traditional values that pose awesome problems for the postrevolutionary leadership.

The case of the Yemen Arab Republic also poses the modernization-
legitimacy conundrum perhaps more sharply than in any other Arab
country. Can a system with one foot planted so firmly in the past and the
other pointing toward the future generate any legitimacy at all? And
if so, what kind of a formula will accomplish the task? To answer
these questions I must first indicate the nature of primordial identifications in Yemen under the imamate because they remain quite
intact in the postrevolutionary republican era. Then I must analyze the
twists and turns in the YAR's short but turbulent history to ascertain
the effectiveness of the two principal legitimizing strategies that have
been tried: the typical nationalist mobilization formula imposed by a
military strongman and an interesting accommodationist formula,
resembling in some ways the consociational aspects of the Lebanese
case. The former is observed during and just after the civil war in
governments dominated by the officers Abdalla al-Sallal and Hassan
al-Amri, and the latter is found in the regime presided over by the
Qadi Abd al-Rahman al-Iryani. In June 1974, however, the Iryani
regime was overthrown in a military coup led by Col. Ibrahim al-
Hamdi, signaling an apparent return to the first model; but insofar
as this coup was also supported by conservative tribal leaders, it
suggested that the search for political community in Yemen would
have its own distinctive if not unique character.

Traditional Yemen: A Tribal Theocracy

We have already encountered the radical, dissenting, character of
Shi'ism in Iraq and Lebanon. We see it again in Yemen where the
Zaydi sect of Shi'ism established an imamate that endured from 898
to 1962. The office of the imam, while common to orthodox Islam as
well, has a particular salience in the Shi'ite community: his authority
is derived in its entirety as a trust from God as long as he does not
blatantly transgress Islamic law and prescript. As Harold Ingrams
succinctly put it, "To be a lawful Zeidi Imam, a candidate must be a
male, free-born, a taxpayer, sound in mind and in possession of all his
senses, sound in limb and free from all physical blemishes, just, pious,
generous, possessed of administrative ability, of the family of Ali (cousin
of Muhammad and his son-in-law), of the family of Fatima (daughter

of Muhammad and Ali's wife), brave and a militant jurist."[35] As a guide and interpreter for the faithful, the imam's authority is not confirmed by inheritance or by raw power but by the bay'a or oath of allegiance which the community confers upon him as the individual most suited (in the judgment of the specialists in religion and the descendants of the Prophet) to play this role. The ruling Hamid al-Din family in practice, however, contested the principle, when in 1927 Imam Yahya designated his son Ahmad as heir apparent. In so doing he weakened the legitimacy of both his office and his family, and he alienated many of the sayyids, descendants of the Prophet in Ali's line who are the putative electors of the imam.

It is a mistake to assume that traditional rule in the Middle East must necessarily be stable, observes C. Ernest Dawn.[36] Yemen illustrates the point with special force. True, the imam and the imamate commanded a remarkable degree of loyalty that extended far beyond the mere threat of coercion; deference and reverence were evident. But at the same time there was a fluidity and an underlying strain of violence that arose in part out of the tradition of dissidence to authority in Shi'ite theology, in part out of Yemen's high degree of tribal fragmentation, and in part out of legal and political ambiguities concerning the rightful succession to authority. The longevity of imamic reigns in the Hamid al-Din dynasty is impressive but possibly misleading. Minor imams could arise in a particular locale and challenge the principal Zaydi imam. A case in point is Sayyid Muhammad al-Hashim al-Dahyani of Sa'da who unsuccessfully challenged the great Imam Yahya (1904–48). The authority of the Hamid al-Din imams was frequently and increasingly marred by dissidence. In 1948 Imam Yahya was assassinated by conspirators supported by numerous elements of the Yemeni elite, traditional and modern.[37] The coup leader, Abdalla ibn Ahmad al-Wazir, only managed to rule for a month before being deposed and executed in a countercoup led by Yahya's son Ahmad. And in 1955, during the long reign of Imam Ahmad (1948–62) another pretender declared himself imam for a few days before suffering a similar fate. The final overthrow of the Hamid al-Din Zaydi dynasty in 1962 and the eventual collapse of the imamate

35. Harold Ingrams, *The Yemen: Imams, Rulers, and Revolutions* (London: John Murray, 1963), p. 27.

36. C. Ernest Dawn, *From Ottomanism to Arabism* (Urbana: University of Illinois Press, 1973), chap. 7, esp. pp. 190–95, 199.

37. Manfred W. Wenner, *Modern Yemen, 1918–1966* (Baltimore: Johns Hopkins University Press, 1967), pp. 93–99.

as the central political structure created a legitimacy vacuum in an inherently unstable political culture, a vacuum which republican institutions were unable by themselves to fill.

Even if Yemen were inhabited exclusively by Zaydis, one might therefore expect a substantial degree of "normal" instability. But Yemen has a very large population of orthodox Sunni Muslims most of whom adhere to the Shafi'i school of Islamic law. The Shafi'is are located along the Tihama coastal plain and in the southern hill country, and they account for half or more of the total population. Most observers in fact think that the Zaydis are a minority—perhaps only one-third the total population.[38] Neither Zaydi nor Shafi'i represent highly militant elements within their respective Shi'ite and Sunni traditions; nevertheless, there are enough differences in ritual (such as method of prayer) and in historical kinship identifications on each side to make the distinctions apparent. In terms of legitimacy, the fundamental issue between Zaydis and Shafi'is is that the latter do not accept the worldly political authority of the imams as having religious legitimacy. These differences have not placed the two sects in perpetual opposition to one another and the Shafi'is have been willing, especially in the twentieth century, to accept the Zaydi imam as a ruler on essentially secular political grounds by virtue of his demonstrated power. Furthermore, as Wenner points out, there have been several occasions when an imam could find support among the Shafi'is against a Zaydi usurper. Still, the community differences have retained an underlying, if somewhat nebulous reality: the Shafi'is, as adherents to the school of Islamic law predominant in Egypt, and heirs to the prevailing orthodox tradition (there was indeed a famous Islamic center at Zabid in the Tihama, dating from medieval times), looked outward and tended to be more cooperative with the Ottoman Turks and later, with the Egyptians, during their various occupations of the country. The Shafi'is, moreover, tend to a more settled, submissive, agricultural way of life in comparison to the Zaydi tribes of the north and east where herding is important and there is a greater degree of clan-tribe autonomy.[39] One of the many consequences of the revolution of the 1960s was the end of formal Zaydi rule: the republicans were largely (though by no means entirely) Shafi'i-supported and the president of

38. Such were the estimates of several civil servants interviewed in Sana in March 1972. Wenner, op. cit., p. 30, suggests an equal division.

39. Dana Adams Schmidt, in his excellent account of the revolution and civil war, *Yemen: The Unknown War* (New York: Holt, Rinehart, and Winston, 1968), p. 189, reflects the widely held view of the peaceful character of the Shafi'i as compared with the warlike Zaydis.

the new republic in the early 1970s was a Shafi'i, the Qadi Abd al-Rahman al-Iryani, a well-known religious scholar and judge. Like the Muslim-Christian cleavage in Lebanon, the Zaydi-Sunni cleavage in Yemen is a theological conflict with deep historical roots and cemented on each side by the web of the clan and tribe; and today it is considerably reduced by cross-cutting cleavages and common interests arising out of modernization and new political orientations toward the Yemen political community as a whole.

But kinship and tribal identifications in particular still bulk large in the Yemeni political culture.[40] The imamate was successful (although turbulent) not only because of the imam's claim to religious legitimacy but also because the ruling family—the Hamid al-Din—was able to retain the loyalty of the principal tribes and to subdue the dissidents. In such a segmented society marked by constant rivalries and tensions among semiautonomous tribes and clans, the imam was required continually to renew tribal loyalties through subsidies, marriages, patronage, and sometimes armed action. These loyalties were never automatic or entirely secure. When the Hamid al-Din family, which was a branch of the original al-Rassi dynasty of the ninth century, took over the imamate in 1891, it largely succeeded in winning the support of the two principal tribal confederations, the Hashid and the Baqil. When Imam Ahmad (1948–62) lost the support of key tribes in 1960, after the incident involving a breach of safe-conduct for the leader of the Hashid federation, a general tribal revolt broke out. The weakening of tribal support facilitated the 1962 revolution; and even though the subsequent civil war, generally speaking, pitted the Zaydi tribes against the Shafi'i republican army some important tribes joined the republican cause. The imamate as a political institution was swept away eventually, but the tribes and tribal divisions remain. Thus, republican Yemen, despite its modern ideology and appearance, also relied heavily for legitimacy upon tribal acceptance. It is a measure of persisting tribal influence that in 1972 the government was forced into conflict with the radical People's Democratic Republic of Yemen, largely under pressure from the tribal leaders who felt injured, insulted, and threatened by the activities of the Aden government. As late as 1976 Shaykh Abdalla al-Ahmar could close the road to Sa'da to government officials if he wished.

Foreign elements, in this case Turkish and British, also have played a part in shaping the legitimacy equation in Yemen as they have in most other Middle Eastern systems. The Turks, who ruled uneasily

40. See the tribal map in Schmidt, op. cit., p. 13.

from 1517 to 1636 and again from 1849 to 1918, were not of course entirely foreign in the religious sense, although to the Zaydis they represented an alien Islamic tradition. But they clearly were alien in a political sense; and a large part of the imamate's legitimacy derives from the armed resistance to the Turks carried out by Qasim the Great in the seventeenth century and by Imam Yahya in the early twentieth century.

The British impact on imamic legitimacy was mixed. Having established important and mutually advantageous commercial interests (such as mocha coffee) in the seventeenth and eighteenth centuries, the British-Yemeni relationship took a more political turn in the 1800s, as Britain's need (discussed in chapter 5 above) to protect its Indian connection against asserted threats—French, Egyptian, Wahhabite—became more intense. By the reign of Imam Yahya, this hitherto amicable relationship began to turn sour because of Britain's increasingly permanent and extensive sway over Aden port and the surrounding sultanates. The imam regarded himself as rightful ruler of all Yemen, even though his authority with the non-Zaydi sultans had long been minimal. The Treaty of Sana (1934) ended a conflict between the imam's forces and British troops and left the Yemen split on the line that divides the Yemen Arab Republic and the PDRY today, but the imam never was required specifically to renounce his claims to the south and tension continued.[41] Thus when in the 1950s Imam Ahmad, through his son Muhammad al-Badr, cultivated relations with Egypt's President Nasir, there was a common anti-British interest that took precedence over the seemingly illogical alliance of the revolutionary and the medieval. And in the 1960s Egypt not only supported the republican revolution (with easy disregard of its one-time support of the fallen regime) but worked with it to support the rebellion against Britain in Aden and south Arabia. Anti-imperialism thus became another building block for Yemen governmental legitimacy (both royalist and republican) in a fast modernizing Arab world.

Post-Traditional Yemen: Revolution or Accommodation?

On November 26, 1962, Brigadier-General Abdalla al-Sallal carried out a coup against the new imam, Muhammad al-Badr. The imam escaped, rallied forces in the rugged northeastern part of the country and commenced a war against the new Nasirite republican regime. The war went on for seven years. From 1962 through mid-1965 the

41. Ingrams, op. cit., pp. 68–70.

fighting was intense and widespread as a large Egyptian expeditionary force attempted unsuccessfully to crush the Sa'udi Arabian–backed royalist resistance. A series of peacemaking conferences and declarations beginning with the Irkwit cease-fire of November 1964 and lasting through the following year were largely inconclusive. Fighting continued intermittently until August 1966 when the Egyptians sought to reassert their flagging military and political influence with a new offensive that included the use of poison gas. But Egypt's stunning defeat by Israel in the 1967 Six-Day War effectively curtailed its military involvement in Yemen, and by the end of that year the Egyptian force had been withdrawn. In the meantime, both the republican and royalist forces had been suffering from internal political instability and fatigue. The royalists besieged Sana in 1968 but failed to take the city, and by the end of 1969 the republican government had gained effective control of most of the country. Reconciliation between the opposition forces took place the following year, and in 1971 the Yemen Arab Republic held its first elections and promulgated a constitution. Although the Egyptian withdrawal had forced the resignation of President Sallal, who had been closely identified with Cairo from the beginning of the revolution and the establishment of a presidential council regime led by the Qadi Abd al-Rahman al-Iryani, it was not until 1970–71 that relative tranquillity prevailed.

Few revolutionary regimes in the Middle East can have faced legitimacy-building problems as serious as those confronting the Yemeni republicans. The vast discontinuities between traditional and modern values and structures were further inflamed by the drawn-out civil war. Sallal, a Zaydi educated in Iraq and committed to the Nasirist type of Arab nationalism, wished to lead Yemen along the path of "unity, freedom, and socialism" through an authoritarian central government. The sacred legitimizing myth of the imamate and, even more important, the nexus of parochial kinship structures behind it had to give way to the authority of a military strongman and a regime clothed in the legitimacy of progressive anti-imperialist Arab nationalism. I have already discussed the difficulties which countries far more modernized than Yemen have had in effecting a break with traditional politics. On the one hand, Nasir's progressive Arabism was widely disseminated by Cairo radio's "Voice of the Arabs," so that it reached many inaccessible places. There was also a small group of well-educated, liberal figures—mainly Shafi'i—who had long opposed the medieval character of the imamate; among the most prominent were Abd al-Rahman al-Iryani and Muhammad Ahmad No'man who became moving figures in the postwar regime. Furthermore, the Egyptian expeditionary force, some 60,000 strong, accelerated the material development of the country simply in pursuit of the war effort and in the process exposed many Yemenis to the ideas and attractions of a more progressive and modern society.[42] And finally there were significant traditionalist elements that had long nursed grudges against the Hamid al-Din family, and they were prepared to join in the revolution despite its secular coloration.

On the other hand, tribalism and religiosity were so deeply rooted in Yemeni society that no mere change of government, even if supported by a large external military force, could replace them easily with a civic culture and loyalty to a modernizing central government. Consider the lack of infrastructure: in 1963–64 the total number of students in secondary schools was eighty-four; and in 1972 there were only 881 kilometers of paved road in a country of some 200,000 square kilometers. The entire civil government in this country of over 5 million consisted of only 17,000 employees in 1971 of whom a mere 415 were college graduates.[43] Although there were a few liberal educated notables, the urban middle class that might constitute a constituency for the revolution was exceedingly small and confined to the three main towns of Sana, Hudayda, and Ta'iz. Nor was there more than an embryonic industrial proletariat: there were only 324 industrial establishments of more than four workers, employing a total labor force of around 6,700.[44] To make matters worse, the longer the Egyptian army remained, the more it came to be resented, even within republican ranks; in fact, by the end of 1964 liberal dissidents were trying to curb the authoritarian rule of "the Egyptian proconsul" Sallal and his equally tough-minded vice-president, Col. Hassan al-Amri. From a republican point of view, the only consolation was that the royalist forces were suffering from similar logistical problems and internal divisions. Moreover, just as many republicans came to resent their Egyptian patrons, so did many of the royalists develop frictions with their Sa'udi backers. Many indeed must have remembered their war with the Sa'udis in 1933–34 in which the imam

42. Schmidt, op. cit., pp. 77–88.

43. Data are from Yemen Arab Republic, Prime Minister's Office, Central Planning Organization Statistics Department, *Statistical Yearbook, 1972* (Sana, April 1973), pp. 91, 143, and 157–58. See also Mohamed Said el Attar, *Le Sous-développement Economique et Social du Yémen* (Alger: Editions Tiers-Monde, 1964).

44. Ibid., pp. 58–59. The point is made by Robert W. Stookey, in an excellent two-part article, "Social Structure and Politics in the Yemen Arab Republic," *The Middle East Journal*, 28, 3 (Summer 1974), pp. 248–60 and 4 (Autumn 1974), pp. 409–18; 1, p. 250.

was forced to cede the Jizan and Najran areas, largely populated by Yemenis.

Yemen clearly was not Egypt and Sallal was no Nasir, so the first republican regime was unable to develop sufficient legitimacy through its reliance on strong personalist authority, revolutionary nationalist symbolism, and an external security force. An opening toward liberalism was attempted in mid-1965 when Muhammad Ahmad No'man was permitted to form a government, but it showed too much independence and a leaning toward rival Ba'thist nationalism; so Cairo returned Sallal to power a year later. But when Egypt was forced finally to withdraw its army, Sallal fell and a regime of liberal politicians was allowed to try its hand.

The new regime of Abd al-Rahman al-Iryani was made up of moderate republicans of the Third Force group which had resisted Egypt's domination of the revolution; in fact, the new president and several of his associates, including Muhammad Ahmad No'man and Muhsin al-Aini, had been detained in Cairo in 1965. The new regime's strategy of legitimization differed markedly from that of its predecessor.[45] Whereas the government of the civil war period was personalist, authoritarian, and committed to a militant Arab revolutionary nationalism, the Iryani regime was built on a philosophy of accommodation. Structurally, the Iryani regime by 1971 had moved toward greater pluralism than its predecessor: there was a 3-man Civilian Presidential Council, a prime minister and cabinet, and a 179-man Consultative Council (*majlis al-shura*). The latter was a quasi-elective body, 20 members appointed by the president and the remainder by a combination of direct election (in the main towns) and indirect election (in the village and tribal areas). Through these structures, two types of accommodation were reached. On the internal level, they brought back the ex-royalist tribal shaykhs into the formal power structure. This reconciliation was symbolized by the role of Shaykh Abdalla al-Ahmar, the principal chief of the Hashid federation (whose membership included both republican and royalist partisans), who served as speaker of the council. On the regional level, the Iryani government sought to steer a relatively nonaligned course between Egypt and Sa'udi Arabia, the external backers of the republicans and royalists, respectively. As for the authority of the president himself, it too reflected a synthesis of the competing ideologies: Abd al-Rahman al-Iryani was a qadi, a religious judge proficient in the Shafi'i school of

45. My discussion of the Iryani regime is based largely upon interviews with YAR government officials and politicians March 1972, October 1974, and May 1976. See also Stookey, op. cit.

Islamic law, a man respected by Zaydis as well as Sunnis for his piety and personal rectitude. At the same time, he had supported the republican cause (even though he had once served the imam) and by the norms of traditional Yemeni politics could be described as progressive. The qadi's authority lay to some extent in his weakness. Unlike Sallal, he had no support base among the officers, nor was he linked to any of the tribes by the traditional bonds. When Col. Hassan al-Amri (a one-time ally) attempted to overturn the regime in the fall of 1971, he was unable to rally his erstwhile supporters among the officers, reportedly because they knew that a coup was unnecessary: the qadi would be glad to resign at any time. His authority, in short, resided in his capacity to act as an honest broker between the two real centers of power, the army, which controlled the main towns, and the relatively autonomous tribes of the north and east.

Unfortunately, the accommodationist posture of the Iryani regime was not conducive to dynamic government. One is reminded of the immobilism and low capabilities that made the traditional pluralist regime in Lebanon perennially unstable. Convenient as the regime was to the modernist and traditionalist camps inside Yemen, it was also vulnerable to criticism from each side for betraying their respective ideals. Some among the republicans who sincerely wanted to revolutionize Yemeni society and politics saw this regime as reactionary for its reconciliation with the shaykhs and its refusal to permit political parties to operate. At least two clandestine radical Marxist movements, the Yemeni Democratic Revolutionary party and the Organization of Yemeni Revolutionary Resisters, founded in 1968 and 1970 respectively, were beginning to agitate and plot against the regime by 1973. Both groups were said to be related to the PDRY-supported Popular Front for the Liberation of Oman and the Arabian Gulf (PFLOAG), which had been conducting a rebellion in Oman's Dhofar province.[46] It was widely believed in the north that the radical regime of the PDRY was encouraging acts of sabotage and terror, such as the assassination of Muhammad Ali Uthman, a member of the Presidential Council, in May 1973. But some conservative tribal leaders were discontented for the opposite reason. They disapproved of liberal political institutions and ideologies. They resented the efforts of the central government to extend its presence and influence in their areas, particularly if the accompanying material advantages were insufficient. While substantial infrastructure development had taken

---

46. Mare Pellas, "Yémen du Nord: La lutte des forces révolutionnaires," *Le Monde Diplomatique,* August 1973, p. 28.

place since 1970, the capabilities of the administration remained very limited, and it was unable either to curb corruption or to institutionalize it to its advantage.[47] A particularly galling issue to the tribal conservatives was the Iryani regime's policy toward the Marxist government of Aden. While the shaykhs were deeply hostile to that regime on ideological grounds and were understandably incensed by Aden radio's propaganda attacks on them by name, the Sana government pursued a policy of avoiding armed confrontation and even pursuing unity talks, in furtherance of one of the few ideological goals which both regimes shared.

The Iryani regime's legitimacy was also impaired by continuing turbulence on the level of regional Arab politics. To be sure, the settlement of the Egyptian-Sa'udi Arabian confrontation eased the external pressures, but other problems remained. Sa'udi Arabia continued to exert conservative influence throughout the northern tribal areas through subsidizing various shaykhs and government officials, much to the discomfort of Iryani's prime minister, Muhsin al-Aini, who was known for his Iraqi Ba'thist sympathies. Yemeni officials felt that Sa'udi Arabia was attempting not only to curb liberal secular political development in Sana but also to use Sana in its struggle against the truly radical regime of the PDRY. While the Aden regime and the Sana republicans were themselves far apart ideologically, there was a recognition by some officials in each capital that mutual cooperation, if not actual unity, was in the interest of both in view of the common potential threat posed by their large, immensely wealthy (although underdeveloped) neighbor. Thus it was that in 1972–73 unity negotiations were underway between the YAR and the PDRY even as Sa'udi-backed tribesmen in the YAR were raiding the PDRY and clamoring for full-scale war, and agents from the PDRY were inspiring sabotage in north Yemen towns. Complicating matters still further were the reported clandestine efforts of elements supported by the Ba'thist regime in Iraq to replace the Iryani regime with a more authentically revolutionary government. Thus torn between still-salient ideological polarities amplified by internal and regional rivalries, the Iryani regime was forced to maneuver constantly to survive and provide a degree of civil tranquillity.

On June 13, 1974, President Iryani's regime was deposed in a bloodless coup led by Lieutenant-Colonel Ibrahim Muhammad al-Hamdi. His accommodationist strategy had brought four years of rare relative tranquillity to republican Yemen, and during that time

47. See Stookey, op. cit. 2, pp. 412–14 for interesting comments on the taxation problem.

significant progress had been made in social, economic, and administrative development. Reforms in central banking, currency, budgeting, and agriculture had been initiated. A modern airport was under construction at Sana, and new communications facilities had been opened. Foreign assistance programs from countries as diverse as China, the Soviet Union, East and West Germany, and the United States, as well as from the United Nations Development Program, were much in evidence. Although there was still a severe shortage of medical personnel, an authoritative local source reported that antibiotics for treating whooping cough and other common maladies were readily available even in remote towns, as were a variety of European contraceptive pills. External private investment was increasing, due in part to a favorable investment law and the new stability; and the newly oil-rich Arab states of the Gulf were beginning to undertake sizeable investment and assistance projects. But useful as it was, the accommodationist formula had not significantly enhanced national integration. Tribal autonomy and dissidence remained a basic feature of Yemeni political life; ideological cleavages were another. The domestic order was still vulnerable to external interference. And despite the considerable progress noted above, the government was too poor, too small, too untrained and too new to co-opt or pacify the numerous elements, conservative and radical, agitating for change. Its last two years were marked by a depressing series of terrorist incidents and political assassinations.

Colonel Hamdi's coup appeared to presage less a systemic change than an adjustment to the Right. Although the country was placed under the rule of a military command council, in classical Nasirist fashion, the new regime also enjoyed the support of important Zaydi tribal elements. The new leader was thought to be more conservative politically than many of the liberals in the Iryani regime and, moreover, was said to enjoy close relations with Sa'udi Arabia. Although Muhsin al-Aini, one of the most radical of the civilian liberals, was brought in as prime minister, he was subsequently forced to resign. On the other hand, key liberal technocrats, including the nephew of the deposed president, were allowed to continue their modernizing policies; and the new government reiterated its commitment to Arab nationalism and the Palestinian cause.[48] In theory, therefore, it appeared that the objective of the coup had been to strengthen the authority of the national government without fundamentally departing from the accommodationist legitimacy strategy of the former regime. These events

48. Interview with Colonel Hamdi, *The Middle East* (London), No. 8 (May 1975), pp. 27–29.

coincided with a certain relaxation of ideological conflict throughout the Arabian peninsula, symbolized by the gestures of rapprochement by Iraq and the PDRY toward their conservative neighbors. This development held out the hope that the intensity of conflict between the two Yemens and within the YAR itself might decrease.

At an informal seminar in June 1976, several prominent Yemeni politicians and administrators reflected on the first two years of the Hamdi regime. All agreed that the parliamentary experiment which it had replaced had failed. The majlis al-shura had become a forum for uneducated, self-interested cliques; and its members were obstructionist and incapable of understanding what development was about. Even the first year of the Hamdi regime had been marked by paralysis and confusion on the administrative level. Matters had improved during the second year as Sa'udi, Abu Dhabi, and international development funds and the new remittance liquidity among ordinary Yemenis began to have an impact. Yemen, despite its poverty, was experiencing a boom in consumption goods, construction, and business. Administrative reform had been highlighted by the transformation of the imam's treasury into a modern Ministry of Finance and by the creation of a Central Planning Organization. A far-reaching expansion and overhaul of the educational system was underway, with assistance from UNDP and UNESCO. Kuwait was financing new schools and the country's first university. An agricultural development authority had been established in the Tihama plain on the Red Sea.

Yet the Yemenis participating in this discussion expressed unease about the political future. It was evident to all that the development boom was creating severe loads on the government's rudimentary administrative apparatus, causing slowdowns, bottlenecks, and frustration among some Yemenis who wondered where the new money was really going. At the same time, ordinary Yemenis were experiencing the same kind of inflation and other problems arising from oil-induced rapid growth which I have noted throughout the Arab countries. Traditional tribal leaders were becoming increasingly aware of the challenge to their authority implicit in certain development schemes. But from the other end of the spectrum, many young Yemenis in the main cities were thought to be ideologically committed toward radical movements of Ba'thist, Arab nationalist, or socialist tendencies, and impatient with the pace and style of the Hamdi regime. Two alternative legitimacy-building courses were identified. One argued for the necessity of building a comprehensive political apparatus to mobilize people for national development and cohesion—something similar in form to the National Front organization in south Yemen or other single-party systems in the area. Without such a structure, it was argued, the regime's development efforts (like those of its predecessor) would founder against the traditionalist opposition. The second alternative called for continued state-directed incrementalist development, with a deliberate deemphasis of the consequences. By keeping a low profile, it was contended, there would be less stimulus for the conservatives to mobilize against the government. While Colonel Hamdi seemed more inclined toward the second of these alternatives, he also seemed to be aware of the efficiency and political problems associated with it. To monitor efficiency, he instituted a number of "corrective committees" which were to observe bureaucratic performance in the various ministries. He also appeared to be lending support to the General Federation of Cooperatives for Development, a hierarchically organized, democratically elected, and ostensibly apolitical association of self-help groups concerned with building roads, schools, and clinics in local villages which the government could not serve. It was not immediately clear whether such organizations could become effective, significant legitimizing institutions. Although still personally popular after two years, Colonel Hamdi confronted a delicate task in devising an ideology and structures to strengthen the fragile legitimacy of the Yemen Arab Republic.

THE PEOPLE'S DEMOCRATIC REPUBLIC OF YEMEN

One of the many paradoxes in Arab politics is the fact that north and south Yemen, both of which assert the desire for one unified Yemen, represent the opposite extremes on the revolutionary republican spectrum. The Yemen Arab Republic, as we have just seen, has evolved along pragmatic, moderate ideological lines under the leadership of a military strongman. Hamdi continues the contraction in the socialist-nationalist goals of the 1962 revolution, and while maintaining the Arab-Islamic synthesis found in all the revolutionary republics, he has tilted in the direction of conservative piety and free enterprise. His parallel tilt in regional relations has been toward Sa'udi Arabia. In sharp contrast, the People's Republic in Aden represents the most radical embodiment of revolutionary transformationist ideology and practice in the Arab world. Leadership has been collective rather than personalist, civilian rather than military. A highly programmatic ideology emphasizing the transfer of wealth and power from the traditional sultans and notables to the peasants, fishermen, and workers has been made operational through an effective single-party organization, the National Front. Planning and administration are more efficient than in the north, a judgment concurred in by international experts and northern officials themselves. While Islam is preserved and observed in south Yemen, the regime lays greatest stress on non-religious developmental and egalitarian goals. Capitalism and free enterprise have only a marginal place in the socialist society of the PDRY. Sa'udi Arabia has been perceived as south Yemen's most deadly enemy and Iraq one of its few friends, but the new weight of Sa'udi Arabia in peninsula affairs was by 1976 beginning to temper even Aden's foreign policy radicalism. So despite the fact that their revolutions were intertwined, north and south Yemen have pursued very different pathways to legitimacy.

The PDRY is almost sui generis in the Arab world because of the extent to which a militant political movement with a powerful ideology has permeated and transformed conventional social structures. To be sure, there have been significant developments in the other revolutionary states. The political elite no longer consists of rich landowners, businessmen, and clerics from the best religious and upper-bourgeois families and tribes; now they are military officers from the middle and lower-middle class. The revolutionary governments have also taken over the economy by expanding their own sources, nationalizing the major industrial concerns and intervening in agriculture. They have imposed a monopoly on political life. But social patterns beyond these alternations at the top have remained more-or-less intact, and mobilization of the masses by government-sponsored parties generally has been ineffective. In the PDRY, the revolution has been far more radical. The old power holders—petty sultans, privileged clans, and clerics—have been displaced at the local as well as the national level. Through a series of spontaneous and violent uprisings, power has been seized by the lowest, least powerful strata—peasants, fishermen, and laborers. Land reform and marketing cooperatives have set in motion a significant redistribution of wealth. Equality and participation (more than nationalism or religion) are the watchwords of this revolution. As for mobilization of the masses, the Political Organization of the National Front, the ruling party, has succeeded in organizing support for the revolution among people who, because of their ascriptive, primordial and parochial orientation and their isolation from modernity, would not appear to make promising cadres. Yet it was among the most isolated up-country tribes and the poorest strata of the labor movement that the NLF was able to develop the base from which it triumphed in 1967 over the more conventional middle-class revolutionaries of the rival Front for the Liberation of Occupied South Yemen (FLOSY). It is this support that has enabled the NLF to survive its first eight years of independence, despite constant pressures by its unfriendly neighboring regimes. Compared to the other revolutionary systems, the PDRY is the most authentically Marxist in ideology. Along with Iraq and Tunisia, it is the least military-dominated single-party regime. It has gone further toward structural innovation on the local level. The National Front organization appears to be effective, penetrative, and coherent, governed by men and women who take their ideology very seriously.

The comparative radicalism of the PDRY is all the more dramatic when viewed against its socioeconomic backwardness. This country of 1.4 million inhabitants, though rich in history, is one of the poorest in the region. On the eve of independence in 1967, there were only 127 miles of asphalted roads; illiteracy outside of Aden was perhaps 95 percent; per capita income in the early 1970s was only around $107.[49] Only six months before independence the closure of the Suez Canal reduced the cargo movements through the big Aden port by 75 percent. On the whole, southern Yemen was an inauspicious place for nation-building of any kind.

Traditional Politics and British Colonialism

If the radicalism of the PDRY is evident in cross-sectional comparisons with other Arab states, it is even more dramatic in longitudinal comparison with the political system of Aden Colony and the south Arabian protectorates. Almost all the regressive features of poverty, colonialism, and parochial traditional politics that characterized Libya in the 1920s and 1930s were operative in southern Arabia well into the 1960s. The one relative virtue of British rule, compared to Italian, was its limited character: British settlers did not push the indigenous people off their land. But that virtue was also a vice inasmuch as little was done to improve social, educational, or economic conditions. A visitor to Aden could literally cross the street from the "favored" area, with its Indian-owned shops stocked with watches and cameras for the tourist trade around Aden port to the "native" area consisting of urban slums and a virtually unimproved hinterland. Indeed, Britain strengthened the authority of the local sultans as the simplest and most expedient strategy for protecting its strategic Aden base. Only as the end of the occupation (which dated from 1839) drew near did Kennedy Trevaskis and other liberal administrators seek to organize a form of self-government under these local despots, but the effort collapsed

49. According to the Arab Information Center, "People's Democratic Republic of Yemen" (New York, 1973), pp. 9 and 13.

almost immediately.[50] This belated attempt to establish a common political identity for Aden together with the sultanates in an independent South Arabian Federation failed partly because of the striking socioeconomic and communal discontinuities in the political culture. Elite fragmentation among the traditional sultans, each a patriarchal kinship ruler with a monopoly of socioreligious status and economic political power in his own domain, was one source of weakness. As Trevaskis put it, "In the tribal world precarious balances of power had come into being as between each clan and its neighbors ... But this wild thing [tribalism] was no fantasy. We had to live with it and our problem was to learn how to tame it."[51] Another weakness was the relative overdevelopment of Aden Colony. The port, in particular, with its large pool of exploited labor, was a strategic center for nationalist resistance. The presence of the transistor radio and the use of broadcasting as a political weapon created a new political consciousness even in the more remote areas and was important in creating a situation favorable to revolution. In his study of political change in a south Arabian town, Abdalla Bujra gives an eyewitness account of how the news broadcasts of the overthrow of the imam in north Yemen exacerbated existing cleavages among the high-status sayyid clan (claiming descent from the Prophet) and the families of lesser position and political influence. He remarks that "the rise of nationalism in south Arabia, and the revolution in Yemen, are both intimately connected with the extensive spread of revolutionary political ideas in rural areas made possible by the transistor radio."[52] With the development of this new communications medium, political events throughout the area took on greater and more widespread salience.

But even without the transistor radio, the regional context came to have a catalytic effect on southern Yemen's traditional polity in at least two ways. One was Egypt's military and political support of the new republican regime in Sana which gave the nationalists a strategic territorial political support base. The other was the ideological and political influence of the Arab Nationalists' movement centered in Beirut. The multiplicity of parochial kinship and religious authority structures, the spread of social mobilization, and the growing percep-

---

50. The story is told by one of the Federation's chief architects, Sir Kennedy Trevaskis, in *Shades of Amber* (London: Hutchinson, 1968).

51. Ibid., p. 87.

52. Abdalla S. Bujra, *The Politics of Stratification* (Oxford: Clarendon Press, 1971), p. 169 and pp. 169–83.

tion of the illegitimacy of Britain's colonial presence imposed a cumulative load on the system. Under these conditions the legitimacy formula contrived by the liberal British administrators and their moderate allies among the Adeni commercial class and the sultans— a formula built upon the value resources of independence, neo-traditionalism and liberal democracy—proved insufficient.

A Marxist-Leninist Experiment

The emergence of a Marxist-Leninist regime in Aden must be viewed in the context of the radicalization of Arab politics that occurred during the 1960s. In the 1950s the main axis of conflict was the struggle between the conservative monarchies and the republican nationalists; and Nasir, with his reformist, military-bureaucratic, pan-Arab nationalism, symbolized the revolutionary orientation. The Ba'th party, although overshadowed by Nasirism in terms of real power, had long advocated a more fundamental cultural and economic (socialist) transformation, and it had attracted a significant following of younger middle-class, educated activists, both civilian and military. In the early 1960s Nasirism waned and the Ba'th came to power both in Syria and Iraq. The third ideological current, the Arab Nationalists' movement, founded in 1948 in Beirut by the Palestinian George Habash and others, arose out of the trauma of the loss of Palestine. Its ideological orientation was pan-Arabism, and it sought the recovery of Palestine through Arab unity. When Nasir emerged as the hero of Arabism in the mid-1950s, the ANM backed him. During the 1950s and 1960s the ANM established groups throughout the Arab east, including southern Yemen.

All three movements underwent a shift toward the Left in the 1960s. In the summer of 1961, just before the collapse of the union with Syria, Nasir introduced his socialist decrees. A radical Ba'th faction, influenced by the Algerian liberation struggle, seized power in Damascus in 1966, and another radical faction came to power in Baghdad two years later. The ANM also underwent radicalization. By 1963 and 1964, it appeared to the ANM that neither Nasir nor the Ba'th were capable of promoting unity or confronting Israel effectively; and the 1967 war amply confirmed these perceptions. Stimulated by these depressing trends, a group of the ANM's younger intellectuals sympathetic to Marxism-Leninism began to challenge the nationalist leadership of Habash and his colleagues. At the same time Habash himself turned leftward, convinced apparently that nationalist symbolism alone would not achieve the desired results: a more comprehensive, "scientific" ideology was needed.[53] As he put it in an interview with this writer in 1970, imperialism is a general phenomenon, whether in Palestine or south Arabia. The poor masses ("not the intellectuals living comfortably, drinking their morning Nescafé") must be mobilized. Armed struggle is a "regrettable" necessity.[54] At the end of 1967 the ANM had transformed itself into the Popular Front for the Liberation of Palestine, and two years later the radical faction led by Nayif Hawatma—still unsatisfied with the Habash "petit-bourgeois" leadership—split off to form the Popular Democratic Front for the Liberation of Palestine.

These events are not as far removed from the south Yemen revolution as they may seem. In 1959 the Arab Nationalists' movement had taken the lead in bringing together several revolutionary groups of southern Arabia into a National Liberation Front; and as the ANM itself shifted to the Left, the NLF too came to adapt an increasingly radical stance. On October 14, 1963, the first armed uprising began in the Radfan mountains, initiating a campaign of guerrilla warfare and terrorism that by the end of 1967 had succeeded both in driving out the British and destroying the federation of shaykhs and sultans which the British had hoped to leave in place. A third important objective had also been accomplished: the defeat of a rival nationalist group, the Front for the Liberation of Occupied South Yemen (FLOSY). FLOSY was basically an Egyptian creation: it drew on the mainstream nationalist movement that had grown up during the 1950s—a period of commercial growth and labor unrest—in Aden port around the Aden Trade Union Congress. The People's Socialist party, under the direction of Abdalla al-Asnag (now the foreign minister of *north* Yemen) and Abd al-Qawi Makawi, came to be the spearhead of the labor and nationalist movement in the early 1960s. Although Egypt initially backed the NLF (Nasir was still on good terms with the parent ANM) and although the NLF was briefly a part of FLOSY after its creation in 1966, the radical currents preponderant in the NLF soon drew it away into bitter rivalry for control of the revolution. From a British point of view, it was FLOSY—supported by Nasir—that was the extremist wing of the local political forces, while the NLF, which was

53. See Robert Anton Mertz, "Why George Habash Turned Marxist," *Mid East*, 10, 4 (August 1970), pp. 33–36. See also the recent study by a former member of the ANM, Walid Kazziha, *Revolutionary Transformation in the Arab World: Habash and His Comrades* (New York: St. Martin's Press, 1975).

54. Interview with George Habash, August 23, 1970.

in reality far more radical, was seen as a possible independent check against the pan-Arab threat.[55]

In late 1967 as the British were preparing to evacuate Aden, southern Yemen presented a revealing cross-section of the ideological currents running in the Arab world. On the one extreme were the twenty-odd sultans and shaykhs whose fiefdoms Britain had been trying for over a decade to weld into a modern federal state. In between there were the moderate upper- and middle-class nationalists of the South Arabian League and notables like Hassan Bayumi. Then came FLOSY, the standard-bearer of establishment revolution, with its emphasis on anti-imperalism, ethnic-nationalism, and state socialism and its denial of the idea of class struggle. Finally, there was the NLF with an increasingly strong Marxist left wing. Abd al-Fattah Isma'il, the ideological leader of the NLF left wing, was particularly scathing toward what FLOSY represented; he is quoted in 1968 as describing the single-party regimes of Egypt, Syria, Iraq, and Algeria as examples of "self-styled socialist parties which are petty bourgeois in ideology and class makeup. . . . The conciliatory politics of the petty bourgeoisie is even more dangerous for the popular national democratic revolution than the overtly hostile politics of the feudal-bourgeois alliance. On the class question the worst thing is the politics of the 'golden mean.' "[56] On June 22, 1969, Abd al-Fattah's faction of the NLF seized power from the relatively moderate ruling faction of Qahtan al-Sha'bi, thus installing the most radical regime in the Middle East.

The Legitimacy Formula of the NLF

Perhaps in no other Arab polity does formal ideology play as important a role in the regime's effort to build legitimacy as it does in the PDRY. In NLF ideology, legitimacy resides with the working class, the peasants, the intelligentsia, and the petty bourgeoisie. According to article 7 of the 1970 constitution, these elements comprise the political basis of the national democratic revolution.[57] Furthermore, the constitution explicitly calls for the state to "liberate society from

55. Joe Stork, "Socialist Revolution in Arabia; A Report from the People's Democratic Republic of Yemen," *MERIP Reports*, 15 (March 1973), 25 pp.; pp. 6–8. See also Eric Rouleau, "South Yemen: Hitched to a Red Star," reprinted from *Le Monde* and circulated with the *Manchester Guardian Weekly* of June 10 and 17, 1972, and reprinted as a pamphlet by the Middle East Research and Information Project.

56. Stork, op. cit., p. 8.

57. *Constitution of the People's Democratic Republic of Yemen* (Aden: The Republic Press, September 1971), 60 pp.; p. 7.

backward tribalism."[58] Another document identifies the "feudal and landed property style" which characterizes a politics dominated by great families as the principal aspect of Yemeni backwardness.[59] It would appear, moreover, that the breakup of kinship authority patterns extends well below the highest political levels. It was this writer's impression after a visit to the Second Governorate (the former Lahij sultanate) outside Aden in 1972 that the Agricultural Reform of October 1970 had indeed been implemented; even the family of the president, Salim Robaya Ali, was limited to three to five feddans like everybody else, and the former sultan's palace now houses government offices and an agricultural school.[60] Certainly, in comparison with the traditional polities, as well as some of the revolutionary regimes, the legitimizing force of kinship in general and the ruler's clan in particular in PDRY is virtually nil. One suspects that family connections, the wasita mechanism discussed earlier, and the deferential attitudes toward traditional leaders (*zu'ama*) are more prevalent, at least at the middle and local levels of politics, in the less radical republics such as Egypt, the Sudan, and the Yemen Arab Republic than in the PDRY.

Religion is also less important as a legitimacy symbol. It is interesting, however, that even the PDRY Marxists do not attack Islam directly the way they battle against tribalism and feudalism. As we have seen, the ideologists in the other revolutionary polities are even more accommodating. Indeed, the PDRY Constitution declares Islam to be the state religion and commits the state to the preservation of Arabic and Islamic culture. But some indications of the low priority given religion by the NLF may be gathered from the fact that these two references to religion (articles 46 and 31, respectively) are buried in the middle of the constitution and not proclaimed as "political foundations" of the state. Interviews with PDRY officials indicated that the NLF policy is to minimize religion as much as possible and to treat it as a cultural characteristic rather than a moral or political force. It is also notable that article 46 also guarantees freedom of belief in other religions.[61] The PDRY leadership stands with Bourguiba of Tunisia

58. Ibid., Article 31, p. 13.

59. "On the Yemeni Working Class Program," mimeographed, 18 pp., courtesy of the General Federation of Trade Unions, Ma'ala, 1972; p. 2.

60. Cf. also the impressions of Stork, op. cit., pp. 11–19.

61. Stork, op. cit., p. 21, discerned "a generally tolerant and confident attitude on the part of the National Front towards religion." He notes that the feast but not the fast of Ramadan was observed, that the chairman visits the main mosque during the Independence Day celebrations, and that religion is included in the primary school curriculum.

as among those Arab rulers that have tried hardest to reduce the influence of religion in politics—harder certainly than Nasir or the Ba'th. But none of the Arab states has gone as far as Turkey, which not only abolished the caliphate but later, in 1928, abolished the clause stating that the state religion was Islam. They have gone far enough, however, to have been attacked by their political enemies in Sa'udi Arabia and the YAR as atheists.

If the PDRY ideology plays down kinship and religion, it shares with the traditional polities an emphasis on history as a source of regime support. The history that is exploited, however, is not the golden age of Arab civilization which the Ba'th emphasizes or the continuity of traditional culture which the shah of Iran celebrates, or the historical nation-building legends of a ruling family, which legitimize the Sa'udi dynasty. In the PDRY, history as a legitimizing tool begins with the revolution, and the myths that are celebrated are associated with specific dates: the coup in north Yemen of September 26, 1962; the beginning of the revolutionary insurgency in the south on October 14, 1963 (the principal Aden newspaper is called *October 14*), the achievement of independence and final British withdrawal on November 30, 1967, and (not least) the corrective movement of June 22, 1969, in which the left wing of the National Front seized power from the incumbent right wing led by Qahtan al-Sha'bi. The regime strives to inculcate in the masses a sense of pride in these events and the various other accomplishments of the revolution.

It also invokes history to induce popular vigilance rather than complacency with these accomplishments. Marxism may be an optimistic theory of history for the long run, but the short run perspective as envisioned by PDRY leaders is dark and full of dangers. The struggle of the exploited classes is of course the central image and the people are constantly reminded of the reactionary elements, internal and external, which are trying to crush the revolution. For example, in March 1972 this writer observed one of the regular drill exercises for the Popular Forces held for employees on a playing field in Tawahi, Aden, every morning before work. Over a thousand workers, male and female, were organized into units of about thirty persons, each under the direction of a young, blue-shirted drillmaster who instructed them in marching and other martial arts. At the time, there was a crisis in PDRY relations with the regime and certain powerful tribes in the YAR to the north and chronic flareups of violence were occurring on the border with Sa'udi Arabia. At the end of the marching drill there was a period of relaxation during which a recent speech of the National Front's general secretary and chief theoretician, Abd al-Fattah Isma'il was broadcast; in it he urged Yemenis to unite to the last man and woman to fight world imperialism, particularly as practiced by the United States, and "regional reaction" as exemplified by Sa'udi Arabia. Elsewhere in the Arabian peninsula the PDRY has often been regarded as an exporter of Marxist, atheist revolution; but an observer inside the PDRY had the strong impression that the mood was defensive. For the NLF, the lesson of history was that victory was not yet secure, so deeper loyalty, vigilance, and further struggle would be required to preserve the revolution.

I have already indicated the relatively nonchauvinist, nonprimordial character of the nationalism espoused by the NLF, especially its left wing, in comparison with the nationalism of the traditional and indeed most of the revolutionary regimes. This is not to suggest that the NLF denigrates nationalism, however. The first sentence of the 1970 Constitution begins, "Believing in the unity of the Yemen, and the unity of the destiny of the Yemeni people in the territory. . . ." But it is careful to specify that the goal is a "united democratic Yemen" which in turn is a step toward "democratic Arab unity." The PDRY's nationalism, while strong, is also selective—it must be democratic, i.e., progressive. The treatment of nationalism is elaborated further by Abd al-Fattah Isma'il in the report of the Fifth Congress of the National Front Political Organization (1972). The front supports the general movement for Arab national liberation because it contributes to the struggle against imperialism and the exploitative capitalist classes. The nationalist movement is a force for democracy. It is recognized that different parts of the Arab world may have their special characteristics, and so a certain diversity of nationalist approaches is tolerable. Unfortunately, however, some of the parties that lead the masses have remained far from the mainstream of political, economic, and social life. Furthermore, the masses in every Arab country have fallen prey to internal divisions. The imperialist and reactionary forces have taken advantage of these weaknesses. The 1967 Arab-Israeli war is an example of how the progressive nationalist cause throughout the area was set back, but fortunately it was not able to tip the scales of power in favor of reaction. The report asserts categorically that the PDRY will not deviate from its patriotic and national duties, and that it will support to the utmost the Palestine resistance and the revolutionary movements in the Arabian Gulf and peninsula.[62]

62. "Political Report of the General Command to the Fifth General Conference of the Political Organization of the National Front," delivered by Comrade Abd al-Fattah Isma'il. March 2, 1972 (Ma'ala, Aden: Republic Press, 1972), in Arabic, 72 pp.; pp. 17–20.

But it is in its rigorous exposition of socialism that the PDRY ideology is distinctive in comparison with other Arab states. Modernity, as we have observed, is very much a part of the legitimacy formula in the traditional polities, but there the predominant values are material development and economic growth. These goals have also been stressed in the revolutionary republics, although there is no decisive evidence that they have out-performed the traditional states in pursuit of them. But in the PDRY conception of modernity, there is far stronger emphasis upon sociopolitical participation at all levels, egalitarianism and sharing of the collective wealth. Once again, the constitution reveals the profundity of the difference in emphasis:

> ... The historical role of the working-class moves upwards and (it) become(s) ultimately the leading class in society. Soldiers, women, and students are regarded as part of this alliance by virtue of their membership in the productive forces of the people. ...
> The National Front Organization leads, on the basis of scientific socialism, the political activity amongst the masses and within mass organization so as to develop society in such a way that national democratic Revolution, which is non-capitalist in approach, is achieved.
> Art. 9: All power serves the welfare of the working people. The working people in the People's Democratic Republic of Yemen exercises its political authority through the People's councils which are elected in a free and democratic manner.[63]

Compared with other Arab constitutions, this is indeed radical. While the constitution guarantees to citizens the rights and protections of liberal Western states, it also stresses the obligation of the citizens to the community. Individuals are rewarded in accordance with their service in behalf of economic and social development (art. 14). Work is not just a right but an obligation as well (art. 35). Citizens contribute towards the public revenue according to their ability (art. 54). "Every citizen shall protect and support public ownership as the essential material basis for the national democratic revolution" (art. 52). The extent to which these constitutional principles are successfully practiced is hard to say, but this writer's personal observation and those of others suggest that the National Front cadres are uncommonly dedicated to their implementation.[64] The main obstacles are poverty and an almost total lack of social and administrative infrastructure outside Aden. But whatever the degree of success, there is no doubt that the PDRY

63. *PDRY Constitution*, Articles 7 and 9, pp. 7–8.
64. Rouleau, op. cit.; Stork, op. cit.

leadership is putting Marxist-Leninist socialism first as a legitimizing principle—ahead of conventional nationalism, Arab socialism, or Islamic socialism. It is sometimes asserted that Arab culture is inherently hostile to socialism: if so, one would doubt that a regime relying so heavily on socialism for legitimacy could survive in a society as poor, fragmented, and particularist as southern Yemen. But the extraordinary success of the National Front in mobilizing the most downtrodden sectors to fight a revolution and the survival of the regime for nearly a decade in a hostile regional environment cast doubt on the validity of such assertions.

The National Front: Legitimation and Control

Ideology, if it is to be fully effective as an instrument of legitimacy, cannot exist in a vacuum: it must be articulated through specific authority structures. In the traditional systems, the symbiosis of kinship as a value and as a structure has brought surprising strength to regimes that would seem otherwise anachronistic. In several of the revolutionary systems, a strong individual leader like Nasir or Bourguiba has vitalized otherwise abstract symbols. In the PDRY, however, the structure which activates the formula I have just described is a revolutionary movement, the National Front. Among the revolutionary states, only in Iraq does the ruling party exercise such complete and unrivaled control and provide such crucial structural legitimacy. To be sure, the Tunisian Neo-Destour is a well-developed party, but Bourguiba overshadows it. Much the same might be said of the Republican People's party and Ataturk during the first Turkish republic. In Syria the autonomy of the Ba'th party has been limited to some extent by military factions. And in the other single-party regimes, the party is either a governmental bureaucracy or ineffectual, or both.

The National Front is the primary political body in the PDRY; the government itself comes second. The governmental executive bodies, the Presidential Council and the Council of Ministers, are made up predominantly of NLF members. A 101-member Supreme People's Council exists on a provisional basis, but there had been no general elections as of the early 1970s, and its membership was determined by the NLF. The various functional groupings—soldiers, workers, students, women, and peasants—were allotted quotas in the council and allowed to choose members through their own organizations. Although only thirty members were NLF members, the front was able to maintain control of the council through its control over the functional groupings.[65]

65. Interview with an official of the PDRY Information Ministry, Aden, March 22, 1972.

National Front cadres penetrate and monitor all the major social organizations of the country, notably the labor federation, civil service, cooperatives, and the army and internal security apparatus. As such, the front performs a number of crucial functions. It sets the guidelines within which political alternatives and discussion must fall. It is a socializing agency for the goals of the revolution. It is an information-gathering and disseminating instrument. Most fundamentally, it is an instrument of control. The front takes internal security very seriously, given its grim but not unrealistic world view. It has applied Leninist principles and East German advisers to upgrade its internal security apparatus. It has not forgotten how Qahtan al-Sha'bi used "reaction-ary" army and security forces to purge the left wing in May 1968. Victims of the left wing's rise to power who have fled the country have charged the regime with unleashing a reign of terror and forcing thousands to take refuge in the YAR. Even sympathetic observers like Rouleau have reported that some of the peasant militia uprisings against landowners were bloody and sometimes degenerated into "sordid vendettas."[66] The darker side of the revolution is also indicated by the assassinations of regime enemies which occur periodically in north Yemen and Beirut, and by mysterious accidents that befall suspect elements in the PDRY itself.[67]

The NLF has been quite successful on the whole in building a coherent and legitimate political order. The ideology of Marxism-Leninism and the structure of the front have been instrumental to this end. The regime appears to have established effective control over the masses and elicited widespread support. Its main problem would seem to be the management of conflict within the top ranks of the front itself and the other progressive forces. This is the same problem which I have identified in the other revolutionary regimes, particularly those in which political religion is so salient. The leadership indicated an awareness of this problem when it called for an enlargement and reorganization of the front in its Fifth Congress Report. In early 1975, it was reported that the front had decided to create a new ruling party, which would include itself, the Communist party, the Ba'th, and representatives of its militia.[68] This development appeared similar to

66. Rouleau, op. cit., p. 9 in the MERIP reprint.

67. An example is the assassination of Muhammad Ali Shu'aiby in Beirut in July 1973. He had left the PDRY early in 1972 and joined an anti-NLF movement. He had just published a book accusing the regime of atrocities. The killer was never found.

68. Joseph Fitchett, "South Yemen Spurns Arab Aid," *Washington Post*, April 20, 1975.

the limited "openings" I have noted in the Syrian and Iraqi Ba'th regimes. The question of personal rivalries also arises. Although any kind of personality cult is unacceptable on ideological grounds, the two strongest figures in the regime, Abd al-Fattah Isma'il, secretary general of the front, and Salim Robaya Ali, the chairman of the Presidential Council, are thought to be rivals. Personal differences are exacerbated by external factors. Following the relaxation of inter-Arab tensions that followed the 1973 war and oil embargo, Egypt and Sa'udi Arabia reportedly offered financial aid if the PDRY would reduce or halt its ideological crusade against the monarchies of the Arabian peninsula. The proffered aid was not inconsiderable: it amounted to about one-fifth of the PDRY's GNP. Salim Robaya Ali appeared receptive to these initiatives. But Abd al-Fattah was true to his oft-stated ideological militance and opposed them. At the Sixth General Conference of the National Front in March 1975, Isma'il's faction predominated and the aid offer was rejected. The Sa'udi initiatives continued, however, and in March 1976 the two countries established diplomatic relations. Lured by a reported Sa'udi aid offer of $400 million, and at the same chastened by the near-collapse of the Dhofar rebellion, it appeared that the PDRY leadership had agreed to moderate its liberationist position in regional affairs.[69] It was not immediately clear what the costs of this tactical retreat to the right might amount to in terms of party and regime cohesion. It was interesting to observe, however, that the regime's closest ally in the region, Iraq, was angered by Aden's new relationship with Riyadh.

The remarkable case of the PDRY suggests that radical political transformation can take place in Arab political culture, even one that borrows ideologically from an intellectual tradition seemingly alien to the Arab and Islamic experience. The secret of its success—which is not inconsiderable in light of the country's poverty, isolation, and hostile political environment—has been organizational as well as ideological. The NLF developed at the grass-roots level during the struggle for independence and was able after independence to retain its coherence and broad-based influence. But a regime which depends so heavily upon a single-party organization to institutionalize a comprehensive ideology needs to have very strong internal mechanisms for interpretation of dogma and resolution of personal rivalries. External

69. Joseph Fitchett, "Saudi-Yemen Ties Seen Breakthrough," *The Washington Post*, March 12, 1976; and John K. Cooley, "Saudi-Yemen Detente Irritates Iran," *The Christian Science Monitor*, May 4, 1976.

conditions also play an important role in shaping regime legitimacy and stability in the PDRY, as they do in so many Arab countries: what the Sa'udis, with their profound antipathy for the radical socialist-nationalist ideological challenge of the Aden government, may have failed to destroy by supporting tribal insurgency against it, they might succeed in undermining with promises of aid.

THE ALGERIAN PEOPLE'S DEMOCRATIC REPUBLIC

The originality and the impatient richness of the Revolution are now and forever the great victories of the Algerian people. This community in action, renovated and free of any psychological, emotional, or legal subjection, is prepared today to assume modern and democratic responsibilities of exceptional moment... The same time that the colonized man braces himself to reject oppression, a radical transformation takes place within him which makes any attempt to maintain the colonial system impossible and shocking. . . . We say firmly that Algerian man and Algerian society have stripped themselves of the mental sedimentation and of the emotional and intellectual handicaps which resulted from 130 years of oppression.[70]

Algeria—the quintessence of the revolutionary polity—finally achieved independence on July 3, 1962, after seven bloody years of insurrection. No country in the Arab world had experienced such lengthy and thorough colonial settlement; none had experienced an independence struggle so traumatic or involving so much mass participation. As Fanon so eloquently described it, this was more than a mere political revolution; it was a psychological and social transformation affecting the family, the status of women, and above all the self-orientation and political identity of the Algerian people. Without denigrating the years of nationalist activity that preceded the uprising that began in November 1954, one can hardly overemphasize the significance of the revolutionary event itself as a source of the legitimizing mythology that has sustained Algeria through its unusually severe postindependence growing pains. Despite serious obstacles, Algeria has emerged as one of the most stable and seemingly successful of the Arab revolutionary republics. But the question remains as to how deep-rooted the stability is and how complete the success. Algeria's political legitimacy may be more fragile than it seems.

70. Frantz Fanon, *A Dying Colonialism* (New York: Grove Press, 1967; originally published in France as *L'an cinq de la révolution algérienne*, 1959), p. 179.

Obstacles to Community

Algeria embarked shakily on the road to independence, lacking many of the building blocks of system legitimacy. Its society had been disrupted, its economy was barely functioning, and its political life was plagued by the personal rivalries within the small revolutionary elite.[71]

Algeria's identity problem arises in part from a lack of historical continuity as a distinct political entity. Prior to the French invasion in 1830 the Regency of Algiers was but a small coastal principality under the Ottoman sultan, and the mountainous tribal areas were societies unto themselves. By way of contrast, Egypt and the neighboring states of Tunisia and Morocco possessed more historical coherence. The identity problem is also a product of France's long occupation and its effort to make Algeria an integral part of France itself. The French occupation of Algeria was far more disruptive of society and culture than any other colonial enterprise in the Arab world, even the British occupation of Egypt. Britain had sent relatively few administrators and had operated through existing structures; France sent hundreds of thousands of settlers who gradually drove out the native tribes and peasantry in much the way American settlers displaced the Indians. The destruction of traditional society has been documented by French scholars such as Jacques Berque and Pierre Bourdieu.[72] Among its more serious consequences were massive migrations to the cities and widespread unemployment. In both rural and urban Algeria—never closely integrated during the colonial period—society and community had broken down.

As if this historical trauma were not enough, there were other challenges to legitimacy in Algerian political culture. One was the cleavage between Arabs and Berbers. Although, as we have been in chapter 3 above, Arab-Berber tensions have on the whole been successfully managed and although the Berbers themselves are divided into four major subgroups—the Kabyles, Shawia, Tuaregs and Mozabites—the existence of a large non-Arab minority presents a potential problem for the regime that pursues Arabization as a legitimizing

71. For a systematic and informative analysis of the Algerian elite, see William B. Quandt, *Revolution and Political Leadership: Algeria 1954–1968* (Cambridge, Mass.: MIT Press, 1969), esp. chaps. 8 and 11.

72. Jacques Berque, *French North Africa* (London: Faber and Faber, 1967; originally published in France as *Le Maghrib entre deux guerres*, 1962), chaps. 8–12; and Pierre Bourdieu, *The Algerians* (Boston: Beacon Press, 1962; originally published in France as *Sociologie de l'Algérie*, 1958), chap. 6.

strategy. The Kabyles in particular, by virtue of their proximity to the capital, their presence in the bureaucracy, and their articulate, educated Francophone stratum are an element to be reckoned with. Berber-Arab differences partially overlap another major cleavage with afflicts the educated sector: the Arab-Islamic versus the Francophone-secular elements. To be a consistent revolutionary in this society is not easy because the Francophone, who ardently believes in rational, secular egalitarianism and who may reject Islamic ideas about education, women, morality, and law, must somehow coexist with his Muslim comrade-in-arms, who is Arabic-trained, committed to an Arab-Islamic renaissance with its implicit rejection of Western decadence, and hostile toward neo-imperialism in all its aspects, including linguistic and cultural. Furthermore, even within the Islamicized population, tensions between the orthodox and maraboutic religious tendencies weaken the integrating functions of Islam. Finally, as Algeria rapidly develops the huge bureaucracy of a welfare state, we observe yet another (again partially overlapping) cleavage between ideology and technocracy. Can the French-educated government sector, with its rationalist but hierarchical orientations, with its predilection for routine and procedure, function compatibly in the service of a political regime with seeks legitimacy through Arabization, Islamicization, and democratic socialism? Algerian political culture is divided in many ways: socially, in terms of income inequality; geographically, in terms of the rural-urban gap; linguistically, in terms of the Arabophone-Francophone difference; and finally in terms of world views which pit Islamic piety against modern secularism. Whoever rules must rely heavily on the military and civilian bureaucracies for internal security and administrative performance, but for popular legitimacy he must draw upon the diverse but somewhat incompatible collection of salient symbols which are found in modern Algerian society.

The problem of building legitimacy has not been easy. Some of the closest observers of Algerian politics have suggested or implied that the achievement of a state legitimate order has yet to be accomplished. For example, C. H. Moore, writing in 1970, contrasted the success of rationalist legitimacy in Tunisia, which he designated "the triumph of reason," with the Algerian "non-party state," in which rationalism was submerged. "Legitimacy is minimal," he declared.[73] W. B. Quandt observed that personality clashes or personal rivalries were more

73. Clement Henry Moore, *Politics in North Africa* (Boston: Little, Brown, 1970), pp. 95 ff. and 118 ff.

important for explaining Algerian political behavior than ideology;[74] furthermore, because the elite was so unstable and the system development so "undetermined" during its first years, it might become either more rigid, authoritarian, and unresponsive or more pragmatic, tolerant, and participant.[75] In assessing the prospects for stability David and Marina Ottaway suggested that President Houari Boumedienne's success in consolidating his personal power after the overthrow of Ahmad Ben Bella in 1965 might not guarantee the longevity of the regime. "Today [1970] Algeria is ruled by a nonelected president, a nonfunctioning Revolutionary Council, and a poorly organized party . . ."[76] They concluded that he would have to find a new, more permanent basis of power, in particular a strong party. But the task was seen as very difficult to accomplish, owing to the heterogeneous nature of the independence movement.[77]

The Primacy of Ideology

In Algeria, as we have seen, some observers doubt that ideology explains much about elite political behavior—not as much as least as personal rivalries and intragroup distrust. It may be true that ideology does not explain elite behavior in any specific sense; certainly it has not prevented serious intraelite conflict, especially in the 1962–65 period. How then does one explain how the Boumedienne regime succeeded in bringing such considerable coherence to the Algerian political process? For by the early 1970s, Algeria ranked with the most stable of the revolutionary systems, Egypt and Tunisia; and this stability had been achieved without Draconian repression. The main source of legitimacy clearly was not personal, for Colonel Boumedienne lacked charisma and a mass following. Nor was it structural, for the revolutionary organizations had become divided among themselves, and the National Liberation Front itself, supposedly the single-party armature of the system, had declined to a position of marginal power.

Ideology, after all, may have played the most important part in nurturing the legitimacy that brought about Algeria's surprising stability. The values which make up the Algerian ideology—national liberation, Arabism, Islam, the Third World, anti-imperialism, and socialism—each with their appeal to particular segments of the

74. Quandt, op. cit., p. 266.
75. Ibid., p. 276.
76. David and Marina Ottaway, *Algeria: The Politics of a Socialist Revolution* (Berkeley: University of California Press, 1970), pp. 282–83.
77. Ibid., p. 285.

society, helped bring together an adequate elite coalition with at least minimal harmony: the military, the ex-guerrillas, the National Liberation Front, and the technocrats. At the mass level, this value constellation may have begun to bridge the gap between traditional and modern orientations through its balanced emphasis on Islam, socialism, and Arabism.

Because the former president, Ahmad Ben Bella, was so well known for his strong liberationist position, supporting anti-imperalist movements in Africa especially, it has been suggested that his successor, Boumedienne, was relatively nonideological. But while the Boumedienne regime moved to establish significant economic relationships with the United States and France, it certainly did not bring about an end of ideology in Algeria. Its support for Third World causes continued. If anything, it increased its linkages with the Arab east, especially after Israel's defeat of Egypt, Syria, and Jordan in 1967. It became perhaps the major supporter of the Palestinian Liberation movement, supplying (by its own official estimate) some 80 percent of *fida'iyin* weapons.[78] On the domestic front, the new regime continued inexorably the program of Arabizing the educational system. Its efforts to implement the principle of state socialism through the development of public corporations like the national oil and gas corporation, Sonatrach, were carried considerably further than during the Ben Bella era. American businessmen saw Algeria's readiness to trade with the number one imperalist power—the bête noire of Vietnam and the Middle East—as evidence of pragmatism. But the militant ideology was still very much present, performing an important legitimizing function for a regime still lacking institutions for participation, legal opposition, and peaceable transfer of power.

Nationalism, Islam, and Revolution

If there is a single key to the relative success of the Algerian legitimacy formula, it is the linkage of traditional Islam, modern Arabism, and revolution to build an Algerian identity. This is the identity that the liberal leader Ferhat Abbas, in a famous speech in 1936, said he could not find: "If I had discovered the Algerian nation, I would have become a nationalist . . . I did not discover it. I looked to history,

78. According to Muhammad Yazid, in an interview in *L'Orient-Le Jour* (Beirut), August 14, 1971. Yazid, one of the major figures of the revolution, had been sent as ambassador to Lebanon and, it was said, to the PLO. In this interview he also gave some examples of Algeria's growing links with the Arab east, noting the use of Lebanese educational, literary, and mass media materials in Algeria's Arabization program, and the fact that the airplanes of Air Algérie were maintained and repaired in the workshops of Lebanon's Middle East Airlines.

I questioned the living and the dead. I could not find it . . . We have therefore pushed aside all the clouds and dreams to definitely tie our future to the French achievement in this country . . ."[79] But even as he was expressing these sentiments, he was being undermined by the Islamic nationalist movements of the ulama and of Messali Hajj, while the French themselves were on the verge of aborting their own liberal-assimilationist plans for Algeria laid down in the Blum-Violette Plan. Abbas was only one of the many Westernized politicians across the Arab world who were to underestimate the appeal of Islamic, anti-imperalist, and ethnic-national values for building political legitimacy in an age of rapid social mobilization; others were Nuri al-Sa'id in Iraq and Camille Chamoun in Lebanon—both nationalists but all outbid by more radical nationalist competitors.

Ferhat Abbas's group, the Democratic Union for the Algerian Manifesto (UDMA), was comprised primarily of secular, middle-class Muslims with a French education. But the Etoile Nord Africaine of Messali Hajj, and its successor organizations, had a largely urban working-class base. The founder, originally a Communist, later emphasized Islam, and so his movement reflected his dual class struggle and religious orientation. In its later form, as the Movement for the Triumph of Democratic Liberties (MTLD), it gave rise to a secret and autonomous Special Organization (OS) which in turn was the primary base for the Revolutionary Committee for Unity and Action (CRUA). This is turn later became the National Liberation Front (FLN) that initiated the revolution in 1954. Although Messali Hajj did not participate in the struggle of the 1950s, he stands never-theless as a patron of mass-based, militant anticolonialism and Islamic nationalism. His organizations served as a structural framework within which the revolutionaries, which Quandt distinguishes from the liberals and radicals more willing to act within the system,[80] worked to implement the doctrine of armed struggle and implant a sense of common identity. Later this militant orientation was elabor-ated by Frantz Fanon, whose analysis of the cultural and psychological paralysis imposed by the West on the native society and personality provides an important insight into revolutionary ideology.[81] But in trying to build positive foundations for Algerian identity upon their militant rejection of Western tutelage, Messali and his successors turned back to the Arab-Islamic character of North Africa's indigenous

79. Cited in Alf Andrew Heggoy, *Insurgency and Counter Insurgency in Algeria* (Bloomington: Indiana University Press, 1972), p. 14.

80. Quandt, op. cit., chap. 5.

81. Frantz Fanon, op. cit., and *The Wretched of the Earth* (London: Penguin Books, 1967).

culture; and once the political rejection of France was complete, it was this historical identity that would help the postindependence regimes overcome the inevitable splintering of the revolutionary front. The second of the two more authentic alternatives to the liberal-assimilationists was the Association of Ulama whose principal leader was Shaykh Abd al-Hamid Ben Badis, a follower of the Salafiyya Islamic Reform movement of Muhammad Abdu and Rashid Rida. The ulama, through their Qur'anic schools, the *madrasas*, had at hand a rather elaborate organizational structure; it is a significant example of the multifunctionality of traditional structures and their relevance for legitimacy. Religious self-purification was the stated objective of these ulama; they were especially concerned with what they saw as the corruption of the marabout orders and brotherhoods. The ulama naturally opposed the Western cultural intrusion and resented the pro-French attitude of some of the maraboutie orders. There were numerous clashes between the orthodox Muslims and the French, for example when the ulama reconverted a mosque used since the conquest as a military supply depot, much to the anguish of the *colon* taxpayers who did not wish to pay for a new one.[82]

After independence, the transition from Ben Bella to Boumedienne brought about a new emphasis on Islam. Part of the difference in emphasis may have been due to the education of the respective leaders: Ben Bella was educated in French schools while Boumedienne studied at the Kitaniyya madrasa in conservative Constantine.[83] Whereas Ben Bella had on occasion slighted the religious nationalists, as many secular revolutionaries in the Arab east have also done, Boumedienne was much more supportive of religion. From a radical secular point of view his position was retrogressive, but as a means of extracting legitimacy at the mass level it appears to have been successful.[84]

The Tradition of Resistance

The salience of the Arab-Islamic tradition for nascent Algerian nationalism is due to more than its historic imprint from medieval times, which I have discussed in an earlier chapter. The tradition of resistance to the long French settler-occupation also played a role which

82. A.-G. Bouvreuil, "Agitation politique et religieuse chez les Musulmans d'Algérie", *Afrique Française*, no. 10 (October 1936), p. 534.

83. Quandt, op. cit., p. 14; Ottaway, op. cit., p. 296.

84. It is interesting to note that a similar controversy on the revolutionary legitimacy of Islamic values has arisen since the late 1960s within Palestinian nationalist circles and that one acute observer of Palestinian politics has attacked the leadership for neglecting Islam as a source of legitimacy. See the review article by Abdullah Schleifer, "Roots of the Resistance", *Journal of Palestine Studies* 2, 2 (Winter 1973), pp. 120–31.

had complex ramifications. On the one hand, the occupation fragmented the predominantly tribal society, but this fragmentation not only paved the way for the imposition of French values and authority patterns, it also broke down tribal parochialism, clearing the path for the subsequent resuscitation of commitments to the broad, orthodox Islamic umma. And although the colonial administrators sought to develop the marabout orders as compliant political structures, they also generated a process, and with it a mythology, of resistance. The preeminent hero of the resistance was Abd al-Qadir, whose valor was exceeded only by his chivalry; both of which were recognized by friend and foe alike.[85] Despite his marabout upbringing and his later reconciliation with the French, he became a symbol of the Arab-Islamic refusal to submit. It is significant that Abd al-Qadir was celebrated in the Arab east as well; upon his release from imprisonment in France he settled eventually in Damascus where he was reversed as both an Islamic scholar and a faithful defender of the Islamic polity. The tradition of resistance, enshrined in song and story, was propagated throughout Algeria by itinerant troubadours and artisans; and since the revolution, particularly since the Boumedienne coup, the Islamic basis of that resistance has become one of the principal legitimizing themes of the regime.

In emphasizing the importance of Arab-Islamic themes in the Algerian legitimacy formula, I do not mean to suggest that a new identity has clearly emerged. The inadequacy of education, communications and political institutionalization indicates that the process of developing such an identity is yet unfinished. The same conflicts between the secular and the religious that divide elites throughout the Arab world are still present in Algeria. The conflict between local religious practice and rationalist orthodox Islam divides generations throughout Algeria, particularly as education and governmental influence spread. The conflict between pan-Arabism or even broader commitments, on the one hand, and a doctrine of "turning inward" toward a particularist Algerian development is also evident. Understandably, the pronouncements and actions of President Boumedienne vis à vis these conflicts have been prudent and deliberately vague.

Regime Performance and Legitimacy

Ideology alone, no matter how congruent with basic values, would not be enough to support a legitimate political order, particularly

---

85. See Wilfrid Blunt, *Desert Hawk: Abd El Kader and the French Conquest of Algeria* (London: Methuen & Co., 1947).

when personal and structural legitimacy is relatively weak. But in revolutionary Algeria geology and technocracy have combined with ideology to bring about an effective level of governmental performance. Rapid economic development has been made possible through the fast-rising revenues from Algerian natural gas and a determination on the part of the leadership to exploit science and technology to the fullest extent. And in the conduct of foreign policy, the Algerians have demonstrated the ability to play a leading role, utilizing simultaneously their revolutionary ideological stature and a well-developed sense of pragmatism. Leadership on the international stage redounds to regime legitimacy at home.

The struggle for independence had left nearly 1 million dead or missing and at least another 2 million uprooted; 800,000 Europeans had fled, including most of the professionally trained infrastructure.[86] Yet from 1964 through 1972, gross domestic product increased by an average of 10 percent annually. Between 1968 and 1972 there was a 70 percent increase in governmental revenue and a 55 percent increase in expenditures. Energy use increased by 75 percent between 1969 and 1973. During the latter period natural gas production tripled and crude oil production increased by a third.[87] Heavy emphasis was placed on industrial development during the first years of the Boumedienne regime and considerable success was achieved. The $7 billion industrial development program (1970–73) which had looked over-ambitious at the time was substantially carried out and a new one double in scope was proclaimed in mid-1973, just before the enormous increase in world petroleum prices.[88] After the oil price increase, the 1974–77 development plan was revised upward to $22.5 billion.[89] A $1.7 billion deal was concluded between Algeria and the American El Paso Natural Gas Company that would bring Algerian natural gas to East Coast cities. Accompanying this growth has been a substantial injection of American, French, and Russian technical and managerial assistance; even while Algerian-American relations were in suspension, big U.S. consulting firms like Kidder, Peabody and Company, and Booz, Allen and Hamilton were engaged in contrast research to Algerian state firms. The agricultural sector, however, was neglected until November 1971, when the government finally launched an

86. Charles F. Gallagher, *The United States and North Africa* (Cambridge: Harvard University Press, 1963), p. 105.

87. "State Capitalism in Algeria", *MERIP Reports*, no. 35 (February 1975), pp. 11–14.

88. As reported in *The Daily Star* (Beirut), June 30, 1973.

89. *The Christian Science Monitor*, May 28, 1974.

agrarian reform program. Agriculture, which employs some 60 percent of the labor force, is due to receive major attention in the "second phase" of President Boumedienne's socialist program. By mid-1973, according to Arab press reports, there were over 3,600 cooperatives involving over 50,000 farmers—still only a small fraction of the 1.3 million agricultural labor force;[90] and the nationalization of large landholdings had only just begun.[91] Obviously, much remained to be done in this sector, and it cannot be said that all the main impediments to economic development had been overcome. Nevertheless, according to some foreign economic experts, an impressive start had been made and official attention was being directed to the persisting problem areas.[92] The Boumedienne regime appeared effectively to have harnessed hydrocarbons in behalf of a development-oriented state socialism. Compared to many other countries in the region, such as Egypt or Morocco, the Algerian performance was impressive and thus contributing positively to system legitimacy.

The second policy area in which the Algerian regime has performed well is foreign affairs. Capitalizing on the symbolic salience of the revolutionary struggle, both Algerian regimes since independence have asserted successfully a claim to leadership of the Third World countries in world affairs. In the early 1970s, Algiers was a meeting place for liberation movements around the world, including Quebec separatists, American blacks, Palestinian nationalists, and numerous other Asian and African groups. It plays a major role in the Organization of African Unity. It has been extremely active in eastern Arab affairs, providing material and diplomatic support for the Arab states, and especially the Palestinian national movement, against Israel. In 1975 President Boumedienne used his good offices to help settle the explosive conflict between Iraq and Iran. While Algeria has not made a bid for hegemony in the Arab world in the manner of Abd al-Nasir, its participation and commitment to the Arab-Israeli struggle since 1967 has been more substantial than that of the Ben Bella regime, apart from propaganda. And the Algerian support for Maghrib unity has been reemphasized by President Boumedienne, although the Moroccan take-over of Spanish Sahara in 1975 has virtually paralyzed the slow progress achieved toward this goal after the Algeria-Morocco border war of 1963. Perhaps Algeria's most important role has been

90. *MERIP Reports*, op. cit., pp. 15 and 18, citing Georges Rassi in *Al-Balagh* (Beirut).

91. *The Daily Star* (Beirut), June 18, 1973.

92. See, e.g., Norman Macrae, "The Socialist Revolutionaries are at Take-Off Point," *The Economist* (London), April 13, 1974, pp. 41-45.

to lead the oil and other raw material exporting countries of the Third World in pressing the industrialized consumer nations to pay more for their exports. As an advocate of a militant oil boycott policy against states supporting Israel, the regime doubtless has gained much stature among its people and in the Arab world generally. Yet its militance is tempered with *realpolitik*: ideological differences did not prevent high Algerian and Sa'udi Arabian officials from touring Europe and the United States together to explain the 1973–74 Arab oil embargo. And in its relations with the superpowers, Algeria has been able to deal profitably with each and yet retain its Third World anti-imperialist, neutralist purity. Not perhaps since Nasir so brilliantly won the hearts and minds of Egyptians and other Arabs through his regional and international initiatives has an Arab regime been as successful as Algeria's in exploiting external conditions for internal legitimacy.

Flaws in the Formula

Revolutionary Algeria epitomizes the ideological-technocratic form of legitimacy. The media and educational curricula are suffused with the symbols of the new Algerian man and society; the regime is the voice of the people, the authentic representative of the masses. At the same time the country is managed by a new stratum of salaried, highly trained bureaucrats imbued with a rationalistic, scientific orientation; and the state dominates the economy and society. While this strategy has succeeded insofar as it has contributed to a fragile stability and a growth of capabilities, it has also generated tension between the ideologues and technocrats. Critics from the Left charge that truly participatory and democratic socialism cannot be achieved in a political system so dominated by an elitist, centralized bureaucracy.[93]

Algerian system legitimacy is also weakened by the narrow authority base of the rulers. In systems like Algeria's which claim to derive legitimacy from the people, the procedure through which a leader or ruling group achieves power, and the method of power transfer within

---

93. One Marxist critic posed the following (rhetorical) questions: "How can a government build socialism using non-socialist cadres and bureaucrats? How can a political party mobilize the masses to participate in a genuinely socialist construction of the country without revolutionary Marxist militants whose devotion and commitment to the improvement of the living conditions of the masses is unflinching? How can a government, regardless of the sincerity of some of its leaders, overcome the mistrust of the disinherited masses without eliminating from the administration or re-educating the bureaucrats who have generated this mistrust?..." Mahfoud Bennoune, "Algerian Peasants and National Politics," *MERIP Reports*, no. 48 (Washington, D.C.: Middle East Research and Information Project, June 1976), p. 24.

the ruling elite have some bearing on the legitimacy accorded to them. Theoretically there is a need for personal and structural legitimacy, as well as ideological legitimacy. But Algeria has been slow to develop either type. Since the days of Ben Bella, Algeria has not had a charismatic leader of the Nasirist type who could command voluntary obedience or even affection and thus confer legitimacy on the whole system. Houari Boumedienne during his early years of rule rarely appeared in public and refused to try and project a cult of the personality.[94] In his later years he was reported to have abandoned some of the collegiality of decision making and arrogated more personal power to himself, but there was still little indication that he could generate the personal legitimacy of some of the leaders examined in the previous two chapters.

Structural legitimacy is also a problem. In the middle 1970s, the rulers of Algeria were a small group of ex-officers and technocrats divided into cliques and factions; and the Algerian political process at the national level was shrouded in mystery. Although some steps have been taken for promoting mass political participation at the local level, only recently has there been progress of this sort at the national level. Indeed, until 1976 there was retrogression. The FLN, which might have served as the linkage institution between the masses and the government, began to wither away as soon as independence had been achieved. In 1967 Ka'id Ahmad, a dynamic personality, took over the leadership, but even he was unable to resuscitate the party; later he was forced out. Its decline also signaled the exclusion of one of the two main revolutionary factions—the *wilaya* guerrilla organizations that had fought inside Algeria. The other faction was the army of the exterior which was led by professional military officers. Its leaders came to be known as the Wijda group, named for the Moroccan border town which served as their base; and foremost among them was Boumedienne. Boumedienne's coup in 1965 brought this faction to power and accordingly alienated many of the former grass-roots, radical revolutionaries of the interior. The Boumedienne group has been described as oriented more toward bureaucracy, planning, and pragmatic management than the wilayists, who placed a higher priority on mass participation, egalitarianism, and social reform. Since 1965 Boumedienne has consolidated his authority within the ruling elite. There has been a remarkable attrition—through

94. For an interesting portrait of Boumedienne, see Edward R. F. Sheehan, "The Algerians Intend to Go it Alone, Raise Hell, Hold Out and Grow," *The New York Times Magazine*, April 23, 1972, esp. pp. 35–38.

imprisonment, assassination, or exile—of possible rivals among the "historic chiefs" of the revolution. The list includes Ahmad Ben Bella, Belkasim Krim, Hocine Ait Ahmad, Muhammad Khider, and Muhammad Boudiaf. In 1967 Boumedienne crushed a military uprising led by a former wilayist, Col. Tahar Zbiri; the colonel fled to Europe. Interviewed later, he accused "Boumedienne and his clique" of having tried to suppress the development of democratic procedures, just as like his predecessor Ben Bella.[95] In December 1974 the mysterious and violent death of Interior Minister Ahmad Medeghri indicated to some observers that even the "Wijda group"—Boumedienne's old inner circle—was breaking up. According to some reports, President Boumedienne was relying increasingly on the army to provide the structural linkages between the regime and the rival masses and to undertake political education.[96] Analysts disagreed as to whether the increasing role of the army was a step toward democratization or simply another phase of the bureaucratization of the revolution; but if the latter interpretation is the more valid, then the prospects for strengthening structural legitimacy in conformity with the ideology of the revolution are less than bright. The inability of the Algerian leadership to broaden and institutionalize its support base and to devise less Byzantine ways of managing intraelite conflict constitutes a serious problem. In March 1976 four prominent former leaders, Ferhat Abbas, Benyoussef Ben Khedda, Muhammad Khaireddine, and Hocine Lahouel, issued a manifesto accusing the Boumedienne regime of autocracy and calling for a more liberal political order and elections.[97] Shortly thereafter the regime issued (and a national referendum approved) a National Pact reasserting the socialist, progressive, and revolutionary character of Algeria's political development. The pact was interpreted as a rebuff to the liberal-conservatives and their demand for a more open system, and yet only a small step toward the Left—not far enough to satisfy the Marxists and their demand for more participation. Characteristically, Colonel Boumedienne appeared to be moving cautiously, trying to maintain his balance under a diversity of pressures. In November 1976 the electorate overwhelmingly ratified a new constitution which

95. Zbiri was interviewed by John K. Cooley in *The Christian Science Monitor*, August 5 and 6, 1969.

96. Joseph Fitchett, "Algeria: Shifts in Policy and Power," *The Washington Post*, March 16, 1975; and *MERIP Reports*, op. cit., pp. 27–28.

97. Paul Balta, "Algeria—A Growing Liberal Opposition," *Manchester Guardian Weekly*, April 18 and 25, 1976.

reaffirmed Algeria's socialist system and a few weeks later Boumedienne—the sole candidate—was elected president.

Even if Algeria's hydrocarbon reserves should last beyond the 1990s and even if there were not serious current problems with production and corruption, material development alone would probably not be a sufficient solution to Algeria's legitimacy problems. Furthermore, the strategy of pragmatic accommodation within a transformationist framework generates costs as well as benefits. There are those who charge that the regime has sold out the revolution by making concessions to traditional religion. Other critics, many of them veterans of the wilaya guerrilla organizations, accuse it of having created a privileged new middle class of military and civilian technocrats bent on stifling democracy through authoritarian bureaucratic government. To these charges the ideologists of the regime reply that Islam is compatible with the revolution and that an effective socialist-democratic society cannot be built without a solid footing in state-managed economic development. Compounding the challenge to legitimacy raised by these larger issues is the question whether the belated effort to develop elite=mass linkages and better procedures for managing intraelite conflict will in fact succeed in coping with Algeria's political culture tensions.

Tunisia

"Harmony, balance, cohesion, tolerance, contentment"—these are the words which spring to the mind of one who, having completed a long and difficult voyage through Arab politics, finally comes to rest in Tunisia. As we shall see, Tunisia too has its legitimacy problem; but compared to the hidden, simmering politics of the monarchies, the volatile, bitter and tragic politics in the pan-Arab core, and the unformed, often capricious and praetorian politics in the peripheral states, Bourguiba's republic appears as a relatively well legitimized political system.

Like revolutionary Egypt, Tunisia since its independence has been shaped by extraordinary personal leadership. Habib Bourguiba has been dubbed by one authority as a "presidential monarch."[98] If anything, Bourguiba bulks even larger as a source of system legitimacy in Tunisia than did Nasir, and certainly Sadat, in Egypt. The leadership in both polities also developed and exploited a formal ideology to

---

98. Clement H. Moore, *Tunisia Since Independence: The Dynamics of One-Party Rule* (Berkeley: University of California Press, 1965), chap. 3.

enhance communal solidarity and allegiance to the regime. Bourguiba, however, was much more the creator of Bourguibism than Nasir was of Nasirism; and the Bourguibist ideology was instrumental and pragmatic while Nasir's was what Apter would call consummatory and totalistic. Furthermore, Bourguiba fashioned a penetrative, broadly based political movement and came to power through it, while Nasir's structure-building took place "from the top down" and was never as successful as Bourguiba's in bridging the gap between elites and masses. Tunisia may be considered as perhaps the most politically modern of the revolutionary Arab states, in terms of secularism, rationality, and institutionalized participation. Certainly it has been one of the most stable. But whereas Egypt after Nasir began moving toward pragmatism and liberalization, Tunisia has lost much of its original broad systemic legitimacy because of the aging Bourguiba's increasingly autocratic leadership. But as the Bourguiba era draws to its inevitable end, the question which confronts analysts is whether the Tunisian legitimacy formula still represents a deep-rooted and mutually supportive combination of the traditional and modern, or whether the extraordinary force of Bourguiba's leadership has masked or even impeded the development of a coherent political order over the long term. To explore this question, I first examine the historical process through which Tunisia gained its identity as a secular nationalist polity and then compare the systemic basis of its present-day legitimacy.

Toward a Secular Polity

Compared to most Arab societies, Tunisia is relatively unmarked by clan and tribal divisions: a century of exposure to European influence and social modernization has helped erase primordial cleavages that were, in any case, less sharply defined than elsewhere. The classical conflict between the mountainous interior and the coastal *sahil* was less intense than in Algeria or Morocco.[99] Nor were there particularly severe religious or ethnolinguistic cleavages, for orthodox Islam and Arabism were relatively unchallenged. Tunisia even had a historical territorial coherence and identity that was stronger than in nearly all the other Arab countries.

While traditionally the kinship basis of authority manifested itself in the patriarchal rule of the bey, this rule was relatively continuous and stable, unafflicted by the internecine parochial struggles experienced by several other Arab patriarchies. In fact, a single dynasty,

99. Moore, op. cit., p. 14.

the Husainids, ruled continuously from 1705 until 1957 when the monarchy was legislated out of existence as the result of strong pressure from Habib Bourguiba. Second, it was progressively limited and transformed, in a process beginning in the middle of the nineteenth century: milestones in this process were the Fundamental Law of 1857 which established rights for Muslims and non-Muslims, the Organic Law of 1861 which, as Nicola Ziadeh tells us, was the first constitution for an Ottoman territory, and the infrastructure developments carried out by the bey's reformist minister Khaireddine.[100] In 1881 France established its protectorate over Tunisia and proceded further to weaken the patriarchal basis of legitimacy by emasculating the office. The rise of the Tunisian national movement in the late 1880s was another landmark event in the shift away from classical kinship-based legitimacy.

The salience of Islam as a component of Tunisian identity and a legitimizing value has been much slower to diminish. Indeed, it suffused the first generation nationalist movement and has persisted even into the age of Bourguibist secularism. As in Turkey and Egypt, the first stage in the movement for national self-assertion was pan-Islamic. The Young Tunisian circle of the 1890s and early 1900s was influenced by the Young Ottomans and by the Salafiyya reform movement of Muhammad Abdu. Ziadeh quotes Ali Bash Hanba, one of the leading early nationalists, writing in his newspaper, *Le Tunisien* (in French), in 1910, as follows:

> Every Muslim is a supporter of Muslim union, and Tunisians, to a man, are partisans of this policy and are attached to pan-Ottomanism, which is a consequence of such an idea and a magnificent manifestation of it. If our modern education has given us a new mentality, we have, all the same, as Muslims, reserved our strong loyalty to our brethren in every country. The Turks and Egyptians inspire us with feelings as much as our nearer neighbors in Algeria or the peoples in further Asia.[101]

Some of the most serious outbreaks of violence against the protectorate in the pre–World War I period, were set off by religious incidents. The post–World War I period witnessed what some scholars see as a second stage of Tunisian nationalism, embodied in the Destour (Constitution) party and a growing drive for independence from

100. Nicola A. Ziadeh, *Origins of Nationalism in Tunisia* (Beirut: American University of Beirut, 1962), pp. 12 ff.

101. Cited by Ziadeh, op. cit., p. 80.

France. But it too retained distinctly religious overtones. Its main leader, Abd al-Aziz al-Tha'alibi, was Muslim shaykh with a learned Qur'anic background; and an important book attributed to him (*La Tunisie Martyre*, 1923) called for (among other things) a resuscitation and expansion of Islamic jurisprudence and education, and it attacked the French for polluting the identity and natural development of the Tunisians.[102]

Bourguiba and his Neo-Destour assumed the leadership of the nationalist movement in 1934, and from that time forward Islam was downgraded as an element in the Tunisian legitimacy formula. After independence in 1956 the Supreme Combatant (as he was and continues to be called) took a number of steps to promote the secular character of Tunisian nationalism. He promulgated a secular personal status legal code in 1956. He gave voting rights to women in 1957. He reformed the prestigious Islamic Zaytouna University and the *habous* (or *waqf*) system of religious endowments in 1959. And in 1961 he tried but failed to convert the month of religious fasting (Ramadan) into a period of mobilization for social development.[103] Apart from Turkey under Ataturk, no contemporary Middle Eastern regime has challenged Islam's influence in social and political affairs as directly as Tunisia under Bourguiba. Not even polities that are otherwise considered quite secularized, like Egypt, or Marxist, like the PDRY, or radical-nationalist, like Syria and Iraq, have matched Bourguiba in the effort to minimize religion in politics.

But if the influence of religion in politics was considerably reduced during the Bourguiba period—the reduction due in part to the prior imperialist and nationalist experiences—it was by no means eliminated. As long as Islamic values remained intact, a political system with a nonreligious or antireligious legitimacy formula would be vulnerable to attack by the partisans of religion. Indeed, the most serious challenge to Bourguiba's autocratic leadership—that of Salah Ben Yussef in 1955–56—was strong in its emphasis on Islamic symbols as well as the ideology of eastern Arab nationalism. While Bourguiba was able to carry out successfully several reforms, he was unable to win his battle over Ramadan, and he was obliged to make a number of gestures toward the "Old Turbans," as he called the religious conservatives, such as having his French Catholic wife convert to Islam in 1960. Certainly the instrumentalities of Bourguiba's successful

---

102. Ziadeh, op. cit., chap. 5, pp. 89–127, esp. pp. 103–4.

103. See Moore, op. cit., pp. 49–55, and Charles Debbasch, *La République Tunisienne* (Paris: Librairie Générale de Droit et de Jurisprudence, 1962), pp. 141–52.

secularism—the well-organized Neo-Destour party, the strong presidential constitutional system, and his own leadership—eclipsed the clerical elite and religious students, as well as other traditional structures like the monarchy, by 1957; but the religious elements were not entirely eliminated. In the post-Bourguiba era, they may reassert themselves, as they have in Algeria and Egypt.

The Nationalist Struggle

Not only does Tunisia's long existence as a continuous political entity facilitate system legitimacy, its more recent historical experience has also constituted an ideological legitimacy resource. The memories of resistance to colonialism are interwoven with nationalism and Bourguibism to provide the sense of community in modern Tunisia. In the formative period of modern Tunisian history from the late nineteenth century up until the end of World War I, the tradition of administrative autonomy, on the one hand, and the disruptive character of the French protectorate, on the other, helped build national identity; moreover, the tension between the two served to accentuate their effect. In the next period, which ended with the armed struggle for independence, the Destour party of al-Tha'alibi popularized the theme of Catholic, colonialist France's negative impact on the growth of Tunisia's authentic culture, society, and political autonomy. The theme proved more durable than the Destour party itself, which shortly disintegrated as an effective structure because of intraelite conflict, a condition which we have seen is virtually endemic in Arab polities. By 1934 Habib Bourguiba had returned from France to form the Neo-Destour and was beginning to apply his organizational genius and his masterly tactic of force-with-diplomacy. In Tunisia, as in Egypt, Algeria, Palestine, Syria, and Iraq, the anticolonial movement took an increasingly violent turn. Tunisia experienced its equivalent of Egypt's Denshwai incident when, on April 9, 1938, French soldiers shot 122 Tunisians in a nationalist demonstration for fomenting sedition. Bourguiba's movement continued to grow in organizational strength and political influence, despite his arrest and imprisonment.

But it is the violent 1950s, when Tunisia crossed the revolutionary divide, that has contributed most to the Tunisian polity's present legitimacy. The assassinations, armed attacks, and subversion carried out by the *fallaghas* (guerrillas) in the 1952–55 period not only pressured France into granting autonomy and later full independence but also forged a sense of national community far more profound than the earlier activities of the bourgeois nationalists. Because Bourguiba's Neo-Destour was the structural vanguard of this struggle, it became the beneficiary of revolutionary sanctity. And Bourguiba, after quickly eliminating his rival Ben Yussef, was able to arrogate to himself a monopoly of the legitimacy accruing from the achievement of independence—more completely so, perhaps, than any other Arab leader besides Muhammad V and Nasir.

The Tunisian legitimacy formula, when analyzed in terms of the political culture values it embodies, stands out as one of the least traditional in the Arab world. Kinship now has little place except through the metaphorical paternalism of the Supreme Combatant. The principal pillar appears to be the historical experience of national resistance and victory. But this nationalism has a parochial focus and it abjures the Arab and Islamic themes that are so prominent in most other nationalisms of the Arab world. One might conclude that the Tunisian legitimacy formula appears relatively impoverished, in terms of the ubiquitous values, symbols, and myths which it does *not* rest upon; but then the question remains, Why has this formula been so comparatively successful? To answer I turn to the political system itself and the personal, ideological, and structural bases of its legitimacy.

Systemic Bases of Legitimacy

Probably no other Arab regime has developed the broad-based systemic sources of legitimacy which are found in this nation of six million. The leadership of Bourguiba—the father of his country—is venerated. The ideology of Bourguibism is didactic, dynamic, and ubiquitous. The structures of government, especially the Destour party, are complex and accepted as the proper procedures for public decision making. Some other states in the region have revered leaders; others have widely and intensely held ideologies; a few even have valued structures. But Tunisia is almost unique in the extent to which it has had all three.

Preeminent among them is the personal leadership of Bourguiba. Forceful leadership can serve as a bridge, and perhaps even as a substitute, for structural legitimacy in newly independent regimes. Notwithstanding the rationality and elaborate structures of the Tunisian system, Bourguiba remains at the very center of the legitimacy equation. Moore has made two revealing observations about Bourguiba, characterizing him (as noted above) as a "presidential monarch," and suggesting that he is not charismatic in the strict sense of the term.[104] Indeed, having replaced the bey and embellished his

104. Moore, op. cit., chaps. 2 and 3, esp. pp. 46–47, 80–81.

presidency with all the trappings of monarchy, including virtually absolute authority, Bourguiba might indeed be designated as a traditional patriarch. Actually, however, he is both more and less than a king: more, in that he has generated his own political religion, Bourguibism, with himself at the center (and in which the scriptures of socialism and democracy are subordinate); but less, in that he has systematically undermined the traditional values which would normally legitimize a monarch.[105] It is also correct to withhold the designation "charismatic," at least in the strict sense of the word, inasmuch as Tunisians do not ascribe to him magical, sacred, or supernatural characteristics. Bourguiba's enormous legitimacy derives from his historical embodiment of the most cherished symbols and values of Tunisian national identity and independence. His accomplishments as an ordinary man have inspired such deference that even the public revelations of his infirmities of mind and body in his later years have not seriously undermined it. In fact, the Destour party and the National Assembly declared Bourguiba president for life in March 1975.

The Supreme Combatant has not been content to legitimize his rule simply on the basis of the accomplishments of the past. Instead, he has attempted to mobilize the Tunisian nation—and in the process to enhance regime legitimacy—by tirelessly promulgating an ideology of national integration and social development. Bourguibism insists upon the need to shake off the traditional values and habits that retard Tunisia's modernization through improving educational opportunities and economic growth and the necessity of pursuing these goals efficiently, through the guidance of wise and authoritative leadership. The unity of the nation has been furthered by the elaboration and further institutionalization of the Destour party, which Bourguiba has always considered as an expression of the whole nation. The party's emphasis on civic training is amplified through various institutions of the state as well: notably the educational system, cultural centers, and the mass media of information and propaganda.[106] In man, says Bourguiba, "there meet the angel and the ape. . . . In order to get him

---

105. A small illustration of Bourguiba's sensitivity at being identified with the trappings of monarchy may be found in his speech, "Chacun de nous est responsable du progrès de la nation" (delivered at Carthage, March 27, 1968). He feels compelled to conclude this speech by protesting references made to "his palace" by the man who introduced him. Asserting that the residence of the chief of state was needed for receiving foreign dignitaries and that it belonged to the state, he insisted that personally he possessed nothing aside from his modest house at Monastir which would one day be transformed into a museum.

106. Some of these efforts are described in Pierre Rossi's laudatory account of *Bourguiba's Tunisia* (Tunis: Editions Kahia, 1967), pp. 89–125.

under control and master him and turn the scale in favor of good, a task of education and moral training is necessary. That is what the Neo-Destour has been out after." And in another place, "Tunisia is on the rationalistic road: the Neo-Destour is the apostle of the reason which allows man to distinguish truth from falsehood and hence to advance on the road to knowledge; putting moral sense in the forefront, it opens up before him the way to good."[107]

For Bourguiba, the molding of good citizens—what the French call *formation politique*—has always been a matter of the highest importance.

> Alors que les réunions publiques étaient interdites, j'affrontais les foudres des autorités coloniales et poursuivais, contre vents et marées, mon action d'éducation politique. Contrairement a l'avis sceptique de certains de mes compagnons de combat, cette action finit par produire d'heureux effets sur les hommes frustes auxquels elle s'adressait. . . . C'est vous dire l'importance d'une formation politique solide. Les étudiants, qui ont un 'bagage' culturel important, doivent pourvoir profiter plus facilement de notre travail de formation et apprendre surtout à aborder les problèmes avec objectivité, sans passion.[108]

In short, the people must learn discipline; they must accept the procedures of the state for the common good. Echoing that fourteenth century Tunisian, Ibn Khaldun, Bourguiba tells the students—among whom are his chief critics—that the history of Tunisia reveals a certain propensity to anarchy, tribal conflict, and raiding. Therefore survival of the nation as a coherent community must come before democracy.

> La démocratie serait une catastrophe si elle devait nous précipiter de nouveau dans l'anarchie et les antagonismes de jadis qui avaient été à l'origine de la colonisation. En voulant accorder a chacun une liberté dont il risque de faire un mauvais usage, nous exposerions le peuple à perdre ce qui est fondamental pour la vie en société: la cohésion de la nation et la pérennité de l'Etat.[109]

An exponent of democratic centralism, Bourguiba encourages the free expression of diverging points of view in the proper forum before a

---

107. Quoted in Rossi, op. cit., pp. 99–100.
108. From "Former des Citoyens Valables," a speech delivered by President Bourguiba at Carthage, December 17, 1967. (Tunis, n.p., n.d.) pp. 11–12.
109. Ibid., p. 18.

decision is taken; but afterwards it must be fully accepted. Under Bourguiba's firm control, the several bureaucracies—party, state, and mass media—through which public expression takes place impose a distinct uniformity on political discussion, presumably in furtherance of this philosophy.

The development of Tunisia's rather meager material resources has also been a cardinal feature of Bourguibist ideology. Officially, Tunisia is a socialist state; the name of Bourguiba's movement-party, the Neo-Destour, was changed to the Destourian Socialist party in 1964. Yet the socialism of Bourguiba's Tunisia is mild by classical standards. The emphasis has been on central planning rather than the nationalization of private business. Unlike the revolutionary socialism of neighboring countries like Algeria and Libya and most countries in the Arab east, Tunisian socialism is distinctly liberal, favoring private enterprise and foreign investment. The investment code promulgated in 1972, in fact, provided a major stimulus to the long-stagnant Tunisian economy.[110] The one major exception to this trend toward economic liberalism occurred in the late 1960s, when Bourguiba's authority was in at least a temporary decline, when Ahmad Ben Salah was allowed to undertake a vast program of agricultural cooperatives. The program generated widespread peasant hostility. Bourguiba deflected this unhappiness squarely onto Ben Salah, forcing his resignation in 1969 and imprisonment in 1970. While socialist symbols are widely diffused through the controlled media and political organizations, it is clear that the regime is far from radical. Indeed, the principal regime opposition, such as it is, strongly criticizes it on these grounds. To the extent that socialism is a legitimizing value among the younger elites and counterelites in Tunisia—as it is in many of the Arab countries—Bourguibism has not effectively exploited it.

Bourguibism has also abjured the pan-Arabism which plays such an important role in legitimizing the other Arab revolutionary states. Tunisian nationalism has always held the highest priority and the French-educated Bourguiba, as we have seen, has striven to infuse a Western rationality into the Tunisian national character. Beyond Tunisia, the chief commitment has been to the Maghrib—Arab North Africa. Perhaps because the main impetus to a broader pan-Arabism has emanated from Cairo, Bourguiba has been reluctant to employ it as a legitimizing value. Bourguiba stiffly resisted Nasirite pressures and he deeply resented Cairo's support for his main rival of the post-

110. *The Daily Star* (Beirut), August 27, 1974.

independence years, Salah Ben Yussef. In October 1958 Tunisia, having just joined the Arab League, withdrew in protest over Egyptian interference in its domestic affairs; later in the 1960s, it withdrew again for a time in reaction to the anger of the other Arab states over Bourguiba's then unorthodox views on Palestine. Furthermore, Tunisia maintained close relationships with the United States, and in the process became one of the major U.S. aid recipients (per capita), during a period when the United States was increasingly excoriated in the progressive Arab camp. Yet Bourguiba has indicated no defensiveness about his anti-imperialist credentials in light of the struggle which he waged against France before independence and at times, afterward. And Tunisian opinion has backed him up. Significantly, Bourguiba was one of the strongest supporters of the Palestinian resistance movement in the late 1960s because he felt it represented a genuine popular uprising in behalf of a just cause, similar to the Neo-Destour in its struggle against France. On balance, however, Bourguibism sought to legitimize itself outside the mainstream of Arab nationalism.

Finally, I must stress the importance of structural legitimacy in Tunisia. The Neo-Destour party in Bourguiba's conception has been the political armature of the nation—not a narrowly partisan organization but the organized expression of the Tunisia nation as a whole. It is the oldest and probably the most elaborately structured party in the Arab world. Founded in 1934, it had grown by 1955, on the eve of independence, into a formidable machine with an estimated 1,000 branches, 32 federations, a National Congress, a Political Bureau (open and clandestine), and a 3,000-man guerrilla army.[111] Western scholars have been impressed with the integrative and socialization functions performed by the party, which is the principal linkage between the people and the government. As one of them wrote in 1967, the party was more effectively becoming "the motor of the state," with Bourguiba the chief conductor.[112] But there are indications that the dynamism of the party, and the structural legitimacy that has accompanied this dynamism, has waned in recent years, notwithstanding its popular origins, its role in the struggle for independence, and its elaborate organization. Since the late 1960s there has been criticism, principally from sudent groups, that the party has become

111. C. A. Micaud, et al., Tunisia: The Politics of Modernization (New York: Praeger, 1964), pp. 69–130, "The Era of the Neo-Destour."

112. Lars Rudebeck, Party and People: A Study of Political Change in Tunisia (London: Hurst, 1967, 1969), p. 257.

structurally arteriosclerotic and mired in its own bureaucratic special interests. Moreover, Bourguiba has continued to insist on the party's conforming to his will. Thus, the same scholar in a postscript written two years later voiced some apprehension that the party would lose its mobilization orientation and cease to play a positive role in the Tunisian system.[113]

Bourguiba's Tunisia stands as one of the most successfully legitimized of the posttraditional, revolutionary states in the Arab world, but its (and his) performance since the late 1960s suggests that problems lie ahead in maintaining system legitimacy and coherence. Debilitated by sickness and age, the Supreme Combatant was becoming increasingly authoritarian and erratic, in the view of many Tunisians, particularly the younger elite. Many saw the imprisonment of Ben Salah in 1970 as excessive and reminiscent of the defeat of Ben Yussef in 1958 and his subsequent assassination. Ben Salah was able to escape in 1973 to Algeria, and he later was said to be organizing resistance to Bourguiba in Europe. Bahi Ladgham, a distinguished patriot, was thought by many to be in line to succeed Bourguiba, but he fell from favor in 1970 after winning praise throughout the Arab world in negotiating the Palestinian-Jordanian conflict. Another prominent leader, Ahmad Mestiri, led a group of predominantly Tunis-based politicians in a move to liberalize the party's and the country's political structures in 1971, but his group was defeated by Bourguiba and his party loyalists from the sahil (coastal plain) area.

A much more radical current of opposition has arisen in the Tunisian student movement, and there were serious troubles in the University of Tunis in 1968.[114] Although the radical socialists of the Tunisian Socialist Action and Study Group were a small minority and forced to function largely in France, they were symbolic of a growing disaffection on the part of Tunisian youth in general toward the regime. Having built an ideological and structural legitimacy that might have eased Tunisia through the transition from the leadership of its founding father, Bourguiba in his later years ironically appears to be weakening

113. Ibid., pp. 265-67.
114. On the student disorders of 1968 see the mimeographed periodical, *Tribune Progressiste*, published by the Etudiants Progressites Tunisiens, and "Perspectives Tunisiennes," No. 4 June 1969), entitled "Les Acquis et les Perspectives de la lutte révolutionnaire en Tunisie," published by the Groupe D'Etudes et D'Action Socialiste Tunisien. For the rebuttal of the Left made by the Destourian students, see the pamphlet "Livre Blanc," published by the Etudiants Socialistes Destouriens, March 25, 1968, in which the opponents of the regime are described on pp. 10-15 as Communists, Ba'thists, the great families of the upper bourgeoisie displaced by Bourguiba, and foreign countries, such as China.

these alternative pillars of legitimacy. Even if the post-Bourguiba leadership remains in the hands of the old Bourguiba loyalists of the Destour, it may be faced with the problem of maintaining both internal party cohesion and the party's tutelary role in Tunisian politics.[115] The possibility also exists of increasing ideological fragmentation represented by groups such as the neo-Marxist socialists, Ba'thist pan-Arabists, and possibly even neo-Islamic nationalist elements. While the major economic upturn of the middle 1970s—generated by tourism, and a liberal investment policy—could mitigate the strains of transition, it is clear from the example of the defunct monarchy of neighboring Libya, among other cases, that prosperity does not guarantee regime legitimacy or longevity.

Without minimizing the autocratic, excessively paternalistic character of Tunisian politics in Bourguiba's last years, it is not difficult to understand the disdain with which many Tunisians regard politics in the rest of the Arab world. A happy combination of cultural homogeneity and historical good fortune have given this country relatively low environmental loads on the system and leadership that was both strong and basically wise. Ideological and structural legitimacy developed hand in hand under the guidance of the Supreme Combatant. The Tunisian system appears to have developed a degree of institutionalized participation that, while increasingly imperfect, is more successful than in any other Arab regime, be it monarchy or republic. I cannot conclude, however, that the Tunisian model is applicable in other Arab societies. In the monarchies, the process of political opening is just beginning and the prospects are for Qadhafis rather than Bourguibas. The pan-Arab core is too obsessed with frustrated dreams to be congenial to a relatively instrumental political style. On the periphery of the Arab world, political culture fragmentation and extremely uneven socioeconomic development create one crisis after another, an atmosphere not particularly conducive to civic politics.

115. It was widely predicted that Prime Minister Hedi Nouira would succeed Bourguiba as president and maintain the regime's conservative orientation.

10

Conclusion

> I think it may be true that fortune is the ruler of half our actions, but that she allows the other half or thereabouts to be governed by us. I would compare her to an impetuous river that, when turbulent, inundates the plains, casts down trees and buildings, removes earth from this side and places it on the other; every one flees before it, and everything yields to its fury without being able to oppose it; and yet though it is of such a kind, still when it is quiet, men can make provision against it by dykes and banks, so that when it rises it will either go into a canal or its rush will not be so wild and dangerous. So it is with fortune, which shows her power where no measures have been taken to resist her, and directs her fury where she knows that no dykes or barriers have been made to hold her.
>
> —Machiavelli

The Arab world is hard to govern. What we have observed in the previous chapters is a society undergoing profound changes. But the political order is lagging behind these changes; instead of directing them into fruitful policy outcomes, it is barely able to manage the social conflict which they engender. Because of an inability to generate structural legitimacy, Arab politics faces two alternatives, neither of them desirable: either the emergence of "control" regimes whose stability is mainly a function of enhanced coercive capabilities or the reemergence of the political turbulence of the 1950s and 1960s. What Arab opinion wants (as its most popular ideologies tell us) and what social mobilization objectively requires is precisely what its political processes have been unable to provide: meaningful institutionalized participation. Without such dykes and canals, political life in the Arab world will continue to be bitter and fear-ridden, subject to the caprices and furies of fortune.

A legitimate political order, theorists tell us, is difficult to achieve unless some basic political culture problems are solved. There has to be some consensus about national identity, some agreement about the boundaries of the political community, and some collective understanding of national priorities. If the population within given political

389

boundaries is so deeply divided within itself on ethnic or class lines, or if the demands of a larger supranational community are compelling to some portion of it, then it is extremely difficult to develop a legitimate order. A second problem concerns authority. What are the bases of right rule? If historical tradition has bequeathed ill-defined or incompatible principles of authority or, worse still, if the gap between principles and practice is widely perceived as immense, then it is no easy matter to establish authoritative as opposed to coercive rule. Moreover, if traditional norms are also incompatible with emerging modern ideas about the proper basis of authority, the problem becomes even more complex. The onset of modernization introduces as well new ideas about the good society itself. If the old order was essentially deferential and extractive, the new one is egalitarian and participant. Ideologies take hold faster than socioeconomic structures can change, which means that new as well as old regimes find it difficult to function. The demand for equality also imposes a new range of administrative burdens on government which, given the underdeveloped character of both government and society, cannot easily be carried: welfare states are hard enough to administer in the industrialized societies.

What are the developmental options available to modernizing political communities in which these three prerequisites for legitimacy are, at best, only partially present? I have indicated three models of change. The transformationist model conceives of a radical assault on established patterns and the creation of a new, integrated order. Political practitioners who want transformation to occur find support from analysts who say that such a transformation is possible and perhaps even inevitable. What I dubbed the mosaic model (which also has its partisans as well as its theorists) envisages the permanence, if not indeed the strengthening, of primordial, parochial elements in the political culture as modernization advances. The mosaic analysis casts doubts on the possibility of radical transformation, and its implications for building political legitimacy point toward the viability of traditional norms and the need for accommodating existing sub-communities. Finally, the social mobilization model depicts the range of political choices as the product of a more complex set of factors. Whether the trend is toward integration or fragmentation of the political culture depends both on the basic configuration of cleavages and upon the speed and evenness of social mobilization. In a culture as complex as that of the Arab world, there may be simultaneous but contradictory trends affecting national identity. Furthermore, while social mobilization is eroding some old structures and values, to the detriment perhaps of an incumbent regime, it is also enlarging the capabilities of a government to enforce its will and provide demanded administrative services. In theory then, as the following diagram indicates, a given rate of social mobilization could give rise to four kinds of political order, depending on whether the political culture was highly fragmented along ethnic or class lines or not and whether the governmental capabilities (relative to system loads) were high or not.

FIGURE 10.1

Alternative Political Orders
(in a situation of rapid social mobilization)

Political Culture Fragmentation

		Low	*High*
	Low	Inert	Unstable
Government Capabilities (relative		I	II
		IV	III
to loads)	*High*	Dynamic	Controlled

Political systems with low fragmentation and low capabilities are relatively stable but inert: their low governmental capabilities are compensated for by their harmonious political culture. Low-capability governments in highly fragmented cultures, however, give rise to an unstable order. Systems with high fragmentation but also with high capabilities are designated as controlled, inasmuch as a high coercive capacity is available (and necessary) to quell internal conflict. The final category, one marked by low fragmentation and high capabilities, is the dynamic order. In an age of modernization and modern ideologies, only this last category, because it possesses both integration and capabilities, can realistically be considered suitable for the development of strong legitimacy as it was defined in chapter 1. This is not to say that such a political order necessarily would generate high legitimacy but only that it would constitute a relatively benign environment for such a development.

Whatever their environment, however, political systems develop a variety of processes for maintaining at least minimum order, legitimate or otherwise; and their elites, consciously or otherwise, compose strategies for maximizing legitimacy. Theory suggests that there are three kinds of legitimacy, personal, ideological, and structural, which can be cultivated or exploited instrumentally to attain the desired goal. For the new states in underdeveloped societies which are rapidly modernizing, structural legitimacy, although the strongest type of legitimacy, is also the hardest to attain. Personal and ideological legitimacy, while usually transitory and superficial, are the types most relevant to difficult political environments. Politics in these new states may be fruitfully understood as a struggle, on the part of regimes and oppositions, to develop a strong legitimacy formula using these instruments.

Arab Politics: The Present

When I look across the Arab world today, I can only conclude that the basic problems of identity, authority, and equality remain unresolved. Because they are unresolved, Arab politics appear to be going neither forward nor backward: the radical future seems unreachable and the traditional past unrecoverable. Politics thus is largely the art of manipulating appealing ideological symbols and trying to generate personal popularity.

When I speak of an identity problem in Arab politics, it is not the problem of "the Arab mind" with all its alleged imperfections. The Arabs are too diverse and free as individuals to be stereotyped so grossly. Nor is the problem that they lack a strong feeling of Arabness. It should be clear from chapter 2 that Arabism has real meaning. In fact it is my impression that the sense of Arabness is spreading as social mobilization proceeds. One obstacle to the crystallization of an all-Arab identity is the sheer objective intractibility of basic all-Arab goals—unity and Palestine. But there is also a serious subjective problem, that of incongruity. Arabs must choose between multiple identities, each of which carries commitments which are incompatible with others. Ordinarily, Arabs (like other people) can manage a number of simultaneous affiliations. The Arabs, as we have seen, are a culturally and ethnically pluralistic people. There is a plasticity and a live-and-let-live tolerance in intercommunal relations. While we have also seen that communal hostility can be triggered by a severe political or social crisis, the Arabs on the whole are successful at managing communal relations. As for the compatibility of religious and political identities, whatever the theorists may say, Arabs seem to have little problem in reconciling Islam with nationalism; in fact, the two appear mutually supportive. The incongruity—and the problem—is political rather than cultural. Arabs unquestionably feel a part of the larger Arab nation and are committed to all-Arab concerns, but they are also proud of being Egyptians, Moroccans, Yemenis, and Qataris, and they cannot but be loyal, to some degree, to the interests of these smaller communities. Certainly the ruling elites in the separate Arab sovereignties are firmly committed to protecting local national interests. How else can one explain the efforts of regimes in Egypt, Jordan, or Syria to suppress militant activity in behalf of all-Arab causes?

While I see little evidence at present of a trend toward Arab unity (in the sense of the political fusion of some or all of the existing states) either at the elite or mass level, neither do I agree with those who believe that the Arab world is on the verge of being permanently fragmented into eighteen or more separate political communities, isolated from each other. All-Arab symbols and concerns remain central, not marginal, in the legitimacy equations of all the Arab states, notwithstanding the undeniable effects of sovereign structures on political behavior. Regime incumbents may act in terms of narrow definitions of local state interests, but this is not true to the same extent throughout the elites, and especially not true of the masses of ordinary people which together make up that inchoate but important element, Arab public opinion. Legitimacy in the Arab world must be approached not just from the standpoint of constitutional law or diplomacy but also from that of sociology. The Arab masses today are far more aware of all-Arab concerns than they were in the early days of the nationalist movement. Arab elites—the growing stratum of the educated—are substantially co-opted into loyalty to specific regime interests, but not entirely so. They are not indifferent to the moral dimension of the Palestine problem, nor can they be unaware of the objective advantages which a more socially and economically integrated Arab world, pursuing common policies in a number of fields vis à vis the rest of the world, would bring. Already the web of intra-Arab relationships and linkages is thickening, despite the frequently envenomed political relationships between different regimes. What we have, then, are some powerful centrifugal and centripetal forces which perpetuate the identity problem, inhibiting a resolution one way or the other. Over and against the pragmatic and parochial character of local loyalties is that perceived bond of an Arab community. We cannot ascertain how the resulting tensions ultimately will be resolved, if at all, without somehow being able to measure how strongly Arabs believe that they are "their brother's keeper" and that "we are all in this together."

The problem of authority (as distinct from control) is severe enough to be designated a crisis. Not only are traditional bases of authority weak and incompatible with one another, they are also singularly inappropriate to the scope and functions of the modern state and nation. Furthermore, they clash with modern principles of right rule. I discerned in chapter 4 four traditional authority patterns—patriarchal, consultative, religious, and feudal. In small, kinship-organized communities like tribes, where face-to-face relationships were normal, patriarchal and consultative mechanisms bestowed legitimacy tolerably well, though they perpetuated chronic intertribal conflict. Religious authority, dispensed through the imperial bureaucracies was at evident variance with the arbitrary, worldly absolutism of the sultan and with various dissident or reformist schools. Finally, there was the pervasive feudal authority pattern and its variants, in which deferential patron-client relationships were rooted in a highly unequal distribution of wealth and status. It is this last pattern which gives traditional Arab political culture its basic "subject" orientation, to use the terminology of Gabriel Almond and Sidney Verba.[1] Subject-orientation, however, is not synonomous with coherence or integration. In fact, traditional Arab political culture also exhibited parochialism—a multiplicity of authorities and authority norms. Given this variety and incoherence, it is not surprising that coercive capabilities rather than legitimacy were dominant in historical authority relationships.

With the implantation of modern ideas about legitimate authority, another and even more serious kind of tension arose, for the traditional patterns were not compatible with the new secular and democratic norms. Moreover, the new sovereign state structures of the Arab world were not congruent with the scope and boundaries of tribal, Islamic, imperial, or feudal domains. While social modernization weakened the old authorities, it did not immediately create authoritative replacements.

Today, as I have shown in the case studies, elements within the modern sector compete with each other for power, and the struggle is unending. The new regimes try to identify themselves with modern authority norms, but they succeed only partially because their actual mode of ruling deviates so obviously from their proclaimed principles. The socially mobilized populations of the modern Arab world can tell the difference between democracy and despotism, propaganda to the contrary notwithstanding. The monarchies and republics of the Arab world today, no matter how benevolent they may be (and many are), cannot be considered representative except in a highly restrictive way. It is a measure of the seriousness of the authority crisis that they

---

1. Gabriel A. Almond and Sidney Verba, *The Civic Culture* (Boston: Little, Brown, 1965), chap. 1, and pp. 17–18.

feel it necessary to proclaim their democratic character when the truth is so obviously different.

There is no reason to doubt the sincerity of Arab leaders who say that they want to democratize their political systems. The key question then becomes, Why don't they? To reply that they are afraid of losing their power is only part of the answer. More than calculations of personal interest are involved. Although they agreed on little else, King Faisal and Nasir both felt that to democratize their societies would have led to chaos, because ruthless and self-interested opposition movements would take advantage of the lack of established structures to create their own dictatorships. Thus, out of a prudent fear of possible chaos, both leaders took care to curb any serious opposition. In short, the insecurity of the ruling elite, based not necessarily on selfishness but on what impartial observers might call a realistic appraisal of the situation, causes it to act autocratically. In the absence of legitimate structures, they cannot conceive of a loyal opposition—the chances are greater that it is subversive. Opposition leaders are right in labeling the incumbents as despotic, but they may be wrong in ascribing the behavior to innate human evil; placed in the same situation, they invariably do the same thing.

The dilemma lies in the fact that Arab society now requires political participation; without it, continued instability is almost certain. But in the absence of established structures, instability is equally certain with it. And chronic turbulence is not a good environment for establishing structures. Reality defies the starkness of logic, however; and the Arab political systems, far from being completely chaotic, muddle through, as we have seen, by generating sporadic personal leadership legitimacy and embracing (with varying degrees of credibility) salient ideological symbols.

The problem of equality has become important in Arab politics as moderization has progressed, and in some areas important advances have been made. From the observations about authority, it is evident that political equality, in terms of broad-based, meaningful participation, remains elusive. But much has been done, particularly in the revolutionary republics, to diminish social and economic inequalities. Not only have the prerogatives of traditional elites been eliminated, governments have carried out substantial redistributions of national wealth through public policy. Tax reforms, welfare programs, free education, subsidies of basic commodities, rent controls, and land redistribution have by no means closed the wide gap in living standards (and some efforts, like that of Egypt, have lagged in recent years), but on balance it would seem that some very significant steps have been taken. The oil-rich monarchies have, to a degree, finessed the equality problem by being able to provide generous welfare programs to all. Nevertheless, income inequality is probably increasing as a thin stratum of the super-rich acquires the lion's share of the new affluence. The salaried middle classes of the petro-kingdoms feel inflation acutely, while the poor (mainly expatriates) benefit the least. Governments also are slowly eroding traditional social inequalities, notably with respect to women, but much remains to be done. Probably the most encouraging but least noticed aspect of Arab political development has been the growth of larger, more effective civil services which are capable of implementing some of the less politically sensitive requisites of a modern society. Enhanced administrative capabilities and welfare-oriented policies have had at least an oblique positive impact on social equality, but this improvement is confined to the "output" side of the political system. On the "input" side, however, I can only discover a lack of movement toward greater equality of political participation. Even considering the modest broadening tendencies of the early 1970s in several of the revolutionary republics— Egypt, Syria, Iraq, the PDRY, and Algeria—it does not appear that equality of participation or freedom of opposition and political expression is likely to become a reality in the near future.

Can the process of legitimation in the Arab world be interpreted in terms of the three developmental models discussed earlier? On the basis of the assessment of the identity, authority, and equality problems and the case studies, I conclude that neither the transformationist nor the mosaic models are valid guides to Arab political development. The achievement of independence and the overthrow of traditionalist governments unquestionably altered political patterns in the Arab world. But it now appears that the revolutionary wave of the 1950s and 1960s has not transformed social and political processes to the extent that many radical ideologists and liberal observers anticipated. Certainly the Rousseauist notion that the slate of political culture could be wiped clean has proved naïve. The rich and often discordant Arab political culture still imposes its constraints on political behavior. Important changes, to be sure, are taking place, but they are taking place much more slowly than the transformationist model would predict. Many radicals now confess disappointment at the loss of transformationist momentum in nearly all the revolutionary republics. Radical optimism about the inevitability of the triumph of the oppressed classes and the beneficient, democratic harmony of a socialist order does not seem to be warranted from the vantage point of the middle 1970s. Have we seen a transformation anywhere in the Arab world comparable to the French, Russian, or Chinese revolutions? Even in the PDRY, Iraq, and Algeria—the most promising cases— the scope and completeness of change does not measure up. Perhaps the Palestinian movement showed the greatest potential, but its own internal failings and its treatment at the hands of supposedly brotherly revolutionary Arab governments suggests that popular mobilization for transformationist ideals, such as occurred in North Vietnam, has hardly begun in the Arab world.

But the mosaic model fares no better in the light of recent Arab experience. It is valid insofar as it emphasizes the relative permanence of ethnolinguistic and sectarian identifications and the intractibility of class divisions. But to extrapolate from this perception the model of an Arab world dominated by parochial, particularist regimes with narrow communal bases and "night-watchman" policy orientations is to envisage a political environment more appropriate to the late nineteenth century than to the late twentieth century. Whatever the failings of the revolutionary regimes, the fact remains that modern, assimilationist values are now accepted throughout Arab society. Assimilation of minorities, either by persuasion or coercion, has been the dominant trend. The interests of ruling elites lie in promoting stronger and, if possible, larger national governments rather than allowing fragmentation. Increasingly, they have the capabilities to promote these interests. Economic logic favors integrated rather than fragmented polities. And security considerations, not without reason, militate against the devolution of very much autonomy to minorities or regions which can be used by hostile outside powers to subvert nationalist governments. The lesson of Lebanon is not that Balkanization is the wave of the future, but that static political systems concerned mainly with accommodating minority elites are inappropriate to the demands of socially mobilized populations and vulnerable to outside manipulation. The eradication of minority cultures is neither morally acceptable nor politically sensible; fortunately there are no Arab regimes or nationalist movements today which advocate such total assimilation. The basic weaknesses in Arab politics do not fall along the dimension of communal identities but on the dimension of class and elite conflicts. The drain on political legitimacy arises less out of secessionist impulses than divisions over the distribution of wealth and power among socioeconomic groups and differences over all-Arab as opposed to local regime priorities. Neo-millets cannot cope with such problems; larger modern political systems at least have a chance.

The social mobilization model best explains Arab political processes.

As late as half a century ago the political order in the Arab world might have been described, in terms of the alternatives presented in Figure 10.1, as inert. An autonomous political life was just beginning and political consciousness was limited. Government, whether Ottoman, colonial, or autonomous, did little; it was not expected to do more than extract taxes and keep the peace. The political and social awakening of recent decades, however, has changed Arab society and politics to such an extent that they now fall (if I may generalize) into the unstable category of Figure 10.1. Social mobilization is politicizing the Arabs: elites are becoming larger and more complex; masses are increasingly sensitized to twentieth-century ideas of nationalism, democracy and government responsibility for welfare and development. While these developments have enhanced the sense of Arabism and local nationalism too, they have also exacerbated latent class conflicts and, to a lesser extent, identity problems. Thus, Arab political culture is both more aware and more fragmented. But government has been slower to develop its capabilities. The first generation of new states has been distinguished by inefficiency and a lack of political wisdom. They have been slow to respond effectively to the new policy and administrative demands and even slower to develop the political structures which might generate a sense of system legitimacy. The result has been widespread instability.

Just as social mobilization has spread, however, so have governmental capabilities increased. In the revolutionary republics, ideology has stimulated the growth of government services; in the monarchies, the increase in oil wealth has provided the means for competing with the progressive camp in the field of social welfare. Internal security capabilities, too, have been improved in both the republics and the monarchies. Even though instability continues, most of the more recent efforts to overthrow regimes have failed. Morocco, Libya, Oman, Sudan, Iraq, Jordan, Sharja (UAE), and Egypt are countries where one or more serious coups or insurrections were unsuccessfully attempted between 1970 and 1976. Where forced regime changes were successful they were intraregime coups ("corrective movements") as in Syria, the PDRY, and (in a sense) the YAR. This evidence suggests that there may now be a trend toward the improvement of governmental capabilities relative to political system loads. If so, several Arab political systems may have moved, in terms of Figure 10.1, from the category of unstable to that of controlled political orders. Polities in this category are beset by severe political culture conflicts (in the Arab case more socioeconomic and ideological than primordial-parochial), but they also have developed relatively strong governments.

FIGURE 10.2

The Arab Polities Classified According
to Alternative Political Orders
(in a situation of rapid social mobilization)

Political Culture Fragmentation

		Low	*High*
		I. Inert	II. Unstable
	Low	Sa'udi Arabia	Bahrain
		Qatar	Morocco
		UAE	Egypt
		Oman	Lebanon
Government			Palestinians
Capabilities			Libya
(relative			Sudan
to loads)			YAR
		IV. Dynamic	III. Controlled
	High	Tunisia	Jordan
		Kuwait	Syria
			Iraq
			PDRY
			Algeria

Although legitimate structures for participation are still lacking in
these regimes, thus perpetuating internal tensions, they are nevertheless capable of maintaining tight security and administering programs with some degree of efficiency. While social mobilization may
favor incumbent regimes over the oppositions at this particular phase
of Arab development, it is doubtful whether regimes will continue
to have the upper hand—a question to which I shall return shortly.

The fourth option in Figure 10.1, the dynamic category, depicts the
situation most favorable for legitimate government. A relatively homogeneous political culture is governed by a relatively capable political
system. In such an environment, the loads are low and there are fewer
objective grounds for the elite insecurity which typically engenders
autocratic behavior. Accordingly, the situation is more favorable for
the risk-taking which must accompany any serious effort to open up

the political process. Such situations do not guarantee but only facilitate
the building of legitimate political structures, and unfortunately they
are rare in the Arab world.

To summarize the Arab situation today (see Figure 10.2) is not easy
without ignoring many of the nuances of the legitimacy struggle which
I have tried to bring out in the case studies. If I may generalize about
Arab politics as a whole, it appears that the Arab governments have
moved in the last half-century from the inert to the unstable category.
But there is a more recent trend in several systems toward improving
their capabilities to load ratio and moving toward the controlled
category. If I break the Arab world down into its constituent parts,
I would place Sa'udi Arabia, Qatar, the UAE and Oman in category
I, inert. Even though social mobilization is rapid and government
fairly rudimentary in terms of capabilities, the loads on the system
are not intolerable because of a relatively homogeneous political
culture. There are certain widely shared assumptions about proper
government and authoritative leadership which permit a certain
legitimacy even without effective government. But as the stresses of
modernization continue, these polities will be pushed toward the
unstable category unless their capabilities improve dramatically. In
that case they stand a chance of moving toward category III, controlled, or even category IV, dynamic.

Most of the Arab polities are found in category II, unstable. Here
we find more serious tensions and governments, both monarchical
and republican, that are hard pressed to cope with them: Bahrain,
Morocco, Egypt, Lebanon, Libya, the Sudan, the YAR, and the
Palestinian movement. Incumbent regimes are hard-pressed to devise
a legitimacy formula to compensate for their relatively low capabilities.
Consequently, in some of these polities, one finds inflated political
rhetoric, sporadic repression, and personality cults. I see here several
cases in which limited efforts at liberalization are being made (Egypt
for example) but which may prove inadequate at representing all the
important political tendencies in the society. The Palestinian movement is less troubled by internal legitimacy problems than by insufficient means to deal with its external enemies.

In category III, controlled, are those systems which have achieved
a certain stability through a combination of ideology and personal
leadership and a relatively capable coercive and administrative
apparatus. Jordan is the only monarchy that I place here, although
Sa'udi Arabia is now working hard to build greater capabilities. The
other states are revolutionary republics which, as I noted in the case
studies, appear to have gone some distance toward developing solid

structural linkages throughout the society: Syria, Iraq, the PDRY, and Algeria. My impression is that there are serious sociopolitical tensions in all four, particularly Syria and Algeria, but that they have, by virtue of their technical capacities and ideological formulas, bought time at least in which to develop more organically based legitimacy. Finally, in category IV, I can classify only two Arab polities as dynamic: Tunisia and possibly Kuwait. In each case, a balanced and functional legitimacy formula has been devised by relatively enlightened leadership in rather favorable environmental circumstances. But in neither is the achievement of dynamic legitimacy necessarily permanent. As we have seen, Tunisia without Bourguiba could face a time of troubles, while the recent developments in Kuwait appear to indicate both the superficiality of liberal structures and the existence of more serious internal tensions than had been apparent.

ARAB POLITICS: THE FUTURE

My speculations about the future of Arab politics are predicated on the belief that social mobilization will continue to enlarge the politically relevant population and generate demands for national self-fulfillment and socioeconomic development. Democratic and egalitarian values will gain new salience both among the younger educated elite and among the masses generally. I see no substantial weakening of traditional communal attachments and, if anything, a strengthening of popular Islam. Although I have tried to indicate a degree of compatibility between the new and old values, I cannot deny that there are tensions too, and these undoubtedly will continue to complicate the struggle for legitimacy.

In the race between loads and capabilities, the loads were predominant in the 1950s and 1960s, but in the 1970s there is some indication that government capabilities have advanced. This development has worked to the advantage of incumbent regimes, monarchical as well as republican. The republics, frustrated at this stage in their development by the natural obstacles to social transformation and the achievement of all-Arab goals, have found themselves outflanked from new critics on the Left as well as old critics from the Right who survived the revolutions. Ideological legitimacy, on which they depended so heavily, has tended to wane with the slowing of revolutionary momentum. Personal legitimacy has proved effective in a limited way but in the long run is ephemeral. Because of the perceived dangers in the political environment, internal and external, regimes have been reluctant to gamble with experiments in structural legitimation through open political participation. In these circumstances, the steady deve-

MONTEREY PENINSULA COLLEGE LIBRARY

lopment of security and welfare policy capabilities has been an important factor for relieving the pressures, but it has also contributed to the bureaucratization and, to some extent, the deradicalization of these regimes.

The monarchies too have found respite in the growth of technical competence. Their problems lie basically in the diminishing salience of kingship and kinship as legitimizing values. They have also been sharply challenged by the radical nationalist wave of the 1950s and 1960s. In response, the kings have moved energetically to assert their own Arab nationalist credentials. By actively supporting the confrontation states against Israel, by imposing the oil boycott, and by publicizing the Arab cause internationally, the royal families of Sa'udi Arabia, the Gulf, Jordan (in its carefully defined way) and even Morocco have won considerable legitimacy for their all-Arab patriotism. The monarchies also face the problem that their form of government is not easily compatible with effective administration. Fortunately, they are small polities with homogeneous populations and manageable administrative problems. Morocco, the largest and least homogeneous, has had the most trouble. Moreover, most of them are wealthy and benefit from generous technical assistance from the United States in almost every field of public administration, from internal security to social security. To an important degree, therefore, they have been able to avoid, or at least postpone, "the monarch's dilemma."

I see, therefore, a distinct convergence in the middle 1970s between the traditional monarchies and the revolutionary republics. The republics are tempering their radicalism while the monarchies enhance their nationalist and welfare-state characteristics.

Is this convergence likely to lead to a more stable Arab politics, less affected by millenarian dreams and ideological conflict than before? Diplomats and analysts concerned with day-to-day developments might be inclined to say yes, but my opinion is different. The basic reason, as I have stated, is that social mobilization is an ongoing, continually disruptive process, creating new elements which will demand a share of influence and the achievement of important goals. They may not be unaffected by traditional orientations and thus not immediately mobilizable for radical politics, but neither are they likely to remain inert. Government control structures may proliferate and bureaucracies grow, giving regimes a temporary respite from political pressures; but these structures themselves are not invulnerable to politicization from opposition movements. There inevitably will be subversive tendencies within the newly trained and enlarged officer corps, and it is not necessarily accurate to classify the new technocrats and bureaucrats as apolitical. The growth of government does not imply an end of ideology or of opposition. In spite of their unforeseen strengths, the monarchies cannot escape what new generations will see as the anachronistic nature of their claims to legitimacy; and, as I have observed, the growing pains of rapid development may yet be difficult for their rudimentary administrations to handle. Although the revolutionary republics have made impressive gains in some spheres, their populations are highly politicized and capable of perceiving the gap between the ideology of freedom and democracy and the reality of autocratic control. Most of these states do not enjoy the luxury of unlimited capital, and their instability has hampered their policy effectiveness.

Another reason to anticipate continuing conflict with established regimes is the permanence of all-Arab issues which demand redress. It is difficult to conceive of a diplomatic solution to the Palestine conflict which, even if it were acceptable to some of the principal Arab governments, would bring the issue to rest in Arab politics. But until it does come to rest, it will always be a legitimacy resource available to the highest bidder and a legitimacy drain on the regimes perceived as abandoning the cause. Similarly, the question of Arab unity in some form or other seems likely to endure without definitive resolution. The Arab polities are too close to one another culturally, strategically, and economically for the developments in one not to affect the others. As long as there remain demands for significant alterations in inter-Arab relations (through fusion or other forms of integration), these demands will jeopardize the legitimacy of established regimes. Even though at present transnational movements like the Arab Nationalists' movement and the Ba'th are in eclipse (at least in their unity efforts), and the drive for unity on the all-Arab, Maghrib, Fertile Crescent, Gulf, and Yemen levels is stalled, it is likely that the idea of unity in some form will continue to appear as an important, legitimate cause within Arab opinion. Regimes which are continually quarreling with one another are not likely to win the respect of people who take this cause seriously. So the continuing salience of unresolvable all-Arab issues will work to the detriment of established political systems and regimes. As the Arab world grows in economic, military, and diplomatic potential, the perception that these goals may now be objectively realizable is likely to stimulate new efforts to pursue them—efforts which can only damage the legitimacy of established orders with a vested interest in the status quo.

If this analysis is correct, we must expect continued turbulence in

Arab politics before reaching the threshold of genuine structural legitimacy. The solution is clear enough. It is the development of meaningful, broad-based participation in the political process in accordance with accepted procedures so that government will be more responsive and responsible to public opinion. I have tried to show, however, that many of the realities of present-day Arab politics make such a solution very difficult to achieve. Of course there are hopeful signs, the most important of which is the appearance of a generation better educated than its predecessors—more humane, well-trained, and socially conscious. But more than the mere existence of such people is necessary. It will take political activists and organizers; leaders that are strong and ready to take risks for the sake of development; and intelligent, disciplined followers to break through the obstacles to legitimacy which are inherent in the Arab political environment.

Appendix

Political Event Data Plots for
Selected Arab Countries, 1948–1967

Source: Charles L. Taylor and Michael C. Hudson, *World Handbook of Political and Social Indicators*, Second Edition, New Haven: Yale University Press, 1972, pp. 154–99. Full descriptions of the variables and collection procedures may also be found on pp. 59–87 and 391–423. Tables showing the number of events reported, by year, are also presented on pp. 88–153. The data were generated and organized with the collaboration of Katherine H. Dolan, Edwin G. Dolan, John T. Dow, and John D. Sullivan.

The variables presented in the plots below may be briefly identified as follows:

Renewals: A renewal of executive tenure is an act that reestablishes or reconfirms the tenure of the incumbent national executive leader or group through the country's conventional procedures.

Adjustments: An executive adjustment is an event modifying the membership of a national executive body that does not signify a transfer of formal power from one leader or ruling group to another.

Regular Transfers: A regular executive transfer is a change in the office of national executive from one leader or ruling group to another that is accomplished through conventional legal or customary procedures and unaccompanied by actual or directly threatened physical violence.

Irregular transfers: An irregular executive transfer is a change in the office of national executive from one leader or ruling group to another that is accomplished outside the conventional legal or customary procedures for transferring formal power in effect at the time of the event and accompanied by actual or directly threatened violence.

Demonstrations: A protest demonstration is a nonviolent gathering of people organized to protest the policies, ideology, or actions of a regime, a government, or political leaders.

Riots: A riot is a violent demonstration or disturbance involving a large number of people and characterized by material damage or bloodshed.

Armed Attacks: An armed attack is an act of violent political conflict carried out by an organized group with the object of weakening or destroying the power exercised by another organized group, usually a government.

Political Deaths: The series deaths from domestic violence records the number of persons reportedly killed in events of domestic political conflict. The data refer to numbers of bodies and not events in which deaths occur.

Sanctions: A governmental sanction is an action taken by the authorities to neutralize, suppress, or eliminate a perceived threat to the security of the government, the regime, or the state itself.

Interventions: An external intervention is an attempt by an actor, whether another nation-state or a rebel group operating from outside the country, to engage in military activity within the target country with the intent of influencing the authority structure of that country. The data are listed by target, not intervening, country.

Algeria

O Renewals
△ Adjustments
□ Reg. Transfers
☆ Irreg. Transfers

Demonstrations
Riots
Armed Attacks
Political Deaths
Sanctions
Interventions

1950   1955   1960   1965

Iraq

O Renewals
△ Adjustments
□ Reg. Transfers
☆ Irreg. Transfers

Demonstrations
Riots
Armed Attacks
Political Deaths
Sanctions
Interventions

1950   1955   1960   1965

Jordan

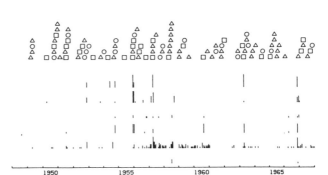

O Renewals
△ Adjustments
□ Reg. Transfers

Demonstrations
Riots
Armed Attacks
Political Deaths
Sanctions
Interventions

1950   1955   1960   1965

Kuwait

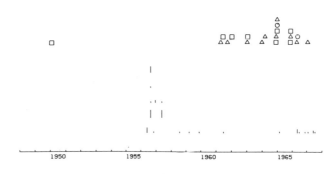

O Renewals
△ Adjustments
□ Reg. Transfers

Demonstrations
Riots
Armed Attacks
Political Deaths
Sanctions

1950   1955   1960   1965

Lebanon

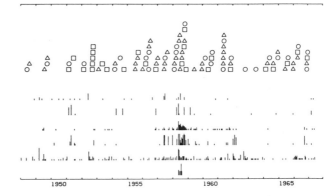

O Renewals
△ Adjustments
□ Reg. Transfers

Demonstrations
Riots
Armed Attacks
Political Deaths
Sanctions
Interventions

1950   1955   1960   1965

Libya

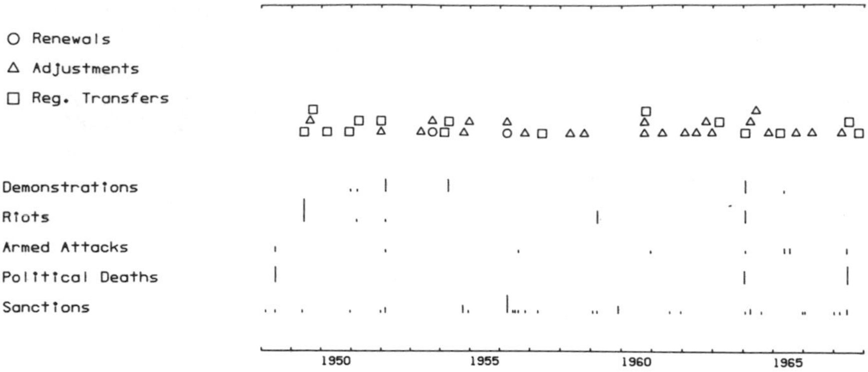

O Renewals
△ Adjustments
□ Reg. Transfers

Demonstrations
Riots
Armed Attacks
Political Deaths
Sanctions

1950   1955   1960   1965

Morocco

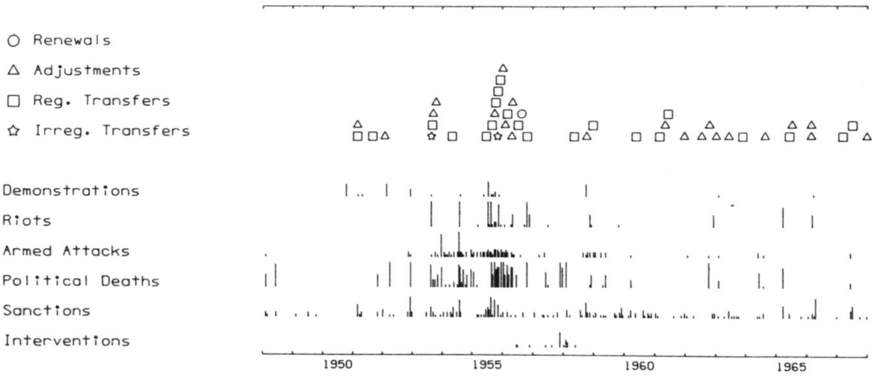

O Renewals
△ Adjustments
□ Reg. Transfers
☆ Irreg. Transfers

Demonstrations
Riots
Armed Attacks
Political Deaths
Sanctions
Interventions

1950   1955   1960   1965

Saudi Arabia

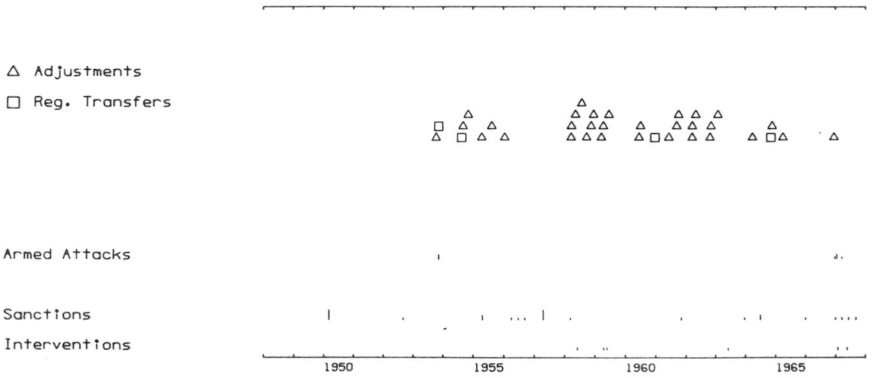

△ Adjustments
□ Reg. Transfers

Armed Attacks

Sanctions
Interventions

1950   1955   1960   1965

Southern Yemen (PDRY)

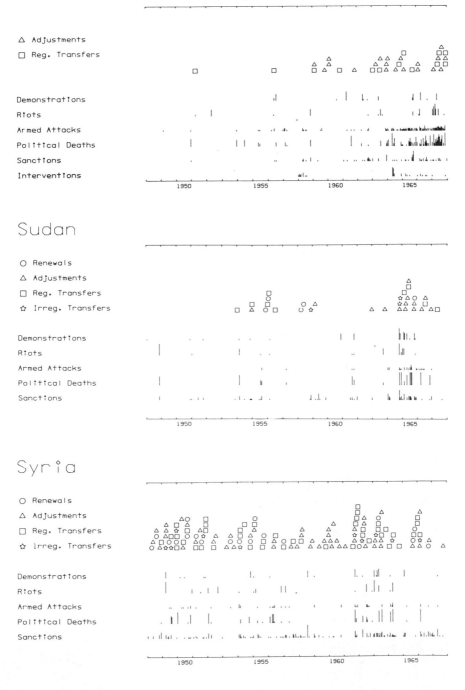

△ Adjustments
□ Reg. Transfers

Demonstrations
Riots
Armed Attacks
Political Deaths
Sanctions
Interventions

1950   1955   1960   1965

Sudan

○ Renewals
△ Adjustments
□ Reg. Transfers
☆ Irreg. Transfers

Demonstrations
Riots
Armed Attacks
Political Deaths
Sanctions

1950   1955   1960   1965

Syria

○ Renewals
△ Adjustments
□ Reg. Transfers
☆ Irreg. Transfers

Demonstrations
Riots
Armed Attacks
Political Deaths
Sanctions

1950   1955   1960   1965

Tunisia

O Renewals
△ Adjustments
□ Reg. Transfers
☆ Irreg. Transfers

Demonstrations
Riots
Armed Attacks
Political Deaths
Sanctions
Interventions

       1950   1955   1960   1965

United Arab Republic (Egypt)

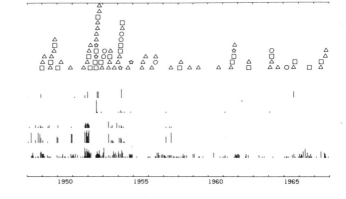

O Renewals
△ Adjustments
□ Reg. Transfers
☆ Irreg. Transfers

Demonstrations
Riots
Armed Attacks
Political Deaths
Sanctions

       1950   1955   1960   1965

Yemen

△ Adjustments
□ Reg. Transfers
☆ Irreg. Transfers

Demonstrations
Riots
Armed Attacks
Political Deaths
Sanctions
Interventions

       1950   1955   1960   1965

Index